of Rɛ

For Philomena

The Threat of Race
Reflections on Racial Neoliberalism

David Theo Goldberg
University of California
Humanities Research Institute

 **WILEY-BLACKWELL**

A John Wiley & Sons, Ltd., Publication

© 2009 by David Theo Goldberg

BLACKWELL PUBLISHING
350 Main Street, Malden, MA 02148-5020, USA
9600 Garsington Road, Oxford OX4 2DQ, UK
550 Swanston Street, Carlton, Victoria 3053, Australia

First published 2009 by Blackwell Publishing Ltd

1   2009

Library of Congress Cataloging-in-Publication Data
ISBN-13: 9780631219675 (hardback)
ISBN-13: 9780631219682 (paperback)

A catalogue record for this title is available from the British Library.

Set in 10.5/13pt Minion by Graphicraft Limited, Hong Kong

For further information on
Blackwell Publishing, visit our website at
www.blackwellpublishing.com

Contents

Preface and Acknowledgments

This is a book about race and its exclusionary, humiliating, and violent expressions, historically produced and contemporarily articulated, yet so often in denial. About the transformational grammars of race and racisms as neoliberal political economy has assumed a more or less firm grip on different societies, across varying regions. I am concerned with what is unique to those geo-regional expressions, and what can be generalized across them.

The numbers are notorious, almost numbing.

Ten million enslaved Africans perished in Middle Passage, on reasonable estimates. Death en passant to a life more often than not worse than death. Starved, worked, beaten, suffocated, diseased to death. Numbers as large again prematurely killed in new world slavery. Systemically, brutally worked, beaten, saddened or maddened into death. Seven million aboriginal inhabitants of Australia wiped out by European colonization and modernization. A lynching every other day in the southern states of the US throughout the 1890s. Ten million battered into death by Leopold's vicious regime in the Congo between 1885 and 1908, half of the population of the area castrated and delimbed and diseased in a brutality matched only by the six million Jews and nameless others gassed and shot and tortured to death by Aryan superiority in the 1940s, for which the Congolese experience served as a pre-cursive laboratory. Each death exceptional in transnational processes of violence and violation all too sadly not. One million people murdered in 1994 in Rwanda in the ethnoracial name of not belonging. In one month. More than 70 percent of the more than two million people rotting in US prisons (up from 200,000 less than 40 years ago) people of color. A percentage eclipsed perhaps only in (post-)apartheid South Africa. Countless lives foreshortened by segregation and apartheid, urban decay and globalized labor conditions, smart bombs and stupid politicians.

All in the name or wake – explicitly or implicitly, structurally or analogically – of ethnoracial configurations and their legacies. People reduced to the abstraction of a group, groups classified as abstracted numbers, belittled, rationalized as animals, treated as beasts by those whose actions would make them better candidates for the designation.

What do these sorts of numbing numbers (repeatable ad nauseam, if one is not already nauseated) say about race and how we have come to think about racial ordering and racial theorizing? About racial futures and their connections with what counts as history? About an ordering, valuing, ways of being and thinking that enable and allow the cults of death and violence, that threaten the wellbeing of so many? And later ignores their legacies. So how are the mentalities of racial being and seeing made, manifested, managed over time, at different times, to different social or governmental purpose? What are their products and productivity, their currency and the value they create, sell, and purchase? What fates does this order(ing) of images and ideas, values and virtues seal, and seal off?

What indeed about color-consciousness and colorblindness, about conscience and connectedness, about community and collectivity? And what about racial cultures and resistance, domination and representation? About racial memory and forgetting, apology, apologetics, and forgiving? About grief and grievance, identity and injury? About racial resonance and suggestibility, refusal and possibility? What, in other words, of that question first asked critically by the likes of Fanon, about the connection between race and culture? What, as Said asks in *Culture and Imperialism*, is culture both productive and reflective of the historical moment(s) in which it is produced? Is there something systematic about the cult(ure)s of race across time so that one can conjure, as Said argues about imperial culture at once more generally and more specifically, a "structure of attitude and reference"?

The set of reflections that follows across the pages of *The Threat of Race*, then, is about retrospectivity and prospectivity, legacy and latency, pasts as horizons of futures. It is about race in structure and representation, order and rationalization, arrangement and narration. It is then also about what race does about itself, how it represents itself and what it does around and in the name of such representation and extension. About the suffocation of history's weight but also about living through and beyond, because and in spite of it. It is, one might say, to pause between, to reflect on the stains and strains of history, of histories. But the book is also about standing up and brushing off. About digging out, and picking up.

In this, my concern is to mold a critical analytics and a critical analytic vocabulary towards comprehending racially driven neoliberalisms and neoliberally fueled racisms: racial regionalizations and critical regionalisms, born again racisms and social prophylaxis, enduring occupations and permanently temporary states, euro-mimesis and Muslimania, mixture and violent duress, political theology of race and racial secularization, racial compulsions and their resistances, socialities of the skin and racial evaporations, racisms without racism and neo-neoliberalism, homogenizing and heterogenizing dispositions.

How, then, to write in the name of and against a title? A title fraught with prospect and promise, with the ambiguities of racial erosion and erasure, on one side, and antagonisms, violence, death, and their charges, on the other? A title in the shadow of which histories are taken to be over, past, evaporated and in denial, yet the conditions of which, as they are buried, misremembered, mis-membered, remain very much alive.

A book of this sort, it may already be evident, conjures if it doesn't emphatically call for a different kind of writing. I have composed a work in which I have tried to retain passion rather than purge it for the preference of a neutral disposition, whatever that might mean, preferring to wed passion to a critical analyticity, commitment(s), and to theoretical reflectivity. I have tried to write with writing in mind. Which is to say with speaking to colleagues and those unknown, shouting at claims from which leave is taken, which leave one not so much cold as furious. How to write with passion and yet remain coolly critical, cutting, incisive? About pressing matters cutting today as deep to the bone as any moment in my lifetime. How to write about complex and difficult matters, but clearly? How to resist and insist, through argument? These are my challenges.

This is a text, accordingly, free of footnotes or explicitly referenced intra-textual citations. Which is different than saying there are no references, or better yet reference points, allusions, conversational interjections. The book is conceived in conversation, with many texts, multiple voices, various expressions of opinion. A bibliography of works consulted, conspired with or against, critically taken up or cast aside, follows each chapter. Where I suggest in passing within the flow of a chapter's argument that so-and-so says such-and-such the general reference will be included in the chapter's bibliography.

We are often in denial about just how collaboratively produced single-authored monographs are. I owe enormous debts of gratitude, from the detailed and definitive to the deep and comprehensive, from the institutional to the invested, the abstract to the personal. The abstract first. The writing was driven in good part by the music in the presence of which it was so often composed. Philip Tabane and the Malombo Jazzmen, Feya Faku, McCoy Mrubata, Greg Georgiades, Paul Hanmer, Wessel van Resburg, Madala Kunene, Tlokwe Sehume, Sibongile Khumalo, Gilad Atzmon, Max Roach and Abdullah Ibrahim, Jack De Johnette and Foday Musa Suso, no doubt among many more. Above all Zim Ngqawana and Gonzalo Rubalcaba. I can only hope the rhythm of the writing resonates with something of their timbre and timing, their inimitable spirit.

Bits of argument and versions of chapters were read in public fora far and wide – across the University of California and the United States, repeatedly in the Netherlands, Britain, Sweden, Ireland, and France, as well as in South Africa, China, Singapore, Australia, and Canada. I learned in other ways from workshops in Costa Rica and Mexico. I am grateful to my generous hosts in each instance and to the critical comments, insights, and thoughtful provocations following from these interlocutions that more often than not prompted me to think anew, to revise and reformulate. If the book took longer as a result to complete, it is inordinately the better for it.

The earlier chapters were much improved also by their reading and commentary from my colleagues in the Critical Theory Institute, Irvine. An insight here or revision there found its way into the book prompted by impromptu conversations often in unlikely settings with friends and colleagues Etienne Balibar, Gayatri Spivak, Ngũgĩ wa Thiong'o, Judith Butler, and Ackbar Abbas. Close friends read or listened, often repeatedly, to my rantings, gently setting me straight and saving me from embarrassment on matters major and minor. The book would be so much the worse but for Ana Paula Ferreira, Michael Hanchard, Angela Davis, Gina Dent, Geraldine Heng, John and Jean Comaroff, Lisa Lowe, Gabriele Schwab, Saree Makdisi, Ronit Lentin, John Solomos, Michael Keith, and Barnor Hesse. A public conversation with Paul Gilroy organized at the University of Manchester by Virinder Kalra (www.archive.org/details/Goldberg_Gilroy) not only happily renewed an old friendship but led me to rethink a couple of points I had thought settled in my mind.

Sadly, our dear friend Tanya Reinhart passed away suddenly before I could share the chapter on racial palestinianization with her. I learned more casually about matters in that troubled region from Tanya and her partner, the inimitable Israeli poet Aharon Shabtai, than from most all else combined. We miss her immensely.

My day job throughout the conception and composition of this book has been administering a research institute serving all ten campuses of the University of California. The incomparable staff not only invariably lightens the sometime tedium of the day-to-day administrative detail and the everyday challenges of fundraising. They have protected my time from the inevitable intrusions of daily demand, without which the manuscript still would not be complete. An unqualified pleasure to work with, knowing that things will be so well done despite my distractions.

In similar vein, the distractions have often been a consequence of matters unrelated to *The Threat of Race*. Through it all I have worked closely with Cathy Davidson, running a national network promoting work at the interface of the humanities and digital technology, and overseeing a series of grants. Cathy, too, has occasionally suffered my writing distractions when I owed her a response or a proposal draft, despite which she was always one to cheer me to completion, sending me relevant articles or urls pertinent to my argument which proved only all the more distracting from our work together. I have long been fortunate to have fabulous research assistants. Kim Furumoto for the earlier parts of the book and Stefka Hristova more recently have been the best of the best. Both have been more interlocutors than assistants. Stefka has been instrumental in making it possible for me to draw on accompanying images and to design the website to accompany the text (see www.threatofrace.org). Muriam Haleh Davis has repeatedly posed probing questions about the argument and conceptual apparatus, prompting me to be clearer than I otherwise might.

Jayne Fargnoli, editor extraordinaire, left me alone when most others would long have called in the chips, prodded me gently along when others might have chided in frustration, cheered me to the finish line when others might have turned out the light. She exchanged reflections about Shaq and Miami's demise, the Knicks implosion, and the Celtics' ascendancy, just the distraction for an author struggling to find his direction. Or found other Blackwell projects to which I might contribute so as to keep her bosses at bay. When I requested Brigitte Lee Messenger to copy-edit the manuscript, the deed was done. Laboring under her own trying conditions, Brigitte as always lived up to the expectation, and then some.

Throughout I have engaged in spirited conversations with a small group of close confidantes. I have burdened them with drafts of chapters and half-baked ideas, troubled them over details disturbing their own time with half-hearted arguments, often while collaborating on something else entirely. Always they have laughed me through my knots, angling me in corrected and renewed directions. Donald Moore has borne all of this burdened by the enormous challenges of his own situation, drawing my attention to points overlooked, a nuance by-passed, inevitably to a reference about which I was unaware. Saba Mahmood and Charles Hirschkind gave me a hearing no matter what part of the world to or from which they were rushing. Conversations with my sometimes skeptical son, Gabe, just leaving his teenage years, occasionally kept me from making claims for which my evidence was less than compelling.

Susan Searl Giroux read and taught the manuscript repeatedly, drew my ideas out in an extraordinary interview, found insights in my work I had not known were there.

Over the past number of years now and throughout the book's formulation I have been engaged in a conversation with my dear friend Achille Mbembe ranging across politics and culture, the postcolonial and post-South Africa, conviction and compulsion. It was out of one such critical conversation before students in a graduate course that I thought to write about the political theology of race. These engagements with Achille, teaching and working together in California and Johannesburg, continuing to be moved by his generative writing and probing thought, have conjured ideas that could have come to me in no other way.

And finally, Philomena Essed has listened to me thinking aloud on these issues on a literally daily basis. Always thinking *with* me, she has more often than not offered me the gift of ideas discovered and uncovered, prompted and polished, helping invariably to deepen insight or abandon thoughts with no nuance and less future. The book's title came together only after months of fretting across meals and travels and conversations over an appropriate characterization. As also many a critical turn or subtle twist, a way of looking or a line of argument. Without her boundless care, support, and generosity, this would be a much lesser book, if one at all.

Amsterdam and Irvine
January 2008

Author's Note

We have created a website to accompany *The Threat of Race*:

www.threatofrace.org

While intended as a stand-alone site, it includes images and links to images informing and embellishing the text, in a sense an essay next to and in conversation with the argument in the book. Somewhat experimental in form, it will incorporate also a forum for commentary and ongoing conversation. We hope you consult it and find it an engaging presence.

I am grateful to Stefka Hristova, Erik Loyer, Shane Depner, and Khai Tang without whom it would still be struggling to see the light of day.

In the following pages I include a critical account of the Royal Belgian Museum for Central Africa in the context of discussing colonialism, racial europeanization, and cultural memory (see pp. 169–75). My analysis was composed on the basis of a visit to the Museum and institutional catalogues and materials predating 2007. The Museum has since signaled a comprehensive commitment to renovate the building and reconceive its exhibits. As an announcement greeting visitors to the Museum today declares, "The aim of the restoration and renovation [due to be completed by 2013] is to bring the Museum in tune with the needs and requirements of the 21th [*sic*] century, but without affecting its charm." Finally realizing that the Museum could no longer continue as an unapologetically colonial institution, the permanent and temporary exhibits already seek to indicate that its leaders are grappling with its troubled past. These developments came about too late to incorporate into the pages of this book. Instead, I have composed a brief supplementary reflection on the anxious, ambivalent attempts now being initiated to save the Museum's troubling "charm." The posting appears on the website accompanying this book (see www.threatofrace.org).

1

Buried, Alive

I find theory exasperating. And I find a confident theory even more exasperating.

Derek Walcott

There is an esteemed tradition of working to end racial configuration in societies long marked by it. This tradition emerged out of resistance movements to racial slavery, subordination, suppression, and segregation both in colonial societies and in postcolonizing social arrangements. Commitments to do away with race, consequently, have long been associated with social movements to end racism. Indeed, a primary prompt to end racial classification and configuration is tied to antiracism.

The connection between antiracial conception and antiracist commitment suggests a complexity I am concerned here to explore. For I shall be suggesting that there are crucial moments when the necessity and complexity of this connection are lost sight of, and antiracism reduces primarily, principally, or completely to antiracial commitment, to antiracialism. At these moments, the end of racism is confused with no more than being against race, the end of race substituting to varying degrees for the commitment to – the struggles for – ending racism. The refusal of racism reduces to racial refusal; and racial refusal is thought to exhaust antiracism.

Now, what is refused in this collapse, what buried, what buried alive? What residues of racist arrangement and subordination – social, economic, cultural, psychological, legal, and political – linger unaddressed and repressed in singularly stressing racial demise? What doors are thus closed to coming to terms with historical horrors racially inscribed, and what attendant expressions of racial grief and group melancholia, on one side, and racial self-assertion and triumphalism, on the other, are left unrecognized? What are the implications of this delinking of race from racism, especially under the contemporary spur of neoliberal socio-economic impetus, for a critical account of the character of the racial state and a critical transformation of racist culture?

Histories

The history of race as an ordering mechanism for modern social arrangement has been widely retold. There is some controversy about the place of race – its conceptual presence, its role, its effects – in what have come to be called the Middle Ages. In the latter part of this period race was emergent rather than fully formed, incipiently invoked to fashion nation formation in the early moments of national elaboration as racial consciousness began to emerge out of – and later can be said to have taken over if not to have replaced – the mix of public religious constitution, the symbolics and architectonics of blood, the naturalizing dispositions – the metaphysics – of hierarchical chains of being, and the ontological orderings in terms of supposedly heritable rationalities. Under medievalism religion was the dominant discourse of public order and intellectual life, while the romantic legends revealed the ways in which public forces got played out in private lives and the imaginary narratives of personal adventure reflected shifting social forces. The sweep from the medieval to the modern, in this sense, can be said to be reflected in the shifts from religion as dominant public frame for structuring and interpreting social life to the civic religion of race as prevailing fabric of public arrangement and imaginative hermeneutics.

Stated thus, it becomes easier to see how much the very notion of the Middle Ages – of an age of darkness caught between the light of classical antiquity and the resurrection of the Renaissance and the learning of the Enlightenment – is so deeply predicated on the presumptive dominance of European historicities, of Euro-dominated temporalities and modernities. And this, in turn, reveals both the centrality of race to the expansive and extensional global order(ing) of European modernity and the (late) modernity of medieval categories of disposition and dominance, imposition and order once racially conceived. To put the latter point another way, as Geraldine Heng has done in her marvelous book, *Empire of Magic*, it could be said that there is much to be learned from medieval narrations about the crusading character of our own all too "medieval" politics of domination, disorder, and cultures of control – without at the same time insisting that the modern is no more than medieval (though in moments of deep despair about our present I am more than tempted by that counter-evolutionist reductionism).

The notion of race, then, was put to work from the fifteenth century on in the Mediterranean countries, especially Iberian. Race quickly came to mark Europe and its wordly extensions in the colonizing and imperializing societies over the next couple of centuries, especially in the drive to state sovereignty and the subsequent centralizing of the war function under state mandate elaborated so provocatively by Michel Foucault in his 1976 lectures on race and modern state formation, *Society Must Be Defended*. Race acquired a more formal codification and consequently socio-intellectual authority from the eighteenth century onwards, as Foucault remarks, increasingly coming to order centralizing state definition and function, institutionalization and practice.

By the late nineteenth century race had assumed throughout the European orbit a sense of naturalness and commitment, a more or less taken-for-granted marking of social arrangements and possibilities, an assumed givenness and inevitability in the ascription of superiority and inferiority, sameness and difference, civilization and vulgar lack. This supposed naturalness meant the ease of racial reference for the relatively powerful and privileged. This easiness of racial ascription served to hide from view – to hide from and for the more racially powerful themselves – exactly the hard work, conceptually and materially, socially and politically, legally and forcefully, it took to set up and reproduce racial arrangements. Science and literature, scripture and law, culture and political rhetoric all worked in subtle and blunt ways to establish the presumption of white supremacy, to naturalize the status of white entitlement and black disenfranchisement, of European belonging wherever the claim might be staked and of non-European servitude and servility.

European expansion accordingly rationalized its global spread in racial terms. Rationalization through race obviously assumed the form of legitimation, of claiming to render this expansion acceptable, even desirable or necessary, to the perpetrators. But it served also effectively to maximize both the grip on power globally – in the colonies or within the European theater of relations – and relatedly the extraction of profit and accumulation of wealth. By extension, this global colonial spread, commercial interaction, and cultural intertwining prompted conceptual seepage into (former) imperial powers. European engagement and enforcement through race, in other words, encouraged the adoption and adaptation of racial conceptualization to give sense to and to rationalize long-existing ethno-class and caste relations and tensions in the likes of China, Japan, and India. In these cases of conceptual assumption, race was pressed into work in new ways on the basis of local ecologies encompassing thick histories of excluding those considered alien, ethnoculturally different, and so racially tainted. In these instances race clearly came to be invested with new, if connected, significance. This can be characterized as networks of racial conception and meaning, of racial value and power.

Thus the *labor of race* is the work for which the category and its assumptions are employed to effect and rationalize social arrangements of power and exploitation, violence and expropriation. Race was turned into a foundational code. But as with all foundations (conceptual and material), it had to be cemented in place. Racial thinkers, those seeking to advance racial representation – scientists and philosophers, writers and literary critics, public intellectuals and artists, journalists and clergy, politicians and bureaucrats – for all intents and purposes became the day-laborers, the brick-layers, of racial foundations.

Conceptions

Like many other commentators on racial matters, I am insisting that there is a conceptual distinction to be acknowledged between racial conception and racism. Racial conception, or what some such as Anthony Appiah have called racialism, is the view that groups of people are marked by certain generalizable visible and heritable traits. These generalized traits may be physical or psychological, cultural or culturally inscribed on the body, and the physical and psychological, bodily and cultural traits are usually thought somehow indelibly connected. Thus racialists more often than not think that racial group members share not only these traits but also behavioral dispositions and tendencies to think in certain ways those not so marked do not share. Appiah argues that such views about racial groups – that they share such characteristics, tendencies or traits not shared by non-members – if unaccompanied by consequential claims of inherent inequality or hierarchy do not amount to racism. Such views, while presumptively mistaken, are not as such necessarily dangerous or immoral. What would further mark racial(ist) beliefs as racist, Appiah insists, would be the added claim to inequality or inferiority as a consequence of being so marked.

In his useful little book, *Racism: A Short History*, George Fredrickson suggests that racism necessarily requires the presumption of inequality or inferiority on the part of those whose assumed difference is deemed intrinsic or unchangeable. But does it?

Consider the racial paternalism of those claiming that others who are supposedly (still) racially immature should be subject to the education and governance of those who take themselves to be racially elevated (a view I have characterized as "racial historicism" in *The Racial State*). The increasingly widespread adoption of racial historicism from the mid-nineteenth century on and its discursive dominance in the latter half of the twentieth century regarding racial matters should serve to qualify the claim that racism necessarily requires a belief in intrinsic or unchangeable inferiority (the view I have called, by contrast, "racial naturalism"). That black or Asian people, as a people, may be thought by racial historicists to be educated ultimately to govern themselves suggests what Ann Stoler calls the "motility" – the shifting meanings and significance – of both racial and racist conception.

The mark of racist expression or belief, then, is not simply the claim of inferiority of the racially different. It is more broadly that racial difference warrants exclusion of those so characterized from elevation into the realm of protection, privilege, property, or profit. Racism, in short, is about exclusion through depreciation, intrinsic or instrumental, timeless or time-bound.

If race (or, ideologically, racialism) is about the manufacture of homogeneities, racisms police their boundaries. Race has historically concerned the fabrication of social homogeneities, their making and their embroidery, arrangement and order, management and commerce. Racism concerns the maintenance of homogeneities' contours, militarizing their borders, patrolling their places of possible transgression.

Underlying racialism, not unlike nationalism, is an abstract presumption of familialism. As Nadia Abu El-Haj remarks in her revealing interrogation of genealogy in the wake of the human genome project, membership criteria "in family, nation and political society are always entangled." The traits or characteristics I take myself to share with those I consider like me conjure an abstract familial connectivity. That I am like them, or they like me, *must* mean that we are familially connected, so to speak. But familiality, by extension, is necessarily conceived, if often silently, by the negation of (racial) otherness, of the differentiated and disconnected, the unlikened and unrelated. Note here the paradoxical relatedness of the racially denied, the constitutive connectedness of the disconnected, the manufactured fabric of familial distinction.

Abstract familial connection – loosely sharing some traits or characteristics or bordered dispositions – becomes the basis in turn for an abstracted familiarity. This connection is well captured in the extraordinary body of *Casta* painting spanning eighteenth-century Mexico, those elaborations of early racial classification schemes predicated on miscegenation I discuss in the chapter on "racial latinamericanization" below, some of which explicitly linked racial types to behavioral, emotional, and moral characterizations. That we are alike in physically predicated ways is thought to entail that we are alike in other ways also. We share benefits, and no doubt burdens too, in ways family members are presumed to do. And perhaps we share more than this, an intuitive set of sensibilities and sentiments, sensitivities and resentments, likes and dislikes. The hint of concrete connectivity, however slight, becomes invested with value well beyond what the concrete bonds of connectivity alone can sustain. I can presume to know you because your somehow looking like me on supposedly crucial markers (skin color, hair texture, facial shape, mannerisms, ways of speaking, even dress and the like) suggests also social dispositions and perhaps even beliefs. If intuition is nothing more than educated and habituated guess predicated on a degree of familiarity, I can claim to know you intuitively on the basis of presupposing peculiarly to be like you. Affiliation, however flimsy its social basis or status, conjures in such cases presumptive filiation. Race and nation, racism and nationalism run together in just these bonded ways. Familiality, no matter how abstract and imagined, is supposed, it seems, to conjure familiarity.

But familiarity, the idiom would have it, similarly breeds contempt. Contempt in this case, we might ask, for whom? And to what end(s)? For those thrown together with one in some way by circumstance – by the very demands of social constitution, if I am right – and whom one accordingly presumes to know, in character and habit, condition and behavior, prospect and limit. In short, ethnoracially. It is the presumption of knowledge, the fabrication of character for those one knows at best partially, in both senses of the term, which both bears and bares the stigma of race in these instances. The end(s), of course, are varied – exploitation or extermination, use and abuse, assertion and order. In short, violence and property, profit, and power, instrumentally but also for their own sakes. Race feeds, fuels, and funnels violence, property, profit, and power, but can also be their modes of expression, the forms in which they manifest.

It is revealing in this sense to read race conceptually as a term of social geography. I mean this not in the disciplinary but in a normative sense. Race is taken historically as (or in terms of) identifying people geomorphically by their supposed phenotypes in terms of their imputed or implied geographic origins and the cultural characteristics considered to be associated with those geographic identifications, those landscapes and their associate characteristics. A Florida-based company, DNA Printgenomics, is one among a growing industry offering "ancestry testing." This is, as they put it, a "Biogeographical Ancestry analysis," a purported DNA test to establish one's racial ancestry or, in the case of mixed race, ancestral proportions. For a mere $158 you can learn "your percentage" of "African-Indo European-Native American-East Asian" (*sic*). A new biopolitical technology meets an older regime of biopower. Race is defined in reified and presumptive terms of "the five major" continental "races" which its website (www.dnaprint.com) characterizes as "Native American, East Asian, South Asian, European, sub-Saharan, etc." It's the "etc." which is the embezzling genomic insurance policy at work here, for in the additive, as Feyerabend once may have put it, anything goes.

When read as mapping social geography in this way, race is taken both to complement and to counter national formation and character. Those whose "racial origins" are considered geographically somehow to coincide with national territory (or its colonial extension) are deemed to belong to the nation; those whose geo-phenotypes obviously place them originally (from) elsewhere are all too often considered to pollute or potentially to terrorize the national space, with debilitating and even deadly effect. But those belonging racio-nationally also share an extra-national raciality, a super-whiteness, as Etienne Balibar has pointed out, complementing the supraracial nationality. Race figures the national even as it transcends it; and in transcending race gives the nation its transcendental character, its larger, ultimately globally extensionalist imperative. Fashioned in the expansive colonial and imperial laboratories of euro-modernities, there's a sense too in which the logical reach of race was inherently extra-national, was drawn inevitably to fulfill itself colonially, imperialistically.

Counters

If this is the historical logic of racial dominance, it suggests too a feature of racial resistance. On the other side then, it is the refusal of living with contempt – and, relatedly, with self-contempt – that gives rise, at least initially, to the impetus for antiracist movements. "The other side," otherness, othering are hardly natural categories, as critical intellectual movements of the past 25 years have shown. Resistance and response are necessarily products of the artifice of alterity, of its making and remaking. If I am different – *that* I am different – in just the ways racially marked may well dispose me in a society taking those markers seriously as much to act against the stereotypifying ascriptions as to act on them, to act them out. No transgression without (in this case) racially fashioned normativity. I am racially characterized, therefore I (am presumed, expected, in fact seen to) think (or not) and act accordingly. And perhaps I do, self-consciously or not.

"I have incisors to bare," Fanon remarks cuttingly, in response to a white French child exclaiming as he might at the zoo, "Look, Mama, a Negro!" Fanon's incisive response – "I bite" – signals acting on, and out, the reifying stereotype, here both racial and racist, and undercutting it, bringing the reader up short, raising the stakes not just of visiting but of creating the zoo or zoo-like environment. If you think there are animals here, the animals bite back.

The weight of race

These tensions between cutting and biting back, alterity and counter, distantiation and embrace – existential as much as analytic, perhaps analytic because existential – reveal what I want to characterize as *the weight of race*. Race is heavy. But the heaviness is layered, volume piled upon mass, the layers or strata composed of varying substances and differentially born. "White man's burden" was the racially historicist rationalization common in the nineteenth century for both the effort and profit of colonial rule. European settlers and colonial rulers were exhorted to sacrifice in the name of empire, just as they were encouraged to educate the less civilized and immature with the view to eventual self-rule (once the cost-benefit calculus of colonial rule tipped precariously away from metropolitan advantage). The weight here was taken to be borne exclusively upon those sagging shoulders of Charles Atlas.

The abolitionist movements, slaves uniting in resistance with white conscience and longer-term self-interest, were the first to reveal in a public way how the load of race weighed so much more heavily upon its targeted populations. Bodies beaten and broken, spirits sagged, life-spans artificially and dramatically limited, whatever prospects for whatever slither of prosperity sliding from grasp because of the racial weights pulling one back. Fingers clawing at the soft sand to pull one onto the bank, to a resting place, a restful place, as the cement about ankles or sand bags upon backs drag one into water already so dark with the bodies of those made kin through race.

The weight of race, as Bourdieu might have put it. That weight borne, as I say, differentially, borne by some for others, killing many for the sake of some, for the salvage and resource and supposed security of those whose weight is borne upon the backs of others. Sometimes a dead weight, one made heavier because the breath has been squeezed out of its subjects, shifting the bearing from those whose fingers have let go, too broken to grab on, to those left clinging, scratched and scarred, half ashore. The weight shifted to those etched with the grief of witness and memory, but also to those forced to grapple with the burden of tasks for which they have been left or left themselves unprepared. The weight of race lingering between the scales of justice bound by a past, present, and future, distributed and redistributed between those marked indelibly by history and those seeking incurably to remake themselves outside of history's cast, untouched by the shadow of their past.

I think here of the differential effects of racial weights taking their toll on blacks and whites respectively in the wake of the vicious murder of James Byrd in Jasper, Texas in 1998, as reflected in the revealing documentary, *Two Towns of Jasper* (2002). Or even more recently of the differentiated weights distributed across targets of the "war on terrorism" and the "clash of fundamentalisms" falling overwhelmingly on Muslims or those mistaken for or identified with them. How in these tensions of racial burden to shed the weight of race?

Though there is a clear conceptual distinction we must mark between race and racism, they are deeply connected conceptually and politically. It may be impossible always – ever? – to sustain the distinction historically and politically. The weight of race is at once a racist weight. A different, if related, metaphor may be equally revealing. Race is the glove in which the titanic, the weighty, hand of racism fits. The cloth may be velvet but it is studded with spikes and soaked in blood. Antiracism, it seems, is at once antiracialism, at least to the degree of de-spiking the glove. Whether the glove, once defanged, can be washed of its bloody legacy remains an open question. But the larger lingering if too often liminal question is whether antiracialism, as so many contemporary commentators and politicians would have it, suffices as a response to the history of racisms.

Antiracialism, antiracism

Antiracialism is to take a stand, instrumental or institutional, against a concept, a name, a category, a categorizing. It does not itself involve standing (up) against (a set of) conditions of being or living, as it is not always clear what those conditions might in fact be for which race is considered to stand as a sort of shorthand. Is antiracialism a counter to claims about biology, or a counter to a social/cultural set of articulations, a mode of expression or its lack, a sense of naturalized entitlement or historically ordered incapacity?

Antiracism, by contrast, conjures a stance against an imposed condition, or set of conditions, an explicit refusal or a living of one's life in such a way one refuses the imposition, whether one is a member of the subjugated population or the subjugating one. It is an insistence that one not be reduced, at least not completely, to or by the implications marked by the imposition and constraint, by the devaluation and attendant humiliation. At the limit, antiracism is the risk of death, the willingness to forego life, perhaps at once the measure of the severity of the imposition, dislocation, and curtailment, and of the seriousness of the commitment. There clearly is no evidence of antiracialism ever commanding that sort of risk.

Since their solidification as coherent social movements in the abolitionist struggles of the nineteenth century, there have been three significant periods of broad *antiracist* mobilization: abolitionism throughout the nineteenth century; anticolonialism and the civil rights movements from roughly the 1920s through the 1960s; and the anti-apartheid and the multicultural movements of the 1970s to the 1990s.

The Haitian Revolution (1791–1803) seeking independence from enslaving French rule might be said to mark the initiation also of antiracist movements. Embracing the racial ambiguities of both American and French Revolutions regarding human and political equality and the Rights of Man, abolitionist slave revolts followed the Haitian example throughout the European orbit, marking most of the nineteenth century. They sought to throw off the yokes of degradation, alienation, economic exploitation, political and legal subordination that combined to fashion the peculiar mode, style, and substance of racist subjugation. The slave revolts thus were not only about inclusion or incorporation into Euro-dominant social orders and civil societies but the very transfiguration of the given and the common-place, of civil society and the state.

Abolitionism, especially in the form of the slave revolts and accompanying maroon secessions, thus constitutes the first of the three major historical examples of antiracist commitment and struggle I am seeking to identify here. Abolitionism, of course, aimed first and foremost to end institutionalized slavery. But the institutionalization of slavery – capture and trade, degradation and exploitation, servility and abuse, violence, the imposition of power, and foreshortened lives – was predicated upon and enacted through racial technologies. Abolitionism accordingly assumed by necessity antiracist disposition, at least in the sense of resisting the balder, more aggressive, and more obvious forms of racial terror. The progressive products of these brave and often dangerous abolitionist social movements were palpable and remarkable. Between the outlawing of slave-trading throughout the British empire (1807) in the wake of the Haitian tragedy and the eventual abolition of slavery in Cuba (1886) and Brazil (1888), the ending of slavery throughout the extended European empire and its satellite societies was effected by the courageous efforts of many men and women, enslaved and free alike. Those hitherto regarded as somehow less than human were admitted, at least nominally, into the family of Man. Their consequent human and legal rights and protections could no longer be denied on the basis of their presumptive inhumanity or natural depravity. Slave-based societies gave way throughout the British, Spanish, French, Dutch, and Portuguese empires. Ultimately, slave-holding and trading were outlawed also in the German and Belgian cases, as well as in the major slave-holding settler societies of the Americas, most notably the United States and Brazil. By the turn to the twentieth century, racially driven enslavement seemed a thing of history.

If abolitionism was the first broad antiracist mobilization, the anticolonial and civil rights struggles amounted to the second. The two – a global anticolonial struggle figured most visibly in Africa and Asia, and the civil rights struggles in the United States – can be thought together here precisely because they are so deeply interconnected historically and conceptually, geopolitically and existentially. This connection should come as no surprise. Colonialism was factored constitutively around racial conception and configuration. How colonizing metropoles and their agents thought about race determined directly the very structures of colonial order and arrangement. And how nationally configured colonies came to be structured influenced the ways in which class, gender, and social relations generally got to be thought and enacted in the colonizing and structuring metropoles. The circulation between national metropole and colonies of state agents and advisors, politicians and civic leaders, corporate entrepreneurs and opportunists, but also intellectuals and churchmen, academics and activists, prompted common conversations both about the structuring of racially repressive regimes and the struggle to undo them. Colonization was racially mandated, mediated, and managed; and racial rule in the colonies shored up and was used to rationalize racial repression in the national metropoles. Racial comprehension, practical as much as theoretical, institutional as much as instrumental, was at the center of both.

The histories of colonial conditions were constitutively tied to the racial histories of metropolitan shaping. The circulation of slave and indentured labor from Africa and Asia to metropolitan Europe and especially the Americas indicates the depth of those linkages. It reveals the causal connections between sources of labor supply, raw materials, and later markets for the making and selling of metropolitan goods, and so the source of metropolitan national wealth and at least economic wellbeing. Global connectivity, interactivity, and mutual constitutiveness were long in place before the notion of globalization became vogue. And racial understanding and its subjugating and exploitative effects were the fabric – that glove I mentioned metaphorically above – of this global connectedness.

In any case, the constitutive connections between American antiracist mobilizations and anticolonial activities were already prefigured in and through the mutual presence at the 1911 Races of Man Congress in London and the ensuing Pan Africanist Congresses of early American antiracist activists like W. E. B. Du Bois and Mary White Ovington, anticolonialists like Kwame Nkrumah (later the first President of free Ghana, who had graduated from an historically black American university), academics like Franz Boas, anti-imperialists like Karl Kautsky, and pacifists like post-World War II Japanese Prime Minister, Kijuro Shidehara. Those working against postbellum racism, segregationism, and accommodationism in the US were already in deep conversation from the early years of the twentieth century with African and Asian anticolonial activists, intellectuals, and leaders. These global meetings constituted a laboratory of antiracist, anticolonial, and anti-imperial ideas, commitments, and organizing.

By extension, anticolonial mobilization gets going as a movement – really a set of movements – just as the civil rights movement in the United States gathers steam, fueled by common cause(s) but then also by the growing en*courage*ment of their respective, if relative, successes. The early mobilizations in each, between, during, and in the immediate aftermath of the two world wars, set the stage for developments in the 1950s and 1960s. These early developments included most notably growing anticolonial assertiveness throughout the various colonial domains and a gathering number of early legal victories around labor (in the 1930s), housing, and educational concerns (in the 1940s) in the US. Nkrumah, Kaunda, and other notable younger African anticolonialists engaged Du Bois at the Manchester Pan-African Congress over which the latter presided in 1945. In the triangulation of the Black Atlantic, Césaire and later Fanon, for example, left Martinique for Africa via Paris, and Fanon spent his dying days in New York; Du Bois circulated between Eastern US urban centers, Germany, Paris and London, and ultimately Ghana. After his legal education in London, Ghandi famously tested his commitment to non-violent resistance in British-ruled South Africa before unsettling colonial India as the principled voice for independence. These circuits of discursive and activist mobilization, multiplied through many biographies and the specificities of particular national sites and struggles, translated in turn into circles of interactive antiracist struggle.

Such interactive movements on the ground were accompanied respectively by the self-defining but also mutually influencing intellectual movements of the New Negro and Negritude. The New Negro, of course, dates back in definition to the earlier period of the Harlem Renaissance, its first formulation in an essay penned by the philosopher Alain Locke in 1925, "Enter the New Negro," and later that year in Locke's widely circulated edited book by the three-worded expression of that title. While emerging from overlapping intellectual and political sources, the discursive influence of "the New Negro" on the conception of the Negritude movement has been variously noted, indeed by principals such as Senghor himself. By the early 1930s, many of the primary writers of the Harlem Renaissance were being read by young African intellectuals studying in Europe, prompted by the presence both of black American cultural producers in Paris, London, and Berlin and of Caribbean and African intellectuals in New York. Aimé Césaire, the first to coin the term "Negritude," in a poem in 1939, had actually written a dissertation in 1930 on the Harlem Renaissance, and was fully informed both regarding the conceptual apparatus and its intellectual, existential, and political commitments, adapting them to the specific conceptual conditions of African anticolonial and antiracist struggles. These ideas spurred, in turn, projects in the 1960s and 1970s by African

Americans, Latinos, Asian Americans, and American Indians (AIM), for example, to shake the dominance of Euro-America, whether conceptually or materially, politically and institutionally.

Both anticolonial and civil rights mobilizations need to be viewed, then, as vigorous, influential, and effective antiracist movements. Anticolonialism, of course, was principally directed at effecting national independence while the civil rights movement was aimed first and foremost at national integration. Both nevertheless sought to undo the histories of racially ordered social structures, legal enforcements, group-driven exclusions, conceptual colonialisms, and racially indexed foreshortened lives in the metropoles as much as in the colonies. Both sought to "decolonize the imagination" and to "provincialize Europe" (which is also to say to deprovincialize what is not European). In this, they sought to strip from the racially subjugated the imposition of infantilizing and demeaning self-conceptions, with varying degrees of success and less dramatic transformative influence on the imaginaries of the oppressing classes. Where anticolonialism altered the geopolitical status quo with palpable implications for former colonial subjects, the civil rights movement altered the political terrain in the US with equally mixed effect for America's racially disadvantaged.

The third antiracist movement I identified above, anti-apartheid, dates back at least to the earliest days of the apartheid regime in the early 1950s. As a broad-based social movement, nevertheless, anti-apartheid is to be comprehended as the combined legacy of the anticolonial and civil rights mobilizations. Global anti-apartheid mobilization, in short, acquires its fuel in the 1970s, especially in the wake of the mid-decade urban youth uprisings in South Africa, and flourishes above all in the form of township refusal, gathering divestment campaigns, cultural and sports boycotts, and growing global isolation throughout the 1980s. It is as a qualitatively distinct if connected mobilization, accordingly, that I consider the anti-apartheid movement to constitute the third major historical moment of antiracist commitment and expression.

Anti-apartheid struggles galvanized a sense of the deep relation of antiracism to democratic political definition; they made palpable the integral connection of antiracist commitments in one part of the world to a progressively transformative politics around race in all other societies marked by the weight of racist histories; and they held out the firm promise that centuries of racist power, privilege, profit, and property would be redressed in some appropriate if not too socially disruptive ways. Those in Europe and North America especially who joined vigorous anti-apartheid protests were driven by a moral and political outrage at apartheid's premises and violently imposed power in South Africa and by the promise, if often only symbolic, of securing racial justice in their own societies. And those governments worldwide that joined the more or less formal diplomatic protest against the apartheid state by imposing travel restrictions or ultimately sanctions were prompted as much by geostrategic realpolitik as by moral outrage and the attempt to appease local national protest and to delink local racial injustices from the volatile mix.

The anti-apartheid struggles, in turn, were linked complexly, as spark and as fuel, as cause and effect, as warrant and as content of multicultural mobilizations wherever those of European descent had ruled on the basis of their ethnoracial (self-)determination. Multicultural movements of the 1980s and 1990s accordingly are to be understood, at least, as the at once irreducible supplement to anti-apartheid antiracisms. Multiculturalisms of course were prompted and fueled as much locally as by these transnational trends to which I am pointing – by the perceived limits of class-determined politics, the fading of the force of trades unions, by circulating migrations, enlarging circles and circulations of globalizing economies and cultures, and by a refusal to be bound by the racial restrictions of past dispensations. This is not to say that what others such as Peter Caws and Stuart Hall have characterized as the "descriptive multicultural" or modern demographic diversity doesn't have a much longer history in western metropoles such as London and Amsterdam, Paris and New York, but notably also in colonial capitals in Asia, Africa, the Middle East, and the Americas, dating back at least to the early onset of European modernities. These urban environments attracted and threw together in more or less vigorous interaction and cultural clash people from across broad swaths of the world in trade and social interaction, political tension and intimate intercourse, intellectual engagement and epistemological distinction, linguistic multiplicity and cultural translation.

Notwithstanding, increasingly self-conscious multicultural social, cultural, and political *movements* are a relatively recent phenomenon, as noted. They take on a characteristic specificity in the context of local, national, and state conditions, globally influenced and textured. The racial dimensions of multicultural developments, themselves complex, may have been inherited in the 1970s and 1980s from anticolonial and civil rights reinventions, but such antiracist prompts were impassioned by re-viewing civil rights and anticolonial commitments in light of the anti-apartheid legacy of the 1980s. Anti-apartheid, then, became the latest way of speaking back, attempting to prise loose the grip of racial effects as much in the form of a dynamic and vibrant multiculturalism on the postcolonial metropoles and its satellites as on apartheid South Africa.

Anticolonial movements often gave way in the former colonies eventually to what Achille Mbembe has insightfully characterized as "the postcolony." In the worst cases, these are withering, debilitating, and abandoned spaces rather than conditions promoting economic independence, demographic upliftment, and the promise of human flourishing. In the extreme they feature the demise of state formation itself, the erosion of all state services and solidarities, safety nets and social securities. Postcolonies are marked by a mix of local affiliations to more or less powerful protective syndicates headed by an aggressive patriarchal figure offering security for those falling under the force of his militia together with the terror among those who invoke his wrath or happen to embody abandoned or unfavorable characteristics, cultures, or affiliations. Of course, not all formerly colonial states have suffered these extreme effects. However, neoliberal economic policies imposed by the dominant powers and global economic institutions upon marginalized economies and societies have tended to push a number of descriptively postcolonial states – those which for various reasons have remained marginal to the extractive conditions of neoliberalizing global political economy – to more or less repressive or anarchic postcolonies.

The civil rights movement in the US, by contrast, clearly has had significantly better if still decidedly mixed results. It has helped to consolidate a more ethnoracially diversified middle class with some economic access and local political power but with definitive limits at the broader national level. These affirmations are offset, nevertheless, by the increasing numbers of impoverished and deprived families of color and a ballooning prison population overwhelmingly black and Latino. The civil rights movement nonetheless managed to invigorate broad antiracist sensibilities alongside expanded civil rights for all, and served as a beacon of sorts, even if a tenuous one, for global standards of ethnoracial civility.

In the wake of anticolonial and civil rights successes, it turns out, there emerged dramatically increased demographic diversification in the former metropolitan colonizing powers as a result of new waves of economic migration, refugees from repression and war, and metropolitan demands for labor in the face of their own aging populations. Multicultural movements thus are cultural expressions of increasing demographic diversity complemented by a more vigorous class mobilization than previously experienced. Multiculturalism sought to secure and embody these ethnoracial shifts in social culture and institutions, to open up socio-cultural arrangements and institutional life to a more diverse set of habits and practices, thus wresting definitional power from narrow homogeneous restriction, repression, and control. In the worst cases, though, multiculturalism has served as a form of appeasement for those increasingly left behind as well as convenient public relations and advertising modalities for corporate interests.

Generalizabilities

A number of general considerations are to be noted about all of the antiracist historical movements I identify here. First, antiracist movements were fueled in all three moments by broad trans-racial, multi-gendered, and generally cross-class coalitions, whether within or across societies. Shored up by international capital and the local racial structures and expressive cultures thus produced and sustained, racial slavery, colonialism, segregation, and apartheid could only be confronted effectively by such broad coalitional mobilization. Abolitionism ultimately was a mix of brave black, brown, and white women and men saving lives via underground railroads, while risking reputations, social status, and life itself over national borders and across oceans.

Anticolonialism and civil rights struggles were global movements. Men, women, and even children engaged in trans- and inter- and multi-racial mobilizations regarding Africa and African America, Asia and Latin America, often (though not always) with a feminist thrust. Long guerilla campaigns in Kenya or Zimbabwe, Algeria or Angola, Mozambique or Vietnam, and a long march in China were matched by civil rights marches in Selma or on Washington, confronting cannon fire in the one instance and water cannon in the other. Anti-apartheid mobilizations offered an even more robust multi-dimensional global and cross-racial movement alongside township mass mobilization beneath asphyxiating tear gas and uprisings before the gun turrets of "Casspirs full of love," as the noted South African artist William Kentridge has ironically put it. These local South African anti-apartheid expressions were joined by multicultural mass rallies in Trafalgar Square, student divestment campaigns on American campuses, art exhibits in Paris and Amsterdam, not to mention Cuban and Palestinian, African-American and Afro-Brazilian solidarities. Antiracist mobilizations were necessarily linked (or served as a prelude) to more obviously recognizable multiculturalisms and, indeed, in many and varied instances their repressions.

Second, like racisms, antiracism in each of these instances is a name for a range of conceptions, activities and practices, coalitions and organizations. As antiracist they share the commitment to undo racism. But it should be self-evident from the above account that what might be meant by the designation, what means might properly be employed, and who might be legitimate contenders as well as objects of critique and action differ on a more or less case-by-case basis. For all this range, however, these antiracist social movements were *political* struggles, in Dipesh Chakrabarty's sense of the term, struggles over the terms of self-representation and self-determination, for "full participation in the political life of the nation."

Third, while it may seem obvious in all three cases that antiracist struggle is also antiracial struggle, this connection in fact is not always so straightforward or clear. Consider the shift from racial naturalism to historicism, from the inherent inferiority claim fueling racial slavery and apartheid to the claim of historical immaturity and unskilled ineptitude, even if admitted moral equality, underpinning much of the white and bourgeois abolitionist movement, condescending anticolonialisms, and the less affirming expressions of the affirmative action debate. Or consider yet again and more recently the begrudging white ceding of political power in the face of apartheid's demise. In the historicist and post-apartheid instances, whites no longer bedeviled blacks by explicit insults of inherent ineptitude so much as they damned them to ongoing impoverishment by dismissals of their lingering lack of skill rationalized away by claims to cultural poverty. In doing so, they were reserving to themselves the differential power to compete and consume, to define and determine.

So, fourth (and as a prelude to the fifth point), all the antiracist social movements were committed to transforming the racial status quo, the prevailing set of stultifying and subjugating conditions of existence for those deemed not white. What the movements ended up doing in each instance, not insignificantly but also revealingly, was to admit, all too often begrudgingly, those hitherto excluded into social arrangements and conditions the definitions of which continued to be dominated by those who had held racial power in the first place. This nominal admission was, for the most part, principally legal. Political, social, and cultural recognition and access were much less compelling and so more ambivalent. What changed little or less so were the criteria of incorporation and the defining power over those criteria. This insistence on controlling the criteria of incorporation, and so on replicating sameness, Philomena Essed and I have analyzed as central to the logic of cloning culture. Former slaves could compete formally for positions from which they were hitherto excluded as slaves and now excluded for the most part by (relative) lack of education, training, capital, accumulated wealth, and social standing. Likewise, though in different ways and to different degrees, with former colonial or segregated subjects and apartheid's discarded. Equal access to unequal resources and possibilities from positions of unequal preparation and power ultimately entails a third-class ticket to nowhere.

It follows that, fifth – and this is the heart of the argument I am insisting on elaborating – in wake of each of these broad antiracist social, political, economic, and legal mobilizations (for each consisted of the combination), antiracism gave way to the dominant trend of antiracialism. Success in doing away with the legal superstructure of racial subjugation gave way (or in) quite quickly to concerns not so much over differential economic or social access and possibilities as considerations of racial categorization and classification, racial preferences and group-conceived possibilities. Why this common shift in each instance? What is represented in these shifts? What is curtailed, simplified, effected, forgotten, denied? In short, how is the bearing of racial weight shifted in the name of its shedding?

Conceived in this way, one could query why the fight against antisemitism doesn't appear as one of the principal expressions of antiracist social movements. The reasons, I think, are revealing. Clearly, the fight against antisemitism has been global and coalitional. And yet, in declaring antisemitism certainly since the Shoah as the constitutive extreme, always the exceptional case, the struggle against antisemitism has characterized itself in the singular, as exemplary, as unlike any other struggle. It has resisted extension to others who for whatever conceptual reasons, strategic positioning, or political gain would have the mantle cover them. There is a generality, a gesture at least to generalizability if not universalism, fueling antiracist social movements: to be free, like others; to be self-determining, independent, treated as a human being, like others. The case against antisemitism, by contrast, turned on the insistence to be left alone, to be free perhaps but even if it meant others' constriction and devaluation, even destruction. The legacy perhaps of a "Chosen People." That's what exceptionalism amounts to. The national(ist) drive to an independent homeland, the grounds for so many coalitional struggles against invasive forces, became for Jews the destruction of homes and hopes for those perceived to stand in the way. And yet one could point to the racial dimensions of Israel's very definition only at risk of being ostracised, of being branded irrational, of being bedeviled as racist, as we'll see in chapters that follow. The difficulty to name the fight against antisemitism as such reveals the point at issue. Anti-antisemitism, assimilation, the War of Independence, or Israel's struggle to survive are either too awkward, too nebulous on one register of antiracist commitment, or speak to a specificity too narrow to the task, on another.

Antifascism fares better. It clearly counts as a broad coalitional social movement, its object(s) and ends are well defined without being too delimiting. And yet one can query whether it properly amounts to an anti*racist* movement. One can certainly think of oneself or others as the victims of fascist repression, as bound or moved by a fascist state, without resorting to racial terms, without that social formation being conceived – at least not principally – racially. Pol Pot's Cambodia or Myanmar today perhaps come to mind. One would be hard pressed to say the same thing about European slavery from the early seventeenth to the late nineteenth centuries, of colonialism or Jim Crow, apartheid South Africa or latter-day multicultural states. Major critical analyses can be written – consider Nikos Poulantzas's *Fascism and Dictatorship*, for one – in which race barely registers a mention. Indeed, Poulantzas himself points out quickly that there can be fascist regimes or state formations from which racism and antisemitism are mostly if not wholly absent. While racial configuration, as I have argued elsewhere, is constitutive of modern state formation, fascism per se is not, Paul Gilroy's sometime suggestion to the contrary notwithstanding.

If race is not a necessary condition for conceiving fascist social formations or states – that it may be a sufficient condition is a different question – it cannot be so for antifascist social movements either. And as Michael Hanchard has pointed out, notable antifascist commitments have been marked more than occasionally by their own racist articulations (one can say this also about antiracist social movements, though more awkwardly). One can be against fascism, give one's life to the cause, having paid scant attention to whatever racial dimensions might be operative at all. Here too one can distinguish antiracism from antifascism by asking not what each resists but what each is for. If anti-antisemitism is reactively about the particularities of letting Jews be, the refusal to be picked out, antifascism concerns the generalities of living free from physical and ideological repression and from the broadly totalizing and insistently homogenizing social, economic, political, legal, and cultural conditions promoting such

reductive statist repression and constraint in the name of the at once masculinized and emasculated nation. Antiracism concerns facing down those
repressive and constraining conditions conceived, mobilized, and effected
in the name of and through racial conception. Intersecting as they all may
be at various historical moments, they remain analytically and sometimes
historically discrete.

To be clear, to reiterate: I am suggesting that in the wake of whatever
nominal successes, antiracist struggle gave way in each instance to antiracial commitments at the expense of antiracist effects and ongoing
struggle. It is telling to note that Daniel Patrick Moynihan noted something
like this emerging shift as early as 1968 in the case of the civil rights wake,
in an article presciently entitled "The New Racialism." The material gains
of the civil rights movement, he was suggesting presciently, were being
stymied or set back by the emerging emphasis on rendering any reference
to race illegitimate, irrespective of the (inclusionary or exclusionary)
motivation or implication. Antiracism requires historical memory, recalling the conditions of racial degradation and relating contemporary to historical and local to global conditions. If antiracist commitment requires
remembering and recalling, antiracialism suggests forgetting, getting over,
moving on, wiping away the terms of reference, at best (or worst) a
commercial memorializing rather than a recounting and redressing of the
terms of humiliation and devaluation. Indeed, antiracialism seeks to wipe
out the terms of reference, to wipe away the very vocabulary necessary to
recall and recollect, to make a case, to make a claim.

Antiracialism, it turns out, takes hold – becomes insistent, one might say
begins to make itself heard – once the antiracist struggles have achieved
their initial but incomplete goals. Antiracialism marks the moment that a
society is accepted into (or even as a momentary moral leader of) the world.
It marks, in a word, the moment of globalization's relative (and repeated)
triumph. To be of the world, in the world, a worldly society, racism nominally has been rejected. Now the category of race must be erased. But we
are being asked to give up on race before and without addressing the legacy,
the roots, the scars of racisms' histories, the weights of race. We are being
asked to give up on the word, the concept, the category, at most the categorizing. But not, pointedly not, the conditions for which those terms stand.
In the beginning was the deed; in the end, to undo the deed, the word should
not be uttered.

Even more ironically, the call of antracialism, while representing the
triumph of the global, is always a *local* call, in a word, the reduction of the

global to the local, the work of the global silently by making the local do its work *only at the local level.* There is no global *antiracial* movement. Look about, find it you will not. Where antiracisms were – how do I lapse here into the past tense? – truly global movements, antiracialism is never more than a local call. Why, it must be asked. What is going on here?

As an end in itself, antiracialism, it turns out for the most part, is whiteness by another name, by other means, with recruitment of people of color to act as public spokespersons for the cause. The targets of racism, by contrast and for the most part, are concerned less with and about the category than with the conditions, the artifice and fabrication, of their restriction and exclusion, their humiliation and degradation. They are concerned, in short, less with the concept of race than with the culture(s) of racism, the cultivating of racisms. Antiracialism is about decategorization, a gesture necessarily by the racially dominant towards those they racially suppress. Antiracism, by contrast, involves itself centrally, among other things, in what Fanon has called decorroboration by the racially repressed of the racially self-elevated. It seeks to remove the condition not indirectly through removal of the category in the name of which the repression is enacted. Rather, it seeks to remove the structure of the condition itself. This is not to say that categorically getting beyond or over race is not a worthy cause. The question has deeply to do with what one takes oneself to be getting over and beyond, and how then to achieve the *aufhebung*, "the overcoming."

The shifts from broad, globally interconnected antiracist social movements in each instance mapped above to local and much narrower antiracialist commitments represent a turn to formalism in the face of impending material shifts of potentially immense proportion. Antiracist social mobilizations in each historical case fueled gathering momentum to open up institutional access and invigorate competition, to transform voting patterns and relations of power, to undo the easy and complacent stabilities of neighborhoods and cultural sedimentation. Privileges came unfixed, profitabilities were imperiled, property desanctified, powers challenged. Antiracist mobilization had sought in each case to end the immobilizing and terrorizing conditions racist order had made manifest and maintained, manufactured and managed. The immobilization under racist repression gave way – if not in – to mobilization, terror turned to transformability, trauma triggered trespass, all threatening if not an overturning at least a turning over.

No sooner had these shifts been successfully signaled, if not fully effected, than the force(s) of racial order reached for the formalism of the law. In the face of instabilities and insecurities, state recourse in each instance quickly reduced to an insistence upon formal equality. There are of course some not insignificant differences between the instances I cite. Nevertheless, at the level of generalization, Reconstruction, "We shall overcome," and "a new South Africa" all gave way in a blur to a state-mandated nonracialism, the drive for some sort of substantive equality to a nominal categorical blindness under but neither before nor beyond the law. Formalism "saved" racism in each case by abandoning (or at least threatening to abandon) race. Call this *born again racism.*

Born again racism is racism without race, racism gone private, racism without the categories to name it as such. It is racism shorn of the charge, a racism that cannot be named because nothing abounds with which to name it. It is a racism purged of historical roots, of its groundedness, a racism whose history is lost. In the wake of the UN Conference on Racism in Durban, Condoleezza Rice (then US National Security Advisor and now the most senior and visible African American in the Bush administration) apparently recommended that those in the United States should forget (about) slavery, as the enactment of civil society, she insisted, necessitates forgetting – really erasing – the past.

Born again racism, then, is a racism acknowledged, where acknowledged at all, as individualized faith, of the socially dislocated heart, rather than as institutionalized inequality. "I understand that racism still lingers in America," declared President George W. Bush, addressing the NAACP for the first time six years into his presidency. "It's a lot easier to change a law than to change a human heart." In short, born again racism is an unrecognized racism for there are no terms by which it could be recognized: no precedent, no intent, no pattern, no institutional explication. That, at least, is the vision. It is a perfectly transparent – a virtual – racism, unseen because see-through. It is a racism of profiles denied, the claim to perfected clones and copies, privatized preferences, policed boundaries, and policy restraints.

The formalism of "separate but equal" in the US historical context couldn't quite pull off that picture. "Separate but equal" rationalized the differential quality for blacks and whites of public accommodations such as railway carriages and public education facilities so long as each group equally had access to some such public accommodations, no matter the differential quality. The legal sleight of hand was to equalize nominal access at the expense of equalizing the standard or quality of accommodations. Equality in this scheme would be preserved so long as a black

person could ride in a third-class carriage or study in a third-class institution no matter that first-class facilities in each case had been reserved
exclusively for whites. A devil's contract, to be sure.

The magic of law's formalism in these instances had to be too heavily
and visibly undergirded by the force of physical violence to remain
broadly and self-consciously comfortable over an extended period. By
contrast, the Racial Privacy Act promoted by Ward Connerly and the same
forces that undid affirmative action in the state of California has captured
all too well the dual logic of constraining public intervention regarding racial
matters. If Ward Connerly and his (reverse robin) hoods would have their
ways, the state would be constrained from registering race, specifically
or abstractly, in any case other than for law enforcement profiling or for
medical research, while liberating private discrimination from public
constraint. There is a double limitation on public intervention: direct
discrimination by public agencies is delimited, but the state and its agencies are almost completely constrained from preventing properly private
discrimination. And where California runs, the rest of the US seems ready
to rush. Racism is crucified in public only to be born again in private. The
implications are volcanic, burying the gains of the civil rights movement
– not to mention of the anticolonial and anti-apartheid struggles in other
national contexts – beneath the rubble of antiracialist eruptions.

There is no history, one might say, without remembrance: no history of
or for those not remembered, whose past is not made present, whose past
is deemed to have no presence. There is no remembering of some pasts –
of those not simply marginalized in a society but marginalized because of
and through their pasts – then, and so no history (for them) either. And
no history of and for them means their absence from the (ethno)national
history that is taken to make up the society's frame of reference, its sense
of itself. The Museum of Ethnography in Budapest lists 23 or so ethnic
groups in the history of Hungary, but not Jews. Jews are absent from the
national narrative of Hungary, at least as told today by that national
museum. This despite the fact that as late as the onset of 1944 there were
approximately 750,000 Jews in Hungary, over 100,000 in Budapest alone.
Today the Jewish population of Hungary is a mere 16,000, the rest largely
annihilated by Nazis and their Hungarian supporters in that fateful final
year of the Shoah.

If you are not memorable, if you have no worthy history, then you are
deemed to have no claim not simply on national remembrance but on the
nation-state itself, because you are seen to have no place in it. On parallel

logic, the death wish of racial classification in the United States and else-where is at one with the absence of racial slavery from national consciousness, with the absence of those cultures considered marginal to the prevailing national narrative. In introducing a bill in the US Senate to promote increased teaching of American history and civics in the wake of 9/11, Senator Lamar Alexander, former Republican presidential candidate, emphasized that "American history has been watered down, textbooks are dull, and their pages feature victims and diminish heroes." This individualization of heroic history, "so our children can grow up learning what it means to be American," is designed to remove the categories for claiming redress, to remove the stain of pained group histories from the national record, to make children American, to nationalize them, by lobotomizing racial violence from historical consciousness. It is, as Norman Mailer has characteristic-ally put it in writing about George W. Bush's belligerence, the case of "white man's unburdening." The logic is fast being generalized: Afghanistan, Iraq, Palestine . . .

Born again racism reappears whenever called upon to do the dirty work of racist politics but purged of its categorical stiffness. Indeed, shed of its stiff categoricality, raceless racism operates in denial, anywhere and any-time. The concern over police profiling, for instance, has quickly shifted from denying its prevalence, if not its possibility, to affirming that there is nothing wrong with profiling for the sake of security and anti-terrorist vigilance. The concern over victims of state violence has shifted from claims of protecting the innocent to dismissive rationalizations of collateral damage (read: they are really not like us, or shouldn't have been there – where "there" just happens to be their home or neighborhood).

Collateral damage, as Mahmood Mamdani remarks, is not an unfor-tunate by-product of war but its very elaboration. One-time concerns about spheres of influence and area studies in geostrategic competition have now given way to narrow concerns about control of strategic global resources and fitting "our" (US, British, Israeli, or begrudgingly European) geostrategic and security interests. The register of race has shifted from the broadly institutional, from which it is at least explicitly excised, to the micro-relational of everyday interactions, on the one hand, and the macro-political strategizing of geo-global interests, on the other. The two in the end go hand in glove, to extend that bloody metaphor I invoked earlier. Palestinians are the most pressed contemporary targets of this dual logic, though anyone today who is or is mistaken for a Muslim is deemed fair game.

This exemplification of the contemporary logic of race reveals what I am driving at: that in the name now even of a denial of formal racial reference, in the shift from racial reference to perverted insecurities, there is the recognition that the histories of racisms, including their histories of the present, are those of terror and death, of death's production, of terror and death in the name of identity and identification. These histories render it impossible to think of race in the absence of racism, to erase race and not have its histories of death and destruction haunt. The racially subjugated are the ghosts of slave and colonial pasts, and by extension of postcolonizing presents. *They* are see-through people, traces of history all but erased from the record. In all the cases of post-World War II wars fought by the US, wars not fought in the United States but always elsewhere seeking to externalize the threat of the strange and the alien, the targets may be characterized in classical ethnoracial terms as not white: Korea, Vietnam, Grenada, Panama, Iraq, Somalia, Afghanistan, Iraq again or without cease in the past decade – not to mention all those proxy wars in Latin America, the Middle East, Africa, and Asia, and not to forget the immediate global war on terrorism. The Balkans, too, resonate at the margins of Europe with thickly, if complex, ethnoracial undertones.

Following Foucault, Ruthie Gilmore has gone so far as to define racism in terms of a relation to death. Racism, she notes, is the likely promotion of the premature death of those individuals and groups subjected to the debilitating terms and conditions of racist configurations and exclusions. There is something unsettlingly significant in her insight: racism both involves the increased probability of premature death for those who are the victims of its violence and foreshortens the lives of those who, but for its institutionalized pressures and effects, for its mark(s), would very likely (inevitably?) live better, longer, more productive, less fraught lives. The death at issue may be physical or social, and where social it renders those suffering it significantly more vulnerable to physical death too. Racism, then, produces the conditions, directly or indirectly, that serve to foreshorten life directly but also foreshorten life's opportunities. Racism of course includes delimbing, whipping, hanging, beating, bombing, shooting or gassing. But it is also targeted or collateral malnutrition (a lack of food and bad food), stress formation, physical debilitation, humiliation, and degradation.

This way of conceiving racism is not meant to belittle or ignore everyday racist micro-expressions such as security guard harassment in stores, sidewalk epithets, refusing or rude taxi-cab or bus drivers and passengers, dismissive, anxious, and unhelpful school teachers, or presumptuous anti-affirmative action litigants. While much of recent accounts about racial matters – in the US especially – have focused on these latter micro-expressions, they are disturbing as much because of their cumulative effects to debilitate and render unwelcome their racially conceived objects, to extend their exclusion, and to heighten the likelihood of foreshortened lives as they are outrageous in themselves. In short, accumulated everyday racisms dispose their object populations, exposing them to extended abjection, rendering them readier, more vulnerable targets of legitimated violence and ultimately unnoticed or overlooked death.

Everyday expressions serve accordingly as a form of what Mahmood Mamdani calls "racial branding," marking a group and its members as vulnerable and thereby disposing them guiltlessly to abject treatment and in the final analysis extermination. Considering racism as the rationalized disposition or vulnerability to premature death is intended to shift the prevailing sense in racial studies that racist violence is now anomalous, largely exceptional, and secondary to the lingering conditions of individuated hate or discriminations. This erosion ignores the relation of the everyday to large-scale institutional violence, of individuated expressions to the likes of ethnoracial cleansing, obliviousness among inhabitants of globally powerful states to terrorizing invisibility, and routine threat to large-scale, state-directed preemptive strikes.

If one's own survival is heightened by the reassuring spectacle of another's death, as Achille Mbembe insightfully puts it in writing about "necropolitics," then national survival is borne out by keeping death at bay, by ensuring that if there is to be death it is the death of those not one's own. Israeli security and survival, in the limit case, have come to be hitched to the demise of those characterized as threatening them. Palestinian death and destruction (of property, institutions, security itself) are evidence – insurance – of Israeli defiance of death. And perhaps vice versa. A cruel and ultimately self-defeating logic, one that is generalizable, revealed especially in its apparently racial production and rationalization. My killing those supposedly racially not like me secures the projection of my racial being; but in predicating my security on a foundation that motivates a counter-killing equally racially predicated, my security is coterminously and at the deepest level an insecurity. Security through the destruction of those not (like) me is tantamount to the insecurity and ultimately threat and fear of death of the self-denyingly secure.

I am concerned in what follows with mapping out some of the more or less programmatic threads of these lingering logics of racial threat and terror, of violence and death, and of the inextricable entanglements of security with insecurity and the undermining of safety. I am concerned to ask, to reveal, what gets unasked in the revelation of these logics, in these linkages, what haunts us as we remember and forget, in what we remember to forget and forget to remember. And to consider the remaining racial effects on how we think and live the social betwixt and between of racial arrangement and order, of racial states. The claim of the evaporation – the death – of race is really a claim not about racial death but about "the end," the disappearance, of racism, seeking to evade thus the violent and deadly ends, all those threats, large and small, geopolitical and everyday, in the service of which racisms continue to be pressed into practice.

The wider project buried in the general line of argument in this book, then, is to insist on a double shift in the study of racial matters: First, from the increasing focus on race and racial classifications to the more troubled, connected, and underlying concerns with racisms, with racially produced exclusions, violence, destruction, and their threat. And second, relatedly, from the growing focus on cultural representations of racial expression to the ongoing and too often overlooked threats and manifestations of violence and violations, disease, death, and destruction activated, represented, and rationalized in the name of race.

Generally conceived, the principal historical prompts for racial conception and derogation have been threefold. For one, race as the marker of difference, distinction, and (potential) debilitation has been caught up with *curiosity*, initially much as nature prompted interest or concern, and later as the lure of cultural fascination. Second, race has served as the mark of *exploitability*, whether as its grounds or its rationalization. Those tagged as ethnoracially different could be made to labor under exploitative conditions, much as work animals might, or might be identified as culturally disposed to excel stereotypically at certain tasks: those of African background at physical tasks and more recently at certain sorts of sport, the English at intellectual labor, Sherpa as mountain guides at high altitudes, Jews at the management of money, and so on. The presumed expertise (or lack) in each case might suggest or rationalize away the supposed use-value identified with each, their supposed (degree of) exploitability.

Finally, in designating difference race carries with it sooner or later the suggestion of *threat*. Whether understood as naturally different or culturally distinct, an ethnoracially identified group might be seen in varying circumstances to conjure or condition, raise or rationalize anxieties about insecurity, possible loss, viral infection, even extinction and survivability.

While curiosity and exploitability have lingered throughout the histories of racial extension, and remain resonant variously within racial reference and mobilization today, it is threat that has assumed overriding contemporary significance in racial matters, absorbing the other two largely into its orbit. Race increasingly and increasingly baldly turned to threat as global condition more or less coterminous with the dominant shift in racial meanings from the natural to the cultural in the post-abolition period as the nineteenth gave way to the twentieth century, and as once distant peoples became (potential) neighbors, competitors, fellow citizens with supposedly divergent political interests. The abolitionist, anti-colonial, civil rights, and anti-apartheid demands for equality in socio-legal rights, educational and economic fair play conjured threat to long-held assumptions of "natural" dominance, settled hierarchies, and cultural superiority. Perceived racial threat fuels fear of loss – of power, of resources, of competitiveness, of life itself – and their attendant antagonisms and aggressivities. This sense of threat, almost invariably tinged with anxiety or exacerbated by paranoia upon racial mediation, tends to articulate self- with social protection, no matter the cost.

All three racial prompts have encouraged, exacerbated, and extended vulnerability, aggression, and violence. But without belittling the suffering prompted by curiosity and exploitability, the aggravations with which they can be identified tend to be mediated by the fact that they each necessitate an engagement – more or less direct interaction – with their objectified subjects. Threat, by contrast, largely does not; in fact, those deemed threatening are held at a distance, whether physically or emotionally, psychologically or politically. Threat undercuts the possibility of such mediation, delimiting engagement to the violence of incarceration or the instrumentalities of incapacitation. In short, threat for the most part seeks distantiation of one sort or another, not engagement, whether spatially or symbolically, materially or rhetorically enacted. But the other side of threat entails also that the group – the "population" – seen as threatening is the one actually threatened: with alienation, intimidation, incarceration, marginalization and externalization of one kind or another, ultimately even with extinction.

It is with a cartographic comprehension of racially emergent and rationalized threats that this book will be concerned, and with their contemporary social arrangements of evasion and evaporation of responsibility but also of the possible conditions and practices of their undoing. In short, *The Threat of Race* concerns itself with changing forms and expressions of racisms across regions and time, contemporarily articulated if historically indexed. It maps racially articulated delimitations, the territorializations and regionalizations, of life's possibilities. It draws out their denials and refusals, material sedimentations and traces, their erasures and evaporations in public memory and from contemporary state accountability, their failures and fragilities. It considers their representations and rationalizations, their silent implications and their coded suggestibilities, their devastating effects but also their courageous resistances, restrictions, and refusals. And it does so with a view to accounting ultimately for the relation between racial evaporation and erasure as explicit conception of state governmentality under globalizing neoliberal conditions today across a broad swath of societies and the increasing difficulty as a consequence of considering racisms critically, of resisting them. *The Threat of Race*, in brief, concerns itself with tracing out the terrains of race, racelessness, racisms, their refinements and redirections under contemporary social conditions.

Bibliography

Abu El-Haj, Nadia 2004: " 'A Tool to Recover Past Histories': Genealogy and Identity after the Genome," Unpublished Paper, December.

Appiah, Kwame Anthony 1990: "Racisms," in David Theo Goldberg (ed.), *Anatomy of Racism*. Minneapolis: University of Minnesota Press, pp. 3–18.

Bourdieu, Pierre et al. 2003: *The Weight of the World*. Cambridge: Polity Press.

Césaire, Aimé 1939/1995: *Cahier d'un retour au pays natal* [*Notebook of a Return to My Native Land*]. Newcastle upon Tyne: Bloodaxe Books.

Chakrabarty, Dipesh 2000: *Provincializing Europe: Postcolonial Thought and Historical Difference*. Princeton: Princeton University Press.

Edwards, Brent Hayes 2003: *The Practice of Diaspora*. Cambridge, MA: Harvard University Press.

Essed, Philomena and Goldberg, David Theo 2002: "Cloning Cultures: The Social Injustices of Sameness," *Ethnic and Racial Studies*, 25, 6 (November), 1066–82.

Fanon, Frantz 1970: *Black Skin, White Masks*. New York: Paladin.

Fischer, Sibylle 2004: *Modernity Disavowed: Haiti and the Culture of Slavery in the Age of Revolution*. Durham, NC: Duke University Press.

Foucault, Michel 2003: *"Society Must Be Defended": Lectures at the Collège de France, 1975–76*. Trans. David Macey. New York: Picador.

Fredrickson, George 2002: *Racism: A Short History*. Princeton: Princeton University Press.

Gilmore, Ruth Wilson 2006: *Golden Gulag.* Berkeley: University of California Press.

Hanchard, Michael 2009: "Racisms as Politics?" in Kim Benito Furumoto (ed.), *Race's Ghostly Words.* Durham, NC: Duke University Press. MS on file.

Heng, Geraldine 2003: *Empire of Magic.* New York: Columbia University Press.

Hilberg, Raul 2003: *The Destruction of the European Jews,* Vol. 2, 3rd ed. New Haven: Yale University Press.

Katzew, Ilona 2004: *Casta Painting: Images of Race in Eighteenth Century Mexico.* New Haven: Yale University Press.

Locke, Alain 1925a: "Enter the New Negro," *The Survey Graphic Harlem Number* (March).

Locke, Alain 1925b: *The New Negro: An Interpretation.* New York: Albert and Charles Boni.

Mamdani, Mahmood 2001: *When Victims Become Killers: Colonialism, Nativism, and the Genocide in Rwanda.* Princeton: Princeton University Press.

Mbembe, Achille 2001: *On the Postcolony.* Berkeley: University of California Press.

Mbembe, Achille 2003: "Necropolitics," *Public Culture,* 15, 1 (Winter), 11–40.

Meeuse, Aik 1981: "Fascisme en Anti-fascisme," in *Oud en Neuw Fascisme.* Amsterdam: Anne Frank Stichting.

Moynihan, Danel Patrick 1968: "The New Racialism," *Atlantic Monthly,* www.theatlantic.com/politics/race/moynihan.htm.

Ngūgī wa Thiong'o 1986: *Decolonizing the Mind: The Politics of Language in African Literature.* Portsmouth: Heinemann.

Pieterse, Jan Nederveen and Parekh, Bhikhu, eds. 1995: *The Decolonization of the Imagination.* London: Zed.

Poulantzas, Nicos 1979: *Fascism and Dictatorship.* London: Verso.

Raffles, Hugh 2007: "Jews, Lice, and History," *Public Culture,* 19, 3 (Fall), 521–66.

Reichman, Deb 2006: "Bush to NAACP: 'I Understand That Racism Still Lingers,'" Associated Press, July 20; www.signonsandiego.com/news/nation/20060720-0912-bush-naacp.html.

Walcott, Derek 2003: "Exasperating Theory," in Okwui Enwezor et al. (eds.), *Creolite and Creolization: Documenta 11_Platform 3.* Ostfildern-Ruit: Hatje Cantz, pp. 19–20.

2

"Killing Me Softly":
Civility/Race/Violence

*Race is, politically speaking, not the beginning of humanity but its end,
. . . not the natural birth of man but his unnatural death.*

Hannah Arendt

Civility's fading (and failing), so commonly supposed as the contemporary condition, has been attributed for the most part to the increasing heterogeneity and diversification of modern urban environments. It has been blamed also for a variety of social ills. These have ranged from charges of selfish and hyper-individualized societies, care-less and increasingly litigious (consider Stephen Carter's flat and flatulently insistent excuse for Christian revivalism), to complaints of societies stricken by runaway crime rates, vulgarity and violence (as in James Q. Wilson's causal connection of crime to rising incivility).

The model of the United States obviously looms large in this imaginary of concern and complaint. And yet European unsettlement over growing numbers of Muslim counter-settlers and threatened intercourse, social and sexual, between European daughters (invariably) and Middle Eastern boys has produced comparable disquiet. The horrors of World Trade Center trauma, pentagonal destruction, and Madrid and London train terror have been attributed variously to the radical incivilities in the name of jihad, on one hand, and to sex, drugs, and free speech, on the other. The post-9/11 revival of Samuel Huntington's "clash of civilizations" rhetoric among American neoconservative warmongers such as Perle, Wolfowitz, Pipes, Feith and the like, or Pat Robertson's urging, while ventriloquizing Jerry Falwell on infidelity, "to speak truth to us brother," are matched by Pim Fortuyn paranoia, head scarf hysteria, and alien invasion throughout Europe.

By contrast, and curiously enough, the depths of despair and fear in the aftermath of terror's traumatizing work miraculously conceived the rebirth of civility in that apparently most godless of cities, Gotham's wormy and now coreless apple. If there is a condition of postmodernity, here perhaps lie its prime symbols, if not most naked expressions: destruction just beneath civility, civilization against jihad, fear entangled with threat, racial death behind the conceptual calls for the death of race.

This supposed cinematic fade to and from the dark ages of in/civility (as the case may be) is contemporaneous with the heterogenizing of supposedly civil(ized) states in the wake of post-World War II decolonization, and the consequent postcolonial counter-migrations from south to north, east to west. It is tied thus also to the asserted and assertive assault of multicultural force(s) on standard profiles of citizenship and its attendant commitments. Indeed, it did not take long to link causally or critically the tragedy of the Manhattan syndrome to heterogenizing globalities, in often complex and contradictory ways. So while the smarmy Falwell/Robertson corporate religiosity (or religious corporatism) signaled the causal connection to a world devoid of godliness, as too does Carter though in less apocalyptic language, James Davison Hunter of cultural war characterization conjured the post-traumatic connection to the shallowness of a politically correct leftish academy bereft of depth or explanation in its wake. Claiming center by equating left with right, an old liberal trick. Politics as usual beneath the façade of a reinvented civility.

Elected to retroject civility (back) into the presidency, George Walker Bush could claim to "leave no child behind" and adult medically uninsured in the name of "compassionate conservatism." With the push of the same pen he could shift public funds to private schooling and HMOs; he could order the devastation of a society in the name of wiping out "weapons of mass destruction" for which no evidence existed or could subsequently be found; and he could criminalize large portions of the world's population so as to "keep the United States secure." (What, for example, have Brazilians, among others, had to do with fomenting global terrorism besides electing a trade unionist president?)

The apocalyptic connection between civility and civilization has been quickly resurrected. So Silvio Berlusconi, controversial (at once past and reborn) premier entrepreneur of Italy and unstinting buddy of Bush, shortly after September 11 exhorted that "we should be confident of the superiority of our civilization because of the religious and human rights generated, something that does not exist in Islamic countries." And in a particularly nasty e-column on the one-month anniversary of world trade devastation equating support for affirmative action with that for terrorists (mockingly titled "Affirmative Action for Osama"), fundamentalist-neocon critic Ann Coulter remarked that:

> Under the affirmative action program now pending before the Supreme Court in *Adarand Constructors v. Mineta*, each of the 12,000 boys born in Pakistan last year who were named "Osama" would be granted preferential treatment over American-born whites. They just have to immigrate here. Our government discriminates against native-born Americans in favor of Pakistanis.
>
> If Islam is not responsible for terrorism, why is Vinnie [the name Coulter gives to her Hollywood composite white cousin fighter pilot flying sorties over Afghanistan] responsible for slavery? I'm just trying to get the rules straight on collective guilt. It's perplexing to hear liberals carrying on so about how peaceful most Muslims are. That's surely true, just as the vast majority of whites oppose slavery. But the very same people who are anxious to quell the rare anti-Arab hate crimes in response to 19 Arabs attacking America are the ones who are usually found ginning up hate crimes against whites for slavery.

Only Muslims, Coulter concluded, are liberally immune from collective responsibility. Lest one be tempted to consider this simply distasteful neocon opportunism to put another nail in the coffin of affirmative action, a week earlier Coulter had implored that "We should invade their countries, kill their leaders and convert them to Christianity." And so "we" have, twice now in just as many years and with decidedly less than definitive, if not decisively radicalizing, threatening results.

Lest this be considered too locally American, recently Martin Amis has repeatedly expressed gross generalizations about Islam and Muslims only less remarked in Britain because, well, more "civilly" stated. Thus Amis has declared the "extreme incuriosity of Islamic culture" and that "there are great problems in Islam." And Dutch parliamentarian Geert Wilders has insisted in his film *Fitna* on linking claims of universalized Islamic violence to Koranic verses in the face of much criticism from the Muslim world and imploring from the Dutch political establishment.

Lest, too, these be considered extreme examples, consider that the United States government recently instituted fingerprinting foreign visitors from 29 countries, including many with no demonstrable link to histories of "terrorism," conventionally understood, and from which list citizens of European states are pointedly excluded (Baader Meinhof, the Red Brigade, the IRA, or ETA, for instance, too faded for official American memory). Sharon's Israel, America's all too often thuggish little sibling in arms, prompted by suicide bombers and Hamas rockets, has terrorized with impunity both Palestinians in territories it now at least half claims as its own and Israeli citizens who object, battering even peaceful women protestors with teargas and truncheons.

Two cases of domestic American airwave abuse should serve to bring the point home. A Ted Koppel "Nightline" special on the 1950s self-taping by Louis Armstrong of his musings about contemporary American life FCC-bleeped all the usual expletives ("shit," "fuck") from the recorded language. Armstrong's repeated use of "nigger," in pointed and painful contrast, remained uncensored. A night or two later on Bill Maher's "Politically Incorrect," airing late night immediately following "Nightline" on ABC until canned after the host had called the WTC suicide bombers "courageous," the topic was a comedian's use of "chink" in a comedy routine (not at all funnily actually, if it ever could be). Again, viewers were subjected to repeated uses of "chink" and "nigger" by the host and two of the evening's four guests, even with all the "appropriate" disclaimers. The open and more or less abusive, even if scare-quoted, circulation of the terms was supported by the network over the explicit protests of the Japanese American and African American guests on the show. Small examples, perhaps, but deeply revealing for all that.

It is these (all too often calculated) slippages between civility and civilizing crusade, civil states and civic violence in the name of (a) race unnamed that conjures the longstanding connection to claimed threats of racial demise and civic fatality, to the ambiguities of racial death, actual as much as conceptual, and to what I mark here as the threat of civic suicide by self-strangulation.

Civility, Civil Society, Civil States

To begin then with what might be tantamount to a cliché: civility assumes almost as many forms as the states – the "civil societies" – which form its ground. Note my pointed collapse here between states of rule and states of being, governmentality and social sensibility (if not sentimentality). Consider, at the broadest level, the contrast between "western" and Islamic modes of civility. After all, and as Achille Mbembe points out, civility is considered a key condition of citizenship, of belonging to (and being at ease with and within) a society, formally and informally. Mbembe's careful formulation – he writes that civility is "known to be," not that it actually is, a "key feature of citizenship" – signals some of the tensions at play here: between the descriptive and normative, "natural" and prescriptive, asserted and forced, presumed and reproduced, commonsensical and imposed. But those tensions between the phenomenological and prescriptive exactly mark out the holy and unholy ground between the local universalized and claims to universality instituted locally, between the civil heterogenized as multiplicitous in expression and the civilized nominalized as singular and unqualified.

There has been a relatively recent renewal of both public and academic discussion about civility and civil society. What is it about social conditions in the past few decades that has bolstered a resurrection of discourses of civility? Why this extensive concentration on civility now? How might these discussions be connected to the insistence on racial evaporation, the death of race, threats in the name of race unnamed or stated and evasion of racisms to which I have drawn attention above? These are questions that have a broader, more general resonance in that a discourse of civility has marked the decades ending and now opening millennia. But they have assumed a more immediate, pressing, and pressed expression in the world-shifting wake of September 11.

For one, civility and civil society have been emphasized in moments where the technologies of destruction and degradation are rife. These latter serve as a kind of counter-force to or recoil from the condition. But they offer also an ideological marker of those contrasting themselves as civil from those they take to deny the condition, or even its possibility. Civility and civil society, not unrelatedly, have been emphasized more extensively also in the wake of globalizing neoliberalism's seeming attack on the state, on the too quickly celebrated demise of the state, as both descriptive and normative matters. If the state's withering before globalization's flourishing is a fait accompli, what else is there as appealing form of social life if not for civil society? Civility itself is a form of presumed homogeneity, or at least predicated on a set of presumptive homogeneous commonalities, not least in the face of perceived threats. Civil wars in states deeming themselves sophisticated, modern, and civilized assume the form of culture wars. They are really civility wars. What, it could be asked here, are the boundaries of the civil? How are these boundaries racially shaped? Why the shift from an earlier social focus on inequalities first to culture and now to civility?

Formulated thus, the emergence of the new seems too tightly tied to the terms of the old. The intellectual fascination with civil society and the attendant virtue of civility of late is not just the desire for the condition (the "state") of relative lack. It is tied also to the relative demise of state theory, of theories of the state over the past nearly thirty years. Globalization supposedly has eroded the hold of states on the lived condition of late modernity (a large supposition, of course, one dramatically undercut by the altogether (re)new(ed) expansionist statist response to September 11). But on this assumption, the generative gap apparently left by the attendant demise of state theory is filled by that social condition of the "not-state" identified since the Enlightenment as civil society and promoted in the name of the individualized disposition conceptualized as civility.

If civil society is the realm of non-state activity, then civility is all one has to fall back on – individually, morally, normatively – where the state recedes and force-flows or the market take over. There is a perverted Hobbesian logic at work here: Where the drive for personal security and fear of one's demise is threatened because of the failure of the state system to protect one, rational choice would have one *not* first and foremost resort to the most violent means necessary for self-protection, as standard readings of Hobbes would seem to suggest. Rather, one would try rationally to generate the diffusion of social civility as the bulwark against initial incursion "from the outside," so to speak. One's security would be the better maintained, sustained, or guaranteed the more likely one could rely on the decent dispositions of those with whom one interacts, both locally and globally, intra- and inter-nationally, as personal politics and the logic of international relations. The discourses of civility and civil society, it turns out, have taken hold in the wake of, as adjunct to, critical rejection of the state in the name of celebrated individualism, of the force of "imperializing" globalization, as Hardt and Negri might put it, but also of the neoliberalist state transformation from a dominant concern with the wellbeing of its citizens to their policing, surveillance, and intensified regulation. Multilateralism, it could be said, is the logic of maximizing the likelihood of unilateral survival.

Civilizing processes, Adam Ferguson argued following Adam Smith in the late eighteenth century, concern the long slow purging of human conditions of discretionary violence. In barbarous nations, insists Ferguson,

> quarrelling had no rules but the immediate dictates of passion, which ended in words of reproach, in violence, and in blows. . . . When they took arms in the divisions of faction, the prevailing party supported itself by expelling their opponents, by proscriptions and bloodshed. The usurper endeavoured

to maintain his station by the most violent and prompt executions. He was opposed, in his turn, by conspiracies and assassinations, in which the most respectable citizens were ready to use the dagger. . . . [In war], [c]ities were razed, or enslaved; the captive sold, mutilated or condemned to die.

By contrast, civilized societies

have mingled politeness with the use of the sword; we have learned to make war under the stipulations of treaties and cartels . . . employing of force, only for the obtaining of justice, and for the preservation of national rights.

George W. Bush reads Adam Ferguson, when he reads at all! Though not without a touch of predictable parochialism: Note at once a central implication of this lingering Hobbesian logic. "Decent dispositions" and "politeness" are better predicted from the familiar, those "one is used to," from those one takes to be more like oneself (and so predictably more prone to behave like one), those sharing one's sense of the civil, the familial, of "our" values, and so potential members of *your* civil society, than those outside your circle of civility. The different become at once the differentiated, and the differentiated the divorceable, the alien and excludable in the self-perpetuating logic or pragmatics of differentiation. The discourses of civility and civil society entail commitment to the rhetorics of civilization, and by extension to the logics of "born again racism" elaborated in Chapter 1 above.

These dispositions to differentiated excludability are magnified in moments of acute crisis or social threat. Thus Tutsis were attacked as the Rwandan state collapsed in the wake of President Habyarimana's mysterious death in an airplane attack, and Muslims in Bosnia became especially vulnerable as the Yugoslav state fractured in the wake of Tito's death. The first person to be falsely accused immediately following the bombing of a US government building in Oklahoma City in 1995 was a local man of Arab descent. And a not untypical sentiment immediately following September 11 is exemplified by the hate mail sent to the Utah attorney general as a result of his insistence on protecting the civil rights of all. The mail read, "Americans have the right to fly Muslim-free." US policy began to enact this perverse liberty, as I write this, with air marshalls forced onto foreign air carriers traversing US air space and planes in flight turned back to their points of foreign departure at the slightest hint of an unrecognizable Arab name aboard, not least because of undifferentiating phonetic spelling of names on airline lists. Self-fashioned threat, or at least its prompting, and attendant fear take over.

Civil society both fuels and is underpinned by a state. But the state form, its principal modality, has transformed from one earlier conceived as care-taker of the population's welfare, its pastoral prescriptive (to use Zygmunt Bauman's term) enacted through modalities of constraining, confining, and containing the undesirable, to that of traffic cop. The traffic cop state polices flows human, capital, and commodity, regulating the political, cultural, and economic. Civil society thus becomes a substantial and substantive focus, the field of flows, shaped and shoved and shifted by the state. It is fash-ioned as "real" – as a sphere independent of, in contrast to, from which criticism can productively be leveled against, the state. Indeed, even by the principal representatives of the state against that very state the apparatuses of which are so readily invoked to undo those rights of citizens deemed civil.

Civil society in this picture accordingly is the sphere, in contemporary parlance and in abstraction from its state-shaping, of non-governmental organizations and new social movements, tax revolts and anti-war pro-tests, of discontent and critique, falling walls and velvet revolutions, failed dictators and people power. So civil society in Eastern Europe in the downfall of communism, in the Philippines or parts of Africa is seen as the reservoir of a democratic possibility in transition from repression to openness, the realm beyond as it is the object of state repression of one variety or another. (It is curious by contrast how little that language is being invoked in respect of Afghanistan – or for that matter Iraq – as though their ruggedness combined with (or giving rise to) their repressive extremisms excludes almost any hope of a civil society and so of any democratic future. Try as we may, too much dirt beneath *those* fingernails.) Civil society accordingly is taken as the realm of face-to-face politics, of spontaneity and struggle, of non- and anti-bureaucratic organizations committed to freeing folks from the yoke of the state.

Civil society accordingly has been thought of as the *non*-state (the *not*-state) and so as the possibility of the "*counter*-state" state or condition of being, a state of being lying outside both of state definition and of state influence. In this negation of state institutionality, civil society seems to reserve to itself the possibility of being always outside of and in contrast to the state. As such, it claims for itself the privilege as critic (*the* critic?) of the state, the state's conscience, though also in placing itself outside of the state the source, the grounds, of state critique. But if always outside of power, the place from which at least potentially "truth" to power is spoken, civil society as radically romanticized independence would appear always easily dismissable, at best the fly on the sovereign's nose (materially in-dependence even as claiming rhetorical independence).

Civil society, in reverse, requires the state for the possibility even of thinking itself, of its very being. Where the state is taken to have broken down completely (Somalia a decade ago, for instance, where civil society was considered, at least in its normative sense, absent also). But equally, as always the outside of the state, this conception of civil society seems to render impossible the humanizing of the state itself, its radical transformation into a lived and livable state of being, of social arrangements not by nature alienating and debilitating, the fabric (as James Scott points out) as much of our freedom as of our unfreedom. If civil society is to be the realm of independence, supposedly of liberty as such and of democratic possibility, then that makes the state institutionally disposed at the least, if not necessarily, to become coercive, dependence-producing, illiberal.

Contrastingly, civilization is served by states, or so the story goes, committed more or less invisibly to making possible the sort of face-to-face life of civic engagement. The state *for* civil society (as opposed to it) becomes a form of self-effacing institutional arrangement, collapsing institutional governmentality with – into – the form of privatized being and in the process projecting a more or less singular form of being, of style or aesthetic, onto state formation, substance onto form. The civil reduced to the homogeneous, civilization in denial of its inevitable discontents, what Slavoj Žižek with characteristic irony might call "decaffeinated sociality." The state subsumption of civil society produces at the limit the current modality of crisis creation, chaos fabrication and management, of state terror to fight the projection of terrorism. The anarchy of the state, state license to terrorize in the name of facing down terrorism, in turn is tied to civil society's acquiescence, the conscience-less comfort of the social soul.

The Violence of Civil Society

Civil society, Mbembe rightly insists then, is deeply embedded in the long-standing tensions between "private lordship and public lordship," between "the affairs of individuals" and "public affairs." Civil society is invoked uncritically, as Mbembe points out and I have hinted above (not unlike the notion of "democracy" in this respect), to conceptualize and describe relations of subjection and their overcoming:

> the origin of civil society is violence – or . . . the necessity of managing it to avoid situations where just anyone may be able to make war and raise taxes, arrogate to himself ownership of public authority, and exercise a relation of domination based on the pure law of arbitrariness.

Respect for rules, censorship of feelings, and control of spontaneous impulses marked dominant Enlightenment conceptions of rationality (or at least one of its dominant strains). As Norbert Elias has long pointed out, Enlightenment rationality thus constituted – and took itself to be constituting – a dramatic shift from the affective states promoted first by religious and then by absolutist states. Civility, Elias emphasizes, is inseparable from, really a complex product of, the transformation of warrior (and I would add church-dominated) into court society with the attendant shifts and persisting postulations in morals and manners, sensitivities and sensibilities.

As modern "enlightened" European states accordingly solidified under bourgeois control and direction, refinement, urbanity, sociability and courtesy – in short, civility – became standards of civil behavior in "imitation of the manners of court nobility," as Mbembe puts it. Increasingly codified in moral and legal arrangements and orders, these central social virtues (refinement, urbanity, sociability, courtesy) became linked to conceptions of the social contract taking hold of the popular political imagination about this time. They became synonymous with – or at least characteristic descriptions or elaborations of – respect for private property legally mandated, and so of the grounds of a civil society. Policing, schooling, and emphasis on legality as modes of social order came to displace raw physical violence as principal modes of civil and state control by the latter half of the nineteenth century. Civil society thus becomes the codification, the socialization, of violence rendered invisible, its "displacement," to use Homi Bhabha's sly phrase. The architecture of states of embedded violence (individualized and institutionalized) rendered standardized relations and modes of violence regular even as they become regulated, structurally *embedded*, in a word, civil.

Conceived in large measure as the face of structurally inscribed and embedded violence, modernizing civility is enacted through racial characterization. By the late eighteenth century, race had begun to take hold across the European orbit as the new civic religion, offering novel threads to the civic fabric(ation) of being and relation. Race provided the artifice of substance to otherwise abstracted social intimacy, fashioning permissible or acceptable contours to civility in the face of – as responses to – rapidly expanding populations, quickening urbanization, intensified demographic and cultural heterogeneities, increasing anonymity, and the collapsing intimacies of close(d) kinship communities.

Conjuring lines of social connectivity threatened by their privatized fading, race quickly came to outline the bounds of civilization, casting the shadows at rationality's limits. Euro-modernity's fragmentation of the social, ironically, claimed resolution through the naturalizing artifice of newly abstracting and fragmenting racial connection and dislocation. The longing to connect, to be part of a civil order, came to be conjured, among other modalities, through racially driven lines of demarcation. Those continuing to fall outside the more or less strictly bounded demarcations of racial connection, civility and civilization, and rational contour have been marked variously if more or less invariably as aliens, strangers without and within, exploitable labor, criminals, infidels, enemies as such and enemies of freedom, destroyers of democracy or more recently and assertively as terrorists.

Conceived thus, civil society is the negotiation of – and therefore, through such negotiation, some sort of engagement with – distinction, with heterogeneity. Heavy racial investments in trans-population identity or sameness, ultimately in cultural or biological clones, thus constitutes the threat of the death – the suicide – of civil society, the end of the necessity of civility as the modes and spaces of negotiation. No need for civility if my neighbors or fellow-citizens are just like me. We are all conforming members of that artifice of familiarity prompted by the racially fabricated sense of familiality mentioned in Chapter 1. No need, alas, even for me. Sameness rules through differentiation; the end of distinction, like the end of history, effecting the unimaginable, dystopic boredom of what Gilroy marks as the Changing Same. Where self and other merge indistinguishably, their contours smudge into cloned figures, the body of the Hobbesian sovereign constituted by all those identical little people making Him up, one just like the other, replaceable avatars in the iconicity of perfect sameness. One might even say that this is the end of the need for the figure of the sovereign, after all, the first and last embodiment of distinction. The end of history (as we know it), indeed!

So, as Achille Mbembe rightfully concludes, civility foregoes any "pressing need for vulgar brute force in the arrangements for maintaining domination and the means to ensure domination," at least historically in the metropoles. Before sameness through obliteration of distinctiveness, one might add, reigns supreme. Among other things, civility serves as a pressure to conform, playing a key part in the social reproduction of consent.

Civility thus is the genteel analogue of what earlier and elsewhere I have elaborated as the expanding hold of racial historicism on modernizing racial imaginaries across the globe. The grip of governing the historically immature to the point of ruling themselves meant that colonial space had to wait well into the twentieth century before loosening at least the direct metropolitan stranglehold on self-determination, challenging John Stuart Mill's two conditions for civility: private property and free expression. The insistent (and later resistant) absence of each in colonial societies, at least largely for the locals if pointedly not for the settlers, has been taken as the persistence, natural or cultural, of illiberal constitution. It is seen as the mark of missing modernity, and as such the sign of incivility, of uncivil states, of culturally driven civil unrest or of civilization's singularly "natural" limits. Driven by "impulse" rather than the ability to "calculate" rationally, the natives are "savage" rather than "civilized," the specter of the state of nature and its shadow of an untimely, ghastly death always threatening to haunt civil society and by extension the state established in its name. It is the persistent paranoias prompted by this haunting that has continued to fuel the steady shift to what in the later pages of Chapter 1 I characterized as the privatizing logics of "born again racism" in the wake of the post-colonial condition. This has consisted in the constantly reconfiguring circuits of de- and re-provincializing the global South and East, and the purposeful re-pressing of standards of civility and civilization.

Civil society, then, is to be understood as the particular ways in which disputes and conflicts are fashioned ("constructed"), approached ("managed"), licensed ("legitimated"), and dissipated ("resolved"). It is the sphere – the mode and manner, the style, the rules and regulations – in, for, and through which "civil" conflict and contrast, dispute and distinction emerge, are classified and conceptualized, comprehended and controlled, massaged and managed. Such a sphere requires a set of emergent or already existing institutional arrangements, premises, modes of thinking and interacting, associations and established forms of engagement filling "the space" – the gap or chasm, field or terrain – at least conceptually, modally, between state and individual, family and economy. The arrangements that became identified as civil society emerged to manage and legitimate the otherwise bald, antagonizing, and often resisting relations of domination – economic, political, legal, cultural – between those occupying differentiated social (class, caste, ethnic, racial) positions.

In short, civil society and its attendant modes of civility are the spaces of accommodation to existing relations of social domination and order, racially inscribed. Civil society, to riff on an oft-cited line about race and class, is the modality in and through which social order is lived, acted upon, acted out.

Civil society accordingly consists of the technologies and informed substance of associations, rules, and regulations of, even resistances to, such conflict and violence management, of lived sociality and social life. It follows that civility is their style, the *aesthetics* of this set of conditions and relations. Civility in this generalized sense amounts to the texture of sociality, the fabric (and fabricated) of the lived, sometimes frayed and sometimes fine, the latter too often tied, if only by negation, to the former. I would say even that civility emerged and has operated as a form of class rule, its privatization.

It may be useful here to distinguish between civility as such and civilities. Civility is the overarching sensibility of the prevailing social order, its modes of perception and deception, interaction and representation. It is what gives the society its "personality," its "character," even its "color." Civilities are the particular expressions of social interaction affirmed as socially appealing, as valorized, which include forms of objection and social movements of resistance to civility. In this, the distinction is not unlike the Aristotelian one between virtue and the (particular) virtues socialized.

The threat (and fear) of violence accordingly always seems to have been lurking behind or beneath – to be shadowing – the concern with civility. "Uncivility," John Keane remarks, was conceived as "the ghost that permanently haunted civil society," its permanent enemy. What happens to civility, it might be asked, when the ordinary calculation of risks becomes the risk society or, more pressingly, when threats to (a) society become the threatened society, and a society projecting "no fear" becomes the society founded upon it? Civilization, always already – historically – racially charged, may be seen accordingly as the undertaking to render violence impotent, as Keane points out, to soften its blow and lessen its impact. It is intended, in short, to vaporize violence, to render its traces virtual. The civilizing process (mission) is considered thus as the process of gradually increasing perfection (progress), of turning uncivil into civil states, of moving in the terms of (European) modernity (Hobbes through Kant) from barbarism, savagery, roughness, vulgarity or the state of nature into civilized, genteel, decent, in short, civil states.

John Keane suggests that the eighteenth-century assumption at work here, that violence is antithetical to civil(ized) society (because normatively reflective of (leftover) antique barbarisms), remains the silent assumption marking almost all theories of civil society. Violence, Keane insists, chronically persists within all extant civil societies. This is surely right, though he fails to comprehend what so many other commentators deny, not that violence persists, which is still to assume that civilization is the purging from society of violence, if only we could get it right. Rather, the more difficult recognition is that modern societies aren't just marked by violence but constitutively founded upon and committed to incorporating and (not quite) covering over the various expressions of violence, civil and state(d). Civilized violence, so to speak, state terror (dropping bombs on more or less defenseless populations in the face of alternatives), is violence rendered civil, the standardizing of forced restrictions or impositions upon those within or outside the society to effect ends at the relative expense of or at least without complete consideration of those targeted or implicated, or enabling less violent possibilities to take effect. To claim not just the mantle but the motivation of the civil, of civilization, for such violence is at least to claim its legitimation if not righteousness, its asserted and assertive justification if not justice. It is a legitimation which in modern social terms is always factored through the cast(e) of race, even as that cast is at once denied.

The logic of modern civilizing processes is reflected, among other things, in the increasing commitment to broadly shared values: the unacceptability of murder, the rejection of violent assault at least as social norms, and so on. As Locke argues in his *Treatise on Government*, the reticence of individuals in the state of nature to have to spend the better parts of their existence fending for themselves and fending off dangers from others is motivation sufficient to prompt them rationally to abrogate most all responsibility – and so too ability (ought implies can) – for social protection to the state. This entails, in other words, that the monopoly over the means of violence, the very defining condition of statehood Weber would later recognize, be concentrated in state apparatuses. In so doing, as Zygmunt Bauman shows, European modernity simultaneously becomes the process of insulating possession of the means and exercise of violence against moral consideration, determination, condemnation.

So there is a constitutive connection between modernization as increasing civility and the potential of the state to be licensed to commit violence, in the extreme even in a genocidal fashion. As the civilizing state assumes the monopoly of the (legitimate) means of violence, the state becomes in some sense (and in a variety of ways and to varying degrees) the embodiment of violence. Counter-intuitively, "civility" and "barbarity" ("Holocaust phenomena," "uncivil abnormality," "terrorism") are caught up together in mutually making and reinforcing ways, the one serving no doubt to delimit the other. In both directions, as the growing popularity of war crimes tribunals, crimes against humanity, etc. in one direction and the quick disposition to violating civil liberties in the name of fighting terrorism in the other both attest. You're either on our side or for terrorism, friend or enemy, forcing out any possibility of critical nuance between those crushing extremes.

Mutilation – the uncivil extreme of violating the body through physical acts – is a form of doing the unrepresentable, that which cannot in some sense be spoken adequately, the changing (mutating) of the body in some basic or radical way. But as also a muting, a silencing, it is, in the extreme, making the identified or identifiable anonymous, lacking identification. Mutilation or bodily violations accordingly are a form of forced silencing, a more or less direct cutting out of tongues. As such, it is anathema to civility, the death of free expression. Mutilation, in short, is the undoing of civility, its counter-condition. Consider here J. M. Coetzee's *Foe*.

Civility, in this context, is precisely about "polite" speech (both the appeal of the civil and its cover). It is about decent speech or exchange, a speech not (too) impolitic but never political, the speech of decency between those with identity, those respectfully identified and addressed. Mutilating violation, counter-civility in the extreme, is exactly about the erasure of address, in both senses of the latter term. Or addressed violently, the mutilated cease to be and have address at all ("no longer to be found anywhere," as Keane says presciently in a different context). They are a "statistic," one anonymously among a number, numbered but unnamed (perhaps living in caves or holes in the ground, in some self-assumed acting out). Thus if civility is about naming, about being named, about being identified in being named and so about having identity (itself an altogether ambiguous condition), mutilation is about – is – the stripping of identity, its purging. Hence the deep relation between purges and mutilation, knotted together in silence, in the silencing that is the logic at the heart of both. Abu Ghraib, Guantanamo, Bagram, solitary confinement and supermaxes more generally . . .

Under Cover of Civility

It begins to become evident here that the emergence of modern forms of civility in the eighteenth century is more than just casually inflected with racial (which is also to say class and gendered) hues. There's a sense in which such modes are structured racially. Relations of racial dominance, their conception and legitimation, are structuring features of modern civil society and modern state formation. The discourses on national character that mark the latter half of the eighteenth century are discourses characterizing national self-conception in deeply marked racial terms. The forms of domination are racially inflected if not (re)produced: conception and concentration of violence, exercise of compulsion, forced delivery of commodities and means of livelihood, allocation of utilities, judgment of disputes, grooming of social members and citizens, moral and social metrics, in short, the entire ethos of the social order, "regimes of privileges and immunities," as Mbembe puts it.

Civil society serves simultaneously as internal limit to and reflection of state institutionalities, a brake on state power even, both as its diffusion through the "private" realm and its "mirror reflection." But its mirror reflection in both senses: as reflecting the character of the state and influence on state image and practice. Institutional state arrangements – forms of governance and rule, and states of being – are entangled in inextricable ways into an "organism" of mutual definition, interaction, influence, and expression, producing what I elaborate below as the rubric of state personality.

Democracy (as an organizing modality of civil society) thus is not a product external to the state, the modes, styles, and substance of representation infused into the state from some perfectly autonomous generating plant that will magically transform the state from outside. It is not some perfectly neutral sphere representing no interests but those of justice. Nor is civility simply a restraining power in the public sphere, simply a mode of social (self-)control, as Edward Shils would have it. Rather, democracy has to be thought of as the very product of the tension between state and civil society, as their interactive expression, the outcome of an engagement where one cannot exist – cannot be defined, cannot express itself – without and without expression in and through the other. The *color* of democracy, so to speak, is that of the civility, the sort of civil society, it promotes.

Thinking about democracy nevertheless does require a sharp contrast between the official and non- or anti-official representations. Democracy is not to be associated simply or reductively with some realm of NGOs outside of the state, wherever that might be, but in the multiplicity of partially overlapping associations, none of which is able to determine (in the final analysis) or to overdetermine outcomes but which in their in-dependence are able to conjure and promote – "to articulate, autonomously and publicly," as Mbembe writes – "an idea of the general interest."

Civility is prompted and promoted among the agreeable, where there is broad social consensus about social arrangements and the shape and content of state arrangements – in short, where social conditions and political infrastructure are largely settled. But resistance, critique, subversion call forth not so much incivility and rudeness as oppositionalities and resistances defined as such, characterized as not belonging because outside the compact, rowdy because already unfitting and unfitted, so not worthy of belonging, stylistically at odds or in contention with the compact. The insistent unworthiness of the uncivil is a product really of a different conception of being and longing, different romantic utopias coupled with the threat – the terror – of subversion.

So civility is founded on a tightly "circular" (and self-contained) order. Civility accordingly is what Mbembe, in a slightly different if related context, characterizes as "the privatization of public prerogatives," thereby enabling power to be socialized, diffused through the state, collapsing stating (state-making, *étatisation*) as order of rule and conditions of being. Mbembe points out, again in pursuing an analysis to explain current conditions of authoritarian rule in contemporary Africa but I am looking to adapt the terms of his account to other more general purposes, that this process of privatization amounts to a "socialization of arbitrariness." It is a cementing of the unnecessary, partial, and partisan, the dominating and coercive, to the benefit of one racial class at the expense of all others, "asserting rights (and the right) over persons and things" – arrogating to itself such power in the absence of consultation or negotiation.

At the same time, this arrogation that is also the arrogance underpinning the restriction of the civil to given and imposed modes of behavior and thought, morals and means, comes to think of itself as bearing a burden – the civilizing mission, white man's burden. This is racial historicism's ambivalent legacy under which we still labor. It comes to be called the price we pay for civilization, for bearing the cross – the proclaimed generosity of charitable rulers over ruled, the former to be the "guide and guardian" of the latter, as Mbembe indicates, quoting Albert Sarrault.

Consider, as Mbembe does, the civic virtue of kindness that of course can also be a vice ("to kill with kindness"). The social policy version of kindness is charity – the displacement of state and social responsibilities to the realm of the private under the rubric of destating (or deva-stating) the social and programmatic efficiencies and private autonomies, as I argue more fully in Chapter 3 in the instance of the US. All those dinner-time phone calls to donate to whomever and the ugly silences and not so silences when you brashly refuse giving to those poor, poor children we should all be helping because the state has been made to fail us all – or at least most of us. Jack Nicholson's *About Schmidt* exemplifies the dark play on emotional emptiness, of alienated need and estranged generosity, at the individualizing heart of privatized sociality. The social commitments of civility thus become the evasion – indeed, the refusal – of civil equality and social justice. For which the dominated are supposed then to be grateful.

Civility as historical process accordingly is not the purging – ending – of violence but its veiling (the iron hand in the velvet glove), the positioning of socially sanctioned violence out of sight – behind walls (e.g., execution, torture, harassment, sweat shops) or "over there" (colonization, foreign wars, desperately cheap factories, in occupied territories), placing curtains between public and private violence, between publics and violence in their name. Civility, in short, becomes a – *the* – mode for monopolizing the means of *public* violence while expressing disinterest in it. As such, it is a principal (and sometimes nominally principled) process for establishing and sustaining modern state domination in the Weberian sense of monopolizing the forms and conditions of expression of legitimate(d) violence and force.

So civility rests – necessarily? – on a certain hypocrisy. It has served – but need it, must it? – as a mask for the conniving egoism and violence of men with a reputation for refined manners. I am reminded here of Gandhi's being asked what he thought of western civilization: "Well," the wise one quipped back, "that would be a good idea." One might generalize that to anyone, to any state, staking the claim to civilization at the expense of others, an all-too deadly game in our times. That non-violence should be the measure of first and intermediate and patient resort does not entail, does it, that one cannot defend oneself as a matter of last resort, indeed, as a matter of resistance and pushing back? It is perhaps the lack of generalization of the distinction that renders so difficult its operationalizability.

The civility of the powerful is "the ally of arrogance," as Jonathan Swift once had it, "having the perhaps unintended effect of producing and reproducing incivility among the powerless." The implication, John Keane adds, is that "the powerful must somehow change their ways and let the 'uncivilized' find their own path to civility." I was in a forum on democracy recently when a middle-class white woman kept insisting that "we don't want *them* (the uneducated) to vote, now do we." Surely the implication is not so much this lingering racial historicism. Rather, it is that civility, as I stressed at the outset, assumes many forms. Resistance, oppositionality, pushing back so often embody and embed counter-civilities, different ways of being-in-the-world, reflective and reflexive of contrasting ways of world-making. The point is how to recognize them all around one, to establish conditions for the mutual engagement and flourishing of the engaged, as well as possible grounds for distinguishing not so much the civil from the uncivil but the just from the unjust, those respectful of the dignity of the different from those violating the grounds of their being. And then how and who to address those in violation? Questions many have come to face all too starkly of late.

Keane concludes that "*all known forms of civil society are plagued by endogenous sources of incivility*," that "incivility is a chronic feature of civil societies, one of their typical conditions, and, hence, normatively speaking, a perennial barrier to the actualization of a fully 'civilized' civil society" (the emphasis is his). This draws attention to the relational distinction between civility and civil society (a surprisingly rare contribution to the voluminous literature on civil society, actually). But, for all that, I would say, more pressingly, that these concerns throw in question the very idea of a "more civilized" civil society. Indeed, they call into question the notion of a separate, stand-apart, idealized private sphere of the civil over and against the state. The civil either is (to be) a defining condition of state formation, a brake on state power *within* the state, as a constitutive condition of its self-expressed formation and being, or the state as a matter of fact will be uncivil not over and against some outside order but as a denial, a negation, of what gets marked as civility as a matter of state *self*-definition – at least to greater or smaller degree. That is the line of argument I have been trying to make out here.

The Spirit of State Personality

The upshot of my provocation is that the focus be centered not so much on civility and civil society as on discrete conditions. The point rather is to consider the scope, shape, quality, internal and external relations and dynamics of the state and its critiques, those critical resistances to overbearing state formation and imperious state reach, to all of which civil society and civility are social expressions and reflections. Elsewhere I have referred to this mix of institutional character and its permissible scope and styles of expression, relation, discontent, and response as the "personality" of the state, as "state character." The state and the social life it shapes, enables, supports or enervates, as well as the global relations states anchor, take on a particular character or hue as a consequence, a disposition towards people defined as and in terms of population or group belonging.

The personality of the state ennobles or disables certain sorts of persons and actions, orders "proper" or "improper" social relations, provides the landscape and the contours of being and longing, horizons of possibility and impermissibility in more or less acceptable or adjustable modes of belonging. In contemporary states, in those states where civility has been so much in contest, the landscape and contours of state personality have been deeply defined and refined in racial terms, figuring a racial character to state personality.

State personality is thus intimately interlaced and interfaced with *national character.* These popular portraits of modern state formation and philosophical conception from the eighteenth century on were painted in racial hues. Consider as an example Latin American (mainly Mexican) *casta* paintings, reflections of and upon prevailing racial hierarchies and the institutionalized and institutionalizing orderings they represent (see Chapter 6 for elaboration). Modern states streamlined identity, ordering character in terms of culture, deeply etched in racial colors. Individual character and state personality were interwoven through the bio-social and bio-cultural ties of citizens. Socio-cultural homogeneity was often tied to ascribed (if not prescribed) biological constitution identified by racial markers. Where threatened, these homogeneities required repeated reinscription in economic, legal, and cultural terms.

Thus state personality is a function of the character of state practices and what the state rhetorically, representationally, commits to. This includes the relations it makes possible and disables, the rationalizations it conjures and the modes of expression it licenses. The contouring of individuated and socialized personhood is promoted through those institutional and cultural policies and practices tailored by the state as the articulation of civility. Civility, then, is one central, even basic sort of social representation and expression of such personality.

I have argued at length in *The Racial State* that the socio-cultural embeddedness of race – its forms and contents, modes and effects of routinization and penetration into state formation and order – has been basic to fashioning the personality of the modern state, not just its modes of governance but equally its modes of being. Race accordingly has been a primary ingredient in the making, molding, and manifesting of modern civility. In offering the conditions of possibility for the enactments and performances of personhood and subjectivity, race figures the presumptive representatives of social civility and who bear its burdens. It orders who (are to) have the pleasures of civility's social networks and civil habits and who suffer its exclusions, who are within and outside its circle of confinements or web of worldly connections. What, from 1780 to the present, has been the racial, class, and gendered make-up of the US Senate, of the South African Parliament from 1910 to 1994, of the British or French Parliaments or German Bund throughout their modern histories, of the legal or accounting professions or of their modern state bureaucracies?

Of course, more or less unbounded by such strings of attachment, deference, and social debt, there is always the possibility to mobilize in the name of counter-racial determinations, of counter-histories and counter-practices to prevailing civil society and state formation. The social space for racial counter-performance, to be sure, is almost invariably contained and restrained. Witness just these tensions and turbulence regarding the French handwringing over headscarves, the phobic clashes of culture, history, and social power between a harried Euro-secularism, founded as it is upon a long tradition of Christian habitus, and sectarian Islami-insecurity, perceived Orientalist inscrutability and fomented fanaticism (themes to which I return substantially in Chapter 5).

Civil society today then has become the dominant domain of what earlier I characterized as born again racisms. These are the racisms continuing to circulate quite ceaselessly in the shadow of racelessness, of raceless states. They are the untouchable racisms of private preference schemes placed off limits to states drawing sharp distinctions between the public and private so carefully critiqued in the past two decades or more of feminist scholarship. So civil society and the civilities on which it is built displace race and the warrant of its exclusions from state practice to privatized and individualized expression, less virile perhaps but certainly more unreachable by critical intervention. Consider who choose to live in gated communities in cities and suburbs, and why, whether in the US, South Africa or Brazil. State personality defers, if not reduces completely, to presumptive conceptions of national character and individualized accusation and recrimination on matters of race, effectively hiding the socio-cultural architecture of racial arrangements from view.

The humiliation and torture of Iraqi prisoners by US and British military and contracted personnel that came to public attention in May 2004 were no doubt made thinkable by the broad ethnocultural characterization of Islamic perversity, aggression, and untrustworthiness long circulated but flagrantly reignited in the wake of 9/11. And yet the prisoner abuse was restricted by the public relations machine of the Bush administration and American military brass, as well as Tony Blair in the British case, to a very small number of soldiers "failing to follow proper procedures." Reduced to the responsibility of a few bad apples, "the sadistic, blatant and wanton criminal abuses" throughout virtually all American-administered Iraqi prisons, as a US army report put it in December 2003 (not unlike maximum security prisons across the US more broadly), could be dismissed as the racial depravity of a few rather than the institutionalized product of a state-licensed national culture responding to (self-promoted) threat. "The practices that took place in that prison," bemoaned President Bush as the story broke, "are abhorrent and don't represent America. . . . They do not reflect American values."

If the President was predictably loath to make the connection to the history of national practice and sensibility, conservative talk show host Rush Limbaugh, addressing his twenty million daily listeners, licensed himself free to do so.

> I'm talking about people having a good time, these people [US guards, military police, and contractual interrogators at Abu Ghraib], you ever heard of emotional release? You heard of the need to blow some steam off? . . . I think a lot of the American culture is being feminized. I think the reaction to the stupid torture is an example of the feminization of this country. . . . It could well be that the whole purpose here, which has been said, was to humiliate these prisoners. And there's no better way of doing it than what was done. These are Arab males – what better way to humiliate them than to have a woman have authority over them? What's the purpose here? What's the objective of this? The objective is to soften them up for interrogation later, later on. As I said, there was no horror, there was no terror, there was no death, there was no injuries [*sic*], nothing.

Assertion, of course, does not necessitate accuracy; and explanation is not justification. These are distinctions clearly lost on the likes of

Limbaugh and his listeners, for whom an Iraqi death in detention apparently is not death, rape is not terror, sodomy with a broomstick is not abuse! And feminization of the homeland is something to be rued, while the feminized humiliation of the enemy for the sake of the fatherland is cause for commendation and celebration. That a woman was the first US soldier to be charged for these prison abuses further deinstitutionalizes the wrongdoing, symbolically displacing it to the person of a woman inherently lacking military discipline. Civility is "saved" for the "Savage nation" by being reduced and restricted to the artifice of a dramatically narrowed ethnonational, masculinized familiality, as much at "home" as abroad. (Asked about Limbaugh's remarks, the White House repeatedly refused to comment.)

This public "privatization" of symbolic violence, displacing it from formal state apparatus to "private" media personality, continues to enable the public circulation of ideas through privatized channels no longer explicitly possible by state representatives. As Slavoj Žižek remarks, Abu Ghraib (and, it could be added, the likes of the Limbaugh legitimation) is deeply revealing of rather than at odds with currently prevailing "American values."

At the same time, the US invasion and occupation of Iraq and the broader anxieties about global Muslim mobilities have drawn attention effectively away from more traditional institutional racisms, most notably against people of sub-Saharan African descent. As in earlier wars directed against those regarded as rogue states, the present intervention continues to structure the lives of black people globally, only now much less visibly. So civil society and civility are generative sites for racisms never dead but repeatedly resurrected as born again, raceless articulations of racist expression.

"Crises" may be manufactured, seized upon, massaged and managed as they are seen to provide especially fertile ground, productive opportunities, for state self-assertion, renewal, and restructuring. Social threat is attributed to an outside. The threat may be taken as the figure of an interior abjection, the alien within, or the unknown stranger, the threat from without. The (invented) threat to state coherence and power – a war on terrorism, most recently – is ascribed in either case to state externalities. Terrorism, in the instance at hand, is always projected as the product of the alien and alienated, those seeking to threaten survival of the state and the way of life for which it takes itself to stand. At the extreme, as John Coetzee muses in his latest novel, deterrence too is conceptually tied to terror, to frightening or terrifying (*terrere*) opponents (if not also critics) into compliance. Fighting terror with terror.

The charge of terrorism has a double effect: It manifests, first, the figure of the outlaw. Outlaws, those literally outside the law, are those nevertheless the law insists on bringing to justice, on pulling the threatening back into its circle of comprehension, and so of containment and control. But, second, the charge of terrorism insists also on an implicit "transcendence" of social distinctions (race, class, for instance). Transcendence here is purchased in the name of a generalizing national character and state security while reconstituting the threat as invasion by the distinct, the different, the dangerous, the outside. Even threats from within are externalized, civilities reinventing themselves only by expulsion, excision, and exculpation. Citizens identified with terrorism in the US have been routinely shipped offshore, to a naval vessel off-limits or to Camp X-Ray at Guantanamo, even if ultimately returned under judicial order.

State security thus buries divisions beneath the symbolics of a common national character, of a civil society premised on shared similitudes, socio-genic commonalities, and on socio-culturally fashioned clones and cloning civilities. As state security is perceived to be increasingly under threat, the appeal to national character, patriotism, and ethnoracial familiality are asserted. This (re)generative tension between externalization and internal transcendence for the sake of staving off threats to the state promotes maintenance of categorical distinctions in the name of homogenizing civilities and supposedly civilizing sameness. This drive to reproduce sameness Philomena Essed and I have called "cloning cultures." Profiling for the purposes of conducting the intersecting "wars" on crime and terrorism are predicated on presumptions of behavioral sameness naturalized. In these intersections are to be found the deep entanglement of civil society and state practice, the defining features of profiled characterization culled from the historic fabric of civil (dis)engagements and socio-legal projection, state enforcement here cementing the renewed histories of stated profiles.

It is worthwhile pointing out in this context that almost every US administration since the beginning of the twentieth century has waged or engaged in a war of one kind or another. These have been invasive and defensive wars, on one hand, and metaphorical or rhetorical ones in service of launching major public policy initiatives, such as the "war on poverty," the "war on drugs," or the "war against crime," on the other. What do the ready invocations of military metaphors for social campaigns say about state character, about the fabric and texture of civility in such a society?

More pointedly, virtually every war conducted by the US throughout its history, material and metaphorical (World War I may be a notable exception), has been coded, if not styled and shaped, at least partly in explicit racial terms: think of the Revolutionary War, the Mexican War, all those Indian wars, the Civil War, the occupation of Hawaii and the Philippines in the 1890s, World War II, Korea, Vietnam, Grenada, Panama, "Desert Storm" (Iraq I), Serbia, Afghanistan, and "Operation Enduring Freedom" (Iraq II). At least from the Civil War on, each was driven as a war by and for the good against evil. They were coded increasingly (and increasingly implicitly, mutedly) as struggles of racial historicisms against the *anciens régimes* of racial naturalisms, of one kind or another. The latest "war on terrorism," in some ways not unlike the Cold War, combines the awesome physicality of the material with the signifying orders of the metaphorical, clearly collapsing state and civil domains into a singular constitutive arrangement through the figure of racial distinction and threat. In a world of racial states, war and defense, terror and deterrence become bound by a reiterative common logic of racial characterization and counter-ascription. Raceless racisms are resurrected as state practice too.

Such wars have served multiple and multiply interactive agendas. They have sought to establish greatness as an emerging world power; to ensure imperial expansion not least to control global resources for a population unbounded in its desires; to claim continuing nobility for a nation obsessed with its place among the *anciens régimes* of power; to reassert state homogeneity for a population increasingly and increasingly assertively heterogeneous; to insist upon its own security by way of policing the world. The wars amount in sum to the *pouvoir nouveau* constantly and loudly having to prove, to assert itself over and against power's latest aristocracy, both domestically and globally.

But there is also another domestic element at work. War or its threat elsewhere makes governing at home easier, keeps the population more or less united, pliant, even domestically docile. "Fighting them there so we don't have to fight them here," President Bush's mantra for the "war on terror," can also be decoded as "fighting them there to keep folks in line here." The militarizing of everyday mentalities, most notable in the US but quietly constitutive of a country like Israel, is pervasive: The print, sonic, and electronic news not only issue daily reports of the military's farings, they are also drenched in statements by military spokespeople and analysis by retired military brass. Air travel experience runs the gauntlet of militarized oversight. Political campaigns, most notably the Presidential election campaign, invariably highlight America's military power and the candidates' respective military history or lack. America reminds itself of its global power by exercising its military might, and we, the people, are re-minded daily of this militarized social mentality by a compliant media. George W. Bush sought re-election by constantly reiterating that he is "a war President," as though no one had noticed.

The crisis of war, which is both a product of and extends military intervention, makes governmentality a form of crisis management, governance little more than a mode of control. The Bush administration's limitless war on terrorism – limitless in every sense of the word – has ceded to itself the definition of limit. It sought the delay or postponement of limit with every upping of the level of alert, of debt-financing, of cuts to domestic social programming, even as limit in each instance may be reached. The war on terrorism is a war of civilizations, the world is told. It is the defense of the civilized against infidelity. Of the brave and the free against the axis of evil. Of Judeo-Christianity against Islam. Of Orientalism, as habitation, against the Orient, as place, as condition, as state of being. It is a war, as a recently killed journalist pointed out, in which "we" nominally mourn the death of "our" soldiers killed in battle while thoroughly discounting, to the point of dismissing, the multiplied deaths of civilians (from) elsewhere as "collateral damage," as the unfortunate cost of self-protection. This, in short, is the logic of a war of races turned loose, its terms of reference at the same time no longer speakable, but rather rendered implicit, coded. It is a war without limit, whether in the case of an expansive war on terrorism, a "coalitional" war *against* Iraq, or occupation of territories for security purposes.

Numerous commentators have noted that states are shaped by the wars that give birth to them. Civil society emerges as the toolbox of techniques holding war at bay and marshalling the population in the face of a war deemed necessary. Foucault notes in *"Society Must Be Defended"* that (civil) society embeds relations of domination, confrontation, and force – relations, that is, of violence. The state seeks as its principal mandate to defend (civil) society against invasion and internal danger. Against all those (threatening) assertions and assaults seen to contaminate from without and within. Against (imagined) penetration and (perceived) pollution by those deemed racially distinct.

The state thus cedes to itself – draws upon for its own defense – the very relations of domination and force it cements in place as the order of the civil domain. As states consolidated "legitimate" power in their own hands, centralizing social control, so they increasingly assumed the "right" exclusively to wage war. They repressed within their territory, within the boundaries under their control, the right to exercise privatized violence. This supposed right is now exercised increasingly in the form of private militias, "resistance" groups such as Hamas or Hizbullah more or less organized as private armies (sometimes assuming a semblance of formal political power or representation), bands of individuals undertaking armed exertion and self-assertion. They make murky the divide between civil society and state, a distinction strong states seek in turn to ensure. The self-reserved rights of states to wage war and the self-asserted insistence of social groups to wage self-protection, resistance, or revolution entail, in turn, what Etienne Balibar characterizes as "a global economy of violence." Increasingly, this global economy of violence has become irrepressible, uncontainable, unrestrictable, threatening not just the projected sources of threat but the rest of us also. State and civil society come to look awfully like each other.

States thus have sought to exert and expand their consolidated power. They exert control in most every corner of their administrative scope. And they reach imperiously beyond the scope of their own territorial boundaries in search of new sources of wealth and of recognition of their awesome power. It is ironic, then, that as states have expanded their reach they more often than not effectively reignite and resurrect dispositions to private war-making. They thus radicalize dissent and determined resistance. Indeed, a resistant life is one refusing to live (more or less completely) the fantasized civilities of social purity, the racially inscribed delusions of social distance, the awkward artifices of apartness. The deeper the repression, the more resilient the resistance conjured, the more passionate the considered counter. "Terrorism" is the intense expression of this ironic tension, extreme at either end of the social self-assertions. Not simply the exception that proves the rule, no longer a state of exception but the establishing norm in the name of exceptionality, "terrorism" conveniently extends the charade of the state as necessarily representing reason and moderation. States accordingly assume and assert themselves by contrast as the institutional embodiment of civility and civilization.

In insisting that civil society and state are necessary conditions for the possibility of each other, constitutive in their interactive expressions of state personality, I am not suggesting that no distinction can be sustained. There is a qualitative difference between what is marked as the sphere of the state and its institutional apparatuses, or at least what gets effected and enacted in their name (messy and internally in tension as they may be), on the one hand, and the spaces of less formalized and less institutionalized arrangements and activities, on the other. Perhaps it could be said that there is a relational distinction between the formalities of institutionalized politics and the informalities of individualized actions. This has been marked variously in the history of thinking about the social as the tension between structure and agency, institutionalization and individualized interactions, even when the latter take the form of serialities or collectivities. The institutional shapes the horizons of possibility for the individual, while individual interventions license *and* limit the possible reaches of the institutional. This renders such normative distinctions less easily sustainable as reified contrasts. The state articulates a civil society; civil society extends definition to the state representing it. Civil society and the quality and range of civilities it embodies impart to the state its peculiar personality, its apparently cohering character, just as the state shapes and massages civil society to "speak" – to *state* itself – in its institutionalizing terms.

Civil society mediates state institutionalities, rendering them livable. It draws attention away from the dourness, the drab bureaucratic repetitiveness, of institutional formalisms. We turn explicitly to institutions only in times of perceived need – "theirs" or "ours." We see ourselves *living in* civil society while looking to the state to look out for us, to mind our backs and behinds, to offer the "safety net" should we fall. Civility, it might be said in these terms, offers the behavioral mediation, the glue, cementing civil society and the state into a model society.

A state purged of civil society, if imaginable in such a "pure state" at all, would be the unbearable condition of life's totalizing institutionalization. It would accordingly also be a life, most notably an institutional life, lacking any civility. Civil society draws attention away from the bureaucratization, the repression, as well as the violence of state institutionalization. Bluntly put, to render livable the experience of state institutionalization, of the state as such, social life at the very least calls forth both acquiescing spontaneity and inventiveness, both agency and affective civilities identified with civil society, both repression and resistance. Institutional arrangements identified with modern state formation make living in the mass conditions of modern societies amenable, if not possible. And social movements mobilizing against state imposition and repression find their fertilization in the sorts of more or less civil engagements of civil society. It would be naïve, in any case, by contrast to think contemporary societies even conceivable in the absence of some sort of institutional arrangements.

Nevertheless, as Michael Hanchard has pointed out, people can be *in* a civil society but not *of* it. They may belong in some nominal or instrumental sense to – be thus claimed by – a society but at best ambivalently, anxiously, devoured as a food too rich or poisoned for the body politic that then sits uneasily, wrenchingly, in society's stomach. Increasingly, as alienation from the state's civil society has spread and deepened, one antidote for growing numbers of the disaffected in this globalizing age and technological facility has been to identify with what Alejandro Colás calls "international civil society" or John Keane "the rise of global civil society." This offers at least a virtual counter-space of action critical of the political reification of the local, on the one hand, effected through the limiting horizons of state formation, identification, and insistence, and of the global, on the other, effected through multinational alliances and actions, state and corporate.

Civil society has various ways to delimit the status of its members, if not of membership itself. What I have characterized as "born again racism" reveals that race continues to serve as a principal modality of such delimitation, even as racial reference is officially silenced. More forcefully still, publicly charging racism is increasingly considered as less than civil. All this also suggests that behind the niceties of civility, violence continues pointedly to characterize civil society. The death of civility is more pressingly the death threatened and effected behind the cloak of civility, in civil society's name, with the acquiescence if not endorsement of the inhabitants, its citizens. The erosion of civility begins to render that social violence naked.

What, it should be asked, then, is the role of civility in effecting violent death, in prompting and promoting violence, and in silently refusing to acknowledge, in denying, civil society's implication? The "suicide" of civil society accordingly has less to do with the vaunted curtailment of civility bemoaned as a function of the "culture wars." I am arguing, rather, that it is more readily about the erosion of civil society's self-proclaimed grounds revealing immediately the deep cleavages, the open scars across the social landscape, festering beneath civility's frayed band-aid. The privatized, individuated self-aggrandizement increasingly identified with civil society's promotion only adds salt to the violence (racial, gendered, class, domestic) promoted in civility's name. The death of civility, while perhaps unimaginable for this among other reasons, would bare the unbearably charged violence waged against all those denied the possibility of a civil death and a decent life.

The Heart of Civility

The complex of relations between civility, civil society, civilization speaks not just to questions of state and society but by extension also to the tensions between affect and cold calculation, empathy and rationality, determination and deliberation. I close this chapter on a sober and somber note, then, by raising a sticky question of heart. The question of heart, so to speak, is at the heart of a society, as one is all too often reminded in giving and taking, in service and its various invisibilities, in the nature of the collective make-up, the "color," of the society and in its attendant denials. Human time bombs have exploded the world over, undercutting in the horror of their amorphous and indistinguishing effects the sharp lines of us and them, the targeting and targeted. The indiscriminate discrimination of the event is horrible and horrifying. As necessary as it especially is in trying times, civility pales in (or as) the extent of a response.

One indication of how pallid a response to the urgency of these times an unqualified recourse to the discourses of and around civility can be, consider that as bombs fall and fall again in reply, the "Battle Hymn of the Republic" re-sings itself into the aesthetic of America's imperious reach:

Glory, Glory Hallelujah, *His* truth is marching on.

This was the "hymn," after all, sung ceremoniously in Washington, DC's National Cathedral at the official memorial immediately following the tragedy that overtook complacency that fateful day of September 11, 2001. The assertive – stated – memorializing of 9/11, afterthought of plans already made well before, is tattooed all over middle earth: Afghanistan, Iraq, Palestine . . . Bellicose noises at one recent point or another about Northern Pakistan, Syria, North Korea, Iran . . .

Where in the name of civility is the multicultural nation here as the "Battle Hymn," "His truth" (whose truth?) marches to the beat of a crusading state – for liberty, for democracy, for Christian values – reduced to the instrumentalities of cleaning up its mess – for a stability its war-making repeatedly has undermined, for an insecure security it is prepared to purchase at the repeated cost of liberty?

A plaintive cry shadows the "Battle Hymn," haunting its practice as pain-filled response in the globalizing theater to the battle call:

DEAR GENERALS
You have bombarded.
Shelled.
Liquidated.
Tortured.
Demolished homes.
Uprooted plantations.
Expropriated.
Starved out.
Arrested.
Imprisoned.
Exiled.
Expelled.
Conquered towns.
Occupied neighborhoods.
Taken over villages.
Imposed curfews.
Closures.
Blockades.

You have tried everything.
You have nothing left. You are bankrupt.
Go home.

Ringing out against one occupation, the voice of the bereft in societies drained of their dignity, this Palestinian protest poem could be said to apply equally to coterminous "Naqbas" elsewhere if deeply connected, those racially inscribing death, destruction, and the demise of the civil in the name of imposed civilities, peace, democracy. One kind of stateless state of being ringing out against another, other, emphatically stated ones.

So civil society is all some postcolonial formations have to fall back on in the face of pointedly stated impositions. It is not only the case, then, that postcoloniality premises the "end of civil society," as Gayatri Spivak recently suggests in commenting on John Coetzee's *Disgrace*. It has perhaps even more clearly prompted the end of *civility* too. Postcoloniality prompts the demise of civility as the habitus of the colonial legacy, unmasking the gentlemanly make-up of the institutionalized violence now privatized in its name. Civilities are the first casualties in the postcolonial "clash of civilizations," of contrasting socialities, racially conceived.

***

I turn in the following chapters to examine relations between various social histories racially fueled and manifest in the hope of uncovering something about the relation between race and death, racial security and threat, civility and power, horror and heterogeneity, historically located. I focus in Chapter 3 on what I call "racial americanization," in the chapter that follows on "racial palestinianization," and in Chapter 5 on race and Europe, on "racial europeanization." In Chapters 6 and 7, I contrast these typifications with those of "racial latinamericanization" and "racial southafricanization," respectively. And in the closing chapter I return to draw generalizations about globalization, neoliberalizing race, and born again and raceless racisms.

Bibliography

Anidjar, Gil 2006: "Secularism," *Critical Inquiry*, 33 (Autumn), 52–77.
Arendt, Hannah 1951: *The Origins of Totalitarianism*. London: Andre Deutsch.
Balibar, Etienne 2004: *We, the People of Europe? Reflections on Transnational Citizenship*. Princeton: Princeton University Press.
Bauman, Zygmunt 1989: *Modernity and the Holocaust*. Oxford: Blackwell.
Bennett, Ronan 2007: "From 'Wogs' to 'Islamists': Martin Amis Does a Coulter," *Counterpunch*, November 27; www.counterpunch.org/bennett11272007.html.
Bhabha, Homi K. 1994: "Sly Civility," in *The Location of Culture*. London: Routledge, pp. 93–101.
Bryant, Christopher 1995: "Civic Nation, Civil Society, Civil Religion," in John Hall (ed.), *Civil Society*. Cambridge: Polity Press, pp. 136–57.
Carter, Stephen 1999: *Civility*. New York: Perennial.
Claestres, Pierre 1987: *Society Against the State*. New York: Zone Books.
Coetzee, John M. 1986: *Foe*. London: Secker and Warburg.
Coetzee, John M. 1999: *Disgrace*. New York: Knopf.
Coetzee, John M. 2007: *Diary of a Bad Year*. London: Harvill Secker.
Colás, Alejandro 2002: *International Civil Society: Social Movements in World Politics*. Cambridge: Polity Press.
Coulter, Ann 2001a: "This Is War: We Should Invade Their Countries," *National Review Online*, September 13; www.nationalreview.com/coulter/coulter 091301.shtml.
Coulter, Ann 2001b: "Affirmative Action for Osama," TownHall.Com Columnists, October1; www.townhall.com/columnists/anncoulter/ac20011012.shtml.
Elias, Norbert 1998: *On Civilization, Power, and Knowledge*. Intro. Stephen Mennel and Johan Goudsbom. Chicago: University of Chicago Press.
Elias, Norbert 2000: *The Civilizing Society*. Oxford: Blackwell.

Essed, Philomena and Goldberg, David Theo 2002: "Cloning Cultures: The Social Injustices of Sameness," *Ethnic and Racial Studies*, 25, 6 (November), 1066–82.

Ferguson, Adam 1776: *An Essay on the History of Civil Society*. Edinburgh.

Fine, Robert and Rai, Shinrin, eds. 1997: *Civil Society: Democratic Perspectives*. London: Frank Cass.

Foucault, Michel 2003: *"Society Must Be Defended": Lectures at the Collège de France, 1975–76*. Trans. David Macey. New York: Picador.

Fraser, Nancy 1990: "Rethinking the Public Sphere: A Contribution to the Critique of Actually Existing Democracy," Paper delivered to the XII World Congress on Sociology, Madrid, July.

Fukuyama, Francis 1993: *The End of History and the Last Man*. New York: Avon.

Gilroy, Paul 1992: *The Black Atlantic: Modernity and Double Consciousness*. Cambridge, MA: Harvard University Press.

Goldberg, David Theo 2002: *The Racial State*. Oxford: Blackwell.

Goldfarb, Jeffrey 1998: *Civility and Subversion: The Intellectual in Democratic Society*. Cambridge: Cambridge University Press.

Greider, William 2004: "Under the Banner of the War on Terror," *The Nation*, June 21; www.thenation.com/doc.mhtml?i=20040621&s=greider.

Gush Shalom 2003: "Dear Generals," Gush Shalom advertisement, *Ha'aretz*, May 23; www.jfjfp.org/indexfiles/gushshalomads.html.

Hall, John, ed. 1995: *Civil Society*. Cambridge: Polity Press.

Hall, Stuart 1980: "Race, Articulation and Societies Structured in Dominance," in *Sociological Theories: Race and Colonialism*. Paris: UNESCO.

Hanchard, Michael 2006: *Party/Politics? Topics in Black Political Thought*. Oxford: Oxford University Press.

Hardt, Michael and Negri, Antonio 2000: *Empire*. Cambridge, MA: Harvard University Press.

Hunter, James Davison 1991: *Culture Wars: The Struggle to Define America*. New York: Basic Books.

Huntington, Samuel 1996: *The Clash of Civilizations and the Remaking of World Order*. New York: Simon and Schuster.

Katzew, Ilona 2004: *Casta Painting: Images of Race in Eighteenth Century Mexico*. New Haven: Yale University Press.

Keane, John 1998: *Civil Society*. Cambridge: Polity Press.

Keane, John 2003: *Global Civil Society?* Cambridge: Cambridge University Press.

Lavie, Avi 2004: "Not For the Faint-Hearted" (on Lev Grinberg), May 7; www.haaretz.com/hasen/spages/424122.html.

Mardin, Serif 1995: "Civil Society and Islam," in John Hall (ed.), *Civil Society*. Cambridge: Polity Press, pp. 278–300.

Mbembe, Achille 2001: *On the Postcolony*. Berkeley: University of California Press.

Meek, James 2005: "They Beat Me From All Sides," *Guardian*, January 14; www.guardian.co.uk/usa/story/0,12271,1390256,00.html.

Naidoo, Kumi, ed. 1999: *Civil Society at the Millennium.* West Hartford, CT: Kumarian Press in cooperation with CIVICUS.

Nimmo, Kurt 2004: "Torture Party: Limbaugh and the Babes of Abu Ghraib," *Counterpunch,* May 8/9; www.counterpunch.org/nimmo05082004.html.

Post, Robert, ed. 2001: *Prejudicial Appearances: The Logic of American Antidiscrimination Law.* With commentaries from Anthony Appiah, Judith Butler, Thomas Grey, and Reva Siegel. Durham, NC: Duke University Press.

Robinson, Paul 2004: "Extremism in the Defence of Liberty," *Spectator,* April 24; www.lewrockwell.com/spectator/spec279.html.

Rouner, Leroy, ed. 2000: *Civility.* Notre Dame: University of Notre Dame Press.

Schechter, Michael, ed. 1999: *The Revival of Civil Society: Comparative and Global Perspectives.* New York: St Martin's Press.

Schmidt, James 1998: "Civility, Enlightenment, and Society: Conceptual Confusions and Kantian Reminders," *American Political Science Review,* 92, 2.

Scott, James 1998: *Seeing Like a State: How Certain Schemes to Improve the Human Condition Have Failed.* New Haven: Yale University Press.

Shils, Edward 1992: "Civility and Civil Society," in Edward Banfield (ed.), *Civility and Citizenship in Liberal Democratic Societies.* New York: Paragon, pp. 1–16.

Spivak, Gayatri Chakravorty 2002: "Ethics and Politics in Tagore, Coetzee and Certain Scenes of Teaching," *Diacritics,* 32, 3–4 (Fall/Winter), 17–31.

Sversky, Gila 2004: "Anarchy in Our Souls," *Gush Shalom,* Sunday, April 25; mailman.gush-shalom.org/pipermail/gush-shalom-intl/.

Tonkiss, Fran and Passey, Andrew, eds. 2000: *Trust and Civil Society.* New York: St. Martin's Press.

Wilson, James Q. 1992: "Incivility and Crime," in Edward Banfield (ed.), *Civility and Citizenship in Liberal Democratic Societies.* New York: Paragon, pp. 95–114.

Žižek, Slavoj 2004: "Between Two Deaths," *London Review of Books,* June 3, 19.

3

Deva-Stating Discriminations, Discriminating Devastations (On Racial Americanization)

When you make slaves you deprive them of half their virtue, you set them, in your conduct, an example of fraud, rapine and cruelty, and compel them to live with you in a state of war.
Olaudah Equiano, *Equiano's Travels*, 1789

Race is commonly assumed in the popular imagination to be an antique notion, a vestige of premodern or at least not adequately *modernized* social assertions and arrangements. I have written extensively against this understanding in earlier work. But in any case, the line of argument in Chapters 1 and 2 illustrates the reformation and reformulation of contemporary racial conception.

I want here to extend this frame of analysis by outlining a set of more or less recent typologies of regionally prompted, parametered, and promoted racisms linked to their dominant state formations. I am suggesting regional models or really mappings rather than ideal types, broad generalizations as contours of racist configuration, each one with its own material and intellectual history, its prior conditions and typical modes of articulation. They are often interactive historically, overlapping landscapes. But it remains nevertheless revealing to delineate them, to distinguish one kind and style as well as their conditions of possibility, expressions, effects, and implications from another. Identifying these mappings in the name of the social places and spaces of their principal origi*nation*, historical manifestation, and regional articulations is not to limit the (partial) influence of their logics and effects on other places, spaces, and regions that might not be readily identified with their coordinates of origination.

Racisms have a history of traveling, and transforming in their circulation. What I register here as more or less discrete in order to identify their socio-material and intellectual conditions of emergence, logics, social manifestations, effects, and implications are in practice, in reality, interactive with each other at various times and places on the ground and across borders and oceans. I will hint throughout at various ways in which this has been the case.

Racial Regionalizations

This way of putting it may be considered odd, may even look contradictory given my now longstanding and assertive avoidance of using the notion of "racialization" analytically or pedagogically. I am asked repeatedly by colleagues and students why this refusal. The usage of "racialization" so broadly in the literature is at the very least ambiguous, and may sometimes be vacuous. One cannot always tell, either explicitly or contextually, whether it is being invoked as a merely descriptive term or with deeper normative, critical thrust. Quite often it is put to work simply to suggest race-inflected social situations, those informed or marked by racial characterization. But lurking beneath the descriptive is more often than not an implicit, unexplained, and almost invariably theoretically unmotivated critical rejection of the normative insinuation in the seemingly neutral description of the social arrangements being characterized as racial or in racial terms.

The lack of specificity here, the emergent ambiguities, blurs the line and so presupposes an answer to a question not even posed: namely, is racial characterization inevitably racist? All too often the use, if not the very conceptualization, of "racialization" determines an answer in the absence of analysis. I want to insist, by contrast, on distinguishing between race and racisms, conceptually as much as politically – as objects and categories of analysis, as analytics or frames of analysis for different contexts, different if related geopolitical regions, as I put it below. To insist on the distinction even as their deep, complex, often tortured connections need disentangling acknowledgment.

In this scheme of things I identify five dominant mappings linked to different, if neither perfectly isomorphic nor absolutely discrete, spatio-historical conditions and expressions. I have called these, somewhat loosely and pragmatically, "regionalizations." Some of my mappings focus on regions (Europe, Latin America) while others on nation states (the US, South Africa). Israel-Palestine finds itself caught between the two, perhaps in more ways than one. In the case of the US and South Africa, the regional influence and global impact of their racial histories and contemporary configurations, if in different ways, go way beyond their narrow cartographical borders. It is this influential reach, more generally, on which I seek to focus and mine for insight in their historical and present-day manifestations. And it is to keep a focus on this trans-statal, if loosely pragmatic, reach that I am using the quasi-analytic category of "regionalization."

The prevailing regional modalities of racial history and arrangement on which I focus include americanization, palestinianization, europeanization, latinamericanization, and southafricanization of racism(s), and by extension of race. This order reveals what would otherwise be less noticed, that each represents a significance that is both historically resonant and politically dominant at specific global conjunctions, but also a logic of historical interaction. While I will of course map out the dominant characteristics of each modality, I begin with a detailed focus on the historical logic of "racial americanization," as much for the way it comes to embody the emergence of "born again racism" elaborated in Chapter 1 as for its own historical significance.

Racial americanization projects itself as *the* model, the one to be emulated, the failure of which bears more significant costs than in each of the other, if related, instances. At the same time, particular countries have taken on elements of such racial modalities developed and finessed elsewhere, out of related histories of racial articulation not quite their own, as will become evident in the elaboration that follows. But though it insists on its exceptionalism, the globally interacting historical analytic on which I insist urges the interactive relation, and therefore influence, of other historically resonant modalities likewise on americanization, thus indicating an exceptionalism disturbingly not too exceptional. There is, nevertheless, a relevant distinction to be attended also between the former two (americanization, palestinianization) and latter three modalities which will be evidenced by the end of this chapter and in the next. I devote the present chapter to racial americanization, and the following four chapters to each of the others respectively.

The oddity I am raising thus seems to come back to haunt me, the return of my own repressed even. How can I invoke the likes of "racial americanization" in the face of my worry about "racialization"? The processes of signification and materialization I aim to reveal and elaborate below that are fabricated and fashioned under the conceptual title offer social embodiment to racial characterization, a specificity produced out of its socially embedded milieu. The specificity, I am suggesting, comes less with the generalizability of "race" or "racisms" as concepts, or as analytics; as concepts, after all, they are generalizations. Rather, the specificity derives from their embeddedness, from the particularities that count for socio-specific determinations. Racial determination, in short, is the multi-determination of social particularities, of socially embedded particulars in regions resonant in racially related, racially conceived, racially significant terms.

Classic racisms were formed and fashioned in the contexts of European expansion, enslavement, and colonization. They were the racisms of self-proclaimed European superiority in pursuit initially of new sources of wealth, a servile labor supply, and exotic goods. Over time this came to include expansive territorialization, settlement, globalizing dominance, and with them new lives for the settlers and new forms of desire, dominance, degradation, even death for those thus made servile. The prevailing geographies of early modern racisms then – until at least the later eighteenth century – are projected as Europe's externality, the colonial outside, provincial extensions vested largely in the rural slaveries of plantation life. Here, the viciousness of the violent structures necessary to uphold the system were hidden just beneath the tranquil façade of settlement: wars, seizures, chains and whippings, death ships and disease, human auctions and forced intercourse. But this violence is revealed variously also in the penning of dehumanizing rationalizations, Sunday sermons, and state edicts. In these classic expressions of racism, race was seen always as a disruption, as the invader, as outsider otherness asserting itself over or inserting itself into local – which was to say, European – homogeneity. Race, as such, was to be kept, if ambivalently, enticingly, at bay.

Racism's more modernizing modes in the wake of abolition and nineteenth-century industrialization, by contrast, are increasingly associated with urbanization and metropolitan life. Modern cities have traditionally been places of migratory attraction and moral repulsion. They have offered the lure of employment and recreational excitement, consumptive novelties and cultural development, radical possibility and intense anonymity. It is this radical heterogeneity that has served more or less simultaneously as magnet and threat, as appealing, even transgressive of conserving inhibition, and repulsion.

The perceived threats to homogeneity, to the reproduction of sameness and identity, to the expected and the usual, to order and control, with which cities are associated historically prompted the institution of controls over urban space, restrictions on entry and movement, limits on access and acceptability. Thus it is in cities that the supposed "need" – the demand – for racial segregation was hardened, if not initiated, becoming the principal sites of formalized segregating institutionalization. Late in the nineteenth century accordingly urban space became the summary motivation and purpose of the drive by whites to segregate – namely, to restrict hetero-geneity and hybridity, to delimit intercourse, to control interaction and rela-tion. This was seen as especially compelling in the Anglo-settler societies, most notably America and South Africa, but also in the likes of Australia.

Racial Americanization

Nation-states are the particular products of modernity. The modern nation-state comes increasingly to be constitutively ordered in and through racial configuration. By the latter half of the nineteenth century, the United States of America emerged as the beacon of modernity, the model of what a nation-state might aspire to in seeking its modernity. Its post-abolition ethnoracial republicanism, civic religion and religious secularism, social segregation and aspirational colorblindness suggested the contours of modern state-making.

Segregations

Segregation emerged as the dominant and formalized modality of racism in the United States as freed slaves moved off the plantations after aboli-tion and into cities, first southern and then up the Mississippi and the east coast, and ultimately also westward. White politicians in the southern Democratic Party machine secured their political power by shielding the white urban working class from competition by newly emancipated black citizens in the late nineteenth century just as the National Party came to power in South Africa in 1948 by securing the wellbeing of the white working and poor classes on the promise of apartheid's racial restrictions on access. The ghettoized segregation widely associated with the height of American racism was a thoroughly urbanized post-Reconstruction development the full effects of which were realized in cities in the 1920s and 1930s, by which time it was being vigorously contested by black social movements and cross-racial coalitions.

Historically, standard American racism at the opening of the twentieth century took the cruel form, then, of a constitutionalized segregation (accompanied by the cultivating ethnocide of assimilating those remaining among American Indians). Contemporary racial americanization, by extension, has informalized apartness, rendering it the effect of privatized preference schemes rather than explicitly institutionalized legalities. Increasingly today, members of different ethnoracially constituted groups – whites, blacks, Latinos, Chinese, Vietnamese, Cambodian, Indian, and Arab Americans – have come "by choice" (principally but not only the choices of whites) to occupy discrete urban spaces. These were at first different neighborhoods but today more often than not are different municipalities, different cities. The choices have been shaped by policy and law to order social opportunities for some while closing them down for others, streaming access in the former case while plugging it up in the latter. This reveals how preferences are molded even as that discriminate sculpting is obviated, rendered obscure and indiscernible in the name of its claimed obsolescence.

Black migration from the south coincided with European immigration to cities like New York, Philadelphia, and Chicago. But it was coterminous as well with Chinese, Japanese, and Filipino settlement especially but far from only in San Francisco, and Chicano migration to Southern California and later across the Southwest to join those already long settled as a result of earlier American territorial annexations. As racial interaction consequently began to increase, African Americans, Latinos, and Asians were becoming progressively segregated within cities. The more black urbanization expanded, the more their racial segregation and restriction within cities was extended. Thus by 1930 the spatial location of segregation already had transformed perceptibly from regional to neighborhood divides.

Until the late 1800s nearly 90 percent of black Americans lived in southern rural counties while almost that proportion of whites lived in northern cities. By 1930 black urban residents tended to live in wards 40 percent black. From 1890 to 1930 black residence in New York surged nearly tenfold from 36,000 to 328,000, in Chicago over twentyfold from 14,000 to 234,000. Chicago neighborhoods just 10 percent black in 1900 were swept by the cold wind of segregation into neighborhoods 70 percent black just 30 years later. By 1950 a majority of African Americans had become city folk, and by 1960 a greater percentage of blacks than whites lived in cities. Between 1920 and 1980 blacks living on the land and working in agriculture declined 96 percent, and by 1981 this figure had almost disappeared to 1 percent.

Already in 1940 ethnic white neighborhoods were far from uniform in their ethnic composition. Neighborhoods in which blacks or Latinos lived tended much more to be overwhelmingly black and Latino. Identifiably "Irish" areas of cities included just 3 percent of the total Irish population, and most of New York's Italians did not live in Little Italy, for instance. By contrast, 93 percent of blacks lived in neighborhoods that in the categorical formation of race in the United States can be characterized as majority black. The construction and containment of Chinatowns within major metropolitan centers at precisely the same time reinforces the ethnoracial logic at work here.

"Racial redlining" acquired formal governmental backing in the 1930s when the Home Owners' Loan Corporation (HOLC), a federal agency, was charged with establishing "residential security maps" for 239 US cities. As Richard Marciano has made evident, these secret maps, composed with input from "competent local real estate brokers and mortgage lenders," ranked zones within cities in terms of their desirability for residential investment. The central criterion underpinning the ranking concerned their ethno*racial* character. The residential security maps coded affluent and desirable lending zones blue, less affluent and less desirable areas yellow, and zones inhabited by blacks – and so deemed undesirable – with the alarmist, high alert red. In 1936, HOLC guidelines made explicit these color-coded residential security maps:

> Blue areas, as a rule, are completely developed. They are like a 1935 automobile – still good, but not what the people are buying today who can afford a new one. They are the neighborhoods where good mortgage lenders will have a tendency to hold loan commitments 10–15% under the limit.
>
> Yellow areas are characterized by age, obsolescence, and change of style; expiring restrictions or lack of them; *infiltration of a lower grade population*; the presence of influences which increase sales resistance such as inadequate transportation, insufficient utilities, perhaps heavy tax burdens, poor maintenance of homes, etc. "Jerry" built areas are included, as well as neighborhoods *lacking homogeneity*. Generally, these areas have reached the transition period. Good mortgage lenders are more conservative in the Yellow areas and hold loan commitments under the lending ratio for the Green and Blue areas.
>
> Red areas represent those neighborhoods in which the things that are now taking place in the Yellow neighborhoods have already happened. They are characterized by detrimental influences in a pronounced degree, *undesirable population* or infiltration of it. Low percentage of home ownership, very poor

maintenance and often vandalism prevail. Unstable incomes of the people and difficult collections are usually prevalent. The areas are broader than the so-called slum districts. Some mortgage lenders may refuse to make loans in these neighborhoods and others will lend only on a conservative basis.

These security maps, a central technology of residential planning and management across US cities from the late 1930s on, became the basis across many years to follow for denying mortgage loans by government and private banks especially to black home seekers and in black neighborhoods. They thus fueled racial residential segregation, urban abandonment, and ultimately capital flight, thus hyper-concentrating racial poverty, slum conditions, and urban blight. Today's gated communities are essentially privatized modalities of redlining, segre*gating* communities informally extended.

Thus the conditions for the reproduction of European immigrant ghettoes have never existed in the way they did in the twentieth century for African-American and Chinese ghettoes. European immigrant segregation ebbed as their migration flow waned, while black and Chinese segregation within the boundaries of confined black and Chinese space increased not primarily as a result of black or Chinese housing preferences but of conscious white avoidance, as manifested in the use of physical violence, intimidation, and the creation of a dual housing market by way of racial covenants and the like. White exposure to blacks accordingly was still self-determinedly minimized through ensuring black isolation in urban ghettoes. Cities became instruments for European immigrant group advancement, but blocks especially for blacks not only residentially but educationally and economically also. Chinese entrepreneurship was left to flourish within the strict confines of Chinatowns, linked as it was to external sources of capital formation in Asia, opportunities definitively denied and unavailable to black ghetto dwellers.

The post-World War II period saw the emergence of nationalized desegregating efforts – in the army, the courts, on the streets, in buses and schools – prompted not only by moral and internal political imperatives but also by geopolitical Cold War competition and assertive local mass mobilization. "National interest" and foreign policy demands strongly encouraged if not necessitated public commitment to race-neutral governmentality.

On the face of it, the federal government also made a huge commitment to producing much needed urban public housing, in 1949 authorizing 810,000 new units over six years. In fact, the federal government became

principally engaged in reproducing segregation. In the postwar modernization boom fueling the economy, federal policy initiatives regarding mortgages and taxes promoted the suburban housing explosion for middle- and
working-class whites. At the same time, federal property appraisal policies
rendered possible bank and mortgage company redlining of inner-city property purchase and development. Government, national and local, massively
promoted private (re)development and gentrification of central business
districts (CBDs) by underwriting loans; incentives to redevelop inner
cities by building housing for the urban poor were almost wholly absent.
By 1962 only 320,000 of the public housing units promised in 1949
(roughly 40 percent) had been constructed. Much more inner-city housing in fact was bulldozed away in terms of the 1949 federal housing law
than was actually built: premonitions of "group areas" apartheid South Africa.
Between the end of World War II and 1960, less than 2 percent of new
housing financed by mortgages guaranteed by federal insurance went to
black homeowners.

From about 1950 on, accordingly, segregation across and not just
within cities began to increase. By the 1980s this trend had become
evident: increasingly members of ethnoracially defined and identified
groups, and not only blacks, while living in different neighborhoods from
whites tended also and emphatically to live in different cities. Their
children now likely attend overwhelmingly segregated schools in different
school districts, growing up literally not knowing each other beyond the
stilted stereotypical images they glean from television and other audio-visual
media. Recent judicial efforts to end the use of racially emphasized means
to desegregate public schools across a broad swath of American states are
already exacerbating the trends to resegregation.

At the very time there was growing desegregation – or at least explicit
effort – in the public sphere, one could say there was publicly subsidized
resegregation in the private. Desegregation never stood a chance. By 1980,
Massey and Hajnal have calculated, blacks living in cities found themselves
in municipalities on average 35 percent black; if black and white residents
were to be evenly distributed across municipalities, 50 percent of blacks in
cities would have to switch places of residence with whites. It is revealing
to note that such calculations somehow are invariably made on the dislocating assumption that blacks, not whites, should move, class somehow
trumping race, Owen Fiss being simply the most recent in a long line to
promote such a plan. The suburban explosion that pulled whites out
of the cities transformed the countryside into sprawling suburbs. These

suburbs eventually became small self-governing cities, the effect as much of the desire to be politically and fiscally autonomous from deteriorating old black-identified cities as of some purely administrative rationality.

In 1950 there were no central cities in the US that were overwhelmingly or even largely black. No city with a population larger than 100,000 had a majority black population. Forty years later there were 14 such cities including Atlanta, Baltimore, Detroit, Gary, New Orleans, and Washington. Eleven more cities had black populations between 40 and 50 percent, including Cleveland, St. Louis, and Oakland. Among cities larger than 25,000 in 1950 just two had majority black populations, a number that had exploded to 40 by 1990. Interestingly, the increase in segregation after mid-century is characteristic only of larger cities with large black populations. There was a noticeable decline in segregation in small cities with small black populations. In the latter cases African Americans found themselves assimilated into dominant white space with little if any noticeable effect on prevailing urban arrangements or culture. By the end of the Civil Rights era, in contrast, geographic isolation of blacks in larger urban settings – the overwhelming majority of black folk – was nearly complete. The occasional resident of color in white residential space, when they could afford it, or of white residents in "nonwhite" space, when they couldn't "do better," or of the even more pointedly noticeable "mixed neighborhoods" are simply the exceptions proving the race-as-class, class-in-race rule.

In a provocative thought experiment in 1971, Thomas Schelling exemplified the segregating implications effected through personal preference expression. (Schelling uses a checkerboard with dimes and nickels though I think the coloring of the chess pieces more provocative.) Take a chessboard: Fill 10 percent of its spaces with black pawns; fill 70 percent of its spaces with white pawns. Assume each black pawn wants at least one neighbor to be a black pawn, and each white pawn wants at least one neighbor to be a white pawn. Segregation sets in within a couple of moves (try it). If each wants both neighbors to be like itself, segregation is produced all the more quickly.

So, rational choice theorists to the contrary, preferences are *not* naïve, discursively unstructured, simply given, or unchanging. Preferences are *ordered* by the dominant discursive culture and terms. In the case of the preference for segregated space, segregation is discursively (re)produced and ideologically massaged. White Americans of all class stripes reportedly prefer to live in neighborhoods which are at least 80 percent white; black Americans prefer to live in neighborhoods which are 50 percent white (which is to say 50 percent not white). Given that those classified and experienced as white make up roughly 70 percent of the population, that leaves vast areas of possibility for all-white areas. The age of late twentieth-century deregulation, alongside rapid demographic diversification especially in cities, prompted a more widespread segregation, one less formally imposed than the more formal attempts of the old activist segregation but produced via the informalities of private preference schemes.

Nancy Denton has demonstrated the debilitating effects of such segregation thus. Take a city, not unrealistically, that is 25 percent black or Latino with a white poverty rate of 10 percent and a black or Latino poverty rate of 20 percent. Absent segregation, the neighborhood poverty rate is 12.5 percent (whites in this hypothetical city make up three-quarters of the population). Where segregation is complete, the neighborhood poverty rate for blacks or Latinos becomes 20 percent. Where class segregation intersects, the multiplier effect on the neighborhood poverty rate of poor blacks or Latinos doubles it to 40 percent. In the face of economic downturns, the black or Latino poverty rate jumps from 20 to 30 percent. The black or Latino neighborhood poverty rate then would double to 60 percent. That means almost two-thirds of the people in the black or Latino neighborhood would live in poverty. Post-Hurricane Katrina New Orleans exemplifies both the multiplier and urban hyper-concentration logic at work here. The same logic applies to predominantly segregated towns or cities. This perhaps is a major underlying reason why, according to a *Los Angeles Times* report, two-thirds of new immigrants to the United States claim to be "white" on the US census no matter ethnoracial background. White, it turns out, is thought to identify what it means to be American. Here, in short, American whiteness represents the assimilative logic of "fitting in," of opportunity and access, of getting ahead and succeeding. Charles O. Lee, the awkward Chinese-American immigrant character in Jonathan Raban's novel *Surveillance*, driving to be "an elite player" in American economy and society, exemplifies the point and its potential pitfalls.

If California is the leading edge of trends in the US, the desert communities stretching from east of Los Angeles to the Arizona border further exemplify these exacerbating divides. The desert areas west of Palm Springs are home to retired whites living in gated communities on artificial lakes. They spend their days on golf courses kept green by water piped in from the Colorado River dividing California from Arizona. East of Palm Springs the terrain dries quickly into dusty desert sand, garbage dumps, toxic sewage cesspools, vast prison complexes. These areas are home to a population overwhelmingly of Mexican immigrants not yet citizens, barely out of their teens and speaking little if any English. Their drastically devalued labor warehoused in settlements like Duroville makes possible the lifestyle of those to the west. Pleasantville and Teflontown meet Duroville along a thinly imagined prophylactic borderline protecting the former from the latter.

Prompted by a mix of fear, restricting potential competition, and cementing power, whites could enthusiastically embrace the ideological shift at the middle of the last century from assimilation to pluralism. Pluralism is experienced as the commitment not only to different histories, cultural values and practices but also to the ideological cliché of "live and let live." This made conceivable and legitimated contrasting urban conditions, and by the same token the abandonment of certain city spaces. The libertarian license to "live and let live" is stressed so long as one doesn't get in the way of institutionalized americanization, at home or abroad. Racial americanization in this context includes nominal commitment to liberty, individualism, market economies, private property and profit, but also historical denial of or disregard for others' suffering and concerns, of one's own privilege and self-assertion, near and far, even at the cruel cost to others'.

Old segregationist racism, from post-Reconstruction to *Brown* (1954), thus was an *activist* segregation produced for the most part by an active intervention in politics, economics, law, and culture self-consciously designed to produce segregated city, town, and neighborhood spaces. To combat this activism, the Civil Rights Movement likewise found itself called to action in every dimension. Prompted by the tensions between political pressures at home and abroad, the period from post-World War II to the 1970s, by contrast, was one of tension and contradiction, promise and projection, expectation and elevation, denial and dashed hope. It was a period of desegregating commitment and the seeds of a resegregating mobilization. The logic of the old segregation supposedly was swept aside – only to be replaced by the whisper of the new, the subtle and silent, the informal and insidious, what I earlier characterized as "the born again." This newly expressed segregation, the newly privatized segregation at the heart of what I am elaborating as the model of racial americanization, is one no longer activist (at least at home) but conservative, a segregation in the literal sense conservationist.

Racial americanization thus proceeds not simply by reducing the social to the preferential, the state to (in)civil society. Preferences are not expressed, enacted, and experienced in a political and institutional vacuum. Rather, public spheres – and the state especially – structure the conditions of possibility in which choices are to be made, preferences pushed and indeed in some cases punished. State structures channel, shape, and mold both the boundaries and the terrain of choice-making and their implication; and preferences expressed and enacted reinforce existing state formation while inflecting and coloring them.

This conservationist segregation, the model of *racial americanization*, proceeds by *undoing* the laws, rules, and norms of expectation the Civil Rights Movement was able to effect, attacking them as unconstitutional, as the only sort of racial discrimination with which we should be concerned today! Racial americanization embraces *race neutrality* even as it licenses "limited" racial profiling for purposes of security maintenance, targeted policing, and medical research as legitimate for combating the moral panics of terror, socially or naturally initiated. In the absence of the Civil Rights spirit, and now in its active undoing, accordingly, the present period *conserves* (and deepens) the hold of racial preference schemes historically produced *as if they were the nature of things*.

Private preference expression is leading to the resegregation of public schools in the US today. They are significantly more segregated than they have been since the 1960s. A Civil Rights Project study under the direction of Gary Orfield shows that as white families are aging, the numbers of black and Latino children are spiraling. Tied to municipal residential segregation, black and brown children are increasingly isolated in impoverished public schools. This dramatic trend is exacerbated by a Supreme Court ruling in mid-2007 regarding legitimate means for achieving racial diversity in public schools. While reaffirming the importance of diversity to education, the ruling nevertheless prohibited the use of race to achieve integrated or diverse school bodies, for instance, by assigning children to schools by race. Children as a consequence resort to attending public schools in their residential neighborhoods, residential segregation thus reproducing educational isolation. The impermissibility of race as a technology of public governance is replaced by private racial preferences, with debilitating outcomes. (Repeated studies reveal the overwhelming educational and socializing value of integrated schooling for children of all backgrounds.)

So racial americanization is produced by seeming to do nothing special. This "doing nothing special" consists of a mix of being guided by the presumptive laws of the market, the determinations of the majority's personal preferences, and the silencing of all racial reference with the exception especially of racial profiling for purported purposes of crime and terror control. The latter silencing fails to distinguish between exclusionary racist designs and practices, on one hand, and redressive or ameliorative racial interventions, on the other, reducing the latter to the former as the only contemporary racist expressions worth worrying about.

William Bennett, hypocritical arbiter of America's moral virtues, exemplifies the logic at play here. He recently responded to a call-in question on his radio show that, while morally reprehensible and ridiculous, aborting all black babies would result in a sharp reduction in the US crime rate. His "hypothetical" projection, effectively genocidal, is protected as the sort of free speech the wall of privatization around civil society is designed to render critically unreachable.

Bennett's "observation" trades on a cache of widespread if no longer explicitly expressed presumptions: that the crime rate in the US is overwhelmingly fueled by black criminality, that such criminality is a more or less natural and so inescapable condition of especially the black poor, but also that it is not unacceptable to issue eugenicist judgments about the implications of hypothetical genocide in the case of African Americans in ways it would mostly not be for any other group today (Muslims included). This latter presumption trades on the Africanity of African Americans, the normalcy if not naturalness of early death in the case of the descendants of the despised continent. Hidden from view here is the marginally less extreme logic on which the claim trades, for it is as surely the case that any aborting of babies of any ethnoracial background would likely reduce the crime rate, given that some percentage of that rate, large or small, is made up by members of every ethnoracial group. Bennett's racial eugenicism advances itself only at the price of the expendability of black lives.

Deva-stating privatizations

The privatization of racially exclusionary and debilitating preference expression that articulates racial americanization today makes it more or less unreachable by state intervention. But to secure the shift, to make it truly unreachable by state amelioration, to restrict the competition for social resources in the face of the increasing heterogenizing of the society, racial conservationists are keen to supplement their gains by a radical curtailment of state possibility.

In this mode, the current commitment by fundamentalist fiscal radicals to defund social programs in education, health care, emergency management and response, popular culture and the arts through extreme forms of tax reduction while increasing military, security, and prison expenditures and investments brings public funding to the point of bankruptcy. Grover Norquist, contemporary Republicans' philosopher-king, has giddily proclaimed that his aim is so to starve government of revenues that he could flush all state-supported social programs down the bathtub drain. The overwhelming social commitment to spiraling support for state institutions of violence, their enactment and (re)enforcement – military, policing, homeland security – in the face of an at best static if not diminishing treasury is burdened most notably by dramatic tax reductions for the wealthiest 1 percent of the population. Increases in such expenditures can only be supported, accordingly, by squeezing social welfare and support revenues.

In the past couple of budget cycles, hyper-conservatives have targeted programs for the poor because these programs offer both easy fiscal and political targets and convenient ideological rationalization. At the same time, defense budgets, whether narrowly or broadly interpreted, have spiraled. Thus, the defense budget for FY2006 amounted to $435 billion, up 5 percent from the previous year and almost 25 percent from its 2002 total of $344 billion. The projected $40 billion worth of cuts in the 2006 budget projections focused overwhelmingly on social programs such as student loans, health care, and welfare for the poor. If one factored into the figure for the defense budget the entire range of institutional apparatuses sustaining military presence at home and around the world, including $35 billion for Homeland Security, funds to fight in Iraq and Afghanistan, and the considerable sums for their respective reconstructions, the total would reach a staggering $900 billion, up roughly 30 percent since 2002, as Higgs calculates it. President Bush's recessionary budget requests for FY2009 continue these trends, increasing defense spending by 8 percent to almost $600 billion and dramatically under-estimating war costs while seriously diminishing spending on social programs.

Funding for education, health, housing, and transportation as well as emergency relief has been cut repeatedly. Since 2003, when it was incorporated into the Department of Homeland Security, the Federal Emergency Management Agency (FEMA) has been reduced by 10 percent (if President Bush had had his way the cuts would have come closer to 25 percent). Between 2002 and 2004, for instance, states cut their budgets supporting public higher education by a total of 10 percent adjusted for inflation. While first-rate public universities today receive roughly only between 5 and 25 percent of their operating budgets from their states, they typically are able to spend half or less than top-tier private universities per student on their education. (Twenty private universities, all with sharply escalating endowments, rank higher than the top public university.) Students of color are overwhelmingly educated at public institutions, when they make it into higher education at all; private universities are overridingly the preserve of wealthier whites (the exceptions proving the rule).

Alongside these cuts, since the onset of the Bush administration in 2001 the federal government has almost doubled federal contracts worldwide with private contractors, looking increasingly to outsource military, state, and homeland security operations. The revenue cuts and private contracting have had a debilitating effect on disaster preparedness and reconstruction, undercutting the agency's ability to sustain support for those most in need, as witnessed in the wake of Hurricane Katrina in 2005. The cuts increasingly ceded to uncoordinated private charities the responsibilities of evacuation, clean-up, reconstruction, and care. The results, abundantly evident, have been disastrous.

As with personal or corporate bankruptcy, this emaciation of the social support sector of government revenues forces a radical restructuring of public programming and state governmentality. The immediate implication of such state restriction and ultimately devastation is to redistribute wealth upwards. The point, explicitly articulated by neoconservative pundits and neoliberal politicians, is to put more wealth into the hands of the already wealthy. Expenditures of the wealthy (largely on themselves), the US public is repeatedly told beguilingly, are supposed to trickle down into jobs for the less well off. (Foreign policy supposedly runs on the fuel of the same logic.) But the mission, as much as any, is also to elevate the decision-making, social engineering, and effective powers of the well off. The social effect of state emaciation, accordingly, is not that social spending should end completely. Rather, in being redirected into private hands, it is fashioned by and for the social and political interests of those with capital to spare and power and influence to peddle.

Now the elevated factions of social class in a racial state like the US have traditionally been white, or more precisely representing the interests of those occupying the structural class position of whiteness (and men). The US Census Bureau reports that in 2000 the top 5 percent of white wage earners received wages almost double those of the top 5 percent of black wage earners.

Unsurprisingly, the largest contributors by far to political campaigns are white men. Under this mandate of radical privatization, funded institutions, programs, and activities accordingly become dramatically less diverse both in their programming, scope, and commitments and notably in their employment patterns. (Barack Obama's fundraising success in the 2008 Presidential campaign has exactly challenged this logic.) Hence the fundamentalist conservative outrage expressed by the likes of Abigail Thernstrom, Ward Connerly, Linda Chavez, and the Center for Individual Rights regarding the Supreme Court's upholding in *Grutter v. Bollinger* (2003) of law schools' limited affirmative action programs for the sake of maintaining a diverse student body. Neoconservative critics committed to a "race-free" America (note, not *racist* free) have blasted the diversity commitments of the Court's majority as "murdering the Fourteenth Amendment" (calling for equal treatment before the law) and as "tortured" (Ward Connerly), as "diversity drivel" (Michael Greve), and discriminatory (Linda Chavez), indeed, even "racist" (Abigail Thernstrom). If it is no longer possible to restrict demographic diversity, the culture wars can be won by defunding progressive cultural commitments, by shrinking the cultural horizons of heterogeneity.

There are additional sociological factors in play underpinning and sustaining the current cauldron of anxieties, paranoias, redirections, and renewed restrictions for some and social possibilities for others around racial matters. Black Americans are no longer the largest minority in the US. Latinos are growing as a percentage of overall population (14 percent and rising more quickly than any other major demographic group), as too are Asian Americans though in far smaller numbers and a lower growth rate. African Americans (12 percent of the population) thus are on the verge of shrinking proportionately, or at least not growing.

Social leverages, relatively speaking, are accordingly shifting. Latinos see themselves connected with some pride to Latin America, or nations in Latin America (most notably at World Cup time, or when the US soccer team plays Mexico or Brazil). Asian Americans see themselves connected as a result of family ties, heritage, and nostalgia to countries in Asia – notably China, Taiwan, Hong Kong, Japan, Korea, the Philippines, and to some extent Vietnam. Those connections are affirming, a sense of pride, regions that represent some success and that, at least in the public imaginary, are less racially inscribed.

African-American connection to Africa, by contrast, is at best imagined, ideological, in any case deeply ambivalent, fueled on one side by pride in

Africa's rich cultural and civilizational legacy, its expansive beauty, even its fortitude in the face of colonial degradation, but on the other side by its current poverty-stricken, famine-common, and war-torn condition. Richard Wright reflects (on) this deep ambivalence throughout *Black Power*, his extended essay about his visit to Ghana as Nkrumah's guest in the period pressuring for independence from Britain. African Americans are deeply connected to Africa through the legacy of slavery and Middle Passage, but as disconnected by the distressing recognition that it was more often than not fellow Africans who sold them into bondage in the first place. More recently, the tale of anti-apartheid jubilation and the success of the new South Africa have paled before Africa's broadening debilitation. And, of late, the concern with overcoming African poverty has become the new white liberal *cause célèbre*. Witness Bono, Angelina Jolie, and their social influence, as important and heartfelt as they may be. Here, black Americans, who have long rallied in support of Africa, are now edged if not elbowed to the (at least publicity but perhaps too political) sidelines.

Related to these demographic shifts and their attendant conditions of possibility and implication, debates about race in the US have shifted quietly if dramatically over the past five years. Today the two seminal considerations regarding the americanizing of matters racial have to do with the twin towers of immigration and terrorism. Their ideological connectivity is evidenced in the remarks of the Republican congressman, Texan John Culberson. In recently sponsoring legislation to arm civilian militias – "boots on the ground," as he puts it ominously – to patrol the Texas border with Mexico, Culberson explicitly characterizes illegal border crossers from Mexico as terrorists (or when speaking more carefully as harboring terrorists). Writing for the *New Yorker*, Ryan Lizza quotes a South Carolina Republican mimicking Ann Coulter in the run-up to the 2008 Presidential primary:

> Some of these people may be coming in here to get jobs washing dishes, but some of them are coming here to hijack airplanes. . . . I can't tell Jose Cuervo from the Al Qaeda operatives by looking at them, because they cut their beard [*sic*] off. . . . I mean, not a racist thing, but they're all brown with black hair and they don't speak English or Spanish and I don't speak Arabic.

These ill-informed identifications evidence the increasing shift of racial inventedness in the wake of 9/11 to the slippery figure of the terrorist as

Muslim. The self-conscious denials about racist expression notwithstanding, these slippages often prompt the (il)logical reversal in the public mind.

Here too relational logics effect ambiguous outcomes. So as the "war on terror" is mobilized globally and critical attention is pressed upon especially radicalized and radicalizing Muslims, African Americans fade into the fabric of America, becoming less African, so to speak, and more American. Iconic black figures such as Colin Powell and Condoleezza Rice suggest the constrictive possibility of climbing effectively to positions of power, of climbing out of African Americanness as the devil's choice might have it. (Obama, by contrast, may just not be African *American* enough for some.) On the other hand, this slow dissolution of African America in the remaking of contemporary America (a dissolution thick with traces, of course) is consistent with longer trends of social invisibilities and disappearances.

Thus, roughly a third of African-American men have suffered through the criminal justice system in one way or another, leaving them at the margins of civil society and largely without voice. African-American youth under 18 tried as adults are ten times more likely than white youth convicted of similar crimes to receive life sentences without possibility of parole (in California it is 22 times more likely). Recent reports indicate that police more and more are arresting children, overwhelmingly black, as young as 6 years old on *felony* charges – charges that include handcuffs, fingerprints, mugshots, and criminal files – for such childish acts as a tantrum at school or riding a bike on the sidewalk. One Florida police chief responded that "a 6-year-old can inflict injury to you just as much as any person."

In Jena, Louisiana, six black teenagers were recently charged with felonies – initially for attempted murder, then dropped to battery – for beating up a white teenager. White students had hung rope nooses from a school-yard tree they considered their turf after a black student (upon seeking the principal's permission!) had mingled with other students there during a lunch break. Knocked unconscious some weeks after the noose hanging, the white student was admitted to hospital, released later the same day, and attended a party that evening. Those who had hung the Klan symbols, strongly suggesting life-threatening violence, received no more than a school reprimand from the district's school superintendent. Even the old oak tree was punished: it got cut down. By contrast, a higher court threw out the conviction for assault by an all-white jury, judge, and prosecutor of one of the black students on grounds he never should have been tried in adult court. The prosecutor nevertheless insisted on keeping the black teenager imprisoned for some weeks while he decided whether to appeal the higher court's decision and to pursue further charges against the youth (which he eventually did not).

A Georgia state court sentenced another black teenager, a top student and star athlete at his school, to ten years in prison on a statutory rape conviction for having engaged in consensual fellatio with a 15-year-old underage girl at a party. After the teenager had served two years in prison, a higher court judge threw out the conviction on grounds that he should have been charged with a misdemeanor rather than a felony. The Georgia attorney general, a white man, refused to release the youth while appealing the higher court decision.

Considered against this broader structural backdrop, the Duke lacrosse team case continues to resonate in troublingly racial terms, vociferous objections notwithstanding. Three members of the nationally acclaimed lacrosse team at Duke University were charged with raping a black stripper, a student mother at the neighboring historically black college hired to perform at a fraternity party. In the wake of considerable national attention that included threats of violence to critics of the fraternity and the lacrosse team, it turned out that the charges were fabricated (though it never became clear exactly what humiliating conduct might actually have occurred at the party). The white district attorney was found to have rushed to prosecution, suppressing counter-evidence in his effort probably to support his upcoming re-election bid. He was stripped not only of his position but also of his law license, and the three accused young men, all white, were exonerated.

What is revealing in contrasting these cases is that the sons of wealthy and connected families, while suffering the trauma of wrongful accusation, nevertheless spent no time in prison, saw their case thrown out within a relatively reduced time frame, with likely no lasting negative impact on their professional lives (indeed, they are filing a $30m lawsuit against the city of Durham, a largely black city with a reserve fund of just $5m). The networks of high-priced lawyers, publicity savviness, access to the media – most notably the blogosphere – and the capacity to mobilize public opinion enabled the reframing of the case in ways much more difficult for those less plugged into these modes of mobilization. Genarlow Wilson, the Georgia youth convicted of rape for consensual oral sex, spent 32 months in prison and five years in and out of courts before seeing his conviction reversed, and like at least one of the Jena 6 remained in prison for months even after reversal before the Georgia Supreme Court ruled against the prosecutor's appeal.

Study after sociological study has shown that white teachers treat the comparable expressive behavior of black students considerably more harshly or dismissively than that of white students. Schools attended largely by black and Latino children – those in inner-city neighborhoods – offer far fewer college eligible courses than dominantly white (neighborhood) schools. This makes access to better colleges more challenging for black and brown students than for whites (for one, it depresses their matriculation year grade point average, thus rendering them academically less competitive). George Lipsitz has insightfully characterized these sorts of privileges as the "possessive investment in whiteness." Affirmative action was a relatively soft intrusion into reversing these constraints, but the increasingly strident attack on supposed preferential treatment over the past 15 years has dramatically limited the program's (potential) impact. This exemplifies the cumulative weight resulting from the interaction between everyday and structural racisms that linger long in societies so deeply marked by histories of racial exclusion and humiliation.

Racial profiling to this day shines a debilitating spotlight especially on young black men in the dark of night. And racially inflected impoverishment (like unemployment rates) gropes at black Americans dramatically more than at others in its spiral upwards (12 percent of Americans but 25 percent of African Americans live in poverty now, mostly without support or health insurance). The "war on poverty" has been edged aside by the "war on crime." The cut of racially charged masculinity, like that of class, continues to run deep in American social life, even as their terms are excised from the social lexicon of legitimate reference. No conspiracy, no racist "intention" or explicit institutionally racist rules. Each outcome legitimated by the individuated details, decisions of individual actors reasoning on the basis of the "best evidence" available to them, including statistical "evidence" regarding crimes, IQ test scores, pass or failure rates, family histories as well as previous criminal records. And yet again and again the children of less-well-off families of color get to do time while their better-off white counterparts at worst get reprimands.

Two further factors fuel the deepening social invisibility to which these accounts attest, leaving African Americans with a social dilemma more acute than members of other demographic groups. First, America continues to walk away from the commitment to affirmative action, as indicated above. The California experiment is indicative of future trends, the resistance to "group preferences" hardening as the proportion of profiled minority populations approaches 20 percent presence in educational institutions or employment settings. Too much presence in this fevered imaginary trans-lates into more competition – for positions, for resources, for visibility, for shaping the agenda. In the wake of Proposition 209 in 1998 banning the use of state funds for affirmative action programs in hiring, promo-tion, and college admission or support, registration of black students at the better-ranked University of California campuses as well as the hiring and retention of black faculty (not to mention the hiring of women in the sciences) have dropped precipitously. It is not over-dramatizing the condition to say that blacks in California are becoming dramatically less visible in higher education as a consequence.

The second factor is even more fraught. Since at least *Brown v. Board of Education*, the Supreme Court desegregation ruling in 1954, the principal stress has been on formal equality before the law. That equals should be treated equally before the law has entailed the veiling of the substantially disequating effects as a result. Those without the means are treated far differently than those with. This can be seen once again in the attempt to make California the laboratory by trying to privatize racial discrimination in the name of protecting it for the most part from public scrutiny. But it is evidenced also in the attacks on civil rights protections specific to named racial groups as "special treatment." Underlying this rejection of special treatment is a drive less to dim the spotlight than to shift it from the public to the private realm, effectively pushing black and brown Americans more deeply into the shadow of social disappearance, eroding self-confidence in the face of expanding invisibilities. Mark Potok and his colleagues at the Southern Poverty Law Center reveal that in the two months following the rally to support the Jena 6 in late September 2007, more than 50 incidents of noose hangings were reported across the eastern half of the country. And since 2000 organized hate groups have increased to nearly 850, up 40 percent. The already vulnerable are made to feel even more so.

New Orleans as national narrative

The fate of New Orleans in the wake of Hurricane Katrina in late summer 2005 illustrates these trends with furious force. A city of almost half a mil-lion, its population as the hurricane hit was 67 percent African American. One in eight Americans now live in poverty and double that number of black Americans; in New Orleans the poverty rate for black residents was closer to 50 percent as a result of the logic of high racial concentration Nancy Denton has identified more generally.

Privatizing the conditions of wellbeing has meant the wealthy white have the best medical care while the multitude has none. The well off live in gated communities high on the hill while the poor in the city as elsewhere have lived in polluted neighborhoods vulnerably below sea level with no garbage collection and few options. (Nationwide, white Americans are 79 percent less likely than African Americans to live in locations threatened by the significant health hazards prompted by industrial pollution.) The powerful drive larger and larger gas-guzzling SUVs while the impoverished have had no public transportation to speak of. The newly rich drink imported bottled water while the struggling have had only polluted tap water. The wealthy can dine daily in restaurants while the poor barely have had anything to eat at all, and could afford nothing by the end of each month as they awaited paychecks or welfare subsistence, or both. The wealthy get tax breaks and stock options while the poor can't even depend on the most rudimentary of educations. The lives of the rich are guarded from those of the poor whose fate is more likely prison than work.

In the case of Hurricane Katrina all this has meant that the federal resources to make the city less vulnerable to the wrath of nature were rendered less and less available while urban decadence could ultimately be drowned in its own vulnerabilities. The well to do could scramble for safety in their air-conditioned tank-sized vehicles while the poor were reduced to a decaying and in some cases deadly domed stadium. The tens of thousands unable to flee the evacuation order in New Orleans as the hurricane bore down were overwhelmingly black, as revealed at the Superdome and Convention Center. Family and other networks could support the mobile while the immobile were left to flounder in a flooded and rotting city, many losing contact even with the family members sharing their fate. The less lucky lost their lives. The wealthier got to watch from afar while the stricken got to share the streets with floating bodies, excrement, oil pollution. The privileged seemed to need no medical care while the poor restricted to the city got close to none, even where doctors from further afield were volunteering their help. The rich were free to roam the country, the poor rounded up and subjected to prison-like conditions even when bussed off to safer turf, their crime nothing else than abject poverty and the color of their skin.

Amartya Sen has famously argued that famines, far from simply natural disasters, are politically produced, the product of strife, war, political conflict and turmoil. It is these latter factors that more or less inevitably prevent the delivery of food and medical aid to avoid or alleviate starvation and death. The same could be said in this case.

In the name of securing the city, New Orleans was quickly turned into an armed military camp. Combat-ready forces went door-to-door urban warfare style, kicking down locked entrances searching for survivors to evacuate at the end of often fully loaded AK47s. While critics were rightly bemoaning the dehumanizing conduct of war abroad, few seemed to notice that for domestic purposes America was mimicking tactics of militarization honed in the desert war. America, in short, has taken to turning itself into armed and gated camps at home. Its regime of social truth today is shaped principally by a military mind-set circulated and recirculated by all those retired generals appearing on the nightly news programs advising the public on how to read the day's events. President Bush even went so far as to make a case for turning over disaster response from civil to military agencies, the latter supplemented by if not subsidizing private enterprise. And privately employed soldiers of fortune, recently repatriated by the likes of Blackhawk Security company from tours of duty protecting politicians and corporate entities in Iraq, invaded the city, requisitioning forcibly abandoned apartments in the French Quarter as headquarters, and firing randomly upon perceived looters with the tacit blessing of the more constrained National Guard.

Post-Katrina New Orleans, in short, is simply Iraq come home.

The rebuilding of New Orleans is proving instructive too. A city with fewer residents for the foreseeable future, it perhaps will be turned into a Disneyland for the oil industry and paying visitors where the racial poor will not be welcomed back (after all, they have been disbursed and dispersed to larger, more heterogeneous cities where their presence ultimately will become less noticed), a nightmare explicitly stated by then head of the US Department of Housing and Urban Development (HUD), Alphonso Jackson, himself ironically (and perhaps tragically) African American. A safe Democratic haven deep in the red-state South is being metamorphosed into another southern Republican stronghold. The working class will service the oil rich and worry free. The pollution will be rendered invisible in landfills and waterways once again to afflict the most vulnerable. A new sports stadium supporting privately owned sports teams valued at hundreds of millions of dollars each will likely be sponsored by public revenues. Mardi Gras will be turned from the conviviality of an organic urban celebration to the plasticity of tourist fanfare. New

Orleans spirit reduced to the cloned parades of Mickeys and Minnies. Welcome back, well, to Anaheim.

For those residents of the Gulf who managed to survive the carnage of nature-culture (or a naturalized politics), life after Katrina will mean putting themselves back together with little government support to rely on, all the public relations rhetoric notwithstanding. It is revealing that a large effort of private giving to hurricane relief has been heralded in contrast to the relatively forlorn and begrudging public revenues enabled, amidst handwringing about having to slow down extending existing tax cuts and rendering permanent the ending of the estate tax. The Bush administration has gone about more or less systematically deva-stating its public welfare activities to the point of constricting its support for the most vulnerable populations in the country.

Thus, those among the hundreds of thousands of Gulf Coast homeowners whose homes were decimated by the hurricane and flooding and who sought federal support to rebuild and revive their properties were directed to apply for low-interest disaster loans from the Small Business Administration (SBA). A staggering 82 percent of the 276,000 loan applications received to date have been rejected, overwhelmingly because incomes are too meager or credit ratings too low to qualify. The loans that have been approved have gone exclusively to wealthier and whiter neighborhoods in New Orleans, those thus more readily able to rebuild. Rejected applicants are eligible for home repair grants from the FEMA but the grant amount in each case is capped at about one-seventh the loan amounts available from the SBA. The likes of New Orleans' black and mixed neighborhoods, mainly the Ninth and Lower Ninth Wards, largely remain empty, mildewed, cordoned-off disaster areas with little relief in sight. Federal policy reinstates the privatized racial divide between the haves and the "would rather not have around."

The respective experiences of universities in the city serve to bear this out. Tulane University, private, overwhelmingly white, and wealthy, was cleaned up sufficiently within the year to welcome back its student body and (albeit diminished) faculty in January 2006; black city schools such as Dillard, Xavier, and Southern, their physical plant more or less completely wiped out by Katrina's flooding, were fortunate enough to reopen considerably later and under much reduced conditions. The federal government has lived up to President Bush's promises to do whatever it takes to rebuild New Orleans at best partially – in all senses of the term.

So post-Katrina New Orleans has simply made bare for all to see what neoliberalizing America amounts to. The impact of redlining can be found etched into the urban landscape of contemporary New Orleans. The Lower Ninth Ward is neither mistake nor oversight. Its destruction by Katrina and its burial by FEMA were as surely the outcome of neoliberal privatization as its neglected condition was a product of the history of redlining, of the segregating racial state.

Privatizing the support system means just that, sustaining and securing the structures of support for private, corporately channeled interests, which in the structure of racial americanization tend to be overwhelmingly white, and less for everyone else, most notably for those who are not.

When Kanye West declared on the national telethon to raise money for the victims of Katrina that George Bush "doesn't care about black people," he personalized and individualized what for the past 20 years has been turned effectively into a deeply institutional rationality. Since the Reagan administration, and exacerbated dramatically under George W. Bush, the state has been restructured in such a way that poor people generally, which means especially black and brown citizens, are not to be taken into consideration, cared for, or exhibited compassion by the institutional apparatuses representing the state.

For conservatives, the effect of the Civil Rights successes in the US was to read the state as being in the service of brown and especially black Americans. It had become, for African Americans, the largest post-segregation employer, the instrument of affirmative action, the educator of choice if not necessity, the guarantor of welfare rights when all else failed (or in this dismissive scheme of things more likely as the first resort), the underwriter of housing for those who might otherwise have none. In short, the state was seen by racial conservationists to have been metamorphosed by the Civil Rights revolution into a black institution, or at least one whose mission was now foremostly to serve the interests of African Americans.

The most effective counter, on the conservationist view, both instrumentally and to avoid being seen as racist, would be to go after the institution of the state itself. Kill Goliath and the philistines with a single fling: Restrict black advancement, thus cutting out the possibility of additional competition; and delimit state power, long a central conservative tenet. And so that it cannot respond to perceived crisis after crisis of racially driven impoverishment – gangs, crack cocaine, HIV/AIDS, educational failure, intensified poverty, urban blight – other than through criminalizing the most vulnerable, the state is being steadily denuded of the resources of response. The state's resources directed at producing greater racial equality are being drowned in Grover Norquist's bathtub.

The social welfare state, such as it was in the context of the United States, fixed an increasing proportion of the national budget in programs to sustain the quality of life for broad swaths of the national population. The social safety net included social security or retirement benefits, health benefits, and unemployment benefits. But it also offered broad support for public schooling and higher education, at least nominally for low-income housing projects, mortgage tax writeoffs for the middle class, and subsidies for a wide range of corporate interests. The deva-stating of public resources and revenues today, by contrast, fixes expanding proportions of delimited state revenues in policing and prisons, and in state security (including immigration restriction). These institutional apparatuses, in short, all target a very different modality of managing those racially defined as not white, and most notably the racial poor.

Americanizing Racial Commitments

Stating the claim

Implicit in this model of *racial americanization* thus is a set of barely stated assumptions, what Slavoj Žižek in a different context might call its circle of presuppositions. First, homogenized apartness is taken as the deracialized norm, the assumed, the natural, the given. Integration, or at least desegregation, comes over as unnatural, literally absurd and irrational in the prevailing order of things, requiring intervention by the state at the cost of individual liberty (the freedom to choose where one lives or is educated, who one hires or works with, where one hangs out, worships or may be laid to rest).

Second, standards (of merit, excellence, morality, civility, civilization) are represented mainly as white, that is, those associated with the structure of whiteness. These are assumed as the norm, as the criteria of judgment, as representing excellence – as what everyone else should aspire to.

Third, whites are projected as the real victims of antiracist excess (of leftist antiracist racism, of political correctness, of liberal soft-headedness, of the ideology of egalitarianism).

And finally, those committed to affirmative action, those against the undoing of antiracist protections and for vigorously heterogeneous public culture, are chided by the agents of rational choice and unfettered individual preference – by racial americanists, in other words – as the cultural elites (the very terms Bob Dole used to knock Democrats in his acceptance speech for the Republican nomination in the 1998 Presidential election), out of touch with the "real" concerns and interests of "real," everyday, working – that is, street wary and weary – white people.

George W. Bush's process of choosing a replacement for the retiring Sandra Day O'Connor, first woman justice to serve on the US Supreme Court, reveals the logic for extending white male privilege and domination under the regime of racelessness. First, be sure to guarantee a genuinely diverse finalist pool. Transparency and the representation of fairness at this stage are imperative, as too the insistence that all the candidates are qualified to serve or for admission. And then one is free to pick the white guy(s) in the pool – perhaps the only white male(s) still under consideration – as the most qualified, the best candidate(s) for the opening(s). Justice Harlan was right already in 1896: white folk, and white men in particular, have nothing to fear competitively from the regime of colorblindness while they continue to control the mechanisms for selection.

Globalizing design

But racial americanization is not simply a movement looking to local conditions. Where it is self-conscious, racial americanization has come to combine domestic with foreign design. In the wake of 9/11, americanization became exportable to those ethnoracially conceived countries or (sub-)continents deemed to threaten its security. The conservationism of domestic racial americanization has been supplemented by an activist agenda regarding externalities, one that has redounded on the fragilities of the domestic mandate in unsettling ways. Domestically, as I have indicated, the commitment is supposed to be to homogenizing racelessness as the rejection of "diversity drivel," where the civilizing standards are those of homogenizing whiteness.

By extension, ethnoracial rationalization as civilizational superiority is readily invoked in the war on terror and exported as the neolibertarian imposition of "living free." Living free means buying (into) the American Dream: privatizing (i.e., corporatizing) national industries, dramatically diminished trade union power, cutthroat competitiveness, a culture of possessive individualism, reduced taxes and scaled-back welfare benefits, strongly encouraged foreign investment with few constraints on taking profits out, the freedom to choose (ultimately to starve) and to put in place US friendly puppets.

Now this foreign extension of racial americanization returns racial configuration to externalities internalized, to race as the outside threat of heterogeneous diversity, as the perceived activist need to reinvent a segregationist logic on an ethnonationalized global scale. Hence the repeated emphases on the infiltration of outside, foreign, terrorizing elements into occupied territories. Rogue states, those premodern avatars of repressive unfreedom or chaotic anarchy, are the new targets of opportunity. Until the American Dream of "living free" is internalized in those civilizational places most resistant to it – notably societies seen to be ordered by the terrors of assertive Islam – they need to be quarantined, segregated into containable and controllable cantons, movement of human and economic capital to and from them constrained and conditioned, filtered and sterilized lest they infect the land of modern liberty.

Muslims are the "new niggers" of this globalizing racial americanization, present-day pariahs. And given that transnational flows are less readily containable and conditioned than they were a century ago, this newly necessitated activism has redounded back on the American "homeland" (how much more an ironically inverted historical invocation of *racially* conceived place can one get?). Recent polls in the US indicated that 39 percent of Americans would have Muslims in the country, whether or not citizens, carry special identification, one-third reject Muslims as neighbors and have a sense of Muslims as terrorists and breeders of hate.

The circulation of terror today knows no borders or boundaries. A talk show host in Washington, DC, in 2007, began a show by suggesting that Muslims in America should be identified by a forehead tattoo or an armband, much like Jews in Nazi Germany. The audience responses were shocking, repeatedly calling for exporting them or placing them in concentration camps. At show's end the host, himself Jewish, admitted to staging the call for identification marks, strongly chiding the audience for being like fascists in Germany during World War II. A revealing moment.

The dictates of national security have been internalized in the form of "homeland security," identifying the transnational uncontainability of an ethnoracially conceived people elsewhere (Muslims everywhere, all two billion, worldwide) into a more strategically manageable grouping (Arabs) geo-graphically locatable in a single, if extended, region (the Middle East). The reifications at work here (as in the Palestinian instance) are revealed by the fact that there are significant populations among Muslims who are not Arab, and likewise of Arabs who are not Muslim.

The transmutations of geostrategic national and localized homeland securities into each other have a double dictate: On one hand, wherever they might be, the terrorists must be eradicated, no matter the collateral damage, or failing that at least kept at bay (though given the need to protect global interests, American presence in any bay has become a vulnerable target). Collateral damage, as Mahmood Mamdani has pointed out, is "not an unfortunate byproduct of war; it was the very point" of terrorizing the general population into submission, a logic destined to bite back the hand that feeds it, as the Iraqi debacle of "Operation Enduring Freedom" is illustrating on a daily basis. That freedom is to be "endured" reveals something of the ironies at work here. It reveals, on the other hand, that the uncivil must be civilized, educated where at all possible in the virtues of the American way, all the while keeping them at arm's length lest they bite back, which they invariably do. The logic of domination, of enduring freedom, dictates it.

This ambivalence between embracing and distancing, between paternalistic rule and the segregative security state, is mirrored by the ambivalence towards racial profiling. Prior to 9/11, racial profiling in the US especially by the police was being rolled back in the face of widespread public consensus that it was unworkable and unjust. Post-9/11, public opinion has swung dramatically, 70 percent now supporting profiling as a means to effect security in the homeland. One-third of people polled in the US responded that all Arab Americans ought to be interned as a bulwark against potential terrorism. In December 2004, a Cornell University study found 44 percent of Americans polled support curtailing of Muslim and Arab-Americans' civil rights.

Think of it: 60 years after World War II, every third non-Arab American one might come across in a random public place in America wants to round up their Arab-American compatriots in a concentration camp, and almost half want Arab Americans considerably restricted in ways other US citizens are not (the numbers are significantly higher for Americans who are Republican, strongly religiously inclined, or watch television news). Paul Gilroy is right at least in this: the *resonances* of fascism die hard.

President Bush's executive order clarifying his administration's policy on racial profiling seeks to capitalize on these tensions. The policy bans profiling by federal law enforcement agents for "routine law enforcement investigations." But the executive order nevertheless enables the use of race and ethnicity in "national security" (including all border) considerations as well as in cases where "trustworthy information" exists identifying specific criminal activity or membership of a criminal organization. So while police cannot target a neighborhood because of its racial composition, border patrol can stop a person on the basis of a racial profile, race can be used to "identify terrorist threats, and stop potential catastrophic attacks," and federal agents can stop racially identified suspects in a particular crime where they claim to have clear evidence that the perpetrator fits the racial profile.

Clearly, this executive order on racial profiling makes explicit in America's global designs what it now extends locally only through sublimation and implication. Doing unto others as you would continue to do unto yourself. The executive order will have no diminishing effect on the racially driven rates of incarceration in America where people of color, totaling a third of the general population, make up more than three-quarters of the spiraling prison population. Racially driven incarceration, in fact, is a cornerstone of the logic of born again segregative racism, of warehousing the poor and managing the unassimilated heterogeny.

The almost random rounding up of Arabs following homeland terror attacks from Oklahoma City onwards is a predictable extension of this logic. A week or so after the release of the Cornell University survey mentioned above, approximately 40 Muslim American members of the Council on American–Islamic Relations, the largest and most prominent Muslim civil rights group in North America, were returning home from a major conference in Toronto (December 26, 2004). They were held at the border crossing for more than six hours by US Border Patrol officials who, citing orders from the Department of Homeland Security, refused to release them until they agreed to be fingerprinted, a violation of law unless citizens are suspected of a crime. "Traveling while Muslim" seems to have become the latest form of state-mandated racial profiling.

Federally fueled profiling in fact proliferates in other significant areas of state administration, most notably in the Pentagon's explicit ethnoracial poverty draft, namely, the targeting of Latinos, American Indians, and non-citizen Mexicans for recruitment to man street patrols in the enduring Iraqi occupation. President Bush's profiling policy thus exemplifies the logic of racial americanization perfectly well: appear to strike racial reference from formal public dictate – indeed, do so with the best of intentions – while endorsing its covert extension, in private and public interactions, especially in cases of national and "homeland" security.

Residential segregation tends to be reflected in and reinforced by what might be called "political segregation." African-American voters tend overwhelmingly to vote for Democratic Party candidates. Of the roughly 200 Republican members of the US House of Representatives, none is black and the three Hispanics are all Cuban American. Of the more than 3,500 Republican members of state legislatures, just 16 are black and 13 Hispanic. Democrats other than white, by contrast, number approximately 70 US Representatives, and 20 percent of Democratic members of state legislators. In recent Presidential elections Republicans accordingly have taken to strategies of discouraging blacks from voting, going so far as to intimidate elderly black people from showing up at polling booths. Thus uniformed state troopers in swing states such as Florida have asserted themselves visibly in the doorways of polling stations to remind African Americans of the historical horrors of casting a vote, and older black people, registered Democrats all, have been visited at home by investigators on trumped-up charges of voter fraud.

Even where Republicans have gestured at diversifying their voter base, much as they might their investment portfolio, their overriding electoral strategy in the face of rapidly heterogenizing multiculture has been twofold. First, because white voters tend largely to vote Republican, to ensure that they vote in elections. And second, to reproduce white legislative majorities – by running almost exclusively white candidates – at more or less all levels of elected government.

In terms of the institutionalization and reproduction of racial americanization, these new forms of segregation have managed to *informalize* what used to be formally produced, both to *realize* and *virtualize* segregative exclusions. Race continues to define, globally as domestically, where one can go, what one can do, how one is seen and treated, one's social, economic, political, legal, and cultural, in short, one's daily experience and prospects. Global circulation, like local city space, is increasingly contradictory: As there is greater heterogeneity and multiplicity, so segregation is refined; as visible openness and accessibility are enlarged, exclusionary totalization is extended; as interaction is increased, access is monitored, traversal policed, intercourse surveilled. As boundaries and borders become more permeable, they are re-fixed in the social imaginary, shifting from the visible to the virtual, from the formalized to the experiential, from the legal to the cultural at a time when the cultural, economically and socially, has become dominant.

Securing social prophylaxis

In short, what Zygmunt Bauman calls the "pastoral" state is being *devastated*. Devastation etymologically means "to lay waste" or "to ravage." The seventeenth-century affiliate term "devastavit" signaled both the offense of wasting a person's estate and the charge of such waste. We are witness to a latter-day version of state *devastavit*. Compassionate conservatives – where neoliberalism meets neoconservatism – have been passionate only about forcing a narrowly ideological agenda on the country's inhabitants, if not the world, and compassionate about little else than the calculation of narrow economic, political, and ideological self-interest. The state is in the process of being structurally transformed from a robust set of institutional apparatuses concerned at day's end to advance the welfare of its citizens and allies, contradictions and all, into a structure of social prophylaxis. It is troubled as a consequence overwhelmingly with securing the most elevated private interests from the perceived contamination and threat of those deemed for various reasons not to belong, to have little or no standing, the welfare of whom is calculated to cost too much, economically or politically.

The state, in short, is being laid waste. Or a specific form of the state, to be precise, for the state at large is being dramatically transformed. Devastating public responsibility, cutting the heart out of it, boils down to discriminating devastations. It drags commitment away from the general wellbeing, at least nominally from the good of all expansively conceived, to the baldly narrowed privatization of particular sorts of preferences, the rest considered only as a variable in the calculation of interests promoted or threatened. New Orleans has simply drawn this contemporary socio-racial dynamic and its debilitating effects momentarily out of the shadows and into the blinding light of day.

National (now reconceptualized as "homeland") security has become the abiding insomnia of American paranoia. The logic of segregation, of isolation, accordingly has come to dominate US foreign policy too. Segregation was never about the complete dislocation of one racially conceived group from another, a final solution of another sort, so much as it was conceived as a logic of ongoing control. Blacks were to be externalized from the social life of whiteness for all purposes other than menial services, demeaning labor, and sometime social entertainment, including sexual experimentation or satisfaction. Likewise with geostrategic calculation.

The US now interacts with others largely in so far and for as long as they service some material benefit or calculation of national interests, or at least not threaten those interests. Self-direction, conjured perhaps also for the racially immature only once schooled in the adult values of national self-determination, is respected really just for those taken to be (or to be capable of being) like the traditional figure of America, those that could be considered racially equal. It would be revealing – a "crucial experiment" – to see how robust American support for Israel would remain were the latter's Jewish population to become overwhelmingly and visibly Mizrahi (Middle Eastern and North African Jews) rather than Ashkenazi (East European) descendant.

The history of segregating others reveals that it necessarily entails more or less extensively isolating oneself, that is, self-segregation. And like repression generally, this too effects a romantic fascination with the denied. Hence the lure to whites of Harlem at the heights of segregating America or of Sophiatown and District Six in apartheid South Africa. Racial americanization is about unilateral Americanism, a new global politics of going it alone or forcing ways of being and doing and thinking on others because, in elevating oneself above all others, one is reduced to the paranoidly assertive insecurity of rendering oneself too sensitive to touch, thus literally untouchable. Targets of opportunity turn on their paternalists, once they figure out there are no free opportunities. Iraq is simply the latest in a long line. This shriveling of possibility reduces the plaintive cry of freedom to turning the self-proclaimed father figure of America into targets. Racial americanization externalized is the fuel – and fear – of terrorism internalized.

Historically America has been long concerned, and at times consumed, with its own sense of security, with defending itself from (perceived) threats internal and external. From the late nineteenth century on, as race turned increasingly to be about the urban, about the social inside, it came to be tied up with society's sense of self-protection, society's *condomization*. Securing the social interior is always sponsored or sustained by a paranoid sense of the outside. One need look no further than racially driven immigration policy, urban design, criminal codes, anti-miscegenation statutes, and more recently to the various enactments around anti-terrorism. Towards the close of the 1980s the military-inspired economy was supplemented by the prison growth industry as the dominant political economy of militarism was challenged by the closing down of the Cold War. By the mid-1990s, and accelerating rapidly and dramatically after 9/11, the security state expanded, supplementing military and prison industrializations, folding the former two into itself, creating something qualitatively different and new.

The security state looks to the outside overridingly as a challenge for condomizing the inside. Its knotted logic thus seeks to leverage externalities from the vantage of – for the sake of controlling – internalities. It ultimately involves the nano-technological mapping of the most inner and complete workings of our bio-being threaded into an expansive, vice-like embrace of anything taken as geostrategically threatening, probingly intrusive, or competitively challenging. Security above all else, executed by the military and its civic extensions or surrogates, supplemented both by an informational apparatus and by prisons publicly regulated for the most part in the breach. This extensive securitizing logic, swarming into even the most nano-scale and intimate domains, potentially into any and every corpuscle and crevice of civil society, inhabits the logic of research or intelligence gathering, governance, subject formation, epistemology, and the securing of belief.

Securitization is the condomizing of a world concerned with its own privatization against invasion by germs unwanted, viruses all around, terror threats unleashed and unrestricted. The dramatic expansion and qualitative transformation of the New York Police Department's intelligence division after 9/11 inhabit this new mode of operation, as William Finnegan reveals. No longer do we inhabit that antique 1980s world of risk assessment and calculation (how quickly that has been superseded). The world faced today is that of threat assessment and universal (indeed, also unilateral) alert, of preemptive invasion and prophylactic self-entombment. Even social benevolence, the doing of good to another for the other's sake, is now purely instrumentalized. The drawback of American generosity is that it is interventionist by disposition, if not design. Do it our way or no way; emulate us or failure will surely follow. A hint of disloyalty will entail a charge of terrorism, with potentially invasive implication.

Prophylactic social regimes are anchored in prompting, licensing, and leveraging expression and legitimation of broad popular fears, whether economic or social in origi*nation*. Social prophylaxis is mobilized to circumscribe and sustain the national commonality of historical and social experience it presumes as originating birthmark of the nation. Condomized social ordering takes root in the reification and promotion of articulated fears, most notably that of social dissolution, even giving articulation to the inarticulate, the hinted at, the suggestive. More often than not, these fears are tied causally to a problematized group at the margins of social belonging (a class, a race, an ethnic or religious minority, a nation considered to threaten strategic interests) and, by extension, to a cohering sense of threatened social order, national belonging, territorial commitment, and cultural aesthetic. In short, the threat is conjured to the very being of the patria, circulated broadly across the population easily turning the differentiation into enmity, the differentiated into enemies.

Condomizing social arrangement follows in seeking to secure authority centrally and increasingly secretly, in the unlimited and unannounced unleashing of purges of the body politic, of its cleansing of the alien virus within and of isolating the externalized enemy without. It often elevates an uncritical and pretty much unchecked militarization as source of social truth, political power, and economic wellbeing. Prophylaxis prescribes measures to prevent or circumscribe the spread of social dis-ease, to limit its reach and range. This prescriptive circumscription thus entails protection of the status quo, of prevailing power from critical challenge, from the threat of its dissolution.

Now this latter logic of social terror internalized, securitization centralized, enmity purged, and militarization elevated, creeping to its extreme endgame in the sustained collapsing of the very distinctions, has cast its securing skin across broad regions in the past decade. It pulls across its social self a fragile material, its elasticity stretched to tearing by resistance to and rejection of its homogenizing mandates wherever its expressions and effects surface. And yet even where reduced to tatters various strands of a repressive and domineering social fabric remain. These strands may be discrete, insecure, and far from firmly fixed in place, to be sure. Yet they remain at hand to be put in repressive play, mobilized as regimes find necessary to patch the condomizing social material where the counters and resistances have weakened the structures of control.

The prophylactic apparatuses make readily available a toolbox of technologies racially shaped and licensed for the management of social heterogeneities, and their perceived challenges and threats. The relative lack of robust public resistances – even the intense resistance to resistance, to criticism – suggests that the possibility of pressing repressive social technologies into service is disturbingly closer at hand than is comfortable to contemplate. And yet contemplating it a progressive critical analysis must.

I turn in the following two chapters to consider the elaboration of racial configuration in contemporary prophylactic social orders taking themselves not to be so configured, namely *racial palestinianization* and *racial europeanization*.

Bibliography

Appiah, Kwame Anthony 2007: "What Was Africa to Them?" *New York Review of Books*, 54, 14 (September 27), 41–5.

Associated Press 2005: "Bush Denies Racism in Katrina Response," *chron.com*, December 13, www.chron.com/disp/story.mpl/nation/3520492.html.

Bennett, William 2005: "Morning in America," transcript reported on *Media Matters for America*, Wednesday, September 28, mediamatters.org/items/printable/200509280006.

Bhattacharyya, Gargi, Gabriel, John, and Small, Stephen 2002: *Race and Power: Global Racism in the Twenty-First Century*. London: Routledge.

Bloomberg News 2004: "Almost Half of Americans Favor Restrictions on Muslims Rights," Friday, December 17; www.bloomberg.com/apps/news?pid=10000103&sid=amRg3O8daYc8&refer=us.

Bonilla-Silva, Eduardo 2004: "From Bi-racial to Tri-racial: Towards a New System of Racial Stratification in the USA," *Ethnic and Racial Studies*, 27, 6 (November 6), 931–50.

Brown, Michael et al. 2003: *Whitewashing Race: The Myth of a Colorblind Society*. Berkeley: University of California Press.

Butler, Judith 2003: "No, It's Not Anti-Semitic," *London Review of Books*, 25, 16 (August 21); www.lrb.co.uk/v25/n16.contents.html.

Butler, Judith 2004: *Precarious Life: The Power of Mourning and Violence*. London: Verso.

Cadenhead, Rogers 2005: "Police Trapped Thousands in New Orleans," *Workbench*, September 9; www.cadenhead.org/workbench/news/2748/police-trapped-thousands-new-orleans.

Carnesale, Albert 2006: "The Private–Public Gap in Higher Education," *Chronicle Review of The Chronicle of Higher Education*, January 6, B20.

Cheng, Anne Anlin 2001: *The Melancholy of Race: Psychoanalysis, Assimilation, and Hidden Grief*. New York: Oxford University Press.

Cockburn, Alexander and St. Clair, Jeffrey, eds. 2003: *The Politics of Anti-Semitism*. Oakland: Counterpunch and AK Press.

Connerly, Ward 2003: "Murder at the Supreme Court: Meritocracy and Equal Treatment RIP," *National Review Online*, January 26; www.nationalreview.com/comment/comment-connerly062603.asp.

Crenson, Matt 2005: "Katrina Rebuild Hinges on Who Will Pay," Associated Press, December 4; www.redorbit.com/news/general/320400/katrina_rebuild_hinges_on_who_will_pay/.

Culberson, John 2005: "Transcript of Culberson's Appearance on MSNBC's The Situation with Tucker Carlson," msnbc.com, October 5; www.msnbc.msn. com/id/9610419.

DeBose, Brian 2005: "HUD Chief Foresees a 'Whiter' Big Easy," *Washington Times*, September 30; www.washingtontimes.com/national/20050929-114710-8545r.htm.

Debusmann, Bernd 2006: "In US, Fear and Distrust of Muslims Run Deep," Reuters, December 2; news.yahoo.com/s/nm/20061201/us_nm/usa_muslims_fear_dc.

Denton, Nancy 1994: "Residential Segregation: Challenge to White America," *Journal of Intergroup Relations*, 21, 2 (Summer), 19–35.

Dreyfuss, Robert 2001: "Grover Norquist: 'Field Marshall of the Bush Plan'," *The Nation*, May 14; www.thenation.com/doc/20010514/dreyfuss.

Eaton, Leslie and Eaton, Ron 2005: "Loans to Homeowners Along the Gulf Coast Lag," *New York Times*, December 15; www.nytimes.com/(2005)./national/nationalspecial/15loan.

Eng, David and Kazanjian, David, eds. 2003: *Loss*. Berkeley: University of California Press.

Finnegan, William 2005: "The Terrorism Beat: How is the NYPD Defending the City?" *New Yorker*, July 25, 58–71.

Fiss, Owen 2003: *A Way Out: America's Ghettos and the Legacy of Racism*. Princeton: Princeton University Press.

Foucault, Michel 2003: *"Society Must Be Defended": Lectures at the Collège de France, 1975–76*. Trans. David Macey. New York: Picador.

Freud, Sigmund 1927/1953: "Mourning and Melancholia," in *The Standard Edition of the Complete Psychological Works of Sigmund Freud*, Vol. 14. Trans. and ed. James Strachey. London: Hogarth Press.

Gilroy, Paul 2000: *Against Race: Imagining Political Culture Beyond the Color Line*. Cambridge, MA: Harvard University Press.

Gold, Steven J. 2004: "From Jim Crow to Racial Hegemony: Evolving Explanations of Racial Harmony," *Ethnic and Racial Studies*, 27, 6 (November 6), 951–68.

"The Great White Influx" 2002: *Los Angeles Times*, July 31, 1.

Gregory, Derek 2004: *The Colonial Present*. Oxford: Blackwell.

Gumbel, Andrew 2003: "Pentagon Targets Latinos and Mexicans to Man the Front Lines in War on Terror," *Independent*, London, September 10.

Guardian Unlimited 2005: "Drowned City Cuts Its Poor," *Sunday Observer*, December 11; observer.guardian.co.uk/international/story/06903,1664630,00.

Haines, Erinn 2005: "Black Lawmakers Vow to Repeal Ga. Voter Law," Associated Press, December 29; news.yahoo.com/s/ap/(2005).1229/ap_on_el_st_lo/voter_id.

Herbert, Bob 2004: "A Chill in Florida," *New York Times*, August 23, A23.

Herbert, Bob 2007: "6-Year-Olds Under Arrest," *New York Times*, April 9, A19.

Higgs, Robert 2004: "The Defense Budget Is Bigger Than You Think," *San Francisco Chronicle*, January 18; www.independent.org/newsroom/article.asp?id=1253.

Hirsch, Arnold 1993: "With or Without Jim Crow: Black Residential Segregation in the United States," in Arnold Hirsch and Raymond Mohl (eds.), *Urban Policy in Twentieth-Century America*. New Brunswick, NJ: Rutgers University Press, pp. 65–99.

HOLC 1936: Division of Research and Statistics with Cooperation of the Appraisal Department, San Diego, October 20.

Jackson, Jr., John, ed. 2005: "Racial Americana" (Special Issue), *South Atlantic Quarterly*, 104, 3 (Summer), 393–606.

Kestin, Sally, O'Matz, Megan, and Maines, John 2005: "FEMA Reimbursements Mainly Benefit Higher-Income Groups," Sun-Sentinel.com, December 11; www.sun-sentinel.com/news/local/southflorida/sfl-fema11xdec(2005).

Leonhardt, David 2007: "The New Affirmative Action," *New York Times Magazine*, Sunday, September 30; www.nytimes.com/2007/09/30/magazine/30affirmativet.html?_r=1&th&emc=th&oref=slogin.

Lipsitz, George 1998: *The Possessive Investment in Whiteness: How White People Profit from Identity Politics*. Philadelphia: Temple University Press.

Lipsitz, George 2006: "Learning from New Orleans: The Social Warrant of Hostile Privatism and Competitive Consumer Citizenship," *Cultural Anthropology*, 21, 3, 451–68.

Lizza, Ryan 2007: "Return of the Nativist: Behind the Republicans' Anti-Immigation Frenzy," *New Yorker*, December 17, 46–51.

Mamdani, Mahmood 2001: *When Victims Become Killers: Colonialism, Nativism, and the Genocide in Rwanda*. Princeton: Princeton University Press.

Mamdani, Mahmood 2002: "Good Muslim, Bad Muslim: Apolitical Perspective on Culture and Terrorism," *American Anthropologist*, 104, 3, 766–75.

Marciano, Richard and Goldberg, David Theo 2008: *T-RACES: Testbed for the Redlining Archives of California's Exclusionary Spaces*. www.salt.sdsc.edu/T-RACES/index.htm.

Massey, Douglas and Denton, Nancy 1993: *American Apartheid: Segregation and the Making of the Underclass*. Cambridge, MA: Harvard University Press.

Massey, Douglas and Hajnal, Zoltan 1995: "The Changing Geographic Structure of Black–White Segregation in the United States," *Social Science Quarterly*, 76, 3 (September), 527–42.

Mbembe, Achille 2003: "Necropolitics," *Public Culture*, 15, 1 (Winter), 11–40.

"The Michigan Decisions" 2003: *The Chronicle Review, Chronicle of Higher Education*, July 4, 10–12.

Mohl, Raymond 1993: "Shifting Patterns of American Urban Policy since 1900," in Arnold Hirsch and Raymond Mohl (eds.), *Urban Policy in Twentieth-Century America*. New Brunswick, NJ: Rutgers University Press, pp. 1–45.

Moore, Donald 2005: *Suffering for Territory: Race, Place, and Power in Zimbabwe*. Durham, NC: Duke University Press.

Nossiter, Adam 2006: "Conservative White Voters Hold Sway in New Orleans," *New York Times*, May 7; www.nytimes.com/2006/05/07/us/07orleans.html?_ r=1&oref=slogin.

Orfield, Gary and Lee, Chungmei 2007: *Historical Reversals, Accelerating Segregation and the Need for New Integration Strategies*. A Report of the Civil Rights Project/Proyecto Direchos Civiles, August. www.civilrightsproject.ucla.edu/.

Pace, David 2005: "More Blacks Live with Pollution," Associated Press, December 13; news.yahoo.com/s/ap/(2005).1213/ap_on_he_me/unhealthy_air.

Parents Involved in Community Schools v. Seattle School District No. 1, et al. June 28, 2007.

People 2005: "The Long Shadow of Jim Crow: Voter Intimidation and Suppression in America Today: A Report by the PFAW and NAACP," *People for the American Way*; www.pfaw.org/pfaw/general/default.aspx?oid=16367.

Post, Robert, ed. 2001: *Prejudicial Appearances: The Logic of American Antidiscrimination Law*. With commentaries from Anthony Appiah, Judith Butler, Thomas Grey, and Reva Siegel. Durham, NC: Duke University Press.

Potok, Mark, Visconti, Luke, Frankel, Barbara, and Holmes, Nigel 2007: "The Geography of Hate," *New York Times*, November 25; www.nytimes.com/ 2007/11/25/opinion/25potok.html.

Raban, Jonathan 2007: *Surveillance: A Novel*. New York: Pantheon.

Rosen, Charles 2005: "The Anatomy Lesson: Robert Burton's *The Anatomy of Melancholy* (1621–51)," *New York Review of Books*, 52, 10, 55–9.

Rosenberg, Matthew 2003: "US May Study Israeli Occupation Tactics," Associated Press, September 19, 2003; story.news.yahoo.com/news?tmpl=story&cid= 540&e=33&u=/ap/20030918/ap_on_re_mi_ea/israel_us_iraq_1.

Schmitt, Carl 1922/2005: *Political Theology: Four Chapters on the Concept of Sovereignty*. Trans. George Schwab. Chicago: University of Chicago Press.

Sperling, John 2004: *The Great Divide: Retro vs. Metro*. Sausalito, CA: PoliPoint Press.

Steinberg, Stephen 2007: *Race Relations: A Critique*. Stanford: Stanford University Press.

Stoler, Ann L. 2009: "Deathscapes of the Present: Conversing with Achille Mbembe . . . and Michel Foucault," in Kim Benito Furumoto (ed.), *Race's Ghostly Words*. Durham, NC: Duke University Press. MS on file.

US Newswire 2004: "American Muslims Fingerprinted by US at Canadian Border; CAIR Calls for 'Profiling' Probe, Says Incident Chills Religious Freedom," December 29; releases.usnewswire.com/GetRelease.asp?id=41075.

Volpp, Leti 2002: "The Citizen and the Terrorist," *UCLA Law Review*, 49, 5, 1575–600.

Wright, Richard 1954: *Black Power: A Record of Reactions in a Land of Pathos*. New York: Harper Brothers.

Younge, Gary 2006: "Big Business Sees a Chance for Ethnic and Racial Cleansing," *Guardian*, Thursday, April 20; www.guardian.co.uk/print/0,,329460874-103677,00.html.

4

Targets of Opportunity (On Racial Palestinianization)

For death is to see death.
  Mahmoud Darwish, *Memory for Forgetfulness*, 1995

Palestinians as a people and Arabs more generally, more regionally, as a pan-national self-identification emerged in *modern* terms first in the earlier decades of the twentieth century as expressions of anti-colonial and autonomous sensibilities, interests, and commitments. The heterogeneity among Arabs living throughout the region sought a more cohering identity in the face of intensifying British and French colonization after World War I, the discovery of large holdings of oil, growing anti-colonial movements in Africa and Asia, and ultimately the founding of Israel. The name "Palestine" was reinvoked by the British in the early 1920s upon receiving a League of Nations mandate to rule over the territory after Ottoman imperial control in the late nineteenth century had folded it into the southern extension of Syria.

British modernization, as Salim Tamari has pointed out, accordingly transformed a complexly secular, cosmopolitan, broadly communitarian order under Ottoman rule – especially in cities such as Jerusalem and ports such as Jaffa and Haifa (but also more regionally in Beirut and Damascus) – into a more segregating, ethnoracially and religiously discrete and divided set of communities in contest with each other for resources, space, and political favor. Classic colonial divide and rule, ethnoracially fueled. This regional transformation of heterogeneity into the logos of an assertedly homogeneous ethnoracial polity, of ethnoraciality, its promptings and its implications, is what I trace here in the name of racial palestinianization.

The Order of Racial Palestinianization

These delimiting senses of collective selves solidified interactively at mid-twentieth century as the struggles in the area over and with an emerging Israel and its territorial assertions intensified. The realization of Israel in particular, first as an idea whose roots were planted and then the landscape of which was carved out squarely in the territory until the moment of Israel's inception known as Palestine, united the longstanding and -suffering inhabitants of the area interactively as target of restriction and self-protection.

Thinking racially

Israel was an anomaly at its founding, reflecting conflicting logics of world historical events at the time between which its declarative moment was awkwardly wedged. On the one hand, it mimicked rather than properly mirrored the logics of independence fueled by decolonizing movements, though perhaps curiously closer in some crucial ways to Pakistan than, say, to India or other decolonizing societies of the day. On the other, it embodied *in potentia* as structural conditions of its very formation *some* key features of what coterminously was emerging as the apartheid state. In what follows, I am less identifying Israel as representing the apartheid state as I am tracing the ways in which, in conception and practice, it has come not just to embody apartheid elements but to represent a *novel* form of the racial state more generally.

In the latter spirit, Palestinians were the indigenous inhabitants of Palestine. They were indigenous in the sense of being and being "found" in the area, both by the nineteenth-century colonizing powers and by the increasing convergence of Zionist-inspired Jews in the territory after the Balfour Declaration of 1917 and especially in the wake of World War II. This is not to say Jews weren't present in the area prior to the migrations from the 1880s, only that the numbers were small and overwhelmingly Sephardic, locally born and bred. Identified as the direct kin of biblical Philistines, by the mid-twentieth century Palestinians as a people were often seen as philistines as much in characterization as in scriptural name, conceived in the representational struggles as bloodthirsty and warmongering, constantly harassing modern-day Israelites, debauched and lacking altogether in liberal culture. Terrorists, it seems, historically all the way down, to the toe-nails of time. Goliath cut to size by David's perennial craftiness and military prowess.

Israel came to be seen as an exemplary instance of what Michel Foucault, though in a different context, memorably has called "counter-history," as a historical narrative of insurrection, against the grain, establishing itself in the face of formidable and threatening power directed against it. Israel is forged out of a "biblical history of servitude and exiles," as a "history of insurrections" against state-imposed or -sanctioned injustices. In this, Israel held out hope and the promise of justice prevailed. Its founding narration, in short, is a complex of the history of struggles (Foucault uses the term "race wars" but it is clear from the examples he cites that he really has in mind group, even class, struggles) in which Jews were invariably the quintessential pariah, they who did not belong, but mixed with the civilizing European imperative, the white man's burden, of what I have characterized as "racial historicism."

Moses (Moshe) Hess, important for introducing Engels to the socialist fold and one of the first to articulate the Zionist vision, implored "the Jewish *race*" in 1862 to

> be the bearers of civilization to peoples who are still inexperienced and their teachers in the European sciences, to which your race has contributed so much. . . . [Jews are to be] mediators between Europe and far Asia, opening the roads that lead to India and China – those unknown regions which must ultimately be thrown open to civilization . . . [Jewish] labor and industry [in Palestine] will turn the ancient soil into fruitful valleys, reclaiming it from the encroaching sands of the desert . . . (My emphasis)

Theodore Herzl, the father figure of the Zionist social movement, concurred: "The immigration of Jews signifies an unhoped-for accession of strength for the land which is now so poor; in fact, for the whole Ottoman Empire." The Zionist vision for Israel, as Ella Shohat has remarked, represents the modernizing imperative in a region seen as still marked by the biblical backwardness of its Arab inhabitants.

Israel, it is accordingly apparent, has been thought – has thought of itself in part precisely – from its initiating modern conception explicitly as racially configured, as racially representative. And those insistent racial traces persist despite the post-Holocaust European repression of the use of race as social self-reference or -representation, as I make evident in the chapter to follow. In this, and as much as any other modernizing state, Israel accordingly has been caught in the race-making web of modernizing statehood. States assume their modernity, as I have argued in *The Racial State*, through racial articulation.

Israel, far from an exception, is a modern racial state knotted with and in constitutive contrast to the prehistory of Palestinian antiquity, of its historicized racial immaturity. Israel represents modernization, progress, industry and industriousness, looking to the bright future, the civilizing mission of the best that has been thought and could be taught. Palestine represents the past, failed effort where effort at all, antique land still tilled by hand and the perennial failure of governance, a place constantly in the grip of its time past and passed. The larger relational condition, a state racially characterizing itself in its founding self-representation, is one in which the state of the latter, materially as much as metaphorically, is fueled by the racially conceived, tinged (one might say singed) imposition of the former.

But this civilizing mission and self-determining drive thus initiated through Jews in the name of European civilization is one with a twist. Israel was forged, of course, in the fire and fury of all those migrations, the experiences of expulsions and exiles, arrivals and starting over, assimilations and abjected evictions, wrongful convictions and threatened extinctions. The war of races in which the Jew is the hounded, the perennial foe and fugitive, becomes in Israel's founding a protracted conflict in which the Jewish State, Herzl's dream, is turned into oppressor, victimizer, and sovereign. Vulnerable, victim, and vanquished become pursuer, perpetrator, predator. The State is transformed, as Foucault says, into protector of the integrity, superiority, and more or less purity of the homogenizing group, what Foucault marks as "the race." State sovereignty defends itself above all else so as to secure the group, its ethnoraciality, even to protect its purity, perpetuity, and power, for which it takes itself to exist and which it seeks to represent.

In "The Future of an Illusion" Freud notes that a culture in which the wellbeing of one group in the society is predicated on the subjugation or "suppression" of another will prompt intense hostility on the part of the suppressed. The deeper the hostility, the more likely the disaffected will act to destroy the culture, and in the extreme will reject the very premises on which the culture founds itself. Such an oppressive culture, Freud concludes, neither is likely nor justly "deserves" to perpetuate itself (as oppressing culture, as a state of oppression). A prescient insight, some 75 years ago.

Despite debatable stories of early Zionist settlers driven by socialist ideals of peaceful coexistence with local Arabs on land commonly tilled and towns cohabited, by the early 1970s Golda Meir could claim rhetoric-ally that the Palestinian people did not exist. Romantic coexistence in these parts has always gone arm in arm with assertive claims to territorial and political sovereignty, on both sides of the conflict. In Israel's triumphant War of Independence (what Palestinians characterize as "Al-Naqba" or "the catastrophe," a root meaning curiously more or less synonymous with "Shoah"), Israeli gains expanded the territory ceded it by the original UN Partition Resolution by almost one third. It widened its cartographic waistline, evicting 750,000 of the 850,000 or so Arabs living within enlarged Israel in order to ensure a Jewish majority. The moral qualms over eviction-driven expansion are well characterized in novelist Yizhar Smilansky's short story depicting the Sartrean dilemma faced by a young soldier caught between executing evicted Arab villagers and contributing to securing Israel's infant existence. That dilemma seems now to have been resolved overwhelmingly in favor of the latter national prerogative.

In short, a dominant faction of the Israeli political establishment has been committed since earliest Zionist settlement, intensifying with the de-claration of Israeli independence in 1948, not simply to deny Palestinian existence but to make the claim true, to act in its name and on its terms. An Israeli military planning document, known as Plan D (or Plan *Dalet*), formulated in the run-up to Israel's War of Independence in May–June 1948, sought "destruction of [Arab] villages by fire explosives and mining" after the villages had been surrounded and searched, resistance destroyed, and "expelling the population beyond the boundaries of the State."

Under Arafat, of course, Palestinians not only asserted a coherent iden-tity, but also sought to reciprocate that denial: the state of Israel does not, should not, exist. But as duplicitous and dirty-handed as the Palestinian patriarch turned out, and however rhetorically insistent concerning Israel's denial and demise, it is a whole lot more difficult, it would seem, to activate denial of the existence of one whose semi-automatic is at your nose than it is to insist that a stateless people, a nation of refugees from – while on – its own land, has no rights. It is not that might makes right in this case, if any; it is that might manufactures the conditions and parameters, the terms, of political, and by extension historical and rep-resentational, possibility.

The Zionist fight against the British continues to be framed as a battle against colonial imposition. As Martin Sicker points out, it was touted at least until 1948, and from today's vantage point somewhat ironically, as the struggle for "the liberation of *Palestine*" from British rule. Once the British vacated the territory, the ensuing Arab–Israeli war in 1948 was posed as a war of survival. Survival and security have been the dominant Israeli dispositions ever since. But Samera Esmeir reminds us that this relational logic of death and emergence reveals that birth in this instance is predicated on death, destruction, and eviction, moral and territorial.

Thus Meron Benvenisti reports that something like 200 Arab villages were abandoned in May 1948, and another 60 in June. By the time the dust had settled, nearly half a million Palestinians had been reduced to refugees, fleeing expanded Israel, never to be allowed to return. Israel came into being, came to be, by virtue both of Jews staring at their own individual and collective extinction and of Palestine's constriction, if not cessation, at least of its realization if not of its idea. That latter deathly denial, rationalized in the name of the former, is as much a part of Israel's history as it is repressed in, if not excised from, its official record. It is this tension between denial and repression that fuels Israel's sense of Palestine, and so of itself also.

There is a sharp distinction, often lost, between the notion of self-hating Jew and that of self-critical Jew. To criticize Israel as a state formation, and the Israeli state and governmental policies as enacting, enabling, or turning a blind eye to particularly vicious expressions of humiliation, dehumanization, and degradation, as Judith Butler has pointed out, emphatically counts as the latter without amounting to the former. To criticize the government of Israel and its policies, even to criticize the partial grounds on which that state was founded, is not to criticize Jews as such, nor is it to place Jews anywhere and everywhere at risk, notwithstanding the reported spike in recent antisemitic attacks in the likes of France. It is not even to place Jews in Israel at risk. Quite the contrary; it is to point out the way in which such policies and governmentality manifest the very insecurity they claim to undo.

That there remains always the possibility of an Israeli government that does not discriminate against its own Arab citizens and Palestinian non-citizens, as numerous courageous groups and individuals within Israel itself are working under very trying conditions to secure, entails that criticism of Israeli state policy and actions need not be – and often is not – antisemitic. To make out an argument, even, for a single non-ethnoracially configured state incorporating Jews and Palestinians alike is not to call for the demise of Jews or the dissolution of Jewry. Israel was made by a mix of Jews wanting a place to call home, if not always to be at home, in a world stricken by the guilt of deathly antisemitism. The idea of Israel subsequently came to tie Jews to one way of being in the world, to a singular commitment, the reifying stereotypification from which it was supposed to take leave.

Curiously, some radical Jewish Old Testament literalists call for ending Israel as we know it today in favor of reinscribing some originary biblical formation. And while they might be called crazy, I have never heard them characterized as antisemitic. So it is an irony that the considerable vehemence expressed by those in charging Jewish critics of Israel as "self-hating Jews" suggests an intense hatred of the very Jews at whom they are leveling the charge. The lance of "antisemitism" may just redirect uncomfortably.

To put it thus implicates Jews qua Jewishness as much in the necessity of critiquing the injustices in which the Israeli state engages as the refusal to criticize. More pressingly, the insistence that there be no such critique implicates silent and silenced Jews anywhere in that state's persistent injustices. This is a particularly knotted, if not inverted, expression of the traditional tensions between universalism and particularity, of selfhood and alterity, strangeness and alienation. The Israeli state is founded in the name of all Jews. That fact alone cedes to each Jew the responsibility not simply to defend Israel, no matter what; it demands of each also the critical attention to the especially egregious injustices the state exercises in the name of all.

As the Chosen People, self-anointedly so, Jews are the objects of both envy and scorn. Jews' "right to return" is magically drawn into a landscape apparently never abandoned as the Arab right is buried in the rubble of a landscape to which they assertedly never laid claim and from which they have recently been exorcised. Their homes are bulldozed away, their right to live, to *be*, in either Palestine or Israel, is always in question, under threat, uncertain, no matter how deep any ancestral, familial claim.

The "right of return" presupposes a belonging, a longing to be, a sense of security in a common place uniquely and always *ours*, a security coterminously common and false. For if all Jews were indeed to avail themselves of "return," it likely would be easier today to wipe Israel out with one blast, and with it all Jews, as Iranian president Ahmadinejad has called for, than it could have been under the Final Solution. The project of homogeneity, the artifice, the labor to realize a state of homogenized commonality, of familiality and familiarity, in its name, are, synonymously, the ultimate threat to the group's existence. The "wandering Jew," accordingly, of "going and resting" as Gabriel Josipovici has so elegantly put it, of settlement and unsettlement, is as accurate a characterization of the Jewish experience, Israel or no, as there is to find. It has opened Jews to being cosmopolitan and target, worldly post-national and vulnerable victim, exuberantly diverse and exclusionarily (even stultifyingly) homogeneous, engaged citizen and arrogant aggressor, progressive political critic and subjugating settler. That deathly weight of race, its anxious ambivalences, remarked upon in Chapter 1.

Religious interest groups in Israel and other supporters elsewhere of a restrictively ethnohomogeneous Israel consequently are concerned to control the conception and administration of "the true and pure Jew." This is a commitment not that logically far removed in the end from the likes of the "one drop rule." This idea of Israel requires "the Palestinian prob-lem" to justify itself as the *Jewish* state, much as Germans required the racial logics of "the Jewish problem" and America "the Negro problem" to con-stitute themselves in earlier moments as self-projectedly homogeneous. In the face of its own increasingly radically Jewish heterogeneity – radically Jewish and radically heterogeneous – and so in the face of its own inter-nal implosion, Israel seeks its familial artifice by projecting a threat both internal and purged to its shifting and shifted boundaries, at once within and without. From its earliest formative conception, a dominant order of Zionism articulated "the Jewish race" as creating coherence, artificing ini-tially discursive homogeneity of and for "the Jewish people" in the face of a scattered and diffuse "nation." At the risk of dramatic over-generalization, if homogeneity tends to humiliate, heterogeneity tends to humble.

Israelis now require the Philistine, as Sartre once said about the Jew himself in France: if he didn't exist, he would have to be invented, as indeed he has been. *He* has been: for the figure of the Palestinian, of the threatening suicide bomber, of a refugee rabble reducible to rubble, is over-whelmingly male, supported by women considered, unlike their military-serving Israeli counterparts, too weak and too late to do anything about the state of affairs, the affairs of state. If men suffer for the state, or for the nationalist idea of one, women suffer more immediately for men martyred to the nationalist mandate or sacrificing and sacrificed to state security, and for the families they are left to feed, materially and spiritually. Few women walk the streets of the territories, on either side of the catastrophe, of "the troubles," to borrow a telling phrase from another not so distant time and place.

The project of Israel accordingly became the materialization of this homo-genizing fabric. Israel as such cannot live with the Palestinians, purging them persistently from green-line Israel, but cannot live without them, conceptually as much as materially, existentially as much as emotionally. Israel is no longer as dependent on Palestinian labor as it once was, a result of importing other others – Filipinos, Romanians, Thais – to do the dirty work for a pittance (though cheap labor at hand would still be economically preferable to the import). The presence of Filipinos and Thais likewise makes it possible for Israelis to think of Israel as cosmopolitan, as an ethnically heterogeneous late modern state evidenced by the ready availability of Asian food. Middle Eastern cuisine no longer dominates the eating culture of Israeli fare as it once did, especially in the larger cities and hyper-modern commercial strips of the residential suburbs.

Israelis nevertheless need Palestinians to command militarization, American support and weaponry, even its own sense of victimized self. They "need" Palestinians in another sense too. September 11 revived Israel's renowned but at the time flagging technological revolution and computing industry by selling its products especially to the US as servicing Israel's vaunted security system. Israel's export of security products to America, among others, is up fivefold this decade, ranging from surveillance devices for airports and cities to tamper-proof biometric IDs and techno-securitized walls. Here, too, as Naomi Klein has pointed out, Palestinians have proved indispensable, as guinea pigs, experimental subjects for perfecting the technological apparatuses of securitization.

Israeli armed forces in the territories have increasingly strangled the flow of Palestinian goods from one Palestinian town to another, and have decimated and confiscated Palestinian fields for the sake of erecting a security barrier and separation wall. There are something in the order of 500–600 Israeli military checkpoints in the West Bank. These consist of concrete watchtowers and armored vehicles from behind the anonymity of which the movement of Palestinian daily life is manipulated at official whim, opened up or closed down at invisible military command, as Avi Mograbi's extraordinary docu-contrast, *Avenge but One of My Two Eyes* (2005), reveals in excruciating detail. Movement – of people, goods, money, water, sewage, automobiles, ambulances – is turned on and off, opened up momentarily and closed down just as quickly. Often on nothing more than military whim. The Palestinian territories beneath Sharon's boot and vision, and those of his political offspring, have suffered more than 50 percent unemployment, with 60 percent of the population living below the poverty line (a mere $2 per day). Health problems have spiraled, and securing health care is almost as hazardous as the health condition one might be seeking care to cure.

Israel's current crisis, as the Palestinian one too, consequently, is as much economic as political, as much about the decimation of Palestinian survival and consumptive capacity as about Israeli self-security. It is a self-exacerbated crisis fed by a complex of factors. These include a contradictory collective egoism, exacerbated by perceived Palestinian intransigence and violence, and underpinned by a return to presumptions of racially conceived Palestinian in- or infra-humanity on one side and insistent Israeli assertiveness on the other. "All Muslims are murderers," Israeli cabinet minister Boim declared knowingly in 2004. Well, what does that make all Israelis? Israel necessitates for itself the refusal of Palestine's realization, and as that necessity is insisted upon and enacted, it contradictorily fuels the separatist pipe-dream of Palestine, of an independent Palestinian state rather than mutually recognized respect and a common coexistence.

Here, then, is the knotted dilemma facing the region: Israel's sense of self, statehood, and security is predicated on restricting the scope of the same for those from whose landscape of life, loves, and longing the state of Israel was carved out. And Palestinian possibilities, in point of fact the very idea of a coherent Palestinian corpus, of Palestinian national aspirations, acquired a spirit, its very conception, as explicit resistance to and rejection of Israel's stake, at the extreme, of its being as such. They need each other, at least rhetorically if not psychologically, as perpetual grounds and justification for their own existence as much as in seeking to undermine the possibility of the other. It's as though existence of each is measured by the extent of the other's demise. The lopsidedness in repressive power of course renders Palestinian destitution more concertedly palpable than the reversal, at least at present.

This curious, conflicted, and quite unconventional mix of sensibilities and commitments, logics and laborings continues to mobilize especially American support for Israel. Israel has been seen as anti-colonial and nationalist but in its drive for survival and security as deeply dependent on American support. As such, Israel is never anti-American, as so many others in the Middle East have been or become. Since the 1967 war the region has fallen increasingly into a quasi-colonial condition and its predictable resistance. Israel is seen and comprehends itself rather as kindred spirit, one with America, sharing a supposedly common Judeo-Christian set of sensibilities, dispositions, and values, sometimes now characterized as a civilization in the way Herzl and his colleagues were wont to do over a century ago, and more recently a common set of regional interests.

Israel is taken as an outpost of European civilization, a frontier of sorts, in an altogether hostile and alien environment. Brothers to Christians, keepers of the faith and holy sites, a flourishing democracy in the land of Christ and region of alien autocratic regimes. A defender against irrationality and irreverence of life surrounded by infidels, a tower of strength and stability fueling American industry. Readers of the same book(s) and lovers of the same culture. Israel is the only state outside of the European continental land mass to participate in the Eurovision Song Contest, for instance. In this scheme of things, it seems, Israel must be European, presumptively white. But in keeping with contemporary racial americanization, with born again racism, Israel's whiteness is transparent, virtual, invisible.

American evangelicals, major determinants of George W. Bush's political direction locally and globally, assumed the clash of civilization conception of foreign policy between the west and the rest, most notably between Christianity and Islam. They helped to turn support for Israel into something of a crusade. Abraham, the story goes, was promised by God all the territory between the Nile in the south and west and the Euphrates in the north and east. As Max Nordau, Herzl's assertive assistant, put it in addressing European Jews in 1907, "We shall seek to do in Western Asia what the English did in India" – and then catches himself by adding, "I mean the cultural work, not rulership and domination. We aim to come to *Eretz Israel* as messengers of culture and we aim to extend the moral boundaries of Europe all the way to the Euphrates."

In short, race, racelessly conceived in relation to and through religion, steers the interests of geostrategic positioning. Evangelical Christianity can seek superciliously to satisfy its own apocalyptic vision while asserting its support for Israel. Their sharing a mutual goal is predicated on a putatively common heritage, religious and cultural, evidence of America's distance from its own antisemitic history.

The history of enmity between Jews and Arabs, as Gil Anidjar so revealingly parses it, accordingly is a European history, a history long constituted within Europe and across its orbits, one the traces of which are streaked through the landscape and culture of contemporary Israel. It is a history in the (re-)making. Israel/Palestine thus revealingly figures the condition of postcoloniality, nervously straddles its fissures, on structural more than temporal registers.

The Europeanness of politically and religiously dominant Israelis renders the Promised Land and its members, in the minds of most Americans (not least evangelical Christians) and in the dominant Israeli imagination, as normatively white. Israelis occupy the structural positions of whiteness in the racial hierarchy of the Middle East. Arabs, accordingly – most notably in the person of Palestinians – are the antithesis, a fact rendering the ambivalent situation of Arab Jews especially troubled, as Ella Shohat has demonstrated. Historically, politically, religiously, and culturally, Arabs are neither Jew nor (as such) white.

At the same time, the Jewishness of Arab Jews is complexly undercut by their Arabness. Popularly referenced as "Mizrahim," Yahouda Shenhav makes evident just how racially indexed such reference nevertheless remains by pointing out that it literally translates as "Easterners," itself code for "Orientals." Abba Eban, longtime foreign minister (1966–74), warned that "One of the great apprehensions which afflict us is the danger of the immigrants of Oriental origin forcing Israel to equalize its cultural level with that of the neighboring world." In the complex codes of Israel's race-less racial history, Mizrahim occupy a status as not-quite-white, more so than Palestinian citizens of Israel, to be sure, but less so than the white-ness, the Europeanness, of Ashkenazis. Mizrahim look a little like Israel's post-apartheid "Coloureds."

Prior to 1948, Jews living throughout what would become Arab states numbered somewhat short of one million. Today, that group collectively numbers just 8,000 people, a mere 1 percent of what it was prior to Israeli statehood. The Arab Jewish population of Israel, by contrast, has grown to almost 40 percent. They are in significant part de-Arabized (to riff on Shenhav's term) and de-nationalized, in order to be re-nationalized as they are re-oriented. To a degree Arab Jews became pan-ethnicized in Israel, Zionized in their pan-ethnicity even as their different national histories disarticulate their respective experiences. But they continue to occupy ambivalent, even anxious status in Israeli socio-economic life. A "neces-sary minority," given the country's broader demography, incorporated but significantly poorer and less powerful on every social index, a valuable intel-ligence commodity, given their ethnolinguistic backgrounds and cultural understandings, as Shenhav's account makes clear.

This ambivalence runs to the very early days of the state. "We do not want Israel to become Arab," declared Ben-Gurion in a fit of forthright-ness. "We are bound by duty to fight against the spirit of the Levant society." Yet, because Jews, de-Arabized or not, they are better treated, considered to belong, with more access, rights, political representation, and increasingly political power and acceptance than non-Jewish Arab Israelis.

Palestinians, by contrast and especially in the territories, not unlike the racially marginalized and unwanted in racially oppressive social arrangements generally, have been evicted from the Kantian Kingdom of Ends. Ben-Gurion repeatedly affirmed the right of Palestinians to self-determination, even as he insisted in the spirit of racial historicism that they were incapable of developing or ruling the country, that they had no right of ownership over then-Palestine, that they were to be expelled.

This erosion of the right to a presence, even while acknowledging an abstract right to self-determination, underpinned the steady eviction from the Kingdom of Moral Ends. Over time, then, and perhaps as a response to politics on the ground, Palestinians came to lose as a consequence any claim to moral protection, to being a beloved neighbor. A senior Israeli military officer during the second intifada implored Israeli military personnel chillingly to be "Judeo-Nazis" in order, somewhat ambiguously, "to beat the Palestinians." Another officer, even if self-consciously, opined uncannily in the daily press that "If our job is to seize a densely packed refugee camp or take over the Nablus Casbah . . . [we] must above all else analyze and bring together the lessons of past battles, even – shocking though this might appear – to analyze how the German Army operated in the Warsaw Ghetto."

The term "Judeo-Nazi," now readily rhetorically circulated among more vehement Palestinian critics of Israel, was actually coined by the late critical Israeli philosopher and rabbi Yeshayahu Leibowitz to refer to the unfortunate behavior of a group of Israeli soldiers in the wake of the Six Day War. Generally, the association by critics of Israeli state practices in any way with those of the Nazi brings howls of protest, dismissing such references as insensitive at best, downright antisemitic at worst.

It wasn't always so. In a new biography of Menachem Begin, Avi Shilon reports that in the 1960s longtime prime minister David Ben-Gurion characterized Begin, himself later to become prime minister, as "Hitlerite" and "racist." And an open letter to the *New York Times* damned the Herut Party, founded by Begin in 1948 and a forerunner to the conservative Likud Party today, as emulating "Nazi and Fascist parties." The letter was signed by, among others, Albert Einstein and Hannah Arendt, firm if not uncritical supporters of Israel both. More recently, by contrast, the forcing by Israeli soldiers at a checkpoint of a Palestinian man to play "a sad song" on the violin he was carrying conjured images among Israeli citizens of Jews forced to play music to accompany mass murder in Nazi camps. And yet the outcry in Israel following publication of this "incident" was less against the humiliation of Palestinians than for desecrating the memory of the Holocaust. It is disturbing, as a consequence, that having been coined by a prominent Israeli in a critical register initially, the term "Judeo-Nazi" has come to be occasionally embraced by some, even if ironically, as a term of the realm.

Palestinians (as Arabs more generally) are the new necropolitical targets of the world, heel on the face, eating dust when they have anything to eat at all. Desert people, which is to say deserted, reduced to philistinism, untrusted because normatively untrustworthy. And once deserted, having nowhere to turn, no one to appeal to but a few folks of conscience, they are fair game.

In August 2003, Israel introduced a disturbing new law: In the name of security, of not wanting to be overrun demographically, and so of the untouchable Jewish logic of survival, any Arab Israeli citizen marrying a Palestinian would be *required* to move to the Palestinian territories to live, or to leave the country altogether. Ethnoracial purging – deeply connected to but subtly differentiated from ethnic cleansing – is the process of removing, evicting (what Ghada Karmi calls "vanishing") almost all Palestinians identified as such from green-line Israel. Since 1967, the Arab population of Jerusalem has declined from 72 to 28 percent. Palestinians born, bred, and residing on property they have long owned within the boundaries of "Jewish Jerusalem" are declared by the state residents of the West Bank. They may be registered accordingly as "absentee landlords" in the very houses in which they (illegally) reside, their property subject to confiscation.

Where ethnic cleansing involves wiping a country "clean" of an identifiable ethnic minority by wiping (many or most of) them out, ethnoracial purging involves forcing a considerable percentage of group members out of the national territory and so of the moral imaginary. They are moved further away, outside of national boundaries, more and more into enclosed enclaves, even within what is regarded as their own territory. Radically minoritizing the remainder, ethnoracial purging lies between the national(ist) purification of ethnic cleansing, on one side, and bantustanization, on the other. In a casual exchange, Philomena Essed has distinguished between *weeding out* and "rooting out," the former repetitive task of revisiting the removal of persistent pests, the latter seeking to sterilize and condomize the territory against any possible return. Israel has long vacillated between these two modalities. In either case, racial palestinianization provides the prototype – the rationales and representations, the logics and models, in short, the roadmap – for strategic social prophylaxis, for ethnoracial eviction and ethnoracial culling.

Palestinianizing the racial

As Sartre remarks about antisemitism, then, so we can observe about palestinianization, that it is not simply an idea or set of ideas but as much a *passion*. Racial palestinianization turns on a revulsion and repulsion related to dispositions of abjection, horror, hatred, anger, inferiorization. The Palestinian's vulgarity and aggression are the source if not the totalization of Israel's woes. Were it not for the Palestinian there would be no terror, no threat, no insecurity, no challenge to Israel's very existence, no recession, no economic burden, no refugee problem, no insecurity regarding demographic swamping, no limit on Jewish settlements in Judea and Sumaria. The Holy Land would be complete, unified, God's historical promise fulfilled. But perhaps too there would be no Israel (as we now know it)!

Racial palestinianization is thus a conceit about contemporary conditions in terms of a projected past conceived in terms of the politics of the present. The Palestinian is a Philistine, with philistine values, interests, and desires, a primitive in the sense of never having evolved beyond ancient whims, drives, capriciousness, viciousness, and the irresponsible impulses to which they give rise. The Palestinian is driven by nothing but unprovoked hate and anger, incapable of a higher order of values, of deeper causation, of responsibility as a product of free choice. Palestinianization, like the projection of "Palestine," in short, is a state of passion, its only rationality purely instrumental, crudely calculated and cruelly calculating, consequential, awe-ful. It is a state in which justification, reasonableness, freedom, and justice are feared, from which they have been expunged.

Racial palestinianization is a projection, then, from arrogance and the racial labor of impotence. It is the disposition that arrogates to itself the source of universal and absolute judgment, ultimately over life and death, the quality of living and dying, over the state and civil society, the conditions of existence and civility. But it is a tenuous self-arrogation, one prompting death and destruction, on both sides, in the name of its execution that can never be satisfied or satiated. In creating the philistine, racial palestinianization licenses and unleashes the action-figure of its very invention. Samson, after all and altogether ironically, was the original suicide "bomber."

Supporters of the Kach Movement, the remnants of the outlawed political party in Israel initiated by the late Rabbi Meir Kahane and now listed as a "terrorist organization" by various western governments, rally support around the Samsonite injunction to avenge his blindness. In gatherings that resemble small heavy metal concerts in sweaty stuffed halls, a biblical professor longhair urges the adoring crowd to

> Strengthen me
> That I may avenge one of my two eyes
> Revenge upon Palestine
> Revenge, Revenge, Revenge
> Upon Palestine
> For God's sake.

Committed to reinstating the imagined biblical boundaries of Israel, these assertive extensions of Israeli sovereign power in the name of some antique theological imaginary of Jewish flourishing serve to render mainstream Israeli control over all aspects of Palestinian living and dying seemingly respectable, moderate, responsible self-protection.

By contrast, Arafat's interminable history, of course, was one of too often tragic and occasionally comic mistimings, miscues, and misdirections. The consequences were more than often bitter, even devastating, as much for his own people he claimed to represent as for Israelis he clearly did resent. Orientalize the Palestinian, philistinize him, and he will act out accordingly. The Arab is a dog, Arik had always said, the prototypical Judas; she a whore, the quintessential Delilah. He will howl, keeping you awake at night; she will infect you, blind you, sucking away your strength. Kill as many "worms" as you can, the Sharonites have always implored, for fear they will otherwise overrun you. Take their land, for it is ours. Destroy their houses, villages, olive groves, for they do not belong. We should have done so long ago; let's finish it now.

Racial palestinianization accordingly is the prevailing response to a state of perpetual war. Indeed, it *is* a state of war declared perpetual, a war made the normal state of affairs. Permanent war enables a state of emergency suspending all rights for the target population. But insofar as it is a permanent war, suspension is tantamount to evisceration: rights continue to exist in name only, shadow conceptions of a world lost, never to be reinstated. But if sovereignty is defined in terms of the power to define the exception, then turning the exception into the norm effectively eviscerates the very grounds of sovereignty, as Wendy Brown has commented. As norm, as given, as the naturalized state of being, the exceptional ceases to be, well, exceptional, the power to define exceptionality is rendered irrelevant, powerless. In making war permanent, the (once-)sovereign has made itself dependent – on the Enemy, on maintaining the Enemy as such. The ground on which the sovereign stands, makes its stand, has become quicksand.

Israel has perfected the bifurcated condition its principal patron now tries to emulate: a permanent war elsewhere – its horrors hidden from view, complaint or criticism cordoned off behind the Wall or across the Ocean while the specter of peace and prosperity is maintained at home. But such a state – or states because the bifurcation necessitates always a doubling, two states of being, one here, the other there, one in peace but threatened always by the chaos beyond – requires, as Foucault says, that "truth functions exclusively as a weapon" in the relationship of force. Perpetual war licenses "a rationality of calculations, strategies and ruses."

Force enables one to speak, to interpret the truth, to elevate one's own proposals and claims to the status of truth while denouncing the other's as lies, illusions, errors, as deluded even. Palestinianizing the racial thus involves also transforming truth into a relationship of force, speaking truth in the name of power represented racially. A group is racially branded, as Mahmood Mamdani reveals, when it is set apart as racially distinct thus rendering easier, and so more likely, its guiltless extinction, at least politically if not quite physically.

Since Sharon ascended to power by climbing the steps to Haram-al-Sharif in Jerusalem surrounded by surging rings of security guards, Israel has sought to dissolve, to destroy, the existence and self-determination of Palestinians as a people, politically, economically, socially, and culturally in a deliberate and deliberative process Baruch Kimmerling characterized as "politicide." Thus, what I have been identifying as ethnoracial purging of Palestinians from green-line Israel has been joined to the logic of institutional politicide in the territories, culminating in almost complete social strangulation.

Dis-tilled landscapes

By 1948 Jewish Palestinians had metamorphosed into Israelis, increasingly independent and self-assertive. Jews everywhere were called to defend their right to exist as Jews in the wake of the real threat of a Final Solution not yet finalized by realizing the State of Israel as the homeland of Jews anywhere. In the Promised Land, Jews made real the dream of Israel, made Jews everywhere proud by building a country unique in spirit, social commitment, and security for the globally insecure. But it did so in more than small part by moving into areas – villages, valleys, hillsides and city sections – left by Palestinians turned refugees, coming to inhabit the spaces fled if never quite abandoned. Transferring Palestinian place into Israeli space has been Israel's life-long project, in the process marking such space with a new set of communal habits, other ways of living and being, other names in a different and differentiating language. Eviction was – is – also an *accent*uation, a shift in horizons of sharing as much as in their shape, of the boundaries as much symbolic as cartographic, in register as much as in registration.

Over the past half-century, then, Israel has managed to evaporate the Arab landscape by renaming, in Hebrew, places removed of Palestinian people though still haunted by the ghosts of those fled. Very often the names are those from the Old Testament. This evaporative renaming thus fabricates Israeli jurisdiction as an ancient biblical claim, reducing Palestinian insistence to return to a delusional, manic vision, to political propaganda, as former Jerusalem deputy mayor Meron Benvenisti characterizes it in his bitingly incisive study of this history of renomination.

Nadia Abu El-Haj points out that the Israeli investment in archaeology as a national interest represents not just a fascination with the past as pastime. Rather, it serves to stake an originary claim to the land, an unbroken material link to the antique imaginary, a legitimation of belonging, and the anchoring ground of the right to return. (*This* is the heart of Abu El-Haj's argument, one never addressed by her misleading critics. In this, the thrust of her argument is about recent Israeli history and the use of archaeology to advance a contemporary nationalist project, not a claim to a supposedly antique Holy Land unpeopled by Jews, which she nowhere contends.) Renaming the landscape in antique terms, then, becomes the imprint of proprietorship. Visions of trumping rights to have been there always. If, as Ruth Kluger has remarked, "we start with what is left: the names of places," then Palestinian beginnings are constantly eroded, upended.

As one example among many hundreds, Susan Slyomovics has written movingly and revealingly of how Ein Hod, an Israeli artist colony established in 1953 by Marcel Janco, one of Dada's initiators, eventually replaced Ein Houd, a pre-existing Palestinian farming village south of Haifa.

This practice has been extended ever since by Jewish settlers throughout the West Bank, enclaving the Palestinian population into enclosed refugee camps in what might have been a common territory, prisoners in what is projected to be their own state. Israel's Samsonite smashing out of its originary claustrophobic territorial constraints has been purchased with almost every flexing at the cost of the increasingly imposed constraints of palestinianized claustrophobia.

The twenty-first century thus is not the first time Arab olive groves, old as the hills themselves, were shoveled away. If the clearing shovel is a tool of the State of Israel's founding, the bulldozer has become a tool of terror, a weapon of sometime (massive) destruction (now, if lopsidedly, on both sides) extending the cycle of violence between suicide bombings and demolished homes, shattered dreams both. Rachel Corrie's disfigured face serves as a haunting testament. Olive groves across stony terraces were stripped away from 1948 onwards, at first blush to make way for banana and citrus plantations, later for the modern marketplace of malls, and more recently yet for the dividing and divisive worlds of a Separation Wall.

Hamas leaders have been biblically "marked for death" in the shockingly honest, if ironic, phrasing of then-prime minister Sharon. And Palestinian families have been made to watch the demolition of their homes, in some cases whole apartment buildings, either where the buildings stand in the line of the Wall's progression or when a family member or building resident has been identified as a terrorist, the latter a practice of the Jewish Haganah (underground militia) dating back at least to late 1947. So as new settlement homes go up in the Palestinian territories – hundreds of new homes slated for the West Bank in October including those in the large, appropriately named settlement, Ariel – Palestinians are made to suffer through the tearing down of theirs. Construction rubble and garbage disposal from the consequent settlements are summarily dumped around Palestinian villages below, increasing the health risks of living in such close proximity to environmental hazards.

Biblical references to the angel of death fade beneath more recent images both of tattooed numbers and death camps *and* now also of demolished homes and the Star of David painted by soldiers on the walls of Ramallah, Nablus, and Jenin residential buildings, accompanied by the unit number of Israeli military battalions indicating the house had been searched. Lives reduced to rubble. Buildings marked for demolition. Bodies tagged for death. Worldly belongings reduced to longings. The stuff of suicidal motivations.

Large bombs are dropped from Israeli jets into dense metropolitan areas, terrorizing entire neighborhoods while targeting militant organizers for assassination. Every targeted assassination and its collateral killing, *like the counterpart suicide blasts*, conjures a furious political funeral turned revengeful political rally and a likely suicidal or missile explosion in urban Israel. Traces of homes lost, family fled or buried, hopes tattered, dreams destroyed, homeland now nothing more than someone else's hubris. The logic of deathscape and despair repeated in south Lebanon of late. Traces in the psyche matching traces in the landscape, the one a faint and faded resonance of the other. The apartheid state learned these lessons only at the cost of its own downfall.

The Separation Wall is at once a significant imposition of political control and a unilateral securing of additional territory for Israel as the line of the Wall is mapped in key areas deeper and deeper through Palestinian territory. Israel colonizes fertile fields and generous olive groves falling in areas of divergence between the Wall and green-line with little or no compensation to Palestinian proprietors. The Separation Wall accordingly is the equivalent of a massive, if reverse, enclosure act, transforming the West Bank into a permanent prison camp. The Wall interns both the heart of the Palestinian West Bank and encircles the sprawling refugee camps like Qalqilya and Tulkarm (for illustrative maps, see www.gush-shalom.org/thewall/index.html). Four Arab neighborhoods of Jerusalem, totaling 55,000 residents, are being cut from the city, falling to the Wall's eastern side into the West Bank; at the same time, the Wall will incorporate Maaleh Adumim, the West Bank's largest Jewish settlement, into Jerusalem, adding 30,000 Jewish inhabitants to the city's population.

Israel already has the ability to close both the territories – the West Bank and Gaza – and any of their cities, villages or refugee camps at will, to cut off almost all entrance and exit. Gaza today is more or less a closed concentration camp, almost completely cut off from its exterior but for underground arms smuggling tunnels and the occasional detonation of the border fence allowing inhabitants to cross momentarily into Egypt to stock up on supplies. Consequently, 80 percent of Gazans are dependent to some extent on food aid. The Separation Wall (now accompanied by Israel's recent resettlement of Israelis from Gaza) is designed to make permanent those states of encirclement, of dislocation and immobility of the West Bank as well. The Wall is a monumental icon any future generation will grow up thinking a natural contour scarring the landscape, both seal and sign of social incarceration.

Far from a temporary arrangement, the Separation Wall, then, is the final line in the roadmap of Palestinian politics, supplement to the dots marking Jewish settlements throughout the highlands of the West Bank while expanding the territory of green-line Israel – of what officially counts as the State of Israel – by 10 to 15 percent. The Wall is carefully constructed not to constrict the 29 or so superhighways connecting the illegally established Jewish settlements with Israel proper. These ethnonational highways, restricted to Israelis, allow for quick traversal of the Palestinian landscape beneath, unbothered by the crawling humiliation of Palestinians whose journey between village and town normally an hour or two away can consume a hazardous couple of days negotiating endless roadblocks and the degrading and often destructive whims of military personnel.

Israelis – especially Jewish Israelis – living outside the Wall in Israel proper (but then, what is outside?), accordingly can go about the civilities of their daily affairs oblivious to the oppression of occupation or to the fact that Israeli civil society is predicated on the erasure of its counterpart in the Palestinian territories. In an age where mobility is the key to any economic activity, educational opportunity, and social relation, the Wall is the structure of death, symbolically and socially, economically and existentially.

The more the Wall goes up, psychologically and materially, the more it calls forth suicidal impulses. This perhaps gives a new sense to what Foucault, thinking of an earlier historical moment, has called "the suicidal state." Even the Israeli prime minister now recognizes the challenge, American apologists like Alan Dershowitz notwithstanding. In the wake of the Anapolis meeting in late 2007 to revive two state negotiations, Olmert declared bluntly that if the two-state solution fails, "Israel is finished." He continued: "We [will] face a South African-style struggle for equal voting rights." Curiously and contradictorily enough, the contemporary South African legacy reveals that as any ethnoracially predicated "two-state solution" dissolves and equal voting rights prevail, justice is promoted rather than perishes, and racial tensions fall away. This recognition strengthens the resolution that only a single state is conceivable.

Occupation comes to conjure a double entendre, the possibility of inhabiting a singular homeland the hint of which is simultaneously conceived and killed off. Suicidal nihilism is the Palestinian default mode in response to the Israeli default of racial branding and group area acts. Suicide attacks are destined to destroy the desirable alongside the discarded even as they are a final desperate demand for recognition in the face of a slow, strangulating social death. Encircling imprisonment produces a desperation born of nothing left to lose.

At the latest count, fully one quarter of young Palestinian *men* declared a willingness to engage in this act of brutal finality. An educational counselor working in one of the West Bank refugee camps, upon inquiring of the children where they thought they would be in 20 years, was shocked at the unanimous response: "Buried," they said. These are the children of "lost hope" who have been seen digging up the Separation Wall in sight of armed Israeli soldiers – weapons cocked, trigger fingers twitching – removing pieces of metal making up the Wall in supreme acts of carceral defiance. Where all hope of a better life is undermined, the only substitute for hopelessness is sought from the solace of an investment in the afterlife. That the path to an afterlife projected as meaningful is thought to lie in taking the lives one is against as one takes one's own is simply a measure of the hopelessness, a perversion of the perversion. Where racial palestinianization is fueled in the name of an absolutist sense of security, it produces in the objects of its calculations not fear but defiance of death, not awe but anger, buried perhaps but buried alive, the (social) dead striking back. The Wall at best throws itself at effects, intensifying the very causes it is supposed to deflate.

Targeted assassinations, effectively extrajudicial executions, while aimed rhetorically at all Palestinians, seek in their immediate destructiveness officially and officiously to kill the individual targeted. They do not look to obliterate the ethnoracially identified group, no matter whether or not many Israelis desire Palestinians to disappear completely. And yet, in seven years of the Al Aqsa or second intifada, more than four times as many Palestinians as Israeli Jews have been killed, 60 to 80 percent of whom were not involved in armed actions against Israel or Israelis and almost 25 percent of whom are children (nearly ten times as many Palestinian as Israeli children have been killed since September 2000). The cycle of violent death, the performative aspects of mourning, resentment, bitterness, and the resolution of revenge, serve only to reinforce already hardened responses, on all sides.

Collateral damage, to paraphrase Mahmood Mamdani, is not an exception in the war on terrorism but the exaggeration of its very point. It sends a message not just to the organizers of terrorist acts but to any passive supporters, any bystanders, anyone silently appreciating or vaguely sympathizing with the work of the branded terrorist. Racial branding makes it thinkable, targeted assassinations actualize its instrumentalization,

disappearance its prevailing effect. Disappearance has collateral consequence not taken into account in the cost-benefit calculus of a governmentality as much about annexation as about occupation. Not unlike
behavioral violations in the US, young teenagers, and in some instances
even adolescents, are imprisoned by Israeli authorities for as long as a
year for stone-throwing, their parents uninformed even of their arrest
by Israeli soldiers almost as youthful.

"A young man's war it is," writes Eavan Boland in another context, "a
young man's war"

> Or so they say and so they go to wage
> This struggle where, armored only in nightmare,
> Every warrior is under age –
> A son seeing each night leave, as father,
> A man who may become the ancestor

These experiences are as likely to produce a seething disposition to suicide
bombing upon release as a love of life.

The rationality of domination at the heart of racial palestinianization,
then, is reckoned as the strategies of subjugation and techniques of terror,
the calculation of insecurities, again political as much as physical, global
as much as local. Benny Morris, Israel's best-known revisionist historian,
captures this logic perfectly: "When the choice is between destroying or
being destroyed," he insisted in clarification of his unstinting commitment
to retaining Israeli domination, "it's better to destroy." If the legitimating
logic is on one side of the bitter divide, the neutrality of Morris's formulation suggests that the logic is not restrictable, as though these bifurcated
choices are the only or best ones available.

Central also to the rationality at work is the reckoning of rationalization and obfuscation, of rephrasing and reframing, of renaming and
restating. This is a fragile rationality, indeed, as Foucault remarks more
generally, one deeply insecure because always open to reversals, reprimands,
recriminations, retaliations, revenge. The pathological insecurity at the heart
of racial palestinianization, an insecurity that is simply the extreme
embodiment of the characteristic insecurities of all racisms, calls forth the
most pulverizing responses to any resistance as a way to cover over its own
insecurities. "Society must be defended," to use Foucault's provocative phrasing, sealed from suicidal infiltration, configured against contamination, walled
off from the weight of its own history, plastered against pollution.

Recalibrating resistance

The self-determining response of the Palestinian people was to catapult Hamas into power, the very group to which Israel was instrumental in giving birth, and which now it seeks most to destroy. And to do so less because Hamas has stood up to Israel than that, in the face of relentless Israeli attack, it was seen to succeed, at least within limit, where Arafat's Fatah had hopelessly failed. Hamas delivered social services, providing the garbage collection, medical treatment, and food supplements for the starving, services the long-ruling Palestinian Authority could only complain about not having the resources to provide. In the lead-up to its winning formal political power in a democratic election, Hamas – like Hizbullah in Lebanon – succeeded in making more bearable on the ground the otherwise excruciating everyday existence of ordinary Palestinians in the West Bank and Gaza.

In both cases, Israel sought to recalibrate the cost of such commitment to groups on record calling for Israel's demise, with decidedly discounted because deadly results. This, in turn, has fueled as much bitter anger, frustration, and a social death wish as rejection of the apparent agenda represented by Hamas and Hizbullah. It has turned Palestinian against Palestinian (and to a degree Lebanese against Lebanese), in bitter in-fighting with no clear Palestinian beneficiaries beyond the immediacy of marginally more resources from the west.

Hamas and Hizbullah have been widely characterized recently as "states within states," in good part because of the services they offer, the sense of militarist self-defense they have self-consciously constructed, and the loyal following they have conjured. While there is a sense to this, it is over-simplistic, and predicates the picture on a contrast and competitor to "legitimate" and conventional state formations. I think it more compelling to understand both as representing robust, organized responses from the realm of civil society to the sort of state demise and destruction that an aggressive, militarized neoliberalism has come to signal for those state formations not passing the latter's test for legitimacy. Here, such organizations are as much complements as competitors to states shirking their longer-standing caretaker commitment in favor overwhelmingly of their purely state repressive functionalities. And as competitors for, and to, state power, they are more or less ruthlessly constrained, decimated, marginalized (as has been Hamas's experience since asserting its authority and power in Gaza).

Palestinianizing the Racial

Racial palestinianization is today among the most repressive, the most subjugating and degrading, the most deadly forms of racial targeting, branding, and rationalization, not least in the name of racelessness. It is, as Mandela has commented, a fate worse than apartheid. I have nominated it racial *palestinianization* rather than *israelification* (which would be more consistent with the other modes of racial regionalization I have identified) in order both to connect it to the representational and political histories of orientalism and to indicate its occupational singularities in the order of contemporary racial expressions and repressions. It may help to draw together in some semblance of coherence its various instrumentalities elaborated above, not all of which need be implemented for the modality to persist or prevail.

First, and perhaps most basically, racial palestinianization is committed to land clearance underpinned by an accompanying, if not pre-dating, moral eviction. Territorial clearance in Israel's case has been prompted historically in terms of "redemption of land." This heart-felt historico-moral claim to land redemption, to retrieving territory always already biblically "ours," distinguishes racial palestinianization from classic modes of settler colonialism. Reclamation through settlement is extended by renomination, the shrinkage of Palestinian proprietorship materialized in the disappearance of recognizable title.

Dispossession of homes and groves, territory and terraces, through outright demolition, confiscation, or expropriation manifests homelessness in both the immediate and more nationalist senses of the term, and ultimately a virtually perpetual and perhaps permanent exilic refugeedom. (Fully one quarter of the world's refugees are Palestinian, according to the United Nations.) Traces of lives once lived, of the fabric of lives lost, are etched into the landscape, faint lines seeped into the foundations of the victor's architecture overlaid, phantoms haunting the ecology of the possessor. This population expulsion and transfer, while in some ways not unlike "forced removals" under apartheid, distinguishes racial palestinianization from that modality also.

In his characteristically blunt way, Bennie Morris formulates the two options Israel has always posed to itself regarding Palestine and its people: Create an apartheid-like state, a "homeland," in which most all Palestinians are located with radically reduced rights and power and excluded from property ownership, quality education, and economic opportunities while their cheap labor is exploited to benefit the Jewish minority. Or create a majority Jewish state in Israel by expelling all or the bulk of the Palestinian population preferably to Jordan, Egypt, and Syria but more lately simply to the lock-up facility that today is Palestine itself. Israel has always vacillated between these two modalities. More recently it has opted to forego exploitable Palestinian labor for its replacement by the likes of Filipinos while transferring or displacing as many Palestinians as the world will tolerate from Israeli territory to the carceral condition that is Palestine.

Israel has moved from a single state possibility to establishing a state and a shadow state. The first, overwhelmingly for Jews, tolerates really small Islamic, Christian, and Druze minorities. The shadow state for Palestinians largely lacks self-determination, freedom, a viable economic foundation, and any sort of security for its inhabitants. This is not so much the state form of apartheid as a distinct modality of the racial state in denial about its racial predication: racial palestinianization.

Racial palestinianization is likewise marked by the accompanying establishment and expansion of settlements outside the internationally recognized borders of Israel. Recent reports based on Israeli administration figures by the Israeli anti-occupation group Peace Now on Israeli settlement patterns in the occupied territories reveal that fully 40 percent of the 122 settlements are on land *owned* privately by Palestinians. Israel has allocated Palestinian land unilaterally to settlements. While only a little more than 10 percent of the land so allocated is actually used for settlements, 90 percent of the settlements spill over onto privately owned Palestinian property appropriated with no due compensation and no resistance from the Israeli state. Fully one-third of settlement spread now lies outside of official Israeli allocations.

Three settlements, the first two of which are suburban extensions of Jerusalem, Maaleh Adumim Givat Zeev, and Ariel, sit respectively on 85, 44, and 35 percent private Palestinian property. Israel half-heartedly contests the numbers, though not the fact of land expropriation, which has proceeded on classic Lockean principles. The well-known case of Migron is exemplary. Israeli settlers driving northwards in the West Bank from Jerusalem would regularly lose cell phone service in one mountainous bend of the Jewish-restricted Israeli highway. Fearing for their security, they petitioned to establish a phone antenna, which was placed on private if uninhabited Palestinian hilltop property. Land the Israeli petitioners had previously tried to settle. A small number of settler families followed quickly, putting down roots on territory they claimed to be deserted, quickly blossoming to nearly 50 families and now 180 "residents." One, Aviva Winter, declared to National Public Radio in the US that "You just feel that it's so right, so natural to be here." This land is our land, our birth*right*, the law of nature. Empty, for the taking. Guarded by the Israeli military, serviced by state ministries (water, roads, nursery, postal service). Settlement through an enclosure act.

However these claims are collectively settled through land swaps as part of a horizonless peace negotiation, this is postcolonial state extension by any other terms. Israel has perfected its logic. The authorized settlements are intended to be permanent, indestructible. They serve to extend Israel's reach, to widen its width between the Mediterranean and Jordan, appease its more extreme citizens while providing relatively inexpensive, state-subsidized and protected bedroom communities to newer Israeli immigrants, while squeezing Palestinians yet further. These settlements, Israel's equivalents of Ahwatukee in Arizona or Mesa in San Diego, emulate the American dream, often with American capital investment. But they overlook the increasing squalor of Palestinian daily life in the valleys below. And they are just as segregating: a poll of Jewish Israelis soon after Sharon split from the Likud Party and formed Kadima revealed that 68 percent preferred to live completely separated from Arabs, and over 40 percent would like completely segregated recreational facilities. Recent polls of Jewish Israelis indicate that three-quarters reject an Arab family as a neighbor, and half would refuse an Arab visitor. Among Jewish students, 75 percent believe Arabs are "uneducated, uncivilized, and unclean" (the reverse stereotypes, while notable, are considerably lower). Rooting out has started to trump weeding out. These enclosure acts approach born again apartness, in broad sweep if not in style and detailed substance.

The recognizably red-roofed summit settlements thus serve simultaneously as expanded Israeli residential terrain, offering a counter to the territorial claustrophobia of the homeland's narrow waistline, alongside pervasive "eye-in-the sky" security oversight of palestinianized shantytowns otherwise known as refugee camps. Holding the high ground has long been the logic of militarized dominance and domination. Settlement – the land of ancient debts reclaimed, calling in the historical chips – is accompanied by extended encirclement of Palestinian towns and villages deemed threatening to Israeli wellbeing and security, cutting Palestinians off from one another, effectively undermining any possibility of Palestinian coherence.

Palestinian life is turned into a living hell of perpetual siege and seizure, death and destruction, restriction and constriction. Hence the trading off of settlements between Gaza (already an enlarged hyper-camp) and the West Bank, the settler nostalgia to sustain the former abandoned by the state to the geostrategic calculation to extend the latter.

These forms of totalizing repression, territorializing annexation, and social suffocation claim in the name of the security imperative complete control because convenient and profitable, politically and economically. They cohere with and within two other central, even foundational and interactive, features of racial palestinianization, namely, occupation and militarization. Occupation extends the possibility – the license, the logic – of Israel's political economy as militaristically driven, as a war economy, as a military economic complex serviced by a state. The military orders Israel's regime of truth, as the late Tanya Reinhart made clear shortly before her untimely passing, shaping both how Israelis understand themselves and how the state structures conditions of life and death, the more so in the wake of Ariel Sharon's command. Occupation is both inevitable prompt and outcome of this militarily mobilized state self-conception, in a sense circular analytic implicatures of each other. Occupation is to Israel's military as blood is to the heart, lubricant to the pump. It not only primes the pump; it requires the switch remain incessantly on, demanding that the pumping should not cease or slow down in a state geared to the exercise of its central instrumentality.

Occupation not only licenses every sort of invasive activity conceivable; it likewise seeks to control the air above, the land, and the below-ground materialities too. It accordingly enables the exploitation of all strategic resources of the territory occupied – land, water, labor, produce – with no commensurate respect for political, civil, environmental, or even the most basic of human rights. It is, as Meron Benvenisti characterizes it, a "de luxe occupation," with Israel bearing little of the fiscal cost for running the territories, which they have managed to bill to the developed countries of the world, most notably the Europeans.

People are killed, either as direct or indirect targets, without trial or trepidation, accidentally or collaterally. Curfews are imposed, randomly, 24/7. Schools are restricted, universities shut down, businesses shuttered. Palestinian life has no more value than an input in the geopolitical calculus of securities and losses, bits of manipulable data in the supreme (and extreme) militarization of expertise. Zvika Fogel was Israeli Defence Force (IDF) chief of staff of the Southern Command (responsible for the control of Gaza) from February 2000. In an interview late in 2007, he revealed that the IDF quite consciously "promoted an armed confrontation with the Palestinians" that inevitably resulted in the outbreak of the second intifada in September 2000. The point was to provide a cover for repeated repression, sustained encirclement, persistent control.

Occupation encourages destruction of local, organic social institutions and infrastructure, making it impossible for Palestinians, for the local inhabitants, to govern themselves. Indeed, the point is not simply that they not be self-governing but that they cease to be recognized as local, that they become alien, intruders in their own land. And that occupation be denied, legitimated as historical birthright, as rightful, self-righteous settlement, if one is to believe the likes of Ephraim Karsh.

In short, this is a new modality of occupying state formation made possible conceptually by permanent infantilization, philistinianization. Palestine has been marked as the first "permanently temporary" state, to use Eyal Weizman's incisive characterization. State boundaries are rendered impermanent, flexible according to the occupier's needs and whimsical determinations, visible only to the day's militarized cartographic dictates. Permanent impermanence is made the marker of the very ethnoracial condition of the Palestinian, and through the Palestinian of the possibility of the Arab as such. Lebanon is the latest case in the transformation from the neoliberal political economy of debt creation and regulation to the necropolitical disciplining of an otherwise unruly population through the threat of destructive violence and ultimately immediate and painful death.

Palestinianization's temporary temporality is taken as much as ontological condition as political-military condition. The Palestinian is always between, always ill-at-ease, homeless at home if never at home in his homelessness, if anyone really could be, the explicit embodiment of Levinasian facelessness. Shifting, shiftless, unreliable, untrustworthy, nowhere to go, nowhere to be, the persona of negativity, of negation, of death's potential. He is the quintessential Nobody, as Memmi characterizes the figure of the colonized, the embodiment of enmity, almost already dead. The territory of the state, at any rate, is multiply divisible, broadly between three islands but more locally between multiplying settlements both overlooking and cutting off one local population from another. Indeed, the determination of the local, of who belongs and who does not, of the very meaning of occupier, is being rendered increasingly and deliberately, purposefully, ambiguous, doubtful. Possession is nine-tenths of belonging, of being, to twist a cliché.

This self-estrangement, this *unheimlich* homelessness, is instrumentalized through the elevation of the state's security apparatus as primary mode of governmental rationality and instrumentality. The main modalities of the terrorizing state today include targeted assassinations, expulsions, threatened deportations, collateral damage, perpetual imprisonments and preventive detentions under the most trying conditions, accompanied by incessant provocations. Emergent leadership and political elites are constrained, if not killed. Proliferated checkpoints make Palestinian movement all but impossible, painfully snail-pace, and life miserable. Access especially to and within city centers is open and closed according to the calculation of security risks, military movements, political whim. The population is economically and politically isolated, starved of the means to even a modicum of stable social life. Access to work and workplaces, hospitals and education is severely restricted, availability of food, medicine, and other basic necessities carefully managed and manipulated. People die daily as much from debilitation as from bullets in numbers that don't show up on the administrative daily roster of the dead.

Israel seems to have perfected the security apparatus of almost absolute surveillance predicated on what might usefully be called controlling chaos. The point is to promote panic among a population or crowd of people, at once observing – gaining insight into – the reactions of members of the multitude. Random attacks in and on depersonalized public places, invasions, unannounced searches, bombs apparently missing targets, purposeful collateral damage, deliberate targeted assassination of moderates.

Space itself is open to constant rearrangement. Borders and boundaries are shifted according to harassing security mandates, checkpoints appear and disappear momentarily, buildings are bulldozed at whim, paths created for militarizing purpose not just across landscapes but through Palestinians' personal homes in a process Eyal Weizman theorizes as the *elastic geographies* of "hollow land." All this always visited on those assumed to be ethnoracially distinct, as already possibly suspect, exhibiting habits, behavioral dispositions, and cultural expressions deemed peculiar. And all done as much as possible out of the presence of international media or monitors, giving rise for the most part to what Derek Gregory, in a different context, has called "war without witnesses." The forced absence of neutral witnesses, of almost any observers other than embedded reporters, removes every barrier to violent interventions, targeted removals, terrorizing collective punishments, or directed collateral injuries or death.

The teleology of creating controlled chaos in enclosed environments is to force those present to resort to "natural instinct," to flush out those trying for what is considered terrorizing purposes to blend in by making manifest their cultural habits, their implicit difference, to uncover their hidden agenda. Crowd control becomes a matter of checking out reactions to the randomization of reaction in the face of dramatically unpredictable possibilities.

On a recent visit to Israel we had an impossibly early morning flight that required a 3 a.m. airport check-in. Expecting relative sleepiness at the airport, we were shocked to find ourselves in a terminal busier than any airport worldwide at the height of rush hour. Pressed between seven or eight layers of formal security passage from the drive into the airport until one boarded the flight were irregular lines of people pushing and pulling, stress-making uncertainties about what line one was in or what the line was for, where one was headed or how long it would take. Watching over all of this seemingly random chaos were further layers of all-seeing eyes, some mingling easily in the crowd, others overhead, picking out panic, distinguishing difference amidst sleep-deprived activity: a too quick movement, furtive looks, sweat on the brow, foam at the corners of the mouth, too obvious attempts to blend in, a mixed couple traveling under different names, on different national passports signaling different places of origin. Israel's vaunted security management apparatus, as Ella Zureik calls it, immediately available for export to the rest of the world. The civic equivalent, one might say, of carpet bombing Baghdad. Insecurity manifest through unnerving norms, shock and awe.

The territory of the targeted population is reduced to a state of perpetual siege through closure and curfews, encirclement and sanctions, invasion and repression. Walls are erected, barriers go up, gates are locked, roads blocked, access denied. All critical opposition, and any cross-societal solidarity, is rendered unpatriotic, their "perpetrators" considered traitorous and treacherous, subject to high crimes of treason and incarcerable without trial.

Ornery organic leaders are marginalized or disappeared, by one means or another, their replacements handpicked in the name of a democracy promised or imposed. "We want you to choose your leaders, only not him. Or him. Or him." He'll be good "so long as he has been trained in the west, one of us, understands our ways, is on our payroll." Democracy for the damned, but not of them, as the response to the Hamas electoral victory has more than amply evidenced. If this is the prevailing racial modality for

Palestinians, it is not, as I said, restricted to them, or to assertion only by Israel. As Melani McAlister has remarked regarding the United States, the point has been not merely to support Israel in its palestinianizing ventures, "to act with them," but to emulate Israel in circumstances deemed similar, "to act like them" vis-à-vis the Middle East and Muslims, and perhaps more generally too.

It just may be that we are all, more or less, potentially Palestinians today. But is it also that the potentiality for "palestinianizing" is in each of us too?

Ehud Olmert, Ariel Sharon's successor as Israeli prime minister, has committed Israel wholeheartedly to his predecessor's plan, a mix of containerized Palestinian abandonment alongside regulating the trickle of Palestinian traffic through funneled openings, cattle crossings, easily closed. The mix of containment and funneling perhaps hastening the pace of claustrophobia and heightening the tensions.

As Israel reinvaded Gaza in early July 2006, and was on the verge of intensely hostile action in Lebanon to curtail the activities of Hizbullah, long a needle in Israel's side, Olmert declared revealingly that "the inevitable historical process of separation between Israelis and Palestinians" cannot be stopped. The declaration of historical inevitability, it is known from long experience, must invariably be ensured by bombs, bullets, and boots on the ground. Ethnoracial separation can only be guaranteed with the alienating engagement of deathly weaponry. The viciousness of Israel's response to the sometimes malarial mosquitos of Hizbullah and Hamas buzzing about its nose – effectively 10 pairs of human eyes for every tasteless tooth or suicide sting – only signals the mania of Israel's segregating vision and the painful vacuity of its Palestinian policy (malaria of course can produce significant death; how it is treated will determine whether the treatment is worse than the cure).

All this is the logical ratiocination of a state mobilizing around militarism: Israel is not so much a state that has a military; rather, it is a leading example of a militarily fueled society that codifies and mobilizes a state in its image.

At the same time, Hizbullah has demonstrated that there are forms of effective or at least curtailing resistance both to boots on the ground and to aerial attacks. Eyal Weizman has recently shown how an Israeli military think-tank counter-intuitively mobilized the rhizomatic mobilities of Deleuzian theoretical implications, putting them to work to effect domination over densely populated and architecturally impenetrable Palestinian refugee camps such as Jenin and Balata by controlling the "geometrical syntax" of those packed urban spaces. The "operational theory" at work is for the military to go underground, "to swarm" the city like insects, "walking through walls" of apartment buildings, breaking down barriers linking a kitchen in one lived building to a living room in another, and a bedroom in a third until through these "polycentric networks" lighting upon the targets of their operational opportunity, Hamas or Al Aqsa operatives.

Arguably successful in controlling the refugee camps, the Israeli military pressed into play this "dynamic relational force field" of "thanato-tactics" in invading south Lebanon in the summer of 2006, with decidedly disastrous effects. Highly disciplined and keenly observant Hizbullah fighters figured out the IDF's operational tactics, lay in waiting as a spider might for the swarm of ants and blew up the buildings entered by the Israeli special operations forces intent on walking through walls. The body count mounted, Israel resorted once again to the politically disastrous pursuit of cluster bombing from above with spiraling collateral damage and international recoil from the horrors of innocent death. Before long, but not before far too much carnage, Israel was forced to withdraw.

Similarly, Palestinians in Gaza have conjured a counter to Israel's bombing from above. In the redeployment of force inside Gaza in late 2006, Israel took to announcing that it would target for bombing apartment buildings or homes it claims to house arms caches supporting Hamas-or Fatah-connected guerillas. This announcement, the deific marking for death of the non-compliant sons of the philistines holding Israel hostage, is supposed to minimize collateral damage in the "enemy city" by clearing out the targeted Casbah corridor. But Palestinians, regardless of political affiliation and inspired by Hizbullah's strategies of resistance tinged per-haps with a tiny emergent strain of post-Gandhian anti-violence, have figured out an effective counter-tactics, a living shield set to disrupt the politics of death. When the target is announced a large crowd of Gaza inhabitants from near and far, women and children, young and old, ring the target building, swarming of a counter kind. The Israeli air strikes have been brought to a standstill at least momentarily by weapons of the weak, to use James Scott's telling phrase, undone by the political cost of wiping out large numbers of peaceful protestors. The instrumentalist force field of military calculation encounters the ethical force field of anti-violent global outrage. Hamas itself seems not to have understood its own possibilities. In this specific instance at least a political tactics of sustaining life outwitted a military tactics trained only to protect familial life by producing the death of the familiar stranger, of the enemy.

In the 60 years of its existence Israel can boast extraordinary achievements: election after democratic election, if exercised by and for its citizens alone, which exclude those limited to the occupied territories; enormous industry and modernization, learning and upliftment; the flourishing of desert landscapes, a compelling health care system, great commitment of its citizens to one another and to the idea of the state; an awesome military machine. But it suffers also in these assertive commitments considerable shortcomings: rampant corruption; a bullying aggressiveness; maltreatment or neglect of a rising range of its own citizens; an awesome military machine. The question is whether those achievements now inevitably rest upon its excesses. What Israel has come best to be known for and what it exhausts itself defending is a persistent brutality in its occupying forces that knows little limit and rampant violations of international law. That occupational brutality – an occupation the force of which can only be brutal – requires, as I have argued, at basis a conceptual raciality to sustain it.

Racial Palestinianization

Finally, then, I need to say what it is that makes palestinianization racial. Palestinians are treated not *as if* a racial group, not simply *in the manner* of a racial group, but *as* a despised and demonic racial group. Struggling to maintain the semblance of a fair, judicious, and impartial governing overseer, Britain's Peel Commission, reporting to the League of Nations in 1937 on the Arab "disorders and disruptions" in Palestine of 1936, refers repeatedly to the "*racial* antagonism" between Jews and Arabs (Palestinians). The Commission characterizes Jews as "a highly intelligent and enterprising *race* backed by large financial resources" in contrast to Palestinians as "a comparatively poor, indigenous community, *on a different cultural level*" (my emphases). Addressing the Commission, William Ormsby-Gore, British Secretary of the Colonies at the time, while claiming "to give equal weight to the interests of those two deeply divided, race-conscious and civilisation-conscious peoples," nevertheless projects onto Jew and Arab standard racial figurations already long embodied by the likes of Hess and Herzl. Ormsby-Gore stressed that from the point of view of the Jew, the Arab belongs to a backward people, to what they would call a different and a lower civilisation. From the point of view of the Arab, with his aristocratic ideas, the Jew is called by the name of "Yahoudi," which is a term of contempt.

The Israeli state and its political and military representatives continue to devalue, debilitate, denigrate, humiliate, exclude, and evict Palestinians morally and economically, legally, territorially. And it does so in the name of their ethno-naturalized or ethno-historicizing difference. Palestinians are all terrorists, hiding bombs to aim at Israel beneath their beds, lurking at the border ready to kidnap the stray Israeli soldier, scheming incessantly to obliterate the state of Israel (I am not making this up: these are positions expressed to me, at various levels of volubility, by family long living in Israel). Especially at politically fraught moments, Palestinians in particular, and Arabs more generally (non-Arab Muslims too, if Ahmadinejad is anything to go by), respond with equal contempt, and sometimes in explosive kind, each ratcheting up the anger and frustration of the other.

But between the humiliations and devastations, there are daily examples of dignified resistance, from facing down bulldozers by courageous Palestinian and Israeli peace groups alike in order to hold onto private Palestinian land to protests in villages and border crossings, of making uncomfortable in their offices Israeli bureaucrats administering dehumanizing edicts committed to splitting married couples and families and embarrassing young soldiers brutally enforcing border crossings. Here, perhaps, the fuel for coalitional antiracist social movements to emerge and enlarge, ultimately to flourish.

Israel has been founded and continues to be grounded on land and population clearance, on a rooting out that can never be more than a weeding out, on the ephemeralization of a people the ghostly tracings of which and whom can only continue to haunt Israel's landscape, cultural embodiment, and political calculation. And to haunt Israel's frustration at its incapacity to complete its monolithic mission, totalize its megalomaniacal vision, finalize its idiolectical solution to the Palestinian problem. Fueled by the psychic stress of melancholic negotiation in relation to the long-suffering experience of its European prehistory, Israel's founding and flourishing are at the same time embodiment and extension, resistance and repression, memorializing and masking of melancholic aggressivity, of aggression and aggravation. The immediate effect is no more or less than frustration bombing, intensifying the more it fails to produce its pronounced outcome.

Palestinians in particular, and Arabs more generically, are treated as a subjugated race, directly. Beaten in the name of devaluating stereotypes, concentrated in camps in the name of generalized security, displaced in the name of biblical right (effectively collapsing the historical into the transcendental, the naturalizing), killed in the name of retributive justice. A 2006 report in the mass-circulation Israeli newspaper *Yediot Aharonot* has at least 25 percent of Israeli soldiers admitting to humiliating Palestinians just for the sake of it. Palestinians are ordered in the name of race rendered see-through, of a category in denial, of a conception unmarked because of a history cutting too close to the bone. This, in short, is born again racism revitalized, on the rebound.

Racial melancholia, Anne Cheng argues, is the suffering effected by the loss from failing to live up to the society's self-projection of democratic ideals. In mourning, Freud remarks, one understands the world to have suffered a loss; with melancholia, one experiences it as a loss of part of oneself, fixating on the sense of emptiness. Collective melancholia, I want to suggest by extension, is the exacerbated socio-psychic condition, the social stress, following from multiplier fixations and awkward hesitations: on the failure to realize these social ideals – of democracy, of morality, of justice; on the guilt attendant both to these failings and to the consequent denials "necessary" to sustain the fiction of the idealizations; on extending the historicist *fabric*ation of ethnoracial distinction – whether articulated as natural inferiority or cultural difference – to shore up the façade of commitment to these ideals in the face of their imminent implosion; on the hesitancies between embracing the fictions and their attendant rewards, at least totally, or letting go of them, giving them up, if not quite completely.

Raceless melancholia adds a twist. It screens off the violence of such exclusions even from conscious recognition at the cost of deepening the sense of one's (social) loss through denial, removing the terms of reference for a state the denial of which cannot be completely sustained. Hence the ongoing need to keep invoking the terms it is insisted (ought to) have (or have had) no reference. With melancholia we thus get the inevitable stresses on and of aggression and aggravation: in extending the exclusions and their terms of reference; in sustaining their conjoint denial; in looking repetitiously to reinstate legitimacy in the eyes of others, if not also oneself, while lamenting always its loss.

Melancholia often strikes too those trying to turn resistance into the pragmatics of grievance. For grievance all too readily – if not inevitably – fails to be fulfilling. This is so whether a grievance is formally upheld by the courts or materialized in equalizing institutional access and effects, the materialities of institutional redress offering at best a salve but rarely a resolution to the psychic wounds of historical catastrophes. The fixation on the injury and its social recognition "culminates," Freud says about melancholia more generally, "in a delusional expectation of punishment," whether juridical or deific. The delusional expectation bespeaks a desire for fully recognized membership in a society the excluded intuitively know is incapable of it. Recognized, that is, as having social standing simultaneously as a member of the maligned racial group and as not merely such a member. Almost too much to ask of societies so fixated on the deniability of racial recognition they cannot help themselves but articulate?

Americanizing palestinianization, Palestinianizing americanization

This critique of racial palestinianization is not to advocate for nor self-loathingly to desire Israel's destruction, as so many bristlingly respond to any critical reflection on Israel's modus operandi. I am concerned here insistently to question *not* Israel's being, its right to exist, but rather its *forms of expression* and its *modes of self-insistence and enforcement*. I have been holding up to scrutiny, in short, the presumed singularity of Jewish ways of being on which the Israeli state is presumptuously predicated, a presumption that ironically reinscribes the restrictive, corrosive, even purging logic from which Jews historically have repeatedly fled. A two-state solution predicated on dismantling – effectively crippling – any of the cohering and enabling institutions of one partner state is tantamount to disabling one twin that the other might thrive.

Racial americanization and racial palestinianization thus are deeply related. If the former is a disposition to externalize death for the purposes of elevating life locally, the latter is a disposition to set for others life's very distinct limits through death. Racial palestinianization involves the marking of a population as excess, as superfluous, while refusing to acknowledge, to see or conceive, the death and dominating destruction brought about under the force of racial americanization. Where racial americanization offers historical template and post facto legitimation, racial palestinianization now serves as embodied extension and testing ground for the implementation of its technologies and a trial balloon, a model among others, for how much a state-oiled military can get away with.

Sovereignty amounts in the final determination not just to the power or right to determine the state of exception, as Carl Schmitt so famously has put it. Achille Mbembe, following Foucault, emphasizes that it concerns even more basically power over the right to kill. No doubt the power over exception could be said to entail the power over killing. But the sovereign's defining power over killing remains no matter the declaration of exceptionality. If every state killing is legitimated through the at least implicit declaration of exceptionality, exceptionality must either be instrumentally in service of sovereign power and not its ground, or it is simply moot. The sovereign's defining power to kill accordingly must be more basic than the power over exceptionality.

America has sought to elevate itself to the self-declared world sovereign. Israel then is its troubled double, its frankensteinian shadow, at once mimic and model. This power over death, racially produced and performed, means nothing less than that sovereignty, historically, has manifested itself as the state of whiteness par excellence. Only now the sovereign power over death has become more tenuous, cut adrift from the anchor of classical racial conception, challenged by those willing as a social force to take their own lives as they take those of others in the name of a counter-history.

For a necropolitics gone global, the right to kill is no longer restricted to state institutionalities, challenged as they are now by their own necrophilic, suicidal spin-off action figures. Hobbes limits the sovereign's power over killing – and as such sovereignty – by reserving to every rational being the right to protect oneself against all impending danger. Iraq and Israel-Palestine offer ample evidence of the sociological generalization of the Hobbesian limit case. One can only add, generalizing Gilad Atzmon's deep insight, that these are not simply cases of neighbors not loving neighbors. Those so ready to inflict so much pain on others cannot possibly "like themselves either." The implication of becoming murderous, with no reservation, no self-consciousness, no restraint, can only be a mania of the most debilitating, distorting, self-destructive sort.

America today, in contrast to European colonizing modalities of yesteryear and neocolonial shifts of the mid- to late twentieth century, is a regime, bent on shaping the occupied in its own image. It would not be too awkward to call this a *cloning* (perhaps more pressingly a *clonializing*) regime. Israel is its obedient if occasionally prodigal son, mixing the new modalities of cloned occupation with older settler forms of colonial domination. America seeks to mold the world in its own cultural-political image, to render disparate cultures and countries clones of itself, socially and politically, legally and economically, culturally and axiologically. America the blueprint, sovereign power globally inscribed, the world replete with its more or less cloned variants. As Iraq most recently bares (*sic*) witness and despite some efforts to the contrary, one of the central outcomes of clonializing americanizations turns out to be a devolution into violent, ethnoracially driven separation. Segregation haunts the hand that feeds.

Born again racism gone global thus becomes the attempt to reimpose racial sovereignty in the face of the emerging global challenges to clonializing power. The artifice of racial homogenization is the necessary condition for effecting objectification, othering, and enmity that together form the substance of racial sovereignty. The model has been made most extremely palpable in the *vanishing* of an ethnoracially conceived population that Ghada Karmi has so painfully characterized in the case of the Palestinians. Social movements insistent on the project of heterogeneity – as much on the premises as the political economy, social architecture, and habitus – are committed to dissolving the cultures of racial restriction, disappearance, destruction, and death, their modes of thought and being, seeking to suffocate the stranglehold of racial sovereignty.

The elasticity of democracy in the face of heterogeneous challenges can be seen here, narrow and wide, at the edges and to the core. There are competing conceptions of democracy at work in this. On one hand, democracy as imposition, a democracy of the dominant, extending assumptions of racial historicism where those who have dominated suggest the unreadiness to govern themselves of those perceived as not like them, to claim independence, to shed itself of its own repressions and (pre-)occupations until the dominant clear the dominated, declaring them so ready. This is a democracy of loss imposed and immediately denied, loss manifested but unrecognized, the loss of evasions and facile apologies. These are partial and at least in part empty democracies, forced, despairing. I have been dealing in this chapter with the racial modalities predicated on this set of assumptions and motivations.

On the other hand, there are emergent democracies invigorated by taking their distance from their own more or less recent experiences with racial death, destruction, and domination. They seek in different and not always appealing ways, but seek nonetheless, to come to terms not simply with those unfortunate histories but more pressingly with the terms of vigorously interactive and transforming heterogeneities. Call this in general the democracy of determination mixed with the other side of denial, of dreams drummed up, often deferred, sometimes dashed.

There is loss here too, to be sure, taken up and evaded. But in the end they seek too the gain of national self-determination, casting away as best as possible from traditions of the dominant and imposed. The democracy of determination, determined and desiderative, seeks to break from a democracy of imposed domination, though nothing guarantees there won't be homegrown repressions in the wake of such a break and its attendant articulations. These are the themes with which the compelling film *La Nuit de la Vérité* (2004), for instance, grapples. They are the effects, the outcome of practices of self-willing and collective engagement, not only of resistance but of self-definition also by the racially regionalized in the face of their otherwise overwhelming repression and frustration, debilitating restrictions and oftentimes (self-)destructive reactions and retaliations. Such democracies – in post-apartheid South Africa, if a little uncertainly, more unevenly in the likes of Brazil, and from moment to lurching, destructive and sometimes self-destructive moment in Palestine pushing to break from the grip of Israel's making – seek to break as much with the conceptual architecture (in Eyal Weizman's sense in *Hollow Land*) of debilitating racial characterization as they do with the institutional political edifices built in their name. I turn to a variety of these complex, knotted cases in the chapters that follow.

Bibliography

Abu El-Haj, Nadia 2001: *Facts on the Ground: Archaeological Practice and Territorial Self-Fashioning in Israeli Society*. Chicago: University of Chicago Press.

Ahmad, Aijaz 2000: "Israel's Killing Fields," *Frontline*, 17, 23 (Nov. 11– 24); www.palestina-balsam.it/d03.html.

Aljezeera.Net 2004: "Israeli MP: Arabs are Worms," *AljezeeraOnline*; 209.157.64.200/focus/f-news/1301642/posts.

Amnesty International 2003: *Israel and the Occupied Territories, Surviving under Siege: The Impact of Movement Restrictions on the Right to Work*; web.amnesty.org/library/Index/ENGMDE150012003.

Anidjar, Gil 2003: *The Jew, the Arab: A History of the Enemy*. Stanford: Stanford University Press.

Atzmon, Gilad 2006: "Israel's New Math: 2 = 500,000," *Counterpunch*, July 22–3; www.counterpunch.org/Atzmon07222006.html.

Avneri, Arieh L. 1984: *The Claim of Dispossession: Jewish Land-Settlement and the Arabs, 1878–1948*. New Brunswick: Transaction Books.

Bahour, Sam 2006: "We Can't Go Home Again," *New York Times*, Op-Ed, October 7. www.nytimes.com/2006/10/07/opinion/07bahour.html?th&emc=th.

Barzak, Ibrahim 2006: "Protests Force Israel to Halt Airstrikes," Associated Press, November 19; news.yahoo.com/s/ap/20061119/ap_on_re_mi_ea/israel_palestinians.

Benvenisti, Meron 2003a: *Sacred Landscape: The Buried History of the Holy Land Since 1948*. Berkeley: University of California Press.

Benvenisti, Meron 2003b: "International Community Supports a Deluxe Occupation," *Ha'aretz.com*, Thursday, September 11; www.haaretz.com/hasen/spages/338995.html.

Benvenisti, Meron 2005: "Apartheid Misses the Point," *Ha'aretz.com*, Monday, May 9; www.haaretz.com/hasen/spages/577789.html.

Bhattacharyya, Gargi, Gabriel, John, and Small, Stephen 2002: *Race and Power: Global Racism in the Twenty-First Century*. London: Routledge.

Boland, Eavan 1996: "A Soldier's Son," in *An Origin Like Water: Selected Poems 1967–1987*. New York: Norton.

Brown, Wendy 2007: "Porous Sovereignty, Walled Democracy," Keynote Lecture, Graduate Conference on "Cutures of Violence," Department of Comparative Literature, University of California, Irvine, April 7.

Butler, Judith 2003: "No, It's Not Anti-Semitic," *London Review of Books*, 25, 16 (August 21); www.lrb.co.uk/v25/n16.contents.html.

Butler, Judith 2004: *Precarious Life: The Power of Mourning and Violence*. London: Verso.

Carter, Jimmy 2006: *Palestine: Peace not Apartheid*. New York: Simon and Schuster.

Cheng, Anne Anlin 2001: *The Melancholy of Race: Psychoanalysis, Assimilation, and Hidden Grief*. New York: Oxford University Press.

Christison, Kathleen and Christison, Bill 2004: "On Israel/Palestine: An Exchange with Benny Morris," *Counterpunch*, October 2/3; www.counterpunch.org/christison10022004.html.

Christison, Kathleen and Christison, Bill 2005: "Polluting Palestine: The Settlements and Their Sewage," *Counterpunch*, September 24/25; www.counterpunch.org/christison09242005.html.

Cockburn, Alexander and St. Clair, Jeffrey, eds. 2003: *The Politics of Anti-Semitism*. Oakland: Counterpunch and AK Press.

Cook, Jonathan 2006a: "The Emerging Jewish Consensus in Israel," *Counterpunch*, March 23; www.counterpunch.org/cook03232006.html.

Cook, Jonathan 2006b: "Israel's Indiscriminate Onslaughts," *Counterpunch*, July 19; www.counterpunch.org/Cook07222006.html.

Darwish, Mahmoud 1995: *Memory for Forgetfulness: August, Beirut, 1982*. Berkeley: University of California Press.

De Rooij, Paul 2004: "The Scale of Carnage: Palestinian Misery in Perspective," *Counterpunch*, June 3; www.counterpunch.org/rooij06032004.html.

Dershowitz, Alan 2006: "The World According to Jimmy Carter," *Huffington Post*, November 22; www.huffingtonpost.com/alan-dershowitz/the-world-according-to-ji_b_34702.html.

Eng, David and Kazanjian, David, eds. 2003: *Loss*. Berkeley: University of California Press.

Erlanger, Steven 2006: "Israeli Map Says West Bank Posts Sit on Arab Land," *New York Times*, Tuesday, November 21, A1, A10.

Erlanger, Steven 2007a: "Years of Strife and Lost Hope Scar Young Palestinian Lives," *New York Times*, Monday, March 12, A1, A12–13.

Erlanger, Steven 2007b: "Israeli Settlements Found to Grow Past Boundaries," *New York Times*, July 7; www.nytimes.com/2007/07/07/world/middleeast/07mideast.html?_r=1&th&emc=th&oref=slogin.

Esmeir, Samera 2003: "1948: Law, History, Memory," *Social Text*, 75 (Summer), 25–48.

Federman, Josef 2007: "Olmert: Israel Risks South Africa-like Struggle," Associated Press, November 29; www.usatoday.com/news/world/2007-11-29-olmert-mideast_N.htm.

Feldman, Yotam 2007: "Collision Course" (Interview with Brig. General (res.) Zvika Fogel), *Haaretz Magazine*, Friday, December 21, 8–10.

Fisk, Robert 2006: "Elegy for Beirut," *Counterpunch*, July 22–3; www.counterpunch.org/Fisk07222006.html.

Foucault, Michel 2003: *"Society Must Be Defended": Lectures at the Collège de France, 1975–76*. Trans. David Macey. New York: Picador.

Freud, Sigmund 1927/1953a: "Mourning and Melancholia," in *The Standard Edition of the Complete Psychological Works of Sigmund Freud*, Vol. 14. Trans. and ed. James Strachey. London: Hogarth Press.

Freud, Sigmund 1927/1953b: "The Future of an Illusion," in *The Standard Edition of the Complete Psychological Works of Sigmund Freud*, Vol. 21. Trans. and ed. James Strachey. London: Hogarth Press, pp. 3–56.

Gandhi, Mahatma 1938: "The Jews in Palestine," *Harijan*, November 26.

Goldberg, David Theo 2002: *The Racial State*. Oxford: Blackwell.

Goodenough, Patrick 2006: "Members of UN Body Say Israel's Military Actions Motivated by Racism," *Crosswalk.com*, August 4; www.crosswalk.com/news/1412594.html.

Gregory, Derek 2004: *The Colonial Present*. Oxford: Blackwell.

Gush Shalom 2005: "The Separation Wall," www.gush-shalom.org/thewall/index.html.

Hass, Amira 2003: "What the Fatality Statistics Tell Us," *Ha'aretz.com*, Wednesday, September 3; www.haaretz.com/hasen/pages/ShArt.jhtml?itemNo=336075&contrassID=2&subContrassID=4&sbSubContrassID=.

Herzl, Theodore 1897/1997: "Address to the First Jewish Congress," in Arthur Hertzberg (ed.), *The Zionist Idea: A Historical Analysis and Reader*. New York: Jewish Publication Society.

Hess, Michael 2007: "Alan Dershowitz Claims 'Arab Money Bought' Jimmy Carter," *BBSNews*, January 13; bbsnews.net/article.php/20070113234525132.

Hess, Moshe 1862/1995: *The Revival of Israel: Rome and Jerusalem, the Last National Question*. Lincoln: University of Nebraska Press.

Jews for Justice in the Middle East 2002: "The Origin of the Palestine–Israel Conflict," www.cactus48.com.

Josipovici, Gabriel 1993: "Going and Resting," in David Theo Goldberg and Michael Krausz (eds.), *Jewish Identity*. Philadelphia: Temple University Press, pp. 309–21.

Karmi, Ghada 2004: "Vanishing the Palestinians," *CounterPunch*, July 17/18; www.counterpunch.org/karmi07172004.html.

Karsh, Ephraim 2004: "What Occupation," Aish.com (reprinted from *Commentary Magazine*); www.israel-wat.com/h9_eng6.htm.

Kimmerling, Baruch 2003: *Politicide: Ariel Sharon's War Against the Palestinians*. London: Verso.

Klein, Naomi 2007: "Laboratory for a Fortressed World," *The Nation*, July 2; www.thenation.com/docprint.mhtml?i=20070702&s=klein.

Kluger, Ruth 2001: *Still Alive: A Holocaust Girlhood Remembered*. New York: Feminist Press at CUNY.

Lentin, Ronit, ed. 2005: "Palestine Issue," *Race Traitor*, 16 (Winter), 1–125.

McAlister, Melani 2001: *Epic Encounters: Culture, Media, and US Interests in the Middle East, 1945–2000*. Berkeley: University of California Press.

McGreal, Chris 2004: "Israel Shocked by Image of Soldiers Forcing Violinist to Play at Roadblock," *Guardian*, Monday, November 29; www.guardian.co.uk/israel/Story/0,2763,1361755,00.html.

McGreal, Chris 2006: "Worlds Apart," two-part series, *Guardian*, Monday, February 6 and Tuesday, February 7.

Makdisi, Saree 2008: *Palestine Inside Out: An Everyday Occupation*. New York: Norton.

Mamdani, Mahmood 2001: *When Victims Become Killers: Colonialism, Nativism, and the Genocide in Rwanda*. Princeton: Princeton University Press.

Mamdani, Mahmood 2002: "Good Muslim, Bad Muslim: A Political Perspective on Culture and Terrorism," *American Anthropologist*, 104, 3, 766–75.

Mbembe, Achille 2003: "Necropolitics," *Public Culture*, 15, 1 (Winter), 11–40.

Moore, Donald 2005: *Suffering for Territory: Race, Place, and Power in Zimbabwe*. Durham, NC: Duke University Press.

Morris, Benny 2001: "Revisiting the Palestine Exodus of 1948," in Eugene Rogan and Avi Shlaim (eds.), *The War for Palestine*. Cambridge: Cambridge University Press.

Morris, Benny 2004: "Survival of the Fittest: An Interview," *Haaretz.com*, January 9; www.haaretzdaily.com/hasen/pages/ShArt.jhtml?itemNo=380986&sw=fittest.

Nordau, Max 1907/2002: "Address to the Eighth Jewish Congress," in Peled and Shafir (ed.), *Being Israel*. Cambridge: Cambridge University Press.

Ormsby-Gore, W. 1937: "Minutes of the 32nd (Extraordinary) Session Devoted to Palestine," League of Nations Permanent Mandates Commission, July 30; domino.un.org/UNISPAL.NSF/9a798adbf322aff38525617b006d88d7/fd0553511 8aef0de052565ed0065ddf7!OpenDocument.

Pappe, Ilan 2005: *The Ethnic Cleansing of Palestine*. London: Oneworld Publications.

Peel Commission 1937: *Report of the Palestine Royal Commission*. League of Nations C.495.M.336.1937.VI, Geneva, November 30; domino.un.org/ UNISPAL.NSF/9a798adbf322aff38525617b006d88d7/08e38a718201458b0525657 00072b358!OpenDocument.

Raffles, Hugh 2007: "Jews, Lice, and History," *Public Culture*, 19, 3 (Fall), 521–66.

Reinhart, Tanya 2002: *Israeli/Palestine: How to End the War of 1948*. New York: Seven Stories Press.

Reinhart, Tanya 2006: *The Roadmap to Nowhere: Israel/Palestine since 2003*. London: Verso.

Roberts, Paul Craig 2006: "The Shame of Being an American," *Counterpunch*, July 22–3; www.counterpunch.org/.

Rosen, Charles 2005: "The Anatomy Lesson: Robert Burton's *The Anatomy of Melancholy* (1621–51)," *New York Review of Books*, 52, 10, 55–9.

Rosenberg, Matthew 2003: "US May Study Israeli Occupation Tactics," Associated Press, September 19, 2003; story.news.yahoo.com/news?tmpl= story&cid=540&e=33&u=/ap/20030918/ap_on_re_mi_ea/israel_us_iraq_1.

Sa'di, Ahmad 2003: "The Incorporation of the Palestinian Minority by the Israeli State, 1948–1970: On the Nature, Transformation, and Constraints of Collaboration," *Social Text*, 75 (Summer), 75–94.

Said, Edward 2003: "An Unprecedented Crisis: The Arab Condition," *Counterpunch*, May 2003; www.counterpunch.org/said5202003.html.

Said, Najla 2006: "Do People Know How Much We Hurt?" *Counterpunch*, July 22–3; www.counterpunch.org/Said07222006.html.

St. John, Ronald Bruce 2007: "Apartheid By Any Other Name," *Counterpunch*, February 2; www.counterpunch.org/stjohn02022007.html.

Sartre, Jean-Paul 1948: *Anti-Semite and Jew*. New York: Schocken Books.

Schmitt, Carl 1922/2005: *Political Theology: Four Chapters on the Concept of Sovereignty*. Trans. George Schwab. Chicago: University of Chicago Press.

Scott, James C. 1985: *Weapons of the Weak: Everyday Forms of Peasant Resistance*. New Haven and London: Yale University Press.

Shenhav, Yahouda 2006: *The Arab Jews: A Postcolonial Reading of Nationalism, Religion, and Ethnicity*. Stanford: Stanford University Press.

Shilon, Avi 2007: *Begin, 1913–1992*. Tel Aviv: Am Oved.

Shohat, Ella 2003: "'Rupture and Return' Zionist Discourse and the Study of Arab Jews," *Social Text*, 75 (Summer), 49–74.

Sicker, Martin 1999: *Reshaping Palestine: From Muhammad Ali to the British Mandate, 1831–1922*. Westport: Praeger.

Slyomovics, Susan 1998: *The Object of Memory: Arab and Jew Narrate the Palestinian Village*. Philadelphia: University of Pennsylvania Press.

Smilansky, Yizhar (S. Yizhar) 1990: "Silence of the Villagers," in *Stories of the Plain*. Tel Aviv: Zmora Bitan.

Stoler, Ann L. 2009: "Deathscapes of the Present: Conversing with Achille Mbembe . . . and Michel Foucault," in Kim Benito Furumoto (ed.), *Race's Ghostly Words*. Durham, NC: Duke University Press. MS on file.

Tamari, Salim 1999: *Jerusalem 1948: The Arab Neighborhoods and Their Fate in the War*. Jerusalem: Institute for Jerusalem Studies.

US Newswire 2004: "American Muslims Fingerprinted by US at Canadian Border; CAIR Calls for 'Profiling' Probe, Says Incident Chills Religious Freedom," December 29; releases.usnewswire.com/GetRelease.asp?id=41075.

Volpp, Leti 2002: "The Citizen and the Terrorist," *UCLA Law Review*, 49, 5, 1575–600.

Washington Post 2004: "Building a Wall Around Jerusalem"; www.washington-post.com/wp-srv/world/daily/graphics/barrier_020904.htm.

Weber, Samuel 2005: *Targets of Opportunity: On the Militarization of Thinking*. New York: Fordham University Press.

Weitz, Gidi 2007: "From Rabble-Rouser to Recluse" (Interview with Avi Shilon on his biography of Begin), *Haaretz Magazine*, Friday, December 21, 12–15.

Weizman, Eyal 2003: "Ariel Sharon and the Geometry of Occupation," *OpenDemocracy*, September 9.

Weizman, Eyal 2006: "Walking through Walls," Lecture to Critical Theory Institute, University of California, Irvine, November 8. Paper on file with author.

Weizman, Eyal 2007: *Hollow Land: Israel's Architecture of Occupation*. London: Verso.

Westervelt, Eric 2007: "Six Day War: Legality of Settlements Debated," *National Public Radio*, June 8; www.npr.org/templates/story/story.php?storyId=10816818.

Wilson, Scott 2006: "Israeli Leader Defends Incursion into Gaza," *Washington Post*, July 11; www.washingtonpost.com/wpdyn/content/article/2006/07/10/AR2006071000680.html.

Zureik, Ella 2004: "Israel and Multiculturalism: Enigmas of Departure," openDemocracy.net, August 2; www.opendemocracy.net/debates/article-1-111-2033.jsp.

5

Precipitating Evaporation
(On Racial Europeanization)

> ... *there is no document of civilization which is not at the same time
> a document of barbarism.*
> Walter Benjamin, *Theses on the Philosophy of History*, 1940

I wish to shift registers in a variety of ways: First, from the cases so far discussed in which social arrangements obsessed with securitization are fueled by an omnivorous, pliable, and manipulated set of racially regnant insecurities to those less bound by these logics. And second, from an incessant focus on the logics of more or less explicitly racially repressive cases to those today less totalizingly racial in their articulation and artifactuality, even if their histories of production and proliferation may have been at least equally so.

What, then, has race meant in and to regions with different, if related, histories of racial thinking, expression, imposition, and exclusion? How have Europe, Latin America, and South Africa, respectively, been shaped by racial arrangements – been shaped, in part, as those specific regions? And what today do those regions, and the societies constituting them, contribute (especially in the popular imaginary) to the interactive extensions of racial meanings and to thinking critically about racial structuration, racist exclusions, and social markings, social humiliation and violence?

Racial americanizations and palestinianizations – for they are multiplicitous even as I have identified them in the previous chapter as singularly coherent – concern racist domination and racial denial. Or more succinctly, domination now in the name of racial denial. They involve self-assertive imposition, destruction, and aggrandizement in the name of security, self-protection, and the endurance of democracy underpinned by racial erasure categorically and historically, existentially and formatively. Israel's deep denial of its own implication in racial inscriptions, impositions, and social orderings, save as targeted object and effect of a specific historical conjuncture, is linked in some ways to European racial refusal, as will become evident shortly.

Now relatively undeterred and deregulated flows and mixture have been germane to promoting globalized neoliberal commerce. Within the European theater they have been helped along, if unevenly, by more or less resonant informal social intercourse across racial lines. But the promotion of a racially muted sociality within has been supplemented by a more forceful if sometimes symbolic cementing of racially circumscribed border barricades around "fortress Europe" at its geographic limits.

For Europeans generally, then, race is not, or really is no longer. European racial denial concerns wanting race in the wake of World War II categorically to implode, to erase itself. This is a wishful evaporation never quite enacted, never satisfied. A desire simultaneously frustrated and displaced. As diffuse as they are, racist implications linger, silenced but assumed, always already returned and haunting. Buried, but alive. Odorless traces but suffocating in the wake of their nevertheless denied diffusion.

I suggested in the previous two chapters that the americanizing and palestinianizing conditions regarding race-making and racist derogation linger in their legacies and imposed influences, if not implications, in other regions and states. This has been most notable and pressing in the spatial arrangements so favored in the US and Israel of segregation and separation. While major European cities have seen the informal emergence of segregating residential space, contemporary racial europeanization represents another mode again. I focus in this chapter on the racial evaporations identifiable with europeanization and on their implications. In the chapters that follow I turn to the respective transformational grammars, conceptual and cultural, regional and political, of racial latinamericanization and southafricanization.

Racial Europeanization

Race, I have been arguing, is not simply a set of ideas or understandings. The category represents, more broadly, a way (or a set of ways) of being in the world, of living, of meaning-making. Those ways of being, living, and representation differ across space and time, between the regions with which I have been and am concerned here.

On November 2, 2004, the morning of the US Presidential election that would reelect George W. Bush, Theo van Gogh was murdered on an Amsterdam Street a stone's throw from the Tropenmuseum, the former colonial and now multicultural institution of art and culture. Van Gogh, the great-grandson of Vincent van Gogh's brother, Theo, was a filmmaker best known outside of Dutch circles for a short television film, daringly titled *Submission*, deeply disparaging Islam's treatment of women and homosexuality. The film was made with the equally outspoken Asaan Hirsi Ali, a Somali refugee and vocally lapsed Muslim, one-time darling of Dutch conservatives, then member of the Dutch Parliament even while in semipermanent hiding in the face of a *fatwa*, and *Readers Digest* European of the Year for 2006. Van Gogh was shot and stabbed to death by a bearded man of dual Dutch and Moroccan citizenship, who pinned a note to the dead body. The note, a long, rambling if articulate account of the barriers facing Arab immigrants in the Netherlands, ended with a chilling warning that Hirsi Ali too is a marked woman. She fled for the American Enterprise Institute in Washington, DC, though recently has returned to make futile demands that Dutch taxpayers continue to fund her security detail even while a US resident (estimated at $2 million annually).

The murder sharpened the deepening divide in the Netherlands over immigration, assimilation, national identity, and hostility to those identifiably from the Middle East. In the days following the murder, threats against Muslims and mosques in the country were both sharply up, as too were the calls for local *jihad*. Approximately 5 percent of Holland's 16 million inhabitants are Muslim immigrants or their descendants, largely of Moroccan and Turkish background. Actually this represents one of three pillars of post-World War II and postcolonial Dutch immigration, squeezed between Indonesian first (who overwhelmingly assimilated) and later the Surinamese/Dutch Antilles experience. Over 40 percent of both Amsterdam's and Rotterdam's inhabitants are other than white, with half of those in the cities' schools children of color. At the time of his death, Van Gogh had just completed another film about outspoken anti-immigrant and anti-Muslim sociologist-turned-politician Pim Fortuyn, murdered on a street in Hilversum by an environmental activist (and not, as was often implied in US reports, for his anti-immigrant commitments). Fortuyn, who likely would have become the next Dutch premier at the time (or at least the key opposition leader), was rumored (falsely) to have died 911 days before Van Gogh, a paranoiac symbolism nevertheless not lost on a Dutch public consumed in part by American politics and culture.

Van Gogh's murder, like Fortuyn's earlier, throws into sharp relief issues around race as the unspoken subtext, and the difficulties of raising issues around race and racism in the European context. Europe begins to exemplify what happens when no category is available to name a set of experiences that are linked in their production or at least inflection, historically and symbolically, experientially and politically, to racial arrangements and engagements. In no way to condone the murder or associated threats, the European experience nevertheless offers a compelling case study in the frustrations, delimitations, and injustices of political racelessness.

Eurology

For Europe, the Holocaust is the defining event – the turning-point, perhaps – of race and racially inscribed histories. Not surprisingly, given how many of the twentieth century's seminal intellectuals lived through the disaster or came of age as it unfolded. There could be no neutrality here. The Holocaust signals the horrors of racial invocation and racist summation. In its wake, accordingly, race is to have no social place, no explicit markings. It is to be excised from any characterizing of human conditions, relations, formations. Race, if it has any significance at all, is a category ordering animal life, not inflatable to politics.

Europe's reduction of the racial to the Jewish question – an ironic insistence in the name of evaporation – made it possible at least to raise the ethical question: How could we do (or have done) it, to those (pretty much) like us, those among us, indeed, those who are us? Having sought to annihilate (ethnoracial) difference among us, how much easier to do it to those already at a distance, to those more readily neither among us nor acceptably part of us. The question drives home the point famously stressed by Horkheimer and Adorno: In order to satisfy the Universal, the different had (or have) to be sacrificed. That Abrahamic sacrifice, to be fulfilled, is racially embodied, and coterminously denied.

But in making the Holocaust the referent point for race, in the racial erasure thus enacted in the European theater another evaporation is enacted. Europe's colonial history and legacy dissipate if not disappear. The Holocaust is – it belongs to – Europe. It transpired on European soil, it continues to traumatize political dialogue and debate in Europe, it closes down critical themes in public discourse, it effects certain closures on what can be said and what not. The Holocaust, as Neil Levi and Michael

Rothberg make clear in an otherwise impressive collected volume, is solely about the Jewish experience in Europe; the editors' qualifications notwithstanding, it's as if no other group – not Roma, not gays and lesbians, not the disabled, not communists or political progressives – were targeted too. Colonialism, by contrast, is considered to have taken place elsewhere, outside of Europe, and so is thought to be the history properly speaking not of Europe. Colonialism, on this view, has had little or no effect in the making of Europe itself, or of European nation-states. And its targets were solely the indigenous.

This is a radically anti-relational presumption, one failing to understand how much modern and contemporary Europe has been made by its colonial experiences; how deeply instrumentalities of the Holocaust such as concentration camps were products of colonial experimentation; how notions such as racial hygiene can be traced to racially predicated urban planning around sanitation syndromes by colonial regimes; how the operations of emergency law worked out in colonies like India were reimported into European contexts such as Ireland and later Nazi Germany. As a small but significant symbolic token of how this relational tie between Europe and settler colonialism was sewn through race (what Barnor Hesse terms "onto-coloniality"), recall how whites and those deemed not white in the colonies were formally and informally categorized as "Europeans" and "Non-Europeans" in bureaucratic and popular discourse.

This stress on the Holocaust, however, does account for what Stuart Hall has characterized as historical amnesia, the now deafening silence in Europe concerning its colonial legacy. Colonization, on this view, was a settler phenomenon, the Holocaust a local one. Colonialism implicated at most some European states and populations, the Holocaust marked them all, one way or another. The languages of colonialism were English, Spanish, French, largely; Dutch, German, Portuguese, and Italian a little less so; Auschwitz, as Agamben points out, was witness to all of Europe's languages. Natives are just that, native to other places, alien, foreign. Jews and Gypsies and homosexuals were Europe's other, its own strangeness, its own crippling limb it sought to amputate. Mainland Europeans were largely though obviously not nearly universally complicit. Hence the silence about race today, its censoriousness, its denial. Race is an embarrassment. A family past that has passed, or must be made to pass. Better that it not be mentioned, that it not have to be thought or thought about. Only it doesn't comply, it won't cooperate, it refuses to remain silent.

Race refuses to remain silent because it isn't just a word. It is a set of conditions, shifting over time. Never just one thing, it is a way (or really ways) of thinking, a way(s) of living, a disposition. It is, as I have suggested in regard to racial palestinianization, a passion released or charged (up) and put in gear by events, concerns, troubles. As ways of being, living, thinking, emoting, it is both prompt and product of social tensions and catastrophes.

Each catastrophe is unique. The Shoah, the Nakbah, Rwanda, Cambodia. Each – and unfortunately there are others – has its own conditions of possibility, its singularity, its uniquely tragic effects. Its death-producing uniqueness is precisely what makes of it tragedy.

Auschwitz is a failure of imagination. It always was, from the outset. It exceeds comprehension, as Agamben has put it, no matter how much we know about its details. That is the way of death, the more so with mass, violent death. How could it have happened, even as we know the facts of how it did? How was it allowed to emerge, to take place under our very noses? The paradoxes of racism, as Barnor Hesse has characterized it. Never again, and yet again and again, even now, never more so before our very eyes. Seeing but not; seeing but not believing; believing but believing it immediately not my problem, our problem; seeing and believing but frozen from action, too distracted or busy or unconcerned to do anything about it; acting but not in concert, not concertedly.

Imagination dead imagine.

Death as the limit of the imagination, the image of which never enough, always incomplete, in the face of death driven to silence. A moment of silence for the dead, for imagining the dead, for death itself. As though that is enough in the face of a yawning eternity. Auschwitz stands then for absence, for an absence that promises to extend, endlessly. An absence that is also an abyss, unfillable, thankfully unfulfilled.

An abyss built upon the abyss, the emptiness, of race. Of the historical promise that was always founded upon a flimsy premise. The telos of nature as power nature in the end powerless to deliver. Auschwitz is the promise of race. At Europe's heart. Incomprehensible. Unimaginable. Never to be forgotten. But not to be spoken.

The decisive lesson of the [twentieth] century, as Agamben has it, for so many others. And yet the lesson at the heart of which is the unspeakable, the unmentionable, though thought by almost all. Say it not, but act in its name even as its effects are denied, are in denial. There is no racism because race was buried in the rubble of Auschwitz. Its ghosts everywhere haunting us, acting in and through us, violent convulsions attesting to its power and causing us to take note. Only too quickly to force us back into denial. Moroccans in the Netherlands, Algerians in France, Turks in Germany, Pakistanis and Bangladeshis in Britain. Muselmanns everywhere, and those mistaken for them anywhere.

Jewish cemeteries painted with swastikas, by neofascist youth posing as Arabs; police beating or turning a blind eye to the beating of black men; places of worship fire-bombed, places of residence threatened, places of recreation restricted, rendered uncomfortable. Feeding the homeless in France, but only with pork-based broth so as to make the Muslim and Jewish homeless feel nationally homeless too. And that but today. Everywhere in Europe, east and west, north and south. Decisive indeed. Denied without doubt. Death, as we are now witnessing, in the making.

No race here. No imagination of the racial because the terms are deadened, taken away. And so no conceivable recognition of the marks of its effects, let alone of the effects themselves. Buried. But buried alive. Tolerance expresses these denials directly. Acknowledging begrudged presence as desire of willed absence. The refusal of equality – of standing, of access, of outcome – in the name of an ecumenical largesse, a *hostile* generosity. Tolerance is always expressed towards the tolerated, as I have argued elsewhere, from the tolerating agent's position of power. I have the power and position to tolerate you. I am active; you the tolerated passive, powerless to affect me in my tolerating save to get under my skin, make me even less accepting of your distinction. My social power to tolerate turns on all those like me likewise disposed towards you. Terminating angels. Race disappears into the seams of sociality, invisibly holding the social fabric together even as it tears apart.

Dutch tolerance, in particular, unveiled itself immediately following Theo van Gogh's public murder in the bombing of schools of the different, criminalization of the distinct, demonization of the damned. In 2004, a widely publicized Dutch opinion poll crowned Pim Fortuyn the most important figure in Dutch history. Actually, it was reported a day or two later that an undercount of votes had him second, behind the Dutch national hero of the seventeenth century, William of Orange, ruler, uniter, insurrectionist against the Spanish, *Vader des Vaderlands*. But also, revealingly and less remarked, initiator of Dutch settlement of the Cape of Good Hope in 1652, setting in motion, it could be said, the processes that led three centuries later to apartheid South Africa. Current Dutch populist reactions didn't take long because race was already there, as culture tied to color, habits to headdress, behavior to bodies. The poverty of a universalizing "one-model-fits-all" approach is revealed in one significant response to all of this: Dutch authorities suggested that a required text to be read for citizenship be none other than – *The Diary of Anne Frank*! If these are the decisive lessons of the century that have just been left behind, they are ones not learned, or learned too well, the powers of which either way are still very much at work today in different if not unrelated directions.

Race has been rendered invisible, untouchable, as unnoticeably polluting as the toxic air we all breathe. Unseen yet the racist effects are still suffered. But if unmentionable it is because any terms of reference have been eclipsed (more accurately, it might be said that they have been ellipsed, disappearing in the white spaces between the dots). Not simply legally irresponsible, in Agamben's terms, but ethically so too. There can be no response if the terms of recognition and response are unavailable. There is no possibility of saying the deleterious effects of racial application are even ethically wrong because there is nothing there by which to recognize the phenomena purportedly at issue. Making the charge makes you mad. The anger itself at the lack of discerning language is a sign of your madness. You are mouthing words no one else recognizes. Idiolects and idiocy are taken to go hand in hand.

If racial americanization has privatized race, racial europeanization has assumed a prior step. It has rendered race unmentionable, unspeakable if not as reference to an antisemitism of the past that cannot presently be allowed to revive. A town in southern Germany planned an African cultural event displaying artifacts to be held in the town's zoo. Responding to antiracist condemnations, the zoo director couldn't understand the fuss: "It's the kind of market where you can see African products. So the products are the centre of attention, not the people." This is a sentiment with much wider reach and resonance, as Simon Gikandi has shown with regard to Modernism, generally, and Picasso in particular. "Culture without the cannibals" serves as the subliminal text for the raceless state. Think also of the Dutch disdain at any suggestion that Zwarte Piet, the sambo-esque national mascot in chocolate face that adorns most every public place in the month leading up to Sinterklaas Day (December 6), should be retired from at least public life. "You can't do that, you don't understand our tradition. Zwarte Piet is *our* national pet!" Yes, that's the very point.

The post-World War II period is not the first time racial arrangement and order are disavowed in the European imaginary. Sybille Fischer has revealed compellingly how the antislavery liberation struggles of the

Haitian Revolution were barely remarked upon in European circles, and then always only in demeaning and disparaging terms. In the age of revolution, Haiti's case could not count as an instance. Slaves struggling for their freedom at the time weren't perceived as engaged in the noble reach for liberty as much as they were taken simply to enact the beastly counter of kicking back when abused. Slave rebellions during the Haitian Revolution were seen in European eyes thus as the acts of brutes, read accordingly as vicious and violent rather than as the very human stirrings of and strivings for freedom. Modernity not simply unthinkable to the Euro-imaginary but actively disavowed.

Racially produced and enacted slavery (and indentured labor from Asia in its wake, as Lisa Lowe is now showing), in short, is western modernity's shadow. Outsourcing of jobs, the production of resources and manufactured goods are not recent phenomena but a constitutive feature of modern political economy from its earliest formative moments. Modern slavery initiates outsourcing, hiding the conditions of the cheap production of goods by shipping production offshore, to the South in the case of the US, generally to the periphery. This "elsewhere-ness" hides not only the inhumane conditions under which outsourced production takes place. It thus hides too the conditions making possible less expensive and otherwise more comfortable lives especially for those, or at least for those who could afford it, in the northern hemisphere. And it equally covers over the brutal sources of wealth creation in Europe and the US. Consciousness of slavery, of course, was not completely absent from the European public sphere. This is revealed, for example, in the telling façades of many center-city Bordeaux buildings, or the visible presence of the slave-trading market in Liverpool, or in various material signs of the British slave trade in the port city of Bristol, traces of lives lost. But here too the reminders are provincialized within the archite(x)ture of European space, lingering at the metropolitan margins without troubling prevailing conscience at the centers of power.

Not quite lost as well are the tracks of circulating people and ideas, the babble of French, Spanish, English, Dutch, and Portuguese speakers circulating not just in the Caribbean but throughout much of Asia and Africa also. Race at once de-scribed and reinscribed in these linguistic – and so also cultural – circuits. But the reinscription becomes implicit, coded, immediately in denial. If race at most could be limited to Europe's outside, to what happens when Europe goes elsewhere, goes global, the heterogeneities racial reference simultaneously acknowledges and seeks to hold off could be repressed, restricted, on the soil at home. Race is a problem everywhere else but Europe.

What links Haiti, as the figure of European slavery and of colonialism more broadly, to Auschwitz, then, is racially profiled, produced but also evaporated *death*. The death of Middle Passage a formative step on the path to the camps. Brutalization at the tip of the whip, the chicotte, the leather boot: Port au Prince, 1794, Leopoldville 1894, Auschwitz 1944. Racially entwined in conception and production, ends and effects. But death denied, refused, at both ends. And refused through race. Death dehumanized doesn't add up. The slaughter of brutes reduces to the instrumentalities of labor replacement and body evaporation. How to find able bodies and how to rid itself of disabled ones. How to "factorize" labor and "fabricate corpses."

What to say of death itself, in the face of such denial? Not just about whose death is massified and how the massification was effected. But about death as such? Does death not occur when there is no recognition of the bodies that have died? When the bodies are brutes or bare statistics? Bodies are killed, no one dies, corpses are produced, as Agamben puts it. Death itself is numbed in the face of the staggering numbers. The numeracy dissolves death, liquefying it in a sea of numbers. At a certain point in the count even the numbers cease to signify. What's the difference, really, between 500 and 5,000, a rabbi once asked me. And so between 5,999,999 and six million? Is it not just that our feelings are frozen in these generalizations, overwhelmed by the immensity? Or is it that death itself has been deprived? This could not happen becomes really that it could not have happened? And so it did not? Racial condensation produces death's evaporation. Deadly racisms reduce to racial denials.

Death's deprivation is humanity's too. In losing death we cease to know life. The refusal to see yours as death, as a death like those who are mine, is a failure to admit to one's own humanity. My all too human cruelty becomes the hand God dealt you. Our humanity, with all its limits, its fears, its failings, is vaporized into God's untouchable, unquestionable imperative. God bless the King, the Nation, the Children. The Enemy be damned, condemned, decimated.

In a terse twist, by the same token, death's distillation, its concentration, the recognition of death's enormity in these cases conjures *racial evaporation*. In the case of slavery racial evaporation transpires in the delinking of past from present and future, The concentrated killing of Auschwitz evaporates race in the insistence of the Shoah's uniqueness, its exemplary exceptionality.

Jews, Gypsies, the disabled, gays and lesbians were picked out for destruction by the Nazis and their sympathizers. Jews especially were targeted for systematic annihilation. There is much to be learned accordingly from the Jewish experience of antisemitism and the European drive to their extermination. The foreignization even of those among us; the depersonalization of the damned; the awe-effecting power of a frenzied crowd; the aestheticization of the military in everyday culture and as a consequence its elevation as source – as *the* source – of the regime of truth and order; the ordered pursuits of unquestioning obedience and even ambivalent complicity; the unknowing knowingness of state evil; the deep drive to survive and the human burdens of "succeeding"; the courage of the compassionate in the face of overwhelming pressure and deadly danger; the hanging on to humor when hope has long been lost; the insistence to resist, "to spit in the oppressor's eye," knowing the inevitable, as Anne Michaels puts it; the refusal of memory, and yet its utter necessity.

Traces of lost lives lingering literally in Europe's soil. Simon Wiesenthal has noted that in 10 months, between 1942 and 1943, Germans transported out of the Treblinka death camp alone 25 railway wagons of women's hair, nearly half a million gold watches, 160 tons of gold wedding rings, and many thousands of diamond carats. "All across Europe," continues Anne Michaels in her remarkable novel, *Fugitive Pieces*, "there's [such] buried treasure. A scrap of lace, a bowl. Ghetto diaries that have never been found." What, she asks, "is the colour of a ghost?"

In short, the Shoah in many ways is an exemplary experience, raising in sharp relief the entire range of human responses when faced by a popular state machinery of mass death and desired extinction. And yet; and yet. Antisemitism, alas, is neither the only experience of attempted racial annihilation nor the paradigmatic one. It is not paradigmatic because in matters of racially driven or inflected violence and exclusion, no group's experience is reductively exemplary. Each reveals something both general and unique. Never forget, absolutely, each historical instance. Saying so doesn't belittle even the most extreme case. Quite the contrary, it draws attention to the connections, causal and fabricating, to conditions, expressions, and relations both preceding and following, or following from, the Event.

Rid of race, antisemitism alchemically becomes the sum of Europe's self-conscious admission of a racist past, one it continues to struggle to escape. The influence of the dead, as Anne Michaels might characterize it. So that the dead did not die for nought.

Europe's eugenicist history in the latter part of the nineteenth and first part of the twentieth centuries underwrote the Holocaust, made it thinkable, as too did the long history of Jewish expulsion from European societies, stretching from at least 1290 in England via Mittel Europa purges of the mid-teen centuries to the mid-1890s Dreyfus affair in France. The postwar intellectual clean-up accordingly hitched its cart to purging European intellectual institutions largely of at least explicit eugenicist and antisemitic expression, if not quite so clearly of their biologically determinist leanings. With few exceptions, almost all French (Sartre from roughly 1960 onwards, Memmi, Merleau-Ponty, Lévi-Strauss, among others egged on by Fanon's challenges, and most persistently and formatively Austrian Eric Voegelin even before the war), mainstream European thought about race thus pursued the three interrelated paths I have raced through here: denial of race as socially, politically, and indeed morally relevant; an overriding focus on antisemitism as the real (and almost only) manifestation of racism; and the radical delinking of the intellectual and political histories of colonialism and racism.

Where race reentered the consciousness of Europeans later in the twentieth century, accordingly, it was initially in the very delimited and altogether exteriorized case of opposition to apartheid South Africa. If on its own soil Europe could see race only in the cauldron of antisemitism, apartheid and American racial politics were taken as the sum of racism anywhere. This then expanded in conceiving race as the force of prejudice exercised against newcomers, race still an irrational excess tethered to the historical exemplification of the antisemitic.

Ethnicity is comprehensible, religious tension understandable if regrettable, migration and refugeedom unfortunate but perhaps unavoidable. With apartheid institutionally a thing of history, almost two decades gone now, race is only America's problem, racism its legacy. Religious distinction is a European concern, or more precisely the tension between a growing Christian secularism on one hand and a surging islamicism on the part of newcomers on the other. Racism, so the dominant claim goes, is not.

Racial europeanization thus concerns itself overwhelmingly with racial avoidance as denial of or at least failure to acknowledge its own racist implication. But the postwar racial evaporation both deepened and became more difficult to sustain as the empire came home to the metropoles increasingly from the 1960s on. Two trajectories emerged over time. The first concerned the growing socialization of interracial intercourse in everyday casual relations even as institutional and especially labor market discrimination remained substantively unaddressed. Of course, antidiscrimination law was formalized in policy, only to be largely ignored in application. But daily racial interactions, friendships, relationships, romances – social intercourse writ large – became a matter of course, as happily unremarked as appealingly unremarkable. Black and brown and mixed presence on the street, in stores, in schools, even if not quite at the university, in the boardroom, in the chamber of commerce. Few seem to notice.

But what of a different trajectory from past to present, from the ashes of Auschwitz to violated cemeteries, torched mosques, death threats and *fatwas* in Europe's cities today? What, then, of the trajectory of the Muselmann, of the Muslim?

The Muslim

The figure of the Muslim, alongside that of the Jew, has historically book-ended modern Europe's explicit historical anxieties about blackness. "The Muslim" has haunted the continent from the earliest moments of its modernity, inherited of course from the medieval contest between Mediterranean Christianity and Islam. In Elizabethan England, "the Moor" characterized the mix of religion – godless members of the "sect of Mahomet" – and North African blackness. By the late Enlightenment racial hierarchization of national character, Immanuel Kant could wedge "the Arab," "possessed of an inflamed imagination," between the basest of (Southern) Europeans and the Far East, but significantly above "the Negroes of Africa."

The Muslim, his color and culture a warning against his ever-potential treachery, came to be read as inevitably hostile, aggressive, engaged for religious purpose in constant *jihad* against Europe and Christianity in particular, and later the west and its supposed secularist leanings more generally. This orientalism became racially historicized in the wake of European colonial domination in the Middle East especially in the latter half of the nineteenth century. Nineteenth-century racial historicism conceived of the non-European as historically immature in contrast to European culture and ethos rather than as naturally inferior to Europeans or their descendants. It made of the Muslim the quintessential outsider, ordinarily strange in ways, habits, and ability to self-govern, aggressive, emotional, and conniving in contrast with the European's urbanity, rationality, and spirituality. These are prevailing dispositions that continue to dominate contemporarily.

Today there are a little less than 20 million Muslims living in Europe, short of 5 percent of Europe's total population (depending, of course, on what one includes in Europe's stretch). While numbers are opaque not least because European countries have tended to avoid ethnoracial census tallies, Muslim presence ranges from a high of 9 percent in France, between 5 and 6 percent in the Netherlands, 5 and 4 percent respectively in Denmark and Belgium, to between 3 and 4 percent each in Germany and Sweden and under 3 percent in Britain and Spain. A legacy of post-colonial migration to former colonizing metropoles, refugees from global trouble spots, and vigorous guest worker programs in the wake of aging and upwardly mobile European populations unable to sustain the sort of tax base necessary to extend their retirement benefits. This represents the population push and pull promoted by neoliberal policies at both ends of the strings of attachment, by the shrinking space-times exercising the imaginaries of populations as much in Europe as in Muslim worlds.

Muslim communities in Europe, settling in to second- and third-generation status and supplemented by more recent arrivals, however, tend to be hyper-concentrated in containerizing neighborhoods of urban centers, and relatively young of age. If all Muslim immigration to Europe was closed off immediately, the Muslim percentage of the European population would double every 10 to 15 years, given differential birth rates. A Global Attitudes Survey by the Pew Research Center in Spring 2005 found majorities in Germany and the Netherlands, and significant minorities in Spain, France, Russia, and Poland, expressing unfavorable views of Muslims in their respective countries. These social factors have reflected, if not fanned, renewed local fears of rapid demographic growth, "swamping," and ethnocultural "pollution," tinged with occasional paranoias about European daughters lost to the veil of Islam and Muslim sons to the mania of terrorism. Madrid, Amsterdam, London, . . .

In the United States, the figure of xenophobic exclusion enabling the false sense of commitment to universalism has largely been "the black." In Israel, it has been "the Palestinian." In Europe it has veered between "Jew," "black," and "Muslim," the latter today overwhelmingly the driving force. There is a demographic dimension fueling this, certainly, what might be called the "tilt table" phenomenon. In the case of the US, as I demonstrated earlier, resistance to demographic diversity tends to harden as diversity variously conceived approaches 20 percent of institutional representation.

As the tipping point approaches, the majority white population tilts, visibly increasing its vociferous, vigorous, virile, and often virulent political volume of resistant activities. These take the form most notably of anti-affirmative action campaigns concerning college admissions, employment, and government contracting but also of impeding residential desegregation.

In the case of contemporary Europe, the threshold seems to be significantly lower, the tilting point towards a politics of energetic exclusion becoming evidently exercised as Muslims approach 5 percent of the population. Europe takes itself historically, characteristically, culturally, civilizationally – in a word, racially – to be far more homogeneous than the settler colonial societies that spun off from it. As the demographic table reaches the tilting point, the sort of individuating self-discipline Foucault identifies as the emergent mark of post-Enlightenment Europe gives way to pan-ethnoracial massification, to the dynamic of population manufacture and its repressive regulation.

The flames of these sociological concerns are fueled by the fact that Islam is taken in the dominant European imaginary to represent a collection of lacks: of freedom; of a disposition of scientific inquiry; of civility and manners; of love of life; of human worth; of equal respect for women and gay people. This renunciation of the values of life is thought to become by extension the renunciation of the value of life, of life's renunciation – at least of *this* worldly life – itself. And the counter to these perceived lacks at the edge of anomic Muslim youth has been *culti*vation of an aggressive religiosity, violent rejection of the perceived socio-cultural conditions of their alienation, and establishment of broadly global networks of like-minded groups willing to tear apart the social fabric they so vehemently claim to reject.

The Muslim stands for the European and Europe's legacy as the figure of death's approach, death walking, the plague, the coming of death as such. The Muslim in Europe – not individual Muslims, not even Muslim communities, but *the idea* of the Muslim himself – has come to represent the threat of death. The fear of death on which Hobbes so heavily rested the motivation to (Euro-)modernity's social contract is embodied in the imagined figure of "the Muslim." Delilah and Goliath, philistine precursors both. The memory of Mohammed. Arabian Nights. The fearsome Moor warrior. The leering, conniving, pirating marketeer, deadly knife tucked in belt, hidden between the folds of his *shalwar*. Hijacker of planes; killer of the crippled; rapist of daughters. Above all, now, the suicide bomber and beastly beheader of innocents. The Muslim as the monster of our times. Our nightmare.

The figure of the Muslim has come to stand thus for the fear of violent death, the paranoia of Europe's cultural demise, of European integrity. For the fear for the death of Europe itself. The Muslim image in contemporary Europe is overwhelmingly one of fanaticism, fundamentalism, female (women and girls') suppression, subjugation, and repression. The Muslim, in this view, foments conflict: violence, war, militancy, terrorism, cultural dissension. *He* is a traditionalist, premodern, in the tradition of racial historicism difficult if not impossible to modernize, at least without ceasing to be "the Muslim." Prostrate before an idol, a man self-proclaimed god. Driven by demagoguery, spurning individuality, spurred on by manic collective excitability. Resisting democracy, persisting in theocracy, giving in to if not demanding autocracy. If religiosity in the West – in the US in particular – has become radically individualized and commercialized, religiosity for Islam is seen as collectivized, radicalized, masculinized. The Muslim signals the death of European secularism, humanism, individualism, libertinism.

So much has the figure of the Muslim been tied to Europe's horror of death's threat that the "Muselmann" became the name for those Jews in the Holocaust camps that had left life but had not yet given in to death. The camps' Muselmanner were those who existed, it might be said, alongside death, in death's wake, the moment prior to death's throes, prostrate as if a Muslim praying. Emaciated, moving only to scrounge scraps to eat, caring about nothing but passing through the next moment, and the next, and the next. Wild eyed, lacking almost all will, "men of unconditional fatalism" (to mimic Agamben's citation of Kogon). Lacking dignity and self-control. Indeed, the embodiment of lack, most notably a lack of love, of respect, of spirit for life itself.

As the Muselmann in the camps, so the Muslim in Europe: the figure of the unwanted, the avoided, Europe's untouchables. Just as love of the universal is possible only by abstraction from a defining specificity, so Slavoj Žižek has reminded us with characteristic irony that universal love always necessitates that there is one – the enemy – that is, that has to be, hated. If we can only know our loves by contrast with our hates, the possibility of universal love – of the love of life itself – requires an object of hate sufficient to the cause.

Given the Muslim's masculinity in the dominant imaginary, it is ironic, then, that the prevailing symbol of Euro-Islam, of Islam for Europeans, is the shawl or head scarf. The British begrudgingly came to terms with its presence in schools in the mid-1990s. The French, valiantly seeking to sustain secularism, remain steadfastly opposed. Almost to the point of dramatically curtailing otherwise benign liberties to self-express. The head scarf, more broadly, has come to represent for Europe the threat of reproduction, fear of a Muslim planet. Of Euro-Muslims becoming a major minority, making Europe less secular, less Christian, less liberal. The head scarf, in short, is the symbol of more Muslim *men.* Of anxieties about enigmatic extremism, excessive violence, suicidal mass death.

So the Muslim is taken quintessentially as death's door, death's messenger, death's delivery man. If the Muselmann in the camps was the figure of the living dead, a symbolic grim reaper, today the image of the Muslim is of death's threat, a willingness to sacrifice life, one's own and others', because once compared with the life to come this life is no longer considered having value, worth living. The perceived cause of this-worldly degradation is targeted on the path – as the gate – to other-worldly self-elevation. Martyrdom sacrifices self and other on the altar of a fantasized promise.

The idea of the European excludes those historically categorized as non-European, as being not white. You are here but don't (really or fully) belong. Your sojourn is temporary, so don't grow too comfortable. Hence the constant drumbeat about sending "them" back. Following a large demonstration in Amsterdam's Dam Square to support free speech a few hours after Van Gogh's death, Philomena Essed reports that an angry white man was shouting, revealingly, at a Surinamese Dutch man of color on the street "to go back to your country." Bewildered, the man of Surinamese-Dutch background responded, "What's wrong with you, this *is* my country." A well-known Dutch public figure wrote to the King of Morocco at the same time admonishing him to teach "his people," Moroccans everywhere, to behave. Van Gogh's Moroccan-Dutch killer, it was quickly pointed out in response, was born and bred in the Netherlands. The problem, the rejoinder rightly stressed, was a Dutch one, not Moroccan. Born in, but not of, the society. Being here, but not belonging. Being seen but always only as a Du Boisian problem.

Imagined. Deadened. Can't quite imagine.

Why are the experiences of some alive to us while others fail to be recognized, even perhaps as experiences? Why do we recognize the death or disappearance of some, of those we deem "our own" individually and collectively, more so, more readily than others? We deem some closer, more recognizable, more like or connected to us physically, temporally, culturally, and consequently we more readily commemorate their contributions to our social lives. What brings them closer, elevates them, sanctifies them? Jewish suffering we are exhorted never to forget. At just the moment at which the history of African slave suffering is beginning to draw public apologies from enslaving societies, some in the metropoles, such as French historian Olivier Pétré-Grenouilleau, are insisting loudly that Arab slavery was far worse and that colonized Africans and their contemporary black descendants should be grateful for the civilizing benefits of colonization. Coterminously, Muslim degradation is deeply discounted against the universalizing currency of implementing security, resisting terrorism, restricting immigration.

Central to the history of western metaphysics, as Eric Santner has commented, has been an engagement with the question of being, of substance. Substance, it has always turned out, has been unveiled in relation to changing conceptions of sub-stance or sub-standing, of sub-being or non-being. Being comes to know itself only through what it takes itself not to be, to non-being. And in euro-modern terms, this focus on sub-being or non-being, on creatureliness, has been necessarily elaborated in relation to the sub- or less-than-human, to the racially diminished, of the animal or animal-like. Human being is delineated in contrast to, in repulsion from, the creaturely or beastly that is taken always as the threat to "us," to our wellbeing. The beastly is identified invariably to underscore the condition of human being, and by extension of being human. Being human, while deeply related, is more than simply human being. Where the latter represents an ontological condition, the baseline state of being or existence for the human as such, the former signals the range of practices and habits normatively characterizing what it *means* to be human. Being human signals the culture of the ethical, the content of character, the cultivation of the self not possible for the beast, or for the beastly in us.

Contemporary popular culture in Europe continues to express this beastliness by white Europeans towards those Europeans not figured as white and to those figured as not (or never fully) European. Thus the infantilizing popularity of the *Tintin* and *Zig et Puce* comics of the 1930s and of *Blondin et Cirage* in the 1950s has given way to white soccer fans and some players throughout Europe publicly demeaning black players on European club teams, including those of North African origin, by calling them "monkeys" or "orangutans" or "apes," even spitting at or pelting them with bananas during games. Attending some professional soccer games in Europe today serves as contemporary equivalent of the visit to the World's Fair a century or so ago.

How much longer a leap is it to go from cultural animalization to the burning down of mosques than it was to go from the bestialization of Jews to Kristallnacht? Or from the second-class citizenship of young Caribbean men or the alien status (*vreemdelinge*) of Muslim migrants, whether Jamaicans or Antilleans, Turks or Moroccans, to their permanent expulsion from the European landscape? Far-fetched, insensitive connections? Dutch Minister of Immigration and Integration (*Vreemdelingen Zaken en Integratie*) Rita Verdonk, then French Interior Minister Nicolas ("they are scum") Sarkozy, and German commentator Nagel Tilman have at various times explicitly expressed the case for expulsion. In Switzerland in the run-up to a national election in late 2007, the largest party, the ultra-conservative Swiss People's Party, mailed a poster to every household depicting three white sheep on the Swiss flag kicking off a black sheep. Denying racist intent, the message was lost on no one: people of color (now 20 percent of the Swiss population) do not belong and, in the name of the nation's security, should be excluded or expelled. Clearly, these are views resonating with significant sectors of the white – one might say *echt* – European electorate.

Memorialization

Cultural institutions, it is well known, play a defining role in shaping the social imaginary. Up until the middle of the twentieth century, the cultural projection of Jews in Europe made it possible for Europeans to conjure Jews' absence, their disappearance. Jews, in short, were made the beasts of Europe. Much, of course, changed in the wake of the Holocaust. Cultural institutions commemorating the period have proliferated, reminders of horrors not too distant as well as of the processes of bestialization rendering conceivable the application of the terrible technologies of extinction. Some have gone so far as to deem this, disparagingly, the "Holocaust industry." The concentration camps have been made memorials, impressive museums to the memory – dedications to "never forgetting" – have been erected throughout Europe (most recently in Berlin), and spaces of survival or resistance have been sacralized, such as Anne Frank's hiding place in Amsterdam.

Memorializations of the slave experience within Europe, by contrast, are scarce and usually externalize the reference to the colonial experience. Where they exist at all, they largely ignore the implication of mainland European investment and labor in making the horrors of slavery materially possible, even conceivable (and rarely mention metropolitan profiteering from the condition). The Dutch Slavery Monument, an expressionistic statue commemorating as much the struggle for freedom as the suffering of chains, is hidden discreetly behind a row of hedges in Amsterdam's Osterpark, a stone's throw from where Theo van Gogh was felled but a stiff bike ride from the city center. Easy to miss unless you know where to look. Out of sight, cast from national memory save for the item on the national news each July 1 as the anniversary of emancipation is quietly (or sometimes not so quietly) honored by those whose ancestors suffered the chains. Amsterdam's memorial, revealingly, stands more or less alone across the continental European landscape.

A particularly pernicious instance of cultural bestialization, by contrast, can still be found embodied in the Royal Belgian Museum for Central Africa. The Museum exemplifies just how deep the link between colonial past and postcolonial present can remain. A show piece, if not a white elephant, it still sits in a royal park in Tervuren, a suburban tram ride from EU and NATO headquarters in downtown Brussels. Where most European museums have become more careful in their depiction of European colonial history and contemporary European diversity, the contents and display of the Tervuren Museum look today much as they might have when Leopold II moved it to its present building on his palatial estate in 1910, or certainly as they did at the close of World War II. Proclaiming itself to promoting the "scientific study of Africa," the Museum continues to represent the Belgian colonial adventure in the "Congo Free State" from 1885 onwards in terms of the civilizing mission.

In 2005, in the interests of narratological balance, the Museum mounted a special exhibition, "Memory of Congo: The Colonial Era." The exhibit undertook to represent the Belgian colonial experience. It stressed the modernizing progress Belgians had brought to the "dark continent," emphasizing the introduction of bicycles, railways, trading, air travel, universities, and scientific research. Even more tellingly, the regular entrance foyer to the Museum greets one with a series of larger-than-life gold statues declaring on their pedestals that "Belgium brings the gift of civilization," "of support," and "of economic wellbeing to the Congo." In the name of Belgian beneficence and balance – civilization, support, economic wellbeing, and scientific exploration – the Belgian officer Toeback serving in the Congo Free State in 1891 could declare authoritatively that

With perhaps one exception in a thousand, the black is a dirty brute, a wild animal, wherever he comes from.

Visitors enter the Museum's displays through one of two halls. To the left, one walks through a hall laden with the stuffed "game" of central Africa, including a large elephant. To the right one is drawn into a hall filled with the extraordinary cabinet displays of Central African masks and artifacts. At the center of this room, dominating the display cabinets ordered around it, stands a life-size sculpture in black marble atop a stone base. "The Leopard Man" is a controversial figure, dressed in a leopard skin leotard with a matching hood, eye slits and all, the equivalent of an African klansman. The figure, visitors are informed, is supposed to belong to a group of violent secretive men acting to mediate between warring factions by secretly and silently killing the antagonists and wreaking vicious revenge for wrongdoings. The Leopard Man has his hand raised high above his head, sharp knuckled claws on each finger, triumphant over the man he has just killed lying at his feet. The dead man's buttocks are covered by sackcloth, obviously placed over him by museum curators in an after-thought of prurient discretion.

Central Africa, cannibalistic and savage, the inversion of a European colonialism as necessary in its civilizing mission as it supposed itself necessarily brutish in the implementation of its forced labor system. Men protecting women from *their* men, only to make the saved women "theirs" in one sense of domestication or another. The scientific study of Africa reveals in the first instance nothing more than the barbarity, cruelty, primitivism it supposed to exist when it set out upon its civilizing mission.

In 1904–5, Leopold appointed an investigating Commission into Belgian colonial conduct in the Congo. The Commission was intended to serve as a form of public relations damage control in the face of effective critical attacks led by English human rights activist and later MP, E. D. Morel (he defeated Winston Churchill in an election in the 1930s), and Irish diplomat Roger Casement. Far from exoneration, the Commission's own words serve as indictment, as much of the Museum today as they did at the time of Belgian colonial practice:

> Even if it could be proved that the forced labor system, of all colonial systems, is one that lends itself to improper usage [as though there is a proper usage of forced labor]; even if it could be shown that it is characterized by the highest figures of colonial criminality [as undoubtedly it was], it would still be approved and applied because it is necessary.

One dissenting colonial administrator, his conscience pinched between morality and legality, bureaucratic office and order, doubt and duty, reports revealingly that:

> In Leopoldstad, I had to approve the employment of a group of boys of four to five years of age, "recruited" for the coffee factory in Kinshasa against the will of their parents. I wrote to the King's Attorney that I would no longer use my position for operations of such obviously illegal nature. The Director of Justice [*sic*] replied that I would thus disadvantage those children who wished to work.

Children, no doubt deemed orphans, nominally granted "the choice" to work denied their parents. The latter reduced accordingly to less than children. Constitutionalized cruelty dubiously legitimated by contrasting its bestiality favorably to the cannibalism of the beast:

> It is true that our soldiers were guilty of excesses. They mutilated the bodies of the enemy, whose right hand they hacked off in accordance with native custom. Although such barbaric practices cannot be excused, it must be said that they were nothing when compared with the horrendous cruelty of the natives, who tortured their white and black captives before killing them and using them for their cannibalistic feats.

Native terrorism requires a counter-terrorism equal to the charge. The force of civilization is readily on display in the unguarded declaration of a Belgian colonial officer, Vanholsbeek, in 1895 that

> You can only bring proper civilization through the aid of the bullet.

And the gallows:

> The gallows are put up. The rope has been tied too high. They lift the nigger and put the noose around his neck. The rope twists for a few minutes, then crack, the fellow is thrashing about on the ground. A shot in the neck, and it's finished. This time it didn't make the slightest impression on me! And that although I had turned white [*sic*] with horror when I saw the *chicotte* used for the first time. Africa has its point after all. I would now go into a fight as though I were going to a wedding.

Horror exteriorized in the ghostly figure of whiteness, innocence in the white gown of the wedding. Laboratories of death and technologies of modernity slipping together as a knife into a sheath.

This is the "work of the Belgians" in the name of exploration and science, naturalizing racial necessity and civilizing superiority. It is all but matched at the time by the German colonial power's project to obliterate the Ovaherero, Nama, and Khoikhoi between 1904 and 1907 in what today is Namibia. If the brutes fail to deliver their quota, "exterminate all the brutes," as Joseph Conrad's Kurtz exhorts in the scribbled postscript to his Report to the International Society for the Suppression of Savage Customs. The heart of a chillingly cold and brutal darkness, the "laboratory of modernity" indeed, as Ann Stoler has aptly characterized it. The "scientific exploration of Africa" provides as strong an exemplification as one might find of the significant relationship Paul Gilroy points to in *Against Race* "between the sometimes genocidal brutality of the colonies and the later Nazi genocide in Europe." Every documentation of civilization indeed coterminously the inscription of barbarism.

Native primitivism in the figure of naked bodies and their statuesque representations hints simultaneously at the sexual objectification threaded throughout the Museum, and more generally in Europe's relation to colonial and postcolonial bodies. The representation of fully naked figures in the Tervuren Museum is always of women, repeatedly in fact of African women, and occasionally of children. This emphatically equates once again African adults with infantility, and dialogically reduces Africa to the childish and feminine, but also to nakedness before the penetration of the European colonizer. Thus, and revealingly, the most disturbing of these statues is that appropriately named "Slavery." Here a tall Arab male slaver – mean, sly looking, sharp and frowning – holds beneath him a kneeling naked pubescent African girl whose arm he twists, whip in the other hand. Both figures stand atop a dead young African boy, the sandal of the slaver crushing the breath from boy's body beneath his weight. Another statue elsewhere in the Museum represents a Vuakusa-Batetela man, blanket wrapped about waist, defending from a fully clothed Arab slaver "his" naked woman lying prostrate between the two men. In a not so unconsciously ironic twist, "Slavery" is set in relief against a wall marked "Kinderatelier" ("Children's Studio"), a characterization multiply symbolic perhaps of the entire Museum.

There are only very occasional references to slavery throughout the Museum, and where there are they are *always* to Arab slavers, never to Belgian slavery, Belgian or European engagement in enslavement or in the slave trade. Africans petrified; Arabs enslaving; Europeans civilized. Reinforcing at once the orientalizing sense of Arab viciousness underpinning their market cunning, entrepreneurship, and threatening competitiveness.

One would never know from a Museum visit that Belgium had been engaged in one of the more vicious forms of colonial enslavement. And precisely at the time neighboring European colonial societies to the north and south, the Dutch and French, as well as those further afield to the west, the British, Americans, and the relatively late Brazilians, had moved to outlaw the institution. Johannes Fabian quotes Leopold himself announcing as the intentions of the Geographical Conference of Brussels he hosted in 1876 "to scientifically explore the unknown parts of Africa, to facilitate the opening of routes along which *civilization can penetrate* the interior of the African continent, and to seek means to suppress the *black* slave trade in Africa" (my emphases). Science, civilization, and penetration serve as the repressive replacements of the *black* slave trade, not the enslavement *of* but *by* blacks. In the Belgian Congo enslavement could be said to hide behind the "dark" veil of Central Africa, the curtain of secrecy and obfuscation, distance and strangeness the Belgian state had insisted upon and persisted in creating and maintaining.

Modern European states, in one way or another, are built on the muscles and bones of colonial subjects. The German colonial occupation interned the remaining populations of the Ovaherero, Nama, and Damara in Southwest Africa into forced labor camps rivaling the Belgian forced labor regime in the Congo basin if not quite in its temporal extension. In the first half of 1907, the death rate in these labor camps was 90 percent. *This* Africa remains opaque to European scientific study of the continent, and to the Museum's many visitors. It remains obscure, not least, to the daily school groups brought to learn about the "dark continent," almost never about Belgium's dark past on the continent.

The Tervuren Museum is a merging of the historical and contemporary, as all memorializations tend to be. But the Museum fails – really refuses – to memorialize the murder of ten million indigenous Congo basin people in 25 years (more or less half the region's population); it serves rather as nostalgia for Belgian loss – of the colony, its wealth and prestige, of the power and standing it represented within Europe, explicitly even for fallen colonial agents in the service of the state. The 2005 exhibit on "Memory of Congo" certainly goes further than the permanent museum exhibits in acknowledging some of the human suffering endured by Central Africans associated with Belgian colonialism (not difficult when measured against the hitherto silence). But these costs in lives are more or less equated with – reduced rhetorically and representationally to – the burdens and lost lives experienced by European colonizers.

The Royal Museum stands today accordingly as an archive both of European abhorrence of bestiality and of Europe's own racial beastliness. It leaves a thick trace of the continental legacy of collective investment in extermination of populations dehumanized, bestialized, in one way or another. Yet it signals also the hint of a contemporary struggle over conscience beneath an exteriority of celebration both of lost glory and a much too easy embrace of tolerance. Still, unlike many other European memory institutions, the Tervuren Museum cannot quite bring itself to acknowledge – it continues to repress – Europe's undeniable multiculture, in large part the legacy of its colonial adventures.

The looming figure of the Arab slaver one occasions throughout the Museum not only draws attention away from European investment in the slave trade and possession, it also presages Europe's orientalist fears, the return of the repressed, that have come to dominate the contemporary urban racial landscape clear across Europe. The shift from geographies of the colonial, to use Nezar AlSayyad's useful term, to geographies of economic neo- and cultural postcolonialism conjures new regimes of the racial, novel imaginaries, transforming technologies of restriction and resistance, distinct modes of racist exclusion.

Variations

The shift in Europe's dominant fixation of concern and resentment from the figure of "the black" to that of "the Muslim" reinforces the important point that race is not simply a matter of false views about biology or skin color. Nor is the notion of race simply at odds analytically or existentially with religion. Quite the contrary. Race has to do – it has always had to do – more complexly with the set of views, dispositions, and predilections concerning culture, or more accurately of culture tied to color, of being to body, of "blood" to behavior. Racism is knotted into these identifications, sedimented institutionally even as the categories representing race – cultural or religious, phenotypical or biological – are made mute.

There's a sense, then, exemplified most forcefully in Europe, in which race closes down public political debate just as the public political sphere excises any explicit racial mention, save at the fringes. A telling instance is provided by an election rally for controversial candidate George Galloway, then contesting the seat of Oona King, a black woman close to Tony Blair, representing the high-density Muslim district in East London's Tower

Hamlets early in the new millennium. A strong supporter of Galloway, Al Aqsa, reportedly called King a "black Jewish mongrel," under the thumb of the Bush–Blair–"Jew Sharon" axis of evil. The crowd of 300–400 roared their approval; Galloway got himself elected. Privatized racist expression in but not by the public sphere? Protected speech producing protected acts in response to the deracialization of racist exclusions by public forces? The denial of racist arrangement, racial articulation, and targeted restriction called for on one side matched by racist defamation, resentments, and close to random violence in response.

Race serves as invisible border line demarcating both who formally belongs or not and what can or cannot be said about it. The border line is inscribed not at the level of personal relation, of social and sexual intercourse or the excitement of avant-garde aesthetic expression, but in the crevices of political divides and formal relations of power, of institutional access and full membership in the polity, of educational standards and citizenship requirements. Nonracialism squeezing out any possibility of antiracism.

Demographic or cultural heterogeneity means not simply multiplicity of ethnoracial or cultural groups constituting a state's population. It means equally the multiplicitous making of each group, the mixed making up, influences upon, sources of inspiration and expression, the multi-factored generation within each group. Muslims in Europe are no exception. They hail from different countries, even from different continents (or sub-continents), their sources of religious commitment varying, their class formation distinct, their linguistic traditions not singular, their religious allegiances many, their political affiliations as numerous, their historical influences upon the making of Europe at least as varied as they were influ-ential (Moor, Ottoman, Mongol, Malay). The standardizing European figure of the Muslim belies this range.

If, for Agamben, the Muselmann is the absolutely new ethical figure of the irreducible witness to factorized death yet paradoxically incapable of speaking – the witness, in short, who in witnessing cannot bear (to) witness – then the Muslim, as I am conceiving him here, is the figure of death not worthy of witness. The object of a perfectly transparent death. Death's evaporation. This implies the limits, the end(s) of the ethical as we have come to know it. The end in the unquestioning designation of a class of people whose potentially violent death, destruction, and delimita-tion become unworthy of reflection or comment other than as a new instrumentality: how to avoid the bearer of death; how to kill before being killed?

These are ethical ends or commitments in signaling not so much *what* ethics has come to be for – it is for itself and no other, Kant would have it – as *who* it is for and who not, for whom and where the ethical begins and ends. The figure of the Muslim seems to have conjured the transformation of the ethical from the in-itself, from self-sustaining and self-promoting reason, to the personalization of pure instrumentality. Self-regarding reason, whether in the collectivization of ends or in absolute individualization of religious commitment, has elevated instrumentalization above all else. No limit to terror or torture, death and destruction, incarceration and interrogation, restriction and repatriation so long as they service security of the Chosen People. The one reproduces the other, in a vicious upward spiral. Here we see the link, as much in the logic as in the great chain of being, between historical Europe – "old Europe," to twist the Rumsfeldian turn – and born again American foreign adventure, the "new world," in Bush braggadocio.

There are of course differences in how racisms get to be expressed within contemporary Europe. These distinctions speak to the unevenness of Europe's racial embrace, of racial europeanization. There are differences having to do with national and local specificities; with differing colonial, neocolonial, and postcolonial histories as well as with different experiences of empire; with weightier or lighter legacies of colonizing and scientific racisms; with distinct population presence or absence as a result of migration and refugee crises; with uneven modes of situatedness in relation to postindustrialization and globalization, different experiences of economic decline and reinvention, and contrasting standpoints in relation to World War II and postcolonial decadence and melancholia, resurgence and euphoria. Thus France's particularist universalism and insistent assimilationism in the name of *laïcité* and stridently republican anti-*communarisme* can be contrasted with Britain's conservative liberalism and resentful, melancholic, even decadent multiculturalism; the Nordic countries' insistence on their historical homogeneity with much more porous if still paranoid Mediterranean societies; and Dutch (or Danish) traditions of repressive tolerance with German historical guilt or with persistent East European antisemitism and generally virulent anti-black and Muslimanic racisms. Post-Communist Eastern bloc deindustrialization and rampant neoliberalization dramatically ramified income inequalities, quickly lowering quality of life for many as it heightened expectations for social betterment. These developments thus festered the conditions for which almost invariably the visibly identified and vulnerable pariahs get picked out as the prompts.

British assertive exceptionalism is especially revealing on matters racial, about both specific differences and sustained generalizabilities in relation to Europe. Britain dominated the final century of classic and fading colonial ventures. It figured centrally in the long duration of slave trading, plantation slavery, and their profits and losses, but also in their demise. British politicians, administrators, and intellectuals loomed large in the scripting both of racial naturalism and of the shifts to racial historicism as defining conditions of racial enslavement first and post-abolitionist liberalism later. In the postcolonial turn following World War II, Britain thus predictably became a Euro-destination of choice for colonial subjects turned, increasingly contestedly, British nationals of sorts.

These interactive forces were, until recently, probably more likely, evident, and sustained in Britain than on the mainland continent. So migration to Britain, of the empire striking and writing and shouting back, was larger and more lively as it shifted uneasily from empire to commonwealth, to use Gilroy's insightful characterization. And the criminalization of specifically racist acts – violence and discrimination especially – have perhaps been a bit more vigorous in the last half-decade as a consequence. Blacks in Britain are four times as likely to be stopped on the street by police and questioned or frisked than whites. And they constitute more than 12 percent of the prison population, but just 2 percent of the general population.

The anxieties following the fading of empire and its demographic effects assumed many faces and forces only now manifesting as visibly in other European countries: intensified competition for working-class work; bourgeois disdain for having to struggle for student and faculty positions in elite universities once the presumed privilege of legacies; the flamboyance of foreign capital fueling real estate inflation; the fracturing of a presumptuously homogeneous national culture; the indignity and inconvenience of sometime, if repetitive, urban street riots; the panic around rising crime rates perceived as coterminous, correlated, and at worst causally identified with rising immigration presence and gang formation; the embarrassing losses to former colonial cricket and football teams; and the worries – predicated for the most part on a longer set of experiences – about explosive urban terrorism traced to a too liberal open-door policy.

The failure of confidence that followed what Gilroy identifies as "the loss of the fantasy of omnipotence" gave rise initially to insularity, then to an assertive Thatcherizing streak of "putting the great back in Britain." The Thatcherite reclamation project – not unlike the Reagan one across the pond

– was pushed as sovereign-insistent anti-European-unionization, stressing British heritage and a deep nostalgia for Britain's worldly prowess (not to mention its tradition of profiteering and aggressively defensive warmaking). These sources of British sovereign exceptionalism, and most explicitly and emphatically of the anglicizing of Britain, manifested from the outset in deeply inscribed racial terms tied to the denial of their explicitness and intentionality.

Relatedly, the fractured and fractious homogenizing of a singular Black Britannia, drawing together West Indians, Africans, and South Asians into a blackening singularity as uninvited immigrant presence deserving only disdain and repatriation, eventually tore apart beneath the burden of differentiating histories, competing interests, contrasting relations to the state and civil society, shifting demographic proportionalities, and rising religious and "civilizational" anxieties. But it collapsed also beneath the weight of efforts to "provincialize" England within the configuration of Britain, in relation to Europe, in regard to imperial orders, old and new, and in the reinvented global. The hints of a more troubled and troubling solidarity have begun recently to reemerge, revealed in the fact that of the recent spate of home-grown British bombers bent on spectacular public attacks in the name of Islam, two have been of Jamaican background. The ghosts of racial pasts return to haunt the master's house in unpredictable variations.

Generalizabilities

For all of these internal contrasts, inconsistencies, and temporal registers, it is possible nevertheless to draw broad generalizations having to do with what counts for a regional racial *europeanization*. In addition to the relative intensities of local national parochialisms and exceptionalisms, Europe continues to be considered by the bulk of Europeans as the place of and for Europeans historically conceived. And historically this "Europeanizing of Europe," to use Etienne Balibar's term, presumes Europeans to be white and Christian.

A soup kitchen in Paris discovered quite by chance that Muslim and Jewish needy would not eat soup made with pork. So they started making soup exclusively with pork. Odile Bonnivard, the pork soup kitchen leader, declared unabashedly that "European civilization and Christian culture is our choice," asserting Europeans' right to racial preference, to "Ours before the Others," as her "identity soup" campaign calls itself. The taboo of racial characterization, and the at least official avoidance of racial expression or categorization, reinforce the long historical presumption of Europe as the home of whiteness and Christianity. It follows that any person of color or non-Christian (at least genealogically) in Europe presumptively is not of Europe, not European, doesn't (properly or fully) ever belong. Just as, historically, anyone whose ancestry was considered to emanate from elsewhere was deemed non-European.

In the earliest moments of Europe's modern continental self-formation, Europeans conceived of themselves in contrast largely to Jews and Moors or Muslims. A little later, once African colonization and colonial counter-migrations had each materialized, Europeans elevated themselves on a hierarchical scale the counter-measures for which were provided for the most part by those from "darkest Africa" and the indigenous of Latin America. In the wake of more recent trends, Europeans have come once more to define themselves over and against Muslims from North Africa and the Middle East. Roma, whose distant source was the Indian sub-continent, have never been thought to belong.

If migrations are demographically transforming, sexual desire is perhaps more deeply revealing. The body work may have morphed aside the distancing in time, space, memory, and morality from exterminating modalities of moments past, but sex-workers parading today in Amsterdam's famed red light district, as elsewhere, on display each evening as tourists flock by, drawn by the smell of sex or transfixed on the spectacle, are overwhelmingly from Asia, the Caribbean, Latin America, and Eastern Europe. The former three regions represent exoticized sites of sexual attraction, male and female, the preferred destinations of Europe's thriving tourist sex trade today, a point driven home in the wake of the devastating Indian Ocean tsunami, Christmas 2004. The latter region represents Europe's limits, contestedly European if at all, as the testiness of EU expansion makes all too evident today. The fountain of cowboy capitalism, organized gangs control the sex industry within Europe's borders.

Europe accordingly may be able to acknowledge heterogeneity across the continent – nation-states have different cultures, speak different languages, even a variety of differing dialects, have different histories – but only by denying or repressing ethnoracial heterogeneities within each country. The long lingering legacies of national characterization cement this sense of homogenization. It's not so much a matter of operating non-racially, of "seeing a colorblind future"; it's a matter of repressing the very claim of racial conception at all. Racism, by the same token, is taken as the exception in European societies, the expression solely of the *"far* right," loony extremists, individual or collective, such as the various forms of "national front" or neo-Nazi groups waxing and waning across the continent to the tune of foreign presence and perceived local problems. Exceptional racism reinforces the status quo of exonerated, guiltless institutional forms and responsible individuals more silently and invisibly structuring European societies at large.

The effect of European federalization, paradoxically, is to reinforce homogeneity across the generalization while worrying about (imagined) proliferation of heterogeneity at the level of the local. The proliferating lingua franca of English, seeping across the continent, reinforces the point. The popular slogan to "think globally, act locally" translates for the European dominant into acting *as if* homogeneous in the face of the challenges of the heterogeneous, of ballooning heterogeneity from below. But this hapless homogeneity is made also through various circumscriptions within Europe's borders, restricting belonging – the "true Europe" – to an inner core buffered by at least a couple of bands of the less authentic, the at best partially European the further from the spatiocultural core one cast(e)s.

This response to the perceived menace from the outside can be characterized as "federalizing containership." This consists of a European core around which, as Balibar suggests, are nucleated at least two container rings of states conceived as less or incompletely or not fully European by nature or historical formation. Federalizing containment plays out locally as increased harassment of racial foreigners (and those profiled as not fully belonging). This includes criminalizing not just immigration but (those perceived as) immigrants by state agents with more or less unqualified support by a state citizenry frenzied by fear. Racial europeanization thus resituates the classic mix of institutional and individual racisms, of racisms representative of the state and sewn into the fabric of civil society. Etienne Balibar points out that European states increasingly obfuscate the steadily eroding rights of citizens in the wake of globalized deindustrialization since the 1950s. They do so by contrasting these increasingly "thin" rights to the "empty" or absent rights of foreigners and immigrants. The steadily expanding demands across Europe for immigrants and refugees to meet stringent language and cultural testing suggests just this purpose.

Underpinning these distinguishing contrasts is an at least implicit *national profile,* a cultural preference for the cloned or same and an elevation of those who fit the streamlining profile over those who don't. The national profile licenses what Balibar refers to as a "national preference" reserving jobs, benefits, and rights exclusively and exclusionarily to those consistent with the profile. In the face of dramatic demographic and cultural heterogenizing, the city of Rotterdam's ruling party between 2001 and 2006, "Livable Rotterdam," introduced a "Code of Conduct" that the Dutch government was quick to want to nationalize.

This Code insists on "acceptable normal behavior." It urges that Dutch be spoken in public, including on the streets, at work and school, in community centers, and so far as possible at home. Respect for homosexuals and the equal rights of women are demanded of immigrants, even if local Dutch commitment to these matters more than sometimes suffocates beneath its own formalistic and formulaic gestures. "Livable Rotterdam" wishes to exclude from that city anyone with a criminal record, insufficient income to support themselves, and the inability to communicate properly in Dutch. The national government, not to be outdone, passed legislation requiring all would-be immigrants to complete a course in the Dutch language to be taken at the Dutch embassy in the country from which they are applying for entry, at a personal cost, unaffordable for many, of 350 euros. The naturalization test itself adds another 260 euros. France and Germany, among others, have debated similar language and cultural conduct requirements.

Now "Livable Europe" equates to "Europe for Europeans only," racially embodied and culturally encoded. This is evidenced explicitly also in websites today representing more extreme groups such as the "European National Front" or "Islam-in-Europe." The ironizing website of "The Official Apology" for the "Danish Muhammed Cartoons" (www.danish-muhammedcartoons.com), sporting Confederate flags atop its home page, exhorts "freeing the world from Muslim invasion." It thus implies a free-speaking, Muslim-free continent in the name of Euro-supremacy. Racism in Europe accordingly is not just about actions against racially perceived foreigners (guest workers, refugees, immigrants, etc.). Various European societies struggle over the terms of assimilation and accommodation of immigrants (women, more reliable and reliably non-violent, are considered desirable, or at least acceptable immigrants; the veil aside, men are not), and over the terms of anti-discrimination and anti-hate legislation.

Equally important and interactively, Europe has long nurtured the civic drive to identify the foreign, to uphold the possibility of keeping the foreign foreign, of permanently foreignizing the "(racially) non-European."

The reproductive logic of Euro-racism ensures that those "racially non-European" are never nor can ever *be* European, or at least European enough. The recent language requirements notwithstanding, the turn away from Turkish membership in the European Union and the persistent publication, first in a Danish newspaper and then reiterated in the name of free speech throughout Western Europe, of humorless cartoons demeaning Muslims in 2005–6 are the latest cases in point. No matter how seemingly reformed and romancing democracy, a nation or people identified as overwhelmingly Islamic will conjure anxieties for those taking their values, their invented continental civilization and civilities to be at root Christian.

The immigrant in Europe today is articulated thus in terms of at least three overdetermining and interacting racially driven economies, to riff on Balibar: First, an economy of labor serving as lure into a workforce to perform work no (or very few) locals will and to sustain retirement benefits for an aging population. Second, a moral economy enabling Europe to face itself as sustaining a humanity struggling to meet the moral standards it has set itself for refugees fleeing wars, politically fashioned famines, and natural disasters. And third, a political economy where the local politics of possibility veers, often wildly, between access and begrudging, assimilating acceptance, on one side of the ledger, and aggressive, even violent denial and restriction, on the other. The protection of (the rights accorded) immigrants constitutes not only an important register of "the vigor of citizenship," as Balibar puts it in *We, the People of Europe?*, but also an abstract yet vital metric of the status, the rights, of the local working classes.

Racist violence in Europe assumes a variety of expressive forms. First, foreigners, including legal immigrants, face the state and negotiate its agency from the moment of arrival, if not earlier. They are watched, channeled, documented, obliged, commanded, and pressured in various ways by officials. Their presence, if not indeed their very being, is discussed, negotiated, ordered, and recorded in and through legal forms and forums. The police play a very large role in the more visible forms of their discipline, but the police are far from the only source of misery.

Second, civil society generally keeps an eye out for the social misfit, the unwanted, the foreign, shunning them, whether in schools or on the streets. Noted British novelist Martin Amis seemed to echo popular sentiment when he declared in a series of responses to Terry Eagleton's criticisms of his inflammatory views that

The Muslim community will have to suffer until it gets its house in order. What sort of suffering? Not let them travel. Deportation – further down the road. Curtailing of freedoms. Strip-searching people who look like they're from the Middle East or from Pakistan. . . . Discriminatory stuff, until it hurts the whole community and they start getting tough with their children.

While prevailing members of civil society might be happy to eat from exotic restaurants or purchase gifts or cultural goods to enliven existence and homes, the cultural practices of the different, the strange, and the alien – in short, the foreign (*Vreemdeling* signifies just this ambiguity and ambivalence) – are to be held at arms' length on a daily basis.

Civil society, thus, is the prevailing site of what Philomena Essed and many following her have aptly theorized as "everyday racism," not just for those more recently arrived but equally for people of color European born and bred. There is of course violence too from the other side, largely (as Balibar comments) from second- and third-generation teenagers and young men. These are youth who are immigrants only by default as they are more often than not born in Europe, bred by the mix of immigrant and local working-class culture, suffering the distance from two homes, one European and the other that of the parents or grandparents, twice removed from homeliness. Homesickness takes on an altogether different resonance here, and the response is often a lashing out as a result of the frustrations, the non-acceptance of non-acceptance, of discrimination, and perpetuated exclusions.

Overall, the violence wells up as a result of processes abstract and alienating, making alien those less able or willing to comprehend local habits. Occasionally the outcome is social destruction alongside self-destruction, tightening the spiral of social recrimination, externalization, and sometime soul-searching. But more often than not this racially inscribed violence, now more and more reduced to the social panic of terrorism, is alienated as foreign import rather than home grown, the causes seen to have no grounding in local European conditions of hostility, resentment, and ignorance.

This logic has an even more generalized resonance, expanding beyond the geographic borders to the cultural imaginaries of European racial identification in colonial environments past and not so past. This is evidenced by racist violence initiated in the beachside suburbs of Sydney in December 2005 but spreading in rapid fire clear across the country. Alcohol-soaked white youth, fueled by neo-Nazi groups and the techno-instantaneities of text-messaging mob mentality, attacked Australians of Middle Eastern background. The resulting rampage – youths brandishing machetes, home-made bombs, knives, and guns – and aggressive Arab youth responses gesture back to the state's sometime policy of "keeping Australia white." Now long abandoned as *explicit* commitment in the face of rapid demographic and cultural heterogenizing, the sentiment nevertheless bubbles beneath Australia's dominant self-conception, despite current premier Kevin Rudd's apology for historically abusing Aboriginals. Thus, former prime minister John Howard repeatedly denied the prevalency of widespread racist attitudes in the country, implying predictably that the beach outburst was just a matter of a few rotten eggs.

More broadly, these events can be read also as a perverse sort of reverse reference to what one insightful Arab teenager called "the juvenile revolution" of Arab youth in France a month earlier. In Australia, the French outburst exacerbated already simmering anger over 9/11 as well as the Bali and London transit bombings. Racial europeanization offers once more an extended touchstone, if not template, for racial reference and response gone global.

There is accordingly a quadruple and quadruply interactive set of movements regarding Europe's current affair with matters racial. The first concerns the immediate, informal interactions in daily life between individual people in their immediate intercourse – on streets, in stores, in subways. Here European civilities mix with the now 50-year history of formal racial suppression to produce, for the most part though not absolutely, a casualness about interracial social intercourse, and certainly largely a non-issue (at least in Western Europe) about interracial sex and offspring (save perhaps for the sometime exoticizing of black bodies and sexuality, most notably but not only in the case of Germans). Second, and already hinted at in producing the first movement, there is the official denial of racial classification and reference, a strong suppression of the possibility of racial characterization certainly in official state expression, the silencing of any formal racial reference reinforcing informal civility and casualness. State and civil society, the official line would have it, conform one with another.

The third movement, that interface of the formal and informal, suggests an undertone that is less appealing and less fulfilling. This marks the extended and untouchable exclusions, denigrations, and alienations at once racially presupposed, expressed, and reproduced: the relative lack of educational and employment opportunities, the residential segregations, the public media denigrations, the police profilings, the public handwringings, the informal insults that circulate so readily. Raceless racisms, everyday and every way.

Denied always precisely as racial problems, as racisms, turning them generically into a class or cultural, religious or immigrant problem, as though to be tainted by the charge of racisms, individually or as a society, is just too much to bear, beyond the pale.

For all of this, there is now beginning to emerge as a self-conscious and self-organizing development – too early to call it a new social movement, to be sure, but it may be one in the making – around what "Black Europe" amounts to. What are the historical forces and factors fashioning the possibility of a formation drawing together overlapping historical and contemporary experiences into a common self-determining designation, what collective agencies do they prompt, and to what effect? How might the register of this new racial counter-history revise the mapping of European self-narration, reorder Europe's body politic, rearticulate Europe's racial configuration, opening it up not just to new social possibilities but to reconceived polities? How might one think of Europe's "blackening," both historically and contemporarily, in conversation, inter alia, with African and African-American influences but not reducible to them as frame, prompt, or analytic?

Imagination revived, after the postmortem had signed the death warrant. Buried perhaps, but very much alive.

Yet Europe remains, as I've said, in some awkward sense presumptively European. It remains the fantasized space, the "homeland," of those always ever religiously white, of Christians secularized, of the prophylactically protected inner circle ranging from Anglo-Saxony to the Caucuses, from south of the North Pole to the northern shores of the Mediterranean. As flexible as Europe's cartographic and imagined borders throughout modernity have always been, Europe is thus a theological project, as much of racial as religious conviction. The increasingly brown tinge, oil polluting the water, seeping through and across the map of European whiteness, needs guarding against lest it smudge Europe's long-imagined make-up. That self-threatening clash of civilizations tugs at its sense of population, both its civility and its formal arrangements, promising to unravel its social fabric and removing any possibility of a cover other than mosaic. Europe's dominant imagination is still not able to come to terms with that latter possibility, indeed, increasing likelihood. It is this self-generating, fearful threat that continues to prompt the impossible desire to close the borders, both around nation-states and circumscribing Europe's self-proclaimed racial homogeneity. It seeks repeatedly to condomize itself by making the Different different so as to sustain the Same.

European unification thus has been mediated through racial management. The explicit ceiling on national budgets and deficits has placed downward restrictions on welfare support. An aging demographic and low birth rates have exacerbated the need for a more youthful imported labor pool ("work *force*," racially presumed, exactly primes the paranoia) to sustain expected levels of pension possibilities. The apparent ambivalence among some recent immigrant cultures regarding human rights commitments has enabled some European polities to deflect criticism of their own curtailment of civil liberties. And the fear of rising levels of foreign cultural – especially Islamic – presence and assertiveness has fueled louder assertions of "authentic" European identity articulated in terms of cultural Christianity, racial whiteness, and behavioral civilities. Contemporary Europe reinscribes itself as European precisely through re-cognizing and silently, implicitly re-narrating its racial contours in the face of these potentially fracturing challenges.

Europe's racial self-articulation has long expressed itself in terms of the denial, exclusion, and ultimately the purging of those not white – not European, to be emptily, circularly precise – from first its ideational conception and then also from what it has taken as its territory. These interactive reinforcing modes date back to – and can be seen as the source of – the very idea of Europe articulated at the onset of European modernity in the mid-fifteenth century, predicated as it was on the purging of any Jewish or Muslim mark on its self-articulation. It is reconceived more or less vigorously at different moments, but most notably with polygenic and eugenic formulations in the nineteenth century before assuming the force of a genocidal supernational (and to some degree a supranational) movement some 70 years ago. For it was with the onset and especially nineteenth-century maturation of European modernity that those not "traditionally" European began showing up on and within the continent in numbers sufficiently large to conjure attention and anxiety. Intertwined, familiality and familiarity came under self-proclaimed threat.

In turn, the drive to maintain Europe for Europeans fueled the Nazis, driving the Reich to seek to "cleanse" not only the German *patria* but the extension of Europe more broadly of all polluting presence. And it has fueled political promptings and populist outbursts more recently – from Enoch Powell and later Margaret Thatcher in Britain of the late 1960s and 1970s to the Haiders of Austria and Le Pens of France in the 1990s or the Pim Fortuyns, Rita Verdonks, or Geert Wilders of millenial Netherlands and the Flip der Winters of Belgium. Europe for Europeans, first biologically and more recently conceived in terms of national cultural cohesion, of cohering civilization, of political populism.

Now borders are constituted complexly – through culture, language, political negotiation, geography. This volatile mix is given the artifice of stability through race, the biopolitical technology par excellence, fashioning the foreigner, the stranger, the not-belonging. Europe has long negotiated the lines marking off those who belong, whose being constitutes Europeanness, whose genesis can be traced in some extended sense to Europe, temporally and spatially. Longing is cut off from belonging, the former restricted to economic considerations in the case of the alien, drawing a conceptual boundary cutting off the stranger from the inherent insider, the presumptive siblings of Europe. Borders shift between the geophysical and the symbolic-political. The former are fixed more or less in some continental territorialization, expanding and contracting under the material forces of war and peace, political crises and shifting social contracts. The latter fluctuate over more globally expansive, fleeting and fluctuating symbolic spaces, coming into view or becoming less visible subject to the winds of political tensions, culturalist crises, populist paranoias. Two sides of the same national(ist) coin.

Languages have histories, as Balibar has put it in his wonderfully provocative and insightful essay, "Europe as Borderland." Languages embed sets of beliefs, collective understandings and experiences, institutional expressions. They reflect and shape prevailing socio-cultural and institutionalizing narratives, overriding – even overdetermining – though not necessarily totalizing or even finalizing accounts of historical memory, social arrangement, how things are and are to be done. Languages, in short, entwine the descriptive with the normative in social life.

Europe, of course, is a polylinguistic congress translating more or less fluently among, between, even within the major European language groups and sub-dialects. That's part both of Europe's political heritage, its charm, and its historical tensions, its charged legacy. What draws them together across those differences and divides is a sense, small or large, of Europeanness, of commonness, of familiality and familiarity. Of racial (or trans-racial) commonality, of culture, heritage, interests in relation to – as distinct from – an outside, a not-being-European, the content mixing culture with physical distinction. Even where, as a result of colonization, European languages are spoken in the global outside, they are accented. They are considered odd as much in their "color" as in their character, as much driven by who the speakers physically are seen to be as in their syntax and semantics.

Obviously there have been shifts over historical time. European relation to difference, whether outside in or inside out, has become more nuanced and careful. Nevertheless European entanglements of the nature of culture and the culture of nature remain intricately, intensively, extensively, exclusionarily woven together. The silencing of race is at one with the racial markings of the social forces producing that silence.

Raceless Europe

Europe thus represents what the contemporary project of racelessness implies politically: First, the removal of stigma from interracial sociality, and with it largely the de-eroticization of the racial in interracial sociality and sexuality. This, to be sure, has considerable appeal, not least for those in societies long bruised by these very restrictions and their attendant exacerbations, exclusions, excisions, evasions, and erosions of the social fabric. Second, a shift in the burden of legal proof in the face of charges of *institutional* racism from those making the charges to those being charged. A significant shift, indeed, signaling at least a seriousness about facing up to the challenge. But both lead also to the shift to personalize and individualize racism, to reduce racist violence to a few rotten folks, to restrict apartness especially in residential, educational, and employment arrangements and access to the untouchable segregating schemas of personal preference and the lure of the familial and familiar. In the limit case, it reifies the impossibility, given the absence of a language of characterization, explanation, and condemnation, of identifying the problematic, of addressing wrongs, cutting off – as others have commented in the case of America – grief from grievance.

Antisemitism remains the mark and measure of racism where race has been made to evaporate, its emphatic reappearance – or really re-emphasis, renewed focus – the foil precluding the possibility of addressing, let alone redressing, other equally visible, voluble, and violent expressions. Its silencing, solipsistic, even idiolectical emphasis makes it impossible, as Sophie Body-Gendrot points out, actually to ask, let alone to monitor, how many French Algerians, for instance, are confined to French prisons, what is the ethnoracial constitution of the entrepreneurial class or indeed of the local or national legislature, or what the extent of housing discrimination against people of African (North or sub-Saharan) origin. More than half of the French prison population today consists of French Arabs and

Africans; and the unemployment rate among these groups is three times the national average, in some cities as high as 30 percent. Few know or have noticed. This invisibility produces, inevitably in the absence of counter-movements and -weights, despair in the face of denial, anger in the wake of alienation, violence in the absence of the value of life. The fire each time, as evidenced quite literally in France-wide *banlieue* conflagrations in November 2005, more heated, widespread, less constrained and containable than anything to date.

European civility, as attractive as it may be especially for those of us whose traditions seem significantly more violent and vulgar, is built on a mix of respect and repression. Respect more for the sacredness of the public sphere than for the heterogeneities of the peoples inhabiting it. Repression, more or less subtle, more or less robust, of the edges of expression, its edginess, especially in mainstream fora, of the intensity of really distinct modes and messages, more often than not squeezing out the (ethnoracially distinct) edges, maintaining their marginality, in order to save the middle.

In times of metropolitan crisis, chaos, and tragedy – New York immediately post-9/11, Bali following the nightclub bombing, Sumatra in the wake of the tsunami, the Madrid subway bombings in 2004, the London tube and bus bombings in 2005, followed by Sharm-el-Sheikh shortly after – civility and solidarity take hold at least temporarily, fueled by and reinforcing a fleeting humanity, the shared social tragedy drawing us momentarily into a commonality across difference. But the civility and commonality all too often give way quite quickly to a cynical politics of finger-pointing, threats, dismissal, and violence. We embrace each other in suffering, even as we acknowledge distinction. Death brings the living together, the more tragic and unexpected the more so. But the violence of political death also exacerbates existing tensions, reinforcing calls for reprisal.

Thus the messiness of sensible British civility and appealing calls for civilized respect and solidarity across the religious chasm in the wake of the London bombings targeting all Londoners indiscriminately, Muslim alongside non-Muslim alike, were undercut within a day. With the dust still settling, there were reports of 30,000 hate mail messages berating Britain's Muslims. And with every fear of more bombings to follow, mosques were warned of torchings they would inevitably face. At the same time, more than twice as many Muslims in Britain as non-Muslims are unemployed, and five times as many British Muslims live in overcrowded housing as their non-Muslim counterparts. The dreariness and drudgery of disaffected lives in Britain's or France's depressing, divisively reinvented, and deeply segregated urban surroundings – living in a garbage dump, as one thoughtful young Parisian put it – momentarily undone by the angry thrill of anonymous, if not quite random, explosive violence. The fantasy of *Zabriskie Point* blow-ups brought to life.

There are larger numbers of Muslim people today who are members of European or European-derivative societies than vice versa. This partly has to do with postcolonial reverse migration, and relatedly with widening North–South economic disparities, as Hala Mustafa has pointed out. Culturally and politically, though, these demographic shifts have resulted in European societies assuming characterizations about all their local Muslim populations more readily applicable to many, though not all, of the Islamic societies they have left: intense religiosity, anti-secularism, anti-democracy, deep gender inequities, homophobia, violations of human rights. As though the repression of governments naturally translates into repressiveness of all those people who for whatever reasons have fled from them and taken up life elsewhere.

"The European question," then, is not one of immigration so much as it is one of home-grown radicalization. Of the quest for belonging, and its denial. A striving for more than a formalistic and formulaic equality and the refusal of invisibility. The experience of other immigrant societies reveals that limiting second- and third-generation descendants to demeaning stereotypical reductions and their material restrictions is to play with fire around a powder keg. Why the surprise when it blows up? The projection of debilitating and constraining stereotypes onto those already disenchanted with the drudgery of everyday existence hardly helps make folks feel at home, respected, cared for. Perhaps that too is the point.

Partha Chatterjee has insisted that the "rule of colonial difference" marks the constitutive boundaries of imperious universality, restricting its extension to (the inner core of) European nation-states and perhaps their satellite settler populations. Today, I suggest, the boundedness of universal extension is delimited by the "law of postcolonial distinction," as constitutive of the ex-colonial metropole as was the "rule of colonial difference" in shadowing an earlier global formation. The rule of colonial difference prompted significant, vigorous, coalitional resistances, social movements within and across colonized and colonizing states, with at least partial transnational effects. The law of ex-colonial distinction, by contrast, predicates itself on racial denial and the cosmetic masking – the making invisible – of the institutionalizing causes of racist violence and exclusion fronted by the reifying discursive fabrication of the ever-threatening, panic-producing figure of postcolonial character: the revolutionary; the mugger; the criminal; the gang member; the religious fanatic; the terrorist. A figure (or shifting, shifty figures) both perennially regressive and digressive.

This not only freezes in time and across space who the postcolonial must be and what is to be expected of *him*. It makes it close to impossible to prompt, promote, and produce transnational antiracist social movements drawing on wide support and with reachable goals. Jo Goodey reveals that, but perhaps for Britain, European countries continue more or less robustly to resist collecting data revealing the extent of racist violence. Important as they continue to be, resistant movements accordingly are reduced to reactive modalities – against globalization, against capitalism, against the latest war, against sweat shops, and so on. And when antiracist, largely reacting to local instances of racist violence, contained, limited in scope, size, and so success.

Antiracist social movements, more or less widespread, have waxed and waned across Western Europe: Rock Against Racism, the Anti-Nazi League, or the Anti-Racist Alliance in Britain, SOS Racisme in France, Movement Against Racism and Xenophobia in Belgium, Nero e no solo in Italy. They have been supplemented by the all too often aborted attempts to establish EU-wide movements such as the Anti-Racist Alliance or the Network Against Racism, and so on. These groups have foundered for the most part not only on the lack of resources or on internal debates about whether the leadership would be white liberals or radicals or black people with direct experience. Support tends to swell somewhat in the wake of highly publicized events, such as urban outbursts or the Stephen Lawrence murder and his family's courageous and persistent insistence on a formal inquiry into police conduct and its lack in Britain, or the Van Gogh murder in Amsterdam, neo-Nazi outbursts in Germany, antisemitic events and violent outbursts by youths of color in France, and so on. Those enduring weights of race.

Immediate calls for "restoring law and order" followed by public hand-wringing climaxes with the issue of a formal report at best acknowledging structural impediments to social advancement for people of color, or institutional insensitivities. But those formal public admissions also slide into absolutions, dissolving the energy of the insurgent into the modest, quieting force of the law, reducing resistant antiracist anger each time to the formalisms of antiracial insistence. "We will not tolerate racism" invariably and quite quickly becomes "We cannot speak the language of race." Which is a coded way of saying "We cannot speak of race." And social silence sets in until the next outburst.

Death and violence have marked the European romance with race from its earliest moments. From fears of blood contamination through the necrophilia of scientific skull measurements to the death camps. Threat of death, coterminously social and physical, lingers across a shifting landscape of torched mosques, desecrated cemeteries and synagogues, rape accusations, video viciousness, and resentful reprisals. Not the Holocaust, to be sure, but not to be dismissed as trivial or non-traumatizing either. The global relatedness of racially fueled structures of exclusion and debilitation are a reminder that behind the blunted point of racial europeanization lies the sharp edge both of racial palestinianization and americanization.

The relational frame for thinking through race in the European context has usually been ordered in dualistic terms: anti-black racisms following from slavery and colonialism largely keeping Europe white and blacks out; and antisemitism as embroiled in the long history of exclusion, excision, and ultimately extermination. This dualism has dominated the historical conception and comprehension of Euro-racism at least since World War II, and still underpins common understandings of racial europeanization, as Macmaster among many mainstream analysts exemplifies. These are important constitutive elements of European self-making, implicating slavery, viciousness, and exploitative profiteering as well as exclusion and extermination as central conditions of Europe's legacy.

I have been arguing that there is a third major artery in the historical articulation of racial eurology and the constitutive grounding of Europe as cohering political arrangement, feeding and fueling belligerence, bloodshed, and lately bombs in various directions. This has been the trajectory of European Muslimania, from at least the fifteenth century onwards, entangling with the other dominant threads, feeding (off) and being fueled by conditions faced also by blacks and Jews. These intertwined histories constituting the legacy of racial europeanization – at the very least ethnoracial, cultural, religious, in a word civilizational – remind us that the contemporary euro-panics around "the Muslim," signaling something relatively new, nevertheless also have very deep roots. Those panics, I have been suggesting, continue if in novel ways both to shape and to reflect the ethnoracial instrumentalities of mixing and force that service the financializing flows and seek to delimit the disruptions of contemporary neoliberal sociality.

By the same logic of relatedness, racial latinamericanization and south-africanization follow connected if not always similar trajectories. Their historical, demographic, conceptual, and material distinctions play out in somewhat different, if overlapping, terms, thematically, in expression, and in the politics of racial inscription and racist implication. The racially mobilized regions of Latin America and Southern Africa accordingly offer useful contrasts, historically and politically. I turn in the following two chapters to each respectively.

Bibliography

Agamben, Giorgio 1999: *Remnants of Auschwitz: The Witness and the Archive*. New York: Zone Books.

AlSayyad, Nezar, and Castells, Manuel, eds. 2002: *Muslim Europe or Euro-Islam: Politics, Culture, and Citizenship in the Age of Globalization*. Lanham, MD: Lexington Books.

Asia Pacific News 2005: "Sydney Thugs Read the Riot Act," Tuesday December 13; news.monstersandcritics.com/asiapacific/article_1068635.php/Sydney_thugs_read_the_riot_act.

Balibar, Etienne 2004: *We, the People of Europe? Reflections on Transnational Citizenship*. Princeton: Princeton University Press.

Balibar, Etienne 2009: "Europe as Borderland," in Kim Benito Furumoto (ed.), *Race's Ghostly Words*. Durham, NC: Duke University Press. MS on file.

BBC News 2005: "Row Over German Zoo's Africa Show," Wednesday June 8. news.bbc.co.uk/go/em/fr/-/2/hi/africa/4070816.stm.

Beckett, Samuel 1974: "Imagination Dead Imagine," in *First Love and Other Shorts*. New York: Grove Press.

Benjamin, Walter 1940: *Theses on the Philosophy of History*; www.loki.stockton.edu/~greggr/theses_on_the_philosophy_of_history.htm.

Bennett, Ronan 2007: "From 'Wogs' to 'Islamists': Martin Amis Does a Coulter," *Counterpunch*, November 27; www.counterpunch.org/bennett11272007.html.

Blatt, Jessica 2004: "'To Bring Out the Best in their Blood': Race, Reform, and Civilization in the *Journal of Race Development* (1910–1919)," *Ethnic and Racial Studies*, 27, 5 (September), 691–709.

Bleich, Erik 2003: *Race Politics in Britain and France: Ideas and Policymaking since the 1960s*. Cambridge: Cambridge University Press.

Body-Gendrot, Sophie 2004: "Race, a Word Too Much? The French Dilemma," in Martin Bulmer and John Solomos (eds.), *Researching Race and Racism*. London: Routledge, pp. 150–61.

Bond, Patrick 2004a: "George Bush of Africa: Pretoria Chooses Subimperialism," *CounterPunch*, July 17/18; www.counterpunch.org/bond07172004.html.

Breman, Jan, ed. 1990: *Imperial Monkey Business: Racial Supremacy in Social Darwinist Theory and Colonial Practice*. Amsterdam: VU University Press.

Buijs, Frank J. and Raad, Jan 2002: "Muslims in Europe: The State of Research," essay prepared for the Russell Sage Foundation (October); users.fmg.uva.nl/ jrath/downloads/@RSF%20European%20Research%20on%20Islam%20and%20 Muslims.pdf.

Burton, Antoinette 2003: *After the Imperial Turn: Thinking with and through the Nation*. Durham, NC: Duke University Press.

Camberg, Kim 2005: "Long-Term Tensions Behind Sydney Riots," BBC News, Tuesday, December 13; news.bbc.co.uk/2/hi/asia-pacific/4525352.stm.

Campt, Tina 2005: *Other Germans: Black Germans and the Politics of Race, Gender, and Memory in the Third Reich*. Ann Arbor: University of Michigan Press.

Chakrabarty, Dipesh 2000: *Provincializing Europe: Postcolonial Thought and Historical Difference*. Princeton: Princeton University Press.

Chatterjee, Partha 1993: *The Nation and its Fragments: Colonial and Postcolonial Histories*. Princeton: Princeton University Press.

Conrad, Joseph 1901/1990: *The Heart of Darkness*. New York: Bantam Classics.

Delathuy, A. M. 1988: *De Geheime Documenten van de Onderzoekscommissie in de Congostaat*. Berchem: EPO.

Deutsche Welle 2006: "Dutch-Only Bid Stirs Angry Debate," DW-World.DE, January 25; www.dw-world.de/dw/article/0,2144,1870753,00.html.

Essed, Philomena 1991: *Understanding Everyday Racism: An Interdisciplinary Theory*. Newbury Park, CA: Sage.

Essed, Philomena 2008: "Foreword," in Darlene Clarke Hine, Trica Danielle Keaton, and Stephen Small (eds.), *Black Europe and the African Diaspora*. Urbana: University of Illinois Press.

Evens Foundation 2002: *Europe's New Racism: Causes, Manifestations, and Solutions*. Oxford: Berghahn Books.

Fabian, Johannes 2000: *Out of Our Minds: Reason and Madness in the Exploration of Central Africa*. Berkeley: University of California Press.

Finkelstein, Norman 2000: *The Holocaust Industry: Reflections on the Exploitation of Jewish Suffering*. New York: Verso.

Fischer, Sibylle 2004: *Modernity Disavowed: Haiti and the Culture of Slavery in the Age of Revolution*. Durham, NC: Duke University Press.

Foucault, Michel 2003: *"Society Must Be Defended": Lectures at the Collège de France, 1975–76*. Trans. David Macey. New York: Picador.

Friedman, Thomas 2002: "If It's a Muslim Problem, It Needs a Muslim Solution," *New York Times*, July 8; www.nytimes.com/2005/07/08/opinion/ 08friedman.html?hp.

Gikandi, Simon 2005: "Picasso, Africa, and the Schemata of Difference," in Sarah Nuttall (ed.), *Beautiful Ugly: African and Diaspora Aesthetics*. Cape Town and The Hague: Kwela Books and Prince Claus Fund Library, pp. 30–59.

Gilroy, Paul 2000: *Against Race: Imagining Political Culture Beyond the Color Line.* Cambridge, MA: Harvard University Press.

Goldberg, David Theo 2004: "The Power of Tolerance," in Tony Kushner and Nadia Alman (eds.), *Philosemitism, Antisemitism and "the Jews": Perspectives from the Middle Ages to the Twentieth Century.* Aldershot: Ashgate, pp. 31–48.

Goodey, Jo 2007: "Racist Violence in Europe: Challenges for Official Data Collection," *Ethnic and Racial Studies,* 30, (July), 570–89.

Gregory, Derek 2004: *The Colonial Present.* Oxford: Blackwell.

Habermas, Jürgen 1989: "On the Public Use of History," in Shierry Nicholsen (ed.), *The New Conservatism: Cultural Criticism and the Historians.* Cambridge, MA: MIT Press.

Hesse, Barnor 2007: "Racialized Modernity: An Analytics of White Mythologies," *Ethnic and Racial Studies,* 30, 4 (July), 643–63.

Hinton, Patrick Laban 2002: *Annihilating Difference: The Anthropology of Genocide.* Berkeley: University of California Press.

Hondius, Dienke 2003: "'Become Like Us': The Dutch and Racism," *openDemocracy,* March 12; www.opendemocracy.net/debates/article-10–96–1616.jsp.

Horkheimer, Max and Adorno, Theodor 1979: *Dialectic of Enlightenment.* Trans. John Cumming. London: Verso.

Hunter, Shirleen, ed. 2002: *Islam, Europe's Second Religion: The New Social, Cultural, and Political Landscape.* Westport, CT: Praeger.

Hurvitz, Nimrod, ed. 2005: "Muslims in Europe" (Special Issue), *Haggar: Studies in Culture, Polity and Identities,* 6, 1, 1–135.

Hussain, Nasser 2003: *The Jurisprudence of Emergency.* Ann Arbor: University of Michigan Press.

Jones, Tamara 2005: "Among the Young of Multiethnic Leeds, a Hardening Hatred, Racial Resentment, Lack of Opportunity are Shaping a Generation, Experts Fear," *Washington Post,* Wednesday, July 20, A14; www.washingtonpost. com/wp-dyn/content/article/2005/07/19/AR2005071901784_pf.html.

Kant, Immanuel 1763/1960: *Observations on the Feeling of the Beautiful and the Sublime.* Trans. J. T. Goldthwait. Berkeley: University of California Press.

Koechler, Hans 1996: "Muslim–Christian Ties in Europe: Past, Present and Future," *IPO Research Papers. Second International Seminar on Civilizational Dialogue:* "Japan, Islam and the West," Kuala Lumpur, September 2–3; i-p-o.org/ ice.htm.

Kumar, Krishnan 2002: "The Nation-State, the European Union, and Transnational Identities," in Nezar Al-Sayyad and Manuel Castells (eds.), *Muslim Europe or Euro-Islam: Politics, Culture, and Citizenship in the Age of Globalization.* Lanham, MD: Lexington Books, pp. 53–68.

Kundnani, Arun 2002: "The Death of Multiculturalism," *IRRNews* (Independent Race and Refugee News Network), April 1; www.itt.org.uk/april/ak000001.html.

Levi, Neil and Rothberg, Michael, eds. 2003: *The Holocaust: Theoretical Readings.* Edinburgh: Edinburgh University Press.

Long, Gideon 2006: "Survey Highlights Deprivation of British Muslims," October 6, 2006; news.yahoo.com/s/nm/20061006/india_nm/india271083.

Longman, Jere 2006: "Surge in Racist Mood Raises Concerns on Eve of World Cup," *New York Times*, Sunday, June 4; www.nytimes.com/2006/06/04/sports/soccer/04racism.html?th&emc=th.

Loomba, Ania 2002: *Shakespeare, Race, and Colonialism*. Oxford: Oxford University Press.

Lowe, Lisa 2009: *The Intimacies of the Four Continents*. Durham, NC: Duke University Press, forthcoming.

Macmaster, Neil 2001: *Racism in Europe, 1870–2000*. London: Palgrave Macmillan.

Marechal, Brigitte et al., eds. 2003: *Muslims in the Enlarged Europe*. Leiden: Brill.

Michaels, Anne 1996: *Fugitive Pieces*. New York: Vintage Books.

Milios, John 2005: "European Integration as a Vehicle of Neoliberal Hegemony," in Alfredo Saad-Filho and Deborah Johnston (eds.), *Neoliberalism: A Critical Reader*. London: Pluto Press, pp. 208–14.

Mustafa, Hala 2002: "Islam and the West in an Era of Globalization: Clash of Civilization or Coexistence," in Nezar Al-Sayyad and Manuel Castells (eds.), *Muslim Europe or Euro-Islam: Politics, Culture, and Citizenship in the Age of Globalization*. Lanham, MD: Lexington Books, pp. 91–112.

New York Times 2005: "Australian Mobs Attack People Believed to be of Arab Descent," Tuesday, December 13; www.nytimes.com/2005/12/13/international/asia/13australia.html.

Patterson, Thomas 1997: *Inventing Western Civilization*. New York: Monthly Review Press.

Pedersen, Lars 1999: *Newer Islamic Movements in Western Europe*. Aldershot: Ashgate.

Pew Research Center 2005: "Islamic Extremism: Common Concern for Muslim and Western Publics' Support for Terror Wanes Among Muslim Publics," July 14; pewglobal.org/reports/display.php?ReportID=248.

Phillips, Caryl 1987: *The European Tribe*. London: Faber and Faber.

Pigeon, Gerard 1996: "Black Icons of Colonialism: African Characters in French Children's Comic Strip Literature," *Social Identities: Journal for the Study of Race, Nation and Culture*, 2, 1 (February), 135–60.

Potts, Nina Marie 2006: "Code of Conduct for Immigrants Leads to Tension in Rotterdam," *VOA News*, February 14; www.voanews.com/english/2006-02-14-voa48.cfm.

Raphael-Hernandez, Heike 2004: *Blackening Europe: The African American Presence*. London: Routledge.

Royal Belgium Museum of Central Africa, Tervuren 2005: "Memory of Congo: The Colonial Era," An Exhibition; www.congo2005.be/geheugen/frameset.php?page=tentoonstelling.php&lang=en&menu=1.

Santner, Eric 2004: "On Creaturely Life: From Rilke to Celan," Plenary Lecture to the Seminar in Experimental Critical Theory on Psychoanalysis and Politics,

University of California Humanities Research Institute, August 26. Copy on file.

Sciolino, Elaine 2005: "Immigrants' Dreams Mix with Fury in a Gray Place Near Paris," *New York Times*, Monday, December 12, A1, 12.

Sciolino, Elaine 2007: "Immigration, Black Sheep and Swiss Rage," *New York Times*, Monday, October 8, A1, 8.

Smith, Craig S. 2005: "France Has an Underclass, but its Roots are Still Shallow," *New York Times*, November 6; www.nytimes.com/2005/11/06/weekinreview/06smith.html.

Smith, Craig S. 2006: "Poor and Muslim? Jewish? Soup Kitchen is Not for You," *New York Times*, February 28, A4.

Spiegel 2006: "Holland's New Greeting for Immigrants: 'If It Ain't Dutch, It Ain't Much'," *Spiegel Blog*, January 24; service.spiegel.de/cache/international/0,1518,397021,00.html.

Stoler, Ann L. 1995: *Race and the Education of Desire*. Durham, NC: Duke University Press.

Toporowski, Jan 2005: "Neoliberalism: The Eastern European Frontier," in Alfredo Saad-Filho and Deborah Johnston (eds.), *Neoliberalism: A Critical Reader*. London: Pluto Press, pp. 215–21.

Veenkamp, Theo 2004: "After Tolerance," *openDemocracy*, November 24; www.opendemocracy.net/arts-multiculturalism/article_2239.jsp.

Vertovec, Steve and Peach, Ceri, eds. 1997: *Islam in Europe: The Politics of Religion and Community*. London: Macmillan.

Žižek, Slavoj 2002: "Are We in a War? Do We Have an Enemy?" *London Review of Books*, 23 May; www.lrb.co.uk/v24/n10/zize01_.html.

6

Revealing Alchemies
(On Racial Latinamericanization)

. . . the more the Negro [in Brazil] repudiates his African connections, the more he comes to be like Europeans, but in a modest, inoffensive way, the more we have to do with him.
Quoted in Pierson, *Negroes in Brazil,* 1942

The US, Latin America, and South Africa represent three prominent instances of making worlds anew. Israel/Palestine is another case, though as indicated above one less acknowledged as a deeply racially inscribed one. For each of these world-makings, race has played a constitutive and defining role. For the US and South Africa historically, and now in the Israeli–Palestinian instance, segregation was formalized, if in differentiated ways; for Latin America, not unlike Europe, social and residential segregations were largely informal, reproduced through subtle elisions in the alchemical transitions to nationhood alongside socio-economic standing and choices thus enabled or disabled. Chapters 3 and 4 covered *racial americanization* and *palestinianization* respectively. *Racial europeanization* was elaborated in the previous chapter. I focus here on the various ways Latin America has embodied race and extended racisms, while turning to *southafricanization* in the chapter that follows.

Racial Latinamericanization

Latin America. The region of intense *métissage,* of *mestizaje,* of *mesticagem,* indeed, of the very conception. And of an imaginary conjuring it in the first place. Histories of ethnoracial mixtures and categorical transgression, forced and facilitated. Culturally repressed and resisted. Even as they became practiced, projected, and celebrated as national character in the post-abolitionist period. Categorical transgression morphed into mainstream identity. In some regional nation-states more so than others.

Latin America projected itself, at least ideologically, as nation-building through the racial mosaic, by making nations in the name of constituting the new national character distinctly as racial *metis*. Brazil's Gilberto Freyre the national if not hemispheric voice of *mesticagem/mestizaje* as national identity. Settler-dominated Southern Africa, by contrast, pursued nation-building quite explicitly by racial elevation and restriction, through the insistence on and against the resistances, local and global, to white self-elevation and enduring supremacy.

In the Brazilian case the project of "racial democracy" has been most explicit. It has meant celebration of a new, miscegenated "Brazilian" race amalgamating the prevailing populations of Europeans, Africans, and Indians into a novel composite lauded as the best of all three groups, of their worlds. The standards of this newly crafted "race," biologically and culturally, politically and economically, however, were seen to be set by and on the terms of white European descendants. Thus even as the Brazilian project of racial democracy took itself to be opening up to hybridity and its virtues, the terms of engagement and elevation, success and satisfaction remained deeply indexed to the presumptive superiority of European stock. Those not European were to be lifted up – elevated – through racial mixing with Europeans, newly solicited immigrants from continental Europe. European immigration was to be dramatically expanded so as to dilute the local ethnoracial impact of such mixing, biologically and culturally comprehended. Fool's gold mixed in the right proportions with high-quality gold on this picture produces, well, a distinctly national treasure, a precious "mettle" Freyre would later call a "new race."

This latter model generally conceived, with specific national qualifications and characterizations prompted by local historical and social contexts, is applicable across Latin America. The post-abolition mandate to fuse indigenous with existing Africans whose presence was facilitated by slave legacies into the dominant European demographic was supposed to produce a harmonious and dynamic body politic as much socio-politically and culturally as biologically for most if not all Latin American societies. *Mestizaje*, supposedly melding the color and culture of Afro-Indians with the presumed intellectual and political prowess of Europeans, was pushed as the New World's organic answer to the challenges facing twentieth-century modernity.

Legacies of Latin slavery

Latin American societies solidified themselves, if variably, through the deadly and debilitating sufferings of racially driven slavery. Brazilian slavery was no less awful than its racially prompted and promoted experiences and legacies elsewhere, throughout Latin America or more largely. There was less public and arguably religious inhibition to sexual intercourse than in the US, and more openness to self-purchased manumission, to be sure. But the violence inherent in the very structure of racially inscribed slave society certainly spread across the region. Race marked the new Americas from the founding – the "discovering" – moment, as Quijano remarks, a generative condition of modernity not just in the region but for emergent Europe as well. Race across the region identified not just African slaves but fashioned the debate around the enslavability of indigenous Indians also.

Later, the sub-continent came to characterize itself largely in the aftermath of abolition as the region of "the Latin race" (*la raza Latina*, in the hispano-centric version of it). The "Latin race," drawing together those across the region emergently identifying itself as Latin America, were contrasted explicitly with members of the "Saxon race" supposedly so clearly tied to the United States. What followed slavery's formal demise, however, is more telling of the regional distinction.

Abolition in Latin America spanned much of the nineteenth century, coming comparatively early to some but late to other countries. Argentina abolished slavery as early as 1813, Colombia in 1821, after quite widespread maroon revolt and the impact of free-living *cimarrones* communities. Guatemala followed suit in 1822, Chile and Costa Rica in 1824, Mexico in 1829, and Bolivia in 1831, all before the much celebrated British abolition throughout its empire in 1833–4. Panamanian and Venezuelan abolition followed 20 years later, in 1852 and 1854 respectively (also the year of Peru's abolition). The Dutch abolished slavery throughout their colonial holdings in 1863, slavery in Puerto Rico, still under Spanish rule, lasted another 10 years, and in Cuba until 1886. Brazil, so self-celebrated for its later experiment in "racial democracy," left slavery to linger as late as 1888, giving pause about claims of the benign Brazilian racial experience in slavery's later years and in the wake of its demise.

How, after abolition, did Latin American countries conceive both what Benedict Anderson has characterized as the "political viability" of the nation and its "emotional plausibility"? In commenting upon Anderson's significant silences, Thomas Holt questions how race factored into Latin America's political viability and emotional plausibility. In short, how did race factor into the remaking of modern Latin America? What constitutes the reach of the national *familia*, not just the administrative but the affective threads drawing and holding together the familial and the familiar into effective, productive, viable but also assertively repressive collective agency?

Like Europe, and in some ways deeply related in fact, Latin America came to conceive of itself as a region in the mid-nineteenth century considerably in and through the prism of racial terms. As Aims McGuinness reveals, the "Latin race" took itself to be the socio-cultural group emanating from the Latin-rooted countries of Europe, in contrast with those of supposedly Anglo-Saxon or German background. Here race comes to mean connection to background, comprehended phenotypically, culturally, ethnonationally, "spiritually," and emotionally, in short, dispositionally. Here, racial comprehension is the result and response of lineage historically reinscribed and contemporarily restated.

Counting by race, as the past two to three decades have definitively revealed, at the very least is acutely awkward. Categorical contours are loose, racial reference more often than not contradictory, individual bio-histories even where available murky, mixture more widespread than even individuals themselves realize or understand. The Latin American profile provides a more acute exemplification of these warnings than most everywhere else. The data for indigenous and African populations in the region are less than complete or reliable, skewing dramatically in the direction of their respective undercounts. Accordingly, their interests are discounted in the provision and distribution of state resources such as health care, employment, and schooling. Even more deeply, the law fails to recognize and so give standing more or less throughout the region to indigenous and black populations as such.

Notwithstanding the challenges of enumeration, there is a revealing correlation across Latin America between a state's date of abolition and the relative size of the African-descended population remaining today. With all the relevant qualifications for counting by race, the earlier abolition by a state in the region, the lower tends to be the black or mixed black proportion of the respective state demographic today – or even a century ago.

Thus the Southern Cone societies of Argentina, Chile, and Uruguay have virtually no black populations to speak of, certainly no coherent African-descended groups, while Colombia's black population is just 4 percent. The "*mulatto*" populations (mixed black and white) of the Southern Cone countries hover between 1 and 2 percent at most (Mexico's is only 3 percent), while Colombia's is a considerable 22 percent. By contrast, Cuba, Venezuela, and Brazil, the latest comers to the virtues of abolition, have black populations of 11, 9, and almost 30 percent, and mixed proportions of 51, 38 and less than 15 percent respectively. While these numbers may differ from one study to another, every study (and most notably wherever official state demographics count in these terms) consistently reveals much higher rates in the relevant categories for the latter group of states than the former.

Some might argue that these differences have to do with the fact that societies abolishing slavery significantly later left considerably more time for importation of African slaves, their reproduction and resultant sexual exploitation upon arrival, and so the higher proportions are to be expected. But while part of an explanation, this is less than compelling, revealing just one side of the story. For one, slave trading was outlawed for the most part decades earlier than slave abolition outright, especially in the latter cluster of countries. More significant though is the substantial evidence that freed black populations in countries like Argentina were self-consciously wiped out. The African or African-descended population there just prior to abolition was close to or more than half (depending on the source). Argentinean rulers made a deliberate decision to decimate blacks in the population, largely by having them serve on the front lines of devastating mid-century wars with its neighbors. Today, the black percentage of Argentina's population is effectively zero. The experiences in Chile and Mexico, while perhaps not quite as vicious, are comparable.

The significantly smaller African-descended populations accordingly were by and large rendered invisible through mixture, most notably with indigenous people. And indigenous populations too had been decimated early in the historical experience of European colonization, by a mix of literally being worked to death and succumbing to the introduction of foreign illness for which they had built up little or no physical resistance. Before the introduction of African slavery, the indigenous served as disposable manual labor, to use Anibal Quijano's accurate characterization, suffering as much from debilitating labor demands early on while slaves and then indentured serfs as from conquistador invasion and invasive disease.

Where small African-descended populations have survived intact in Latin American countries they have tended to be highly concentrated in more remote parts of the country – the coastal areas of Colombia, the northwest coast of Ecuador, the plains of Venezuela, the Caribbean coast of Costa Rica but the Pacific coasts of the other Central Americas, and so on. The remoteness of these self-contained pockets is a legacy of marronage, the escape to relatively inaccessible areas by black slaves where maroon communities formed, even thrived, often interacting and sometimes intermarrying with indigenous Indians, and from which resistance struggles against slaveholding colonizers and settlers were launched. These remote hideaways were made spaces of self-liberation, of freedom, of self-determination. They became, in short, spaces of self-proclaimed origination, self-making, self-assertion. Flight, resistance, rebellion, liberation, and self-determination date to the earliest appearance of slave populations at the outset of the sixteenth century. The Haitian Revolution is perhaps the most notable instance of this striving for freedom, but examples dot the history of modern Latin America and the Caribbean. Yet, as Torres and Whitten point out, and the case of Haiti sadly exemplifies, these strivings invariably found themselves subject to the threat of counter-attack, restriction, retrenchment, and persecution.

By the late eighteenth century consciously adopted policies of national whitening were afoot, promoting large-scale European immigration, "amalgamation" of Indians and existing *mestizos/mesticos* with whites, cultural assimilation and civic education. Brazil's now widely remarked post-abolition experiment in producing an assertively European-dominated mixed "Brazilian race" as the new national character had a century-old root in other Latin American societies. The Euro-whitening of Argentina, Chile, Uruguay, and later Brazil constituted a foundation stone of state modernization in each instance, a modernizing tied to emerging republicanism, expanding nationalism, and increasingly exercised militarization. If the "anglicizing" of North America was to produce a "New England," the "latinizing" of the Americas undertook more self-consciously to alchemize the "base metals" of Africans and Indians and the already existing local mixtures into the new "Latin race" through the magic of Euro-catalysis (fueled, ironically, by promoting immigration largely from Northern and Central Europe).

The Americas are unique (alongside Australasia and arguably apartheid South Africa) among racially regionalized colonialisms promoted by European globalization and imperial design in acting forcefully to establish white *majority* settler societies. Throughout Africa and Asia, white settlers remained distinct if ruling minorities, requiring force, violence, severe repression, and the guile of false promises to sustain minoritized racial rule.

The Americas pursued a different tack, equally vicious and violent, but with a distinct and deadly outcome. They involved decimating indigenous Indian and African populations. The former were decimated early in the colonizing of the region, as I indicated above, in the process of securing European hegemony. The latter were dramatically diminished first under conditions of life-shortening enslavement, and then more pointedly following abolition in order to institute and secure white control legitimated as majority rule.

In the eighteenth and early nineteenth centuries in Latin America and the Caribbean, more African women were imported as slaves than there were European women migrating or indeed than imports of African male slaves. The colonial presence of European women at the time was relatively rare. In the first centuries of European colonization of the Americas, European men largely came in search of wealth rather than to settle. They quickly gained formal control of virtually all aspects of the local social order. Given the limited availability of European women as potential partners, they "freely" availed themselves of slave concubines whose resistance, in the majority of cases where affectionate ties didn't prompt or sustain the relationships, could only be enacted on pain of death or significant harm, including rape, thus belying Freyre's once-celebrated thesis of generous treatment by Portuguese men in Brazil of sexually promiscuous slave women. For some women, no doubt, the stressful calculation must have been between significant physical harm and the favors of sexual service, both sides of the balance sheet producing severe psychological distress.

The result, in many instances, was mixed offspring, a fact mitigating prima facie against white majority rule. In contrast to the US, mixed offspring were freed in Latin America, even as their mothers remained enslaved and ensnared in desperately unequal and iniquitous relationships. Indeed, "mottled" offspring, not to put too crude an exclamation on the practice and product, were written into paternal property inheritance, while their slave mothers were excluded, thus creating as much a bifurcated regime of wealth accumulation as psycho-emotional identification and its attendant melancholia.

Slave women could be manumitted largely via the self-effort of buying their own freedom, once a bit older and less desirable sexually and as productive workers. The proceeds for self-purchase – for that's effectively what it was – were produced from minor trading, manufacturing, and selling wares at market. Men were less likely to be freed, or to be allowed to self-manumit (and in any case less likely to have the means), for their physical labor was more likely to linger longer and to become more experienced with accumulated knowledge and skills. As they aged, they would become more trusted interlocutors often, serving as intermediaries or minor foremen for younger workers. As slave men survived over time in the same environment, then, they were likely to acquire more trust to serve slave owners' interests as guards, goons, and guardians. And later in life, men were more able to reproduce slave offspring as needed by slavers and arguably less likely to require the costs of medical care to the same degree as women. At the same time, African-background women married later, if they married at all, being deemed less desirable, more likely married non-black men, and bore fewer children. All this led to a diminishing demographic growth of African-background populations throughout Latin America.

Latin American Indians were mostly if ambivalently read as noble savages, as what Europeans might have been in more primitive times. From the earliest moments of colonization in the Americas they were seen accordingly as salvageable through conversion, as amalgamable through procreation, as assimilable through culture. The fact that Indians were less readily enslavable from the earliest moments of Iberian colonization reveals their slightly heightened status in the great chain of being in contrast with Africans. But this somewhat elevated status was quickly undercut by the fact that Indians, if not enslaved, were nevertheless reduced to no more than the status of serf peasantry, and treated accordingly. In terms of potential inputs for racial mixture, Indians were deemed the source of *mestizos*, and as such evaporable through *blanqueamiento*. In these terms, by contrast, black Africans were considered initially less as noble than as savage, as animal-like, to be used to do animal work, beasts of nature doing the work of nature, as unamalgamable and inassimilable.

More or less until abolition, mixed offspring were taken by Europeans largely as the source of degeneracy, in keeping with prevailing racial views. This view gave way slowly and awkwardly as mixed sexual intercourse and the resultant offspring multiplied, as social intercourse to some degree ameliorated fixed ideas of inferiority, and as *mestizaje* was increasingly elevated as acceptable, then appealing, and at last as a form – even the prevailing form – of national identity. While whites, blacks, and Indians were conceived as non-mixed, as not *mestizo* in the more generic meaning of the term, members of the latter two groups could be mobilized as materials for *mestizaje*, for mixing. Ultimately, blacks – like Indians – were projected to disappear into the general population. Whiteness, by contrast, was set aside in the various social imaginaries as the symbol and standard of intellectual prowess and moral virtue, the milk and sugar that made the coffee sweet and palatable. The history of *Casta* painting reveals that this represents a social commitment with a long historical tail.

Casta *characterization*

The history of *Casta* paintings offers a cultural window into the ambiguating sensibilities at work here, as Ilona Katzew's insightful book on the subject helps to reveal. *Casta* paintings were largely a phenomenon of Mexico, flourishing from roughly 1760 to 1790, before abolition set in, that is. They were a popularizing bourgeois extension of the Latin American colonial practice of *retratos*, of seeking social status through portraiture. But they served also as a reflection and cultural reification of the widespread practice among Spanish and Creole locals in the area to rank racially, to place people in the ranked order of caste according to their perceived or intuited percentage of white (Spanish), indigenous (Indian), and black (African) heritage (or "blood").

The paintings on the surface are edenic family portraits almost invariably of husband, wife, and single child (or occasionally two children) in domestic settings or scenes of nature. They reveal the order of racial rankings explicitly by characteristic inscriptions describing the racial typification of parents and the consequent racial characterization of the child offspring. But they reiterate also the relative usualness of such mixing – by century's close, Pat Seed calculates, fully a quarter of Mexico's population was mixed – and the fading of at least robust formal state restriction, even in the face of social status long tied to European preferences for "purity of blood" (*limpieza de sangre/limpeza de sangue*).

This erosion of censure was long in the making, to be sure, tempering the sometimes severe restrictions on Indian, African, and *Casta* populations well into the eighteenth century. Race mixing came to be common enough, the informal social rejection probably aimed more directly at the offspring than the fact of miscegenating intercourse, which seemed irrepressible.

The standard table of the range of racially revealing inscriptions can be broken into three kinds: white/Spaniard mixing with Indian, of which there are three variations; white/Spaniard mixing with black, of which there are four variations; and Indian mixing with black, of which there are eight variations. The relative acceptance of such mixes at the time was sustained by the elevated standing of white Europeans in relation first to Indians and then to blacks in any standard historical racial hierarchy. The increase in supposed types of mixtures as the "great chain of being" is "descended" perhaps suggests the presumption of fecundity associated with cultures of color. The actual labels typifying the offspring are a poignant mix, in retrospect, of humor and horror.

Here are the three variations from the first category, whites mixing with Indians:

- From Spaniard and Indian, a *Mestizo* is Born.
- From Spaniard and *Mestiza*, a *Castizo* is Born.
- From *Castizo* and Spaniard, a Spaniard is Born.

The use of "Spaniard" (in contrast to, say, "Spanish") conveys the collapsing of national character into racial expression, so widespread in Enlightenment European circles of the day. Notice nevertheless the more subtle, if equally conventional, gendered determination of the rankings of the resultant offspring. A male Spaniard mixing with a *mestiza* woman whose own background mixture in these terms is Spaniard and Indian would produce a *castizo* (or light-skinned *mestizo*) child, one just one-quarter Spaniard (in terms of the presumptuous calculations of racial blood quantum). But a male one-quarter Spaniard (*castizo*) mixing with a female Spaniard will produce an offspring ranked as Spaniard, even though in supposedly ethnoracial terms the Spaniard percentage involved in the latter mix (0.5 plus 0.125) is less than that in the case of a *castizo* offspring (0.5 plus 0.25). In the production of "Spaniardness," male input seems to carry greater potency. A male Spaniard, it would seem to follow, was presumed more ethnoracially fertile than a female one.

From the second category, white or Spaniard mixing with black, we find the following variations, revealing the referential awkwardness and evaluative redirections:

- From Spaniard and Black, a *Mulatto* is Born.
- From Spaniard and *Mulatto*, a *Morisco* is Born.
- From Spaniard and *Morisca*, an Albino is Born.
- From Spaniard and Albino, a Return-Backwards is Born.

Here too there is gendered inequity. Albinos, that more or less uncategorizable class, bleached white on the outside but somehow marked by blackness beneath the visible exterior, are a product of male Spaniard and a woman herself a mix of Spaniard and Spaniard–black parents. (Spaniard–black mixes are termed *morisco*, or light-skinned *mulatto*, the former term derivable from *moros*, or Moor/Muslim.) Following the logic of Spaniard–Indian mix above, one would expect a Spaniard and *morisco* to produce a Spaniard (0.5 plus 0.25 plus 0.125 Spaniard with but 0.125 black). But it produces in this scheme of things the anomaly of albino. A touch of black in a sea of whiteness threatens degeneracy.

If the hint of blackness, in a sense a drop of black blood – just one-eighth in the perverse calculation of proportionalities – is so potentially powerful, what does it say about the presumed racial powerlessness of whiteness? And even more revealingly, the mix of Spaniard with the presumed degeneracy of albino produces a seemingly unsalvageable degenerate, one a couple of degrees more removed even, the "return-backwards," represented figuratively in the paintings as what in the 1950s would have been characterized pejoratively as "Mongoloid" or today as a person with Down Syndrome. The sense whiteness has of its self-elevation and superiority is fragile indeed.

From the third set of mixtures, Indians and blacks, symbolic animalization appears, a function of the biologizing assumptions driving the racial hierarchies at work and of the related color analogies at play:

- From Indian and Black, a Wolf is Born.
- From Indian and *Mestiza*, a Coyote is Born.
- From Wolf and Black, a Chino is Born.
- From Chino and Indian, a *Cambujo* is Born.
- From *Cambujo* and Indian, a Hold-Yourself-in-Midair is Born.
- From Hold-Yourself-in-Midair and *Mulatto*, an *Albarazado* is Born.
- From *Albarazado* and Indian, a *Barcino* is Born.
- From *Barcino* and *Cambuja*, a *Calpamulato* is Born.

That the mix of Indian with black produces a "wolf" as offspring has to do both with the thought that the wolf is imagined to be a hybrid animal, a mix of the dog and cat families, and with the reddish-black coloring of the animal. Similarly with "coyote," where the coloring references a yellowish-gray skin hue, and "chino" (derivative from "Chinois"), the shading of whom is taken to be yellow-brown. *Cambujo*, by contrast, is considered swarthy and dark-skinned, resulting from the darkening mix of black and deepened red.

The quaintness of the category "hold-yourself-in-midair" momentarily draws attention away from the insidious racial implications usually affiliated with animalization. An offspring 7/8 Indian and 1/8 black, "hold-yourself-in-midair" signals the floating in air betwixt and between categories, the insertion of blackness and the unknowability of the precise outcome restricting the otherwise relative hierarchical elevation and advancement that is the prospect of full-blooded Indians.

By the same token, an *albarazado* (a mix just under half-Indian, a little more than a quarter black and a quarter white) was widely characterized as white-spotted or one sick with leprosy, indicating the implication, quite widespread at the time, that any mixture made offspring prone to illness, to the physical and intellectual failings of degeneration. A *barcino* quickly recalls animalization, taking its name from an animal with a brown or reddish white coat or hair with black spots – the examples cited are pigs, dogs, cows, or cats. As a person, a *barcino* is one whose hair is a mix of white, brown, and reddish, reflecting the perceived racial inputs. And finally, a *calpamulato* is one whose physical features tend towards black. The name derives from the region of Calpan where *mulattos* more readily mixed with Indians local to the area.

There are a number of generalizations to note about the genre. First, the overall schematism shaping *Casta*-characterization is an amalgam, hardly consistent or systematic. The categories emerged over time in the referential sociality of everyday life, revealing the underlying dispositions, prejudices, relational rationalities, abjections, anxieties, attractions, desires, cruelties, even humor if not derision. But laced through all of this, holding it together as a schematism of sorts, is the thick racial history of the region, in all its concrete determinations. There is, at the heart here, a sort of horrified fascination, a repellent attraction to interracial intercourse, structured as it is in dominance.

And yet while not always seen as desirable, such mixing came to be more and more usual, increasingly acceptable, and in the end (as slave history later gives way to self-conscious nation-building) it proved to be quite definitive. By the close of the nineteenth century it began to be postulated as national ideal. One might even say regional character. *Casta* paintings, then, illustrate from early on the proliferation of racial categories for which Brazil, especially, and Latin America, more broadly, later came to be so well known.

Second, the representation of poverty predictably grows more evident in the paintings as the scale "descends" through what, in keeping with the characterization of the times, one might call the scale of racial being. So the paintings increasingly exhibit tattered clothing, forlorn and labor-weary dispositions as well as impoverished food in representations of the various mixes of Indian and black offspring. In similar vein, the finery of fashion and fare in the paintings of Spaniard mixes with whomever give way to background figures of scrawny mules in the case of mixes involving *mulatto*es. Race and class mirror as they constrain each other.

The animalizing symbolics play out similarly in the relatively common inclusion of parrots in the paintings. While identified since at least the beginning of the sixteenth century as natural to the local habitat, parrots, of course, are birds of mimicry, most notably regarding speech. The appearance of the parrot suggests that the linguistic and cultural expressions of the offspring can be no more than a copy-culture by the non-European in seeking the elevation of European status. David Hume makes this representation explicit in likening a learned Jamaican to a parrot, "who speaks a few words plainly."

It is revealing, then, that the mark of blackness in *Casta* paintings is often metaphorically literalized. Many mixed women whose skin tone is painted as especially white will have a large dark black dot planted at the temple, a visible reminder of the social bruise of blackness even where skin color has been so toned down as seemingly to enable evasiveness of the racial hold.

We nevertheless find ironically embedded in these regional schemas of racial relationality a more generalizable indication of the *fragility* of whiteness hinted at above. Even as whiteness projects itself, and is projected and experienced, as powerful, as awe-inspiring and awesome, cracks cut to its foundations. Its insecurities speak to its unsurety about its sources and extensions of its power(s), about the easiness of its pollution (just a drop here and there of the oily or dark stuff and there it goes in flames), about its potential implosiveness. At once arrogant and aggressive, whiteness sees itself readily undercut and undermined by the force and fraud of its otherness, easily threatened by the guile of those out to get it but also by the mix of its own lack of agility and responsiveness in the face of challenges from else-where and other-wise. It requires self-proclaimed and -promoting privilege to sustain its privilege, self-declaration to convince itself and others of its elevation, self-assertion in the face of threats to its being and wellbeing, of pushing back from below. Its belonging in any place is a mix of its claim to that place and its longing to sustain itself in and at the head of the place it claims. Its animalization of mixes from which it is absent renders it even more anxious, for in its absence it absents itself from the hushed tones of life outside its circles, of challenges to its hegemony and planned revolts to overturn its power. Racially self-ascribed power is always beset by its paranoid projection that the natives may be getting restless.

So, in short, the repetitive assertion of power and aggression, of assertive domination and cruel suppression, of the thrill of power's expression and the exhilaration of violence are meant to cement the cracks against further erosion, more vivid threats, and even deeper fragility. Yet in its deepening isolation it simply animates the sense of threat, cementing the cycle.

This fragility is offset by a number of compensations. First, the gendering generation of the racial schematism, outlined above, orders the possibility of the paintings' mentality. The *Casta* paintings portray the mixing characters in domestic settings, very often in the kitchen with the woman cooking, or in idyllic garden environments not at all unusual in family portraiture. Women may be "racially elevated" in ranking over the men in some instances, in social conditions generally as much as in specific instances of the paintings, so the stereotypical characterization of white men dominating black women does not hold in these cases. But as I have noted, the *"racial productivity"* of women in such racial elevations is undercut in contrast with the power of white men in these mixtures.

Second, at work in the *Casta* paintings, as in racial regards more generally, is the implicit reference always to the racial outside. If the perceived productivity of racial intercourse, of all kinds, is its elevation of the lesser interlocutor in the relation, the racial outside sets to work the threat of the unmixed because unmixable, the racial barbarian always beyond redemption, civilization, and so upliftment via amalgamation. An ultimately necessary grounding of racism's history of expression, perhaps even of its expressibility, the racial outside is figured in Latin American iconography as the "Barbarian Meco Indians." These are represented as hostile, untrustworthy warriors, going about largely naked and inscribed with ritualistic facial tattoos emphasizing their fierceness. They are heathens beyond reach. A minor part of the *Casta* canon, the best-known paintings by Miguel Cabrera from the 1760s and Ramon Torres from 1780 depict "heathen Indians" and "barbarian Indians" respectively. The object of repeated, incessant, and futile calculations to convert, they leave administrators frustrated, even bewildered. What to do with the "Wild Man"?

One indication has to do with the twofold characterization of "the Indian" in Latin American representation. On one hand, the wild ones were seen as uncontainable wanderers, undesirable workers less because lazy than because unreliable, here one day and gone the next, warriors whose violence and viciousness know no limits, given to using the human skulls of their victims as drinking cups. There is – there should be – no mixing here. But there is at play, in the end more or less decisively, also a counter-view. This is one of the Indian as salvageable, assimilable, available to the possibility of civilizability and convertibility, of pastoral labor. Skilled in the agricultural and hunting arts, to be sure, these skills could be put to work nevertheless in ways that could be marshaled to the use of conventional farming and warfare. It is this latter character that makes for mixing.

Given the fragility of whiteness, the ambiguities about Indianness, and the ambivalences about blackness, a pressing question arises: How is it in the case of Latin America that the projection of racial mixing came to amount to national, even regional, self-characterization?

Dipesh Chakrabarty characterizes almost hegemonic historical accounts of the nation-state in India as emulating – mimicking – the dominant European Enlightenment narrative of developmentalism from subjection to liberal citizenship. The universal march of history was to be represented by the path taken by European nation-states from feudal and absolutist regimes to the triumphal progressivism of bourgeois liberal citizenship. Europe's experience provided the model and the goal, inspiration and telos for universal emulation. Even for the politico-theological insistence that historical telos is always at work. European settler societies (Chakrabarty explicitly speaks of India, but his implication – and mine – is far broader) ultimately embody two broad classes: An elite whose culture and habits, education and civilities aspire at least to the European, and are in that sense "modernizing." And a peasantry or largely indentured class who are not yet modernized, as Chakrabarty formulates it.

Local details of course differ, but the critical account Chakrabarty develops is broadly applicable, notably to both the Latin American and South African cases with which I am concerned here and in the following chapter. The overwhelming proportion of elites in the case of India turned out to be indigenous. Those in Latin America and Southern Africa were by and large limited to the European settler, whether already elite imports or class-elevated by virtue of the preferential treatment European settlers faced in contrast to indigenous locals. Latin America, with some qualification, was more like India than South Africa, though, in that it was left at least half open for surviving indigenous and slave-descendant populations to rise in status, to modernize, and potentially to join the elite, even as they might be seen to be shedding their very "nature" in doing so.

In South Africa, under the boot of apartheid, by contrast, "nature" was taken largely to preclude the possibility of indigenous African modernization. Race, in short, became overdetermining in the latter case, while qualifying in the former.

Latin America differed from both India and South Africa, however, insofar as racial mixing came to define racial latinamericanization. But this mixing became elevated by making the mimicking of the European habitus the defining aspiration, if not the condition of possibility of racial elevation. Where in an earlier historical moment the Indian would be disappeared through violent death, from the late nineteenth century on the vanishing of the Indian was sought through amalgamating metamorphosis, through its own social suicide.

Euro-mimesis

Imperialism inscribed cultural cloning of European values, virtues, and visions. But it likewise sought to institutionalize replication of the imperialist's legal and political arrangements or structures. And it did so in good part, as Philomena Essed has shown in the case of physicians, by encouraging local elites, themselves settlers or their offspring, to assume the lead in such institutionalization by means of education and idea adoption.

This imitation and neo-replication by national elites of European (especially French) high culture and institutional orders ranged over fashion and dress, the arts (including literature, poetry, and theater), laws and modes of civility, in short, more or less the entire social habitus. They were helped along, of course, by national policies to encourage immigration on a large scale from Southern and Central-Eastern Europe, fueled as much by a concern to promote economic development as by the fantasy to elevate the region culturally and eugenically. Quijano notes, for instance, that as the twentieth century opened the European population of Buenos Aires numbered in excess of 80 percent. The culturally cloned socio-cultural order was embedded into a dramatically different social milieu and sets of social relation, fashioning what Brunner aptly characterizes as "peripheral modernity." In these periphractic spaces of modeled modernizing, of *euro-mimesis*, the social products and relations assumed new meanings, becoming conflictual and contradictory as their architects emulated models they sought but couldn't possibly serve to satisfy and embed in conditions inconducive to nurturing the imports.

Now Latin American euro-mimesis took root more deeply and lingered far longer and more replicatively, so to speak, than it did in the US, the latter after all supposedly founded upon its celebrated partial break from the templates of British determination, as much culturally as politically. Consider the comparative rhetorics of attachment and detachment circulating today. But in doing so Latin American euro-mimesis had both to adapt the original template to take root in local conditions and simultaneously repress local counters to its hegemony.

The standard conception of the cloned citizen as nations emerged into independent states throughout Latin America in the late nineteenth and early twentieth centuries fashioned propertied men educated in the European ethos, the values and cultivation of a European sensibility, learning, and commitments, intellectual, moral, cultural, and political. In short, the properties making up what we have come to think of as whiteness, structurally. Those not ethnoracially European, phenotypically or culturally not white (notably those of African or Indian descent), somewhat ambiguously could become white, could be citizens, by taking on the properties of education, social elevation, looking after their economic and physical wellbeing, investment in successful business ventures but also in the moral virtues, religious values, personal health, and nutrition. Those not white could elevate themselves through social-sexual relations with those who were, producing offspring visibly whiter, thus rendering whiter not just the offspring but the parents producing them also.

In a commentary on "Race and Nation in Latin America," Peter Wade suggests an insightful account of such logic over time. A darker woman will have an informal relation with a white (or lighter) man (who himself might have a formally recognized white family). Their offspring will likely be whiter. The mother of the darker woman – the children's maternal grandmother – more often than not will be ignored or otherwise rendered invisible. The children will grow up quite probably seeking out partners at least as light as themselves, given the hardening of such social norms and expectations over historical time. These latter relations in all likelihood will become not just more normalized but more formalized too.

"Progress," as Wade concludes, is achieved multiply: by lightening up, in both senses; by leaving rurality behind, after all presumptuously the place of less and lesser whiteness; by "advancing" to more upwardly mobile social relations and economic activities; by pairing the "weakness" of black or mixed women with the "power" – the strength, the standing – of white men; by purportedly improving the national stock; by embodying – and thus inhabiting, making habit of – the supposed virtues of whiteness.

Upward mobility articulates race with class and gender in the most intricate and intimate of ways. It turns people in more than one manner of speaking inside out and outside in.

This flux in whiteness (by the same token, those in could fall out – and down – in the reverse process) is what marks the racial imaginary of Latin America, what inscribes the configuration of racial latinamericanization, as largely unique. Other regions and the societies making them up, most notably Southern Africa and the US but also and in different ways the likes of Australia and Canada, Japan, and Korea, sought to sustain a contrived sense or semblance of racial purity, defining national belonging in purified and homogeneous terms. They did so by inferiorizing those deemed different, excising them from national identity, amputating them from the body politic, separating them out at most into segregated social segments with radically reduced rights if not gesturing to expel them more or less completely from the space and imagination – the national image – making up the state. This is not to say the commitment to the logic played out perfectly in practice. Its practice was occasionally comic, almost always deeply tragic. But the commitment to a stricter, formalized segregation identified with the societies mentioned above was less negotiable, more straight-jacketed, more fixed across space and time.

Neo-Americanism, by contrast – this production of the new Americas, of Europe's alter, as Darcy Ribeiro nominates it – is at the same time the first *neo-racism*.

Latin American neo-racism makes explicit at the opening of the nineteenth century what Europe was simply beginning to gesture towards. Up to the end of the eighteenth century, thinking about race was driven formatively by the restriction of cultural traits racially defined to a supposedly unalterable biology. With the new century European intellectuals first and social policy considerably later began to shift from this hegemonic racial naturalism to a culturally inscribed historicism, ascribing race to potentially alterable and educable cultural traits and habits. The relative but constrained openness of the "new" world – "open" land for the taking, open horizons for self-making, open possibilities for cultural experimentation and invention – meant cultural malleability could be mobilized for purposes of ongoing social control and especially maintenance of racial elevation and existing relations of power. Cultural elevation through euro-mimesis, educability into civilizing mores of European design and definition, if with local accent, promoted the supposed ascent from indigeneity into whiteness. But this euro-mimesis also meant, even as it cemented into place, that both what could be imagined as the national community and the interests the state could represent were configured in terms of and around the structures of whiteness.

Homi Bhabha has made clear that imitation is never complete, failing always to be fully satisfactory. It lurches, Bhabha says, between resemblance and menace, identification and distantiation. It prompts an abiding sense of failure and lack, of limitation and shortfall, of attendant loss but also of displacement, experimentation, possibility, often at the expense of the already racially marginalized. A sense also of anguish, as Freud emphasizes, without being able to grasp what exactly is beyond reach, what precisely not yours or what ought to be. Those registered as racially different, as bruised, are lured into Euro-likeness while warned that its inner treasures are almost always beyond their reach. White-likeness is a liking of what's white, socially induced, a drive to be white-like, but also a grasping in the dark about its idealized experience, for its treasury. That "playing in the dark," to twist Toni Morrison's title, and the more or less extreme ambivalence both about what one thus is missing and what it is about one that inevitably makes one miss, if only one could put one's finger on it, is the sinking sand, the depressing frustrations, of fixating on the unreachable.

Euro-mimesis characterizes as much a national commitment as a personal choice or striving. Imitation necessarily judges the qualities of the imitated superior to those of the imitating. It accordingly denies or fails to recognize the virtues and values, contributions and characteristics in and on their own terms of those at hand, of fellow citizens and civic contributors unless socio-cultural clones and drones of the imitated.

Frustration follows for the mis- or unrecognized, a swelling fury at the lack of possibilities or cultural closures, a sense of unfulfillment of national possibility, an emerging national malaise at the swelling discontent, whether voiced politically or via criminality and social violence. Threat to wellbeing, if not to being itself, becomes threaded with a menace to society as such. And those experiences of malcontent and melancholy at inevitable failure of mimetic fulfillment seek compensation in other forms of gratification that both engage and exploit, often brutally, those considered non-European.

Euro-mimesis, then, is related to – may overlap with – the standard sense of Eurocentrism, though it is not reducible to it. Eurocentrism makes what is recognized as prevailing European values, norms, and cultural expression, historically understood, not just the point and frame of reference but also, as Quijano notes, the telos, if not endpoint, of world historical progress. It is thought to provide the dominant (and dominating) language and style of expression, elbowing to the margins other ways of knowing and being, conception and expression, where they might be recognized fuzzily if at all. In a sense, Eurocentrism covers its tracks by refusing any other point of reference as viable, as bearer of (universal) truth. It acknowledges no gap between center and provinces other than in the dismissal of practice at a distance.

Euro-mimesis, by contrast, has an inkling of – if it doesn't fully comprehend – the inevitable slippages, the replicative failures of and between European influence, its models, and its copies. It is the source, on one hand, of the doleful sense of loss that affectively follows. And, on the other, it is the prompt of a motivation to do better at it, to improve the blueprint by adaptation to new environments, eventually to undo itself in reaching beyond for something new. This reaching for the horizon of a modernity not yet present, the symbol of a national techno-modernity yet to be realized, conjures the unstinting and later self-ironizing sense, for example, of Brazil as the "country of the future" (*Brazil, nais do futuro*), initially articulated in the 1940s.

Mediating *mestizaje*

It is within these parameters and prevailing interests that *mestizaje* was pressed into service on behalf of a new set of national projects while reinforcing dominant social relations and prevailing relations of racial power. *Mestizaje*, it was quickly seen, could be mobilized actually to promote and produce homogeneity, to reinscribe a univocity and univocality in the face of heterogeneity's radical challenge, to order sameness out of diffusion, differentiation, distinction. Late nineteenth-century commentator Jose Eusebio Caro captures the idea succinctly (as quoted by Peter Wade): "[T]he diversity of races will end, because the white race will absorb and destroy the Indian, the black, the yellow, etc."

So, the making of a new nation, of new nations across Latin America, of alchemical combi-nation, involved drawing those marked as distinct and so threatening to national coherence into fusion, flavoring the national recipe. If to a bowl of white rice you add up to 25 percent black beans and 25 percent red chili peppers, you end up with an inflected, flavored meal – of white rice. Demographic and cultural heterogeneity are filtered into the homogeneous national body, more or less self-consciously.

Blanqueamiento, the process of whitening, embodies this process of homogenization. It reinscribes and extends euro-mimesis not just in new guise but in novel form.

In a social imaginary elevating *mestizaje* to the embodiment of national identity, of national stature, mixture accordingly (as Peter Wade remarks in discussing Norman Whitten's seminal work on Ecuador) serves – or, more tellingly, has served – to excise those deemed not mixed, or not mixed enough, from the social corpus. Indians are assimilated by the process of whitening, or otherwise at least ignored if not devastated. African populations – visibly, productively, and powerfully present from the late sixteenth century if largely in provincialized pockets – are rendered invisible. They are marginalized to remote corners of the nation-state. Once out of sight they are close to being out of the national mind unless they act up politically or are later just made to act "natural" in terms of the tourist economy.

Whitening makes the national and by extension regional Latin American population phenotypically lighter. But it likewise increasingly Christianizes and urbanizes them. The whitening processes of Christianizing and urbanizing are seen to draw the uncivilized into civilization, the uneducated into the virtues (if not viruses) of capitalist accumulation, the unsettled into the potential labor force, if only as a reserve army of labor (or just a reserve army). It transforms those hitherto committed to the natural instrumentalities of use value into exchange, of desiring subjects into the force of consumers. In depopulating rural areas and forests, by extension, the process likewise opens them up to the plunder of natural resources, further fueling industrial growth, stripping indigenes of land and resources, displacing them. In doing so, it tears from the land the resources, human and natural, that might otherwise resist environmental degradation and ecological devastation.

In short, in the name of *mestizaje/mesticagem*, whitening (*blanqueamiento/branqueamento*) inscribes race by deracialization. It intensifies racial dynamics, making white by de-indianizing and de-blackening, bringing into the family of Man almost literally by dehumanizing. Far from a project of purification, whitening becomes a process of proliferation through incorporation, of growth and expansion through ingestion of the indigenous, the devouring of the different as much as the ravaging of resources. Euro-mimesis (and as its legacy the cloning of American culture) is no less, one might say with an ironic twist, than cannibal culture, devouring and digesting the culture considered cultivated and cultivating. It is, to mimic Oswaldo de Andrade's "Manifesto antropófago," an anthopophagic culture.

Mestizaje/mesticagem, then, *is* social, cultural, ethnoracial whitening. It operates through "amalgamating" intercourse and socio-cultural assimilation, but also by way of policy-driven encouragement of immigration from Europe. Latin American *mestizaje/mesticagem*, I am stressing, mixes to submerge blackness and indianness. It dissolves darkness into lightness, self-consciously decreasing Africans and Indians, indigenes of one sort or another, in the demographic profile. This certainly produces the sort of "third space" Edouard Glissant identifies with the necessary cultural entanglements of cohabiting Caribbean creolization. But in the Latin American context it is a space thick with the power of hierarchy, domination, and inequality Stuart Hall rightly attributes to all creolizing histories. As national commitment, creolizing *mestizaje* seeks to bleach out the national imaginary and morphology.

The suppression of indianness also has a material implication, loosening as it does historical claims to the land, opening up the possibility that any family whose legacy in the country goes back more than a couple of generations is an indigene. A touch of Indian in the family profile can't hurt, in that regard, though too much opens up the charge of degeneracy, of the *Casta* characterization of "returning backwards." While conjuring a different genealogy of suppression and resistance than indianness, even black entrepreneurial self-advancement requires partnering with those not black. Money, the Brazilian saying reveals, whitens. This works both in the sense that as black people become wealthier they are perceived more readily as less black, more white, and they are more likely to socialize with those less likely (or less likely perceived as) black. They more probably will marry "up," and will more often than not fraternize with whites or outside of black social circles.

Blanqueamiento/branqueamento thus represents the processes of "normalization," processes that Arlene Torres and Norman Whitten insightfully characterize as "becoming increasingly acceptable" to those already made, perceived, having standing as "white." As Wade reiterates, this reinforces the already prevailing sense that impoverishment is black and Indian, wealth and social standing white. In Costa Rica in 1926, for example, Noam Chomsky points out that local economists complained of fruit-exporting enterprises importing too many black workers who were "darkening the racial composition of the country," introducing disease, criminality, and "mesticiz[ing] our race, which is already darkening," while sending their savings back to Jamaica at the cost to Costa Rica.

As De la Fuente notes, Euro-descended Cubans (not unlike others regionally) have tended to equate blackness with backwardness. Already in the 1930s public spaces such as parks, schools, and clubs were privatized so as to restrict black access. Cubans fleeing Castro for Florida from the revolutionary moment until 1980 tended to be white(r) and wealthier, and remittances to family in Cuba thus tended to flow to those characteristically white(r), making for more elevated experiences in a supposedly egalitarian environment. This longstanding culture of anti-black Cuban racism factors also into accounting for the simmering tensions in Miami between Cuban and African-American communities. Even where socialist Cuba moved vigorously and to a considerable extent effectively to outlaw forms of racism, Afro-Cubans have suffered significantly poorer housing stock, are criminalized to a far greater degree, remain relatively underrepresented in government circles, and black women are more likely driven to sex-work than their white counterparts.

Racism, in classic socialist form, has been traditionally regarded largely as an epiphenomenon ideologically rationalizing class conflict. As Foucault remarks with characteristic flair and insight, nevertheless, state socialisms are as prone to biological (or, we might add, cultural) racism in identifying and incarcerating criminals, the mentally ill, and political enemies as capitalist states have been.

More broadly, *blanqueamiento/branqueamento* accordingly reinforces the sense and sensibility that associating with people publicly regarded as black or Indian is delimiting. Such association, in the earlier characterization of the *Casta* categories, threatens "holding-oneself-in-midair," animalization, "returning backwards." Partnering with whites, sexually as much as commercially, by contrast, is supposedly rewarding. Intersectionality with a vengeance, socio-historically invented and culturally reinscribed.

This self-portrait of racial latinamericanization nevertheless presumes also that whites – Europeans by descent – are not just homogeneous but likewise, and perhaps more deeply even, pure. It presupposes that those who came from Europe had no non-European mixture prior to New World admixture, to Latin American amalgamation. The amalgamation, so the story traditionally would have it, is between European Iberian – creolized culturally if not (and preferably) phenotypically – and black or indigenous. Each untouched by prior mixtures.

But think of it: If mixture was such a mark of local Latin Americans, the Iberian peninsula prior to Hispano-expansion across the Atlantic was hardly impenetrable ethnoracially by those outside of it. Quite the contrary, the population of the peninsula, as Caryl Phillips has also observed in his insightful little travelogue on "the European tribe," is precisely inflected with all sorts of historical influences, demographically and culturally: Moorish, African, Middle Eastern, Islamic, Jewish. The Iberian arrives in the New World already significantly, if silently and denyingly, *mestizaje/misto*.

All this bears out the fact, revealed so compellingly by Marisol de la Cadena, that the notion of *mestizaje* is significantly more complex in its racial politics of meaning and social implication than its usual reductive rendering as "mixed race" or hybridity would have it. Technically and narrowly, *mestizo* has referred to mixtures of Indians with whites, *mulatto* of blacks with whites, *zambo* as the offspring of Indian–black mixing. As I have demonstrated in the *Casta* case, these three categories traditionally have fashioned the base of the Latin American classificatory racial pyramid, the pointed pyramidal apex representing the purified whiteness of civilization, power, and wealth, in short, of social status and wellbeing. The pyramidal base racially represents physical, social, economic, political, and cultural degradation and degeneration, bodily incapacity and behavioral impropriety, economic impoverishment and cultural incivility. But also the source of cheap and largely servile labor on which social wealth at the apex was built.

The multitudinous possibilities of mixture up and down the pyramidal schema, physical and cultural, are reflected in the proliferation throughout Latin America of categories to characterize the racial in-betweens. If Thomas Stephens's very useful and deeply revelatory *Dictionary of Latin American Racial and Ethnic Terminology* is any indication, ethnoracial terms of characterization, not least of color mixture, are voluminous and multiplicitous as much in their shifting meanings over time as in their sheer numbers, range, and reach at any given moment. Their regulatory power is as culturally prolific and diffused through the social habitus, the civil society, of a nation-state as formally inscribed in state bureaucracy and structures.

Mulatto/mulato has been used to refer to any offspring resulting from the mixing of white with black. Or to any person taken to be black-skinned, including metaphorically one suntanned. Or to a person marked by other stereotypically phenotypical characteristics reductively associated with black people, such as tightly curled or "kinky" hair and a broad, flat nose. The term has been used, by extension, to refer also to a person considered to exhibit or embody character traits projectedly black, such as danger, wildness, or boorishness.

By contrast, *ladino* has moved in the other, if related, direction. The term has referred at different times, places, and in different contexts to almost anyone ethnoracially. Blacks (including slaves), whites, Indians, *mestizos*, and *mulattos* have all been nominated *ladino*. But the most usual and generalized meaning has been anyone in the Americas, no matter the background, who is or has taken on cultural traits of whiteness, who has acquired the ability to speak Spanish, and who therefore supposedly has become civilized, or white-like.

Differentiated from both *mulat(t)o* and *ladino*, *mestizo/mestico* references specifically the mixing of white and Indian, whether phenotypically (simply in terms of the offspring of mixed intercourse) or culturally, and even linguistically. The broader implication is that *mestizo/mestico* is more readily marked by European color and character than *mulatto*, the lingering implication of supposedly greater closeness along the hierarchical chain of being. It is revealing, then, that the generic category of *mestizaje/mesticagem* has served more widely and openly for referencing the mergings and mappings of intercourse, biological and social, than say *mulat(t)o*. The translation of *mestizaje/mesticagem* as mixture or hybridity flattens the meaning into simplifying Americanized assumptions, as De la Cadena points out, presupposing racial purity as the idealized measure from which mixture takes its leave.

In the case of racial latinamericanization, I have hinted above, more complex significations are at work. The meaning of the term shifted both over time and from one situation to another. In the latter case, different people with similar profiles might find one characterized as mixed while the other would not be. But the same individual might equally be described as *mestizaje/mesticagem* in one circumstance or time but not in another, by one group but not by another, depending on the individual's personal heritage and relations and of different levels of knowledge of such biographies. Most often, perhaps, the term would reference the *offspring* of perceived biological and cultural mixing. Colonial practice, however, sometimes would also mark as *mestizo* the Creole partner in the mixed relation (that is, the local-born European in the Latin American in contrast with the Caribbean context), usually the man if *Casta* paintings provide reliable evidence. Characterizing a white man in a mixed marriage as *mestizo* signals that he married outside of (really beneath) his standing, producing offspring accordingly always categorically outside the social norm if not social acceptability.

Here profound ambivalence accompanies the characterization. On one hand, the connotation of mixture, of *mestizaje/mesticagem*, implies the veiled dismissal of being "mixed up," gone native, driven by passion alone, taking leave of one's senses, and so irrational. But beneath this moralizing disgust and dismissal – and perhaps too the degeneration thought to be their source – lies also the hint of envy at the throwing off of convention, the pleasure of passion that has come so broadly to stereotype the popular figure of latinamericanization. *Mestizaje/mesticagem*, in short, and as De la Cadena rightly concludes, threatened the undoing of classificatory schemas, prompting even while marking their inherent instability.

The ambivalence about *mestizaje/mesticagem* across Latin America seemed to have receded from roughly the 1930s onwards, once the grip of eugenics and the terrors of degenerationism had weakened. Racial mixture in Brazil especially, and across Latin America more broadly, assumed firmer footing as ideological possibility and prospect from the late 1940s on, finding fuel in the UNESCO race statements of the period, predicated as the latter were on reconfiguring race as culture and race mixing as a virile response to biological racism. In some countries, however, those where the pull of *mestizaje* turned out weakest, this was driven by the disappearance of African-descended populations and fierce repression of almost any presence of Indians (Argentina, Chile, Uruguay). In others (Brazil, Mexico, Peru), *mestizaje/mesticagem* was elevated as the defining condition of national character represented in the ideological commitment from the 1950s on to racial democracy.

While considering itself a "melting pot" (*cristol de razas*), the case of Argentina reveals how deep denial can cut. Census counts obfuscate, as the undertaking has traditionally been to enumerate "national origin" rather than race or color, however classified. Nevertheless, the country registers itself as 97 percent white and 3 percent *mestizo*, Amerindian, or other (combined), almost invariably undercounting *mestizos* and Afro-Argentines. Certainly, policy in the nineteenth century strongly encouraged European immigration while self-consciously seeking to eliminate anyone not considered white, as I argued earlier. European immigration continues to be encouraged, and discrimination persists against anyone else. By all accounts, discrimination against anyone not considered white is common, as well as anyone from elsewhere in Latin America. That the country presumes itself white actually prompts the commonplace that anyone not white in the country must be from elsewhere, and so is taken not to belong. Antisemitism is likewise common. The melting pot supposedly melted the racially marked undesirables largely out of the ethnoracial mix of the body politic.

Argentina illustrates how societies that have self-consciously effected a national order of racelessness through effective elimination of those taken not to be white later are led to celebrate the lingering culture of the largely obliterated. From the 1970s onwards, not least as a side-effect of the spreading global resistance to apartheid, racism got to be acknowledged. Slowly but surely, indigenous and Afro-cultural expressions came to be celebrated, as the presence of living cultural practitioners had all but disappeared. Public commitment to anti-discrimination measures combined with enamorment of the cultural ways of those largely rendered invisible.

Here, conveniently, could be found a way to stave off the charge of racism (though neo-Nazi groups from across the region have migrated to Argentina's vigorous protection of the Internet's virtual freedom of expression): "My society is against racism, so I cannot possibly (have) be(en) for it either. 'Our' anti-discrimination laws, policies, and practices provide evidence of the anti-discrimination commitment." How can one discriminate if there are anti-discrimination laws and policies in place? The appropriate policies without the people in question become the projected yardstick of evasive racelessness as social commitment.

While the demographic profiles differ, Venezuela represents another, complementary feature of a more generalized Latin American mode, namely, the troubled institutionalization of a policy of whitening. In the 1950s, a little later than Brazil and Argentina, for instance, Venezuelan dictator Marcos Perez Jimenez introduced the prevailing national ideal of whitening, both demographically and culturally, importing significant numbers of Western European immigrants. The accompanying europeanizing of local culture as the national imperative underpinned the subsequent erasure of race from explicit national reference and policy with the end of the dictatorship in 1958. This simultaneously silenced any attempt to penalize racial discrimination. From 1999 onwards Hugo Chavez, himself of mixed African, indigenous, and European heritage, has attempted partially and with limited success to address the consequent social exclusions of Afro-Venezuelan and indigenous people.

Most Venezuelans would claim to be *mestizo*, not in the technical sense of being the product of European and indigenous family mixtures but more broadly and informally of being (racially) all mixed up. As largely a mixed population, the claim continues, there really is no – the implication is that there could not possibly be, or be a place for – racism, for that would be to self-denigrate. The demography is more measured, however, at least according to a pan-Latin American survey that does not claim objectivity but a broad consistency across the sub-continent. Insofar as numbers can be determined at all in the absence both of formal definitions and of reliable census-taking, *mestizos* make up 19 percent of Venezuela's population, *mulattos* – the mix of black and white – 38 percent, blacks 9 percent, whites 30 percent, and indigenous just 1 percent. At the time of slavery's abolition in March 1854, African-descended people numbered approximately 400,000, roughly 40 percent of the population, 25,000 of whom at the time were slaves. Today, relatedly, race largely maps onto socio-economic class.

The overwhelming members of Venezuela's elite, politically and economically, have tended to be white or at least light skinned, while those inhabiting the poorer classes have tended largely to be darker. Most incarcerated in Venezuela's prisons, by the same token, are Afro-Venezuelan. This is not, of course, to say that whites overwhelmingly are wealthy and powerful and blacks not; only that being wealthy largely correlates with being white, and being dark(er) largely does not correlate with wealth, social privilege, or power. It also implies, more tellingly, that being white disposes one to privilege, that there are fewer barriers to social advancement and decent health than for those not white. Whiteness and blackness, as I have indicated more generally, are structural conditions of possibility and restriction, not simply social identities.

These are the classic, bare social arrangements that we know generally to structure the life worlds of racial states and racist exclusion. Where differentiated demography so closely maps onto social and economic privilege and disprivilege along class-articulated racial lines, we can now safely say from a long legacy of geopolitical exemplification that there racism presumptively structures the society, in one form or another. Popular forms of reference become quite revealing. Thus, the common dismissive derogatory term for black people among Venezuelans is, well, "monkeys"!

The local response to Hugo Chavez's presidency in this context is as revealing racially as it is politically and economically, a touchstone of the complex history of racial politics in the country. Historically, both the first and second constitutions of independent Venezuela in the 1820s and 1830s excluded African-descended and indigenous people from citizenship. A century later African and indigenous Venezuelans were still being characterized as lazy. Today, school textbooks continue to talk of both groups in the past tense, thus naturalizing their condition as fixed in some irretrievable and regressive past, as though having nothing to contribute to nor forming a constitutive part of the vibrancy of contemporary Venezuela.

As I suggest, then, *mestizaje/mesticagem* has served as the means, the enablement, of euro-mimesis. Where *mestizaje/mesticagem* is the national commitment, the official imagination, the state's public face, euro-mimesis is its embodiment, its manifestation in the practices of everyday life and cultural expression. *Mestizaje* has preserved Euro-cultural determination, artifices of gentility and decency, fixing in place the horizons of possibility, securing the marks of modernity, morality, and progress while inflecting them with the aesthetic appeal of honey-tinged color. Creole kissed by color, as the projected imaginary of the public sphere would have it. Less café con leche than caramel-colored and -tasting chocolate milk, sun-splashed rather than sun-seared.

This dispositional openness to *mestizaje/mesticagem* – abstractly to hybridity, mixture, and social metamorphosis; concretely to Euro-cultural extension and white domination – is more crimped in those states where African-descended people have constituted a significant presence, whether demographically or culturally (to some degree Costa Rica and Venezuela, as we have seen, but especially Colombia, and most notably Brazil and Cuba). Here, spatial marginalization and provincialization of black communities were complemented by a softer, more ambivalent insistence on *mestizaje/ mesticagem*.

The fact that *mestizaje* has become over time the most widely used generic word for the process of hybridization and that this term is derivative of the substantiation of white–Indian mixtures (*mestizo/mestico*) reveals the assumptions at work here. White–black offspring are nominated *mulat(t)o*. The correlate terms for *mestizaje* – *mulatismo* or *mulateria* – to characterize the process reproducing such mixtures are rarely heard on mainland Latin America in contrast to, say, Cuba, where the history of black–white mixing has been far more widespread, given the prevailing demography. In Latin America, the *mestizaje/mesticagem* that made for *mulat(t)os* was de-emphasized, less forceful – dare we say, less desirable – than in the case of Indians. And yet where it did occur, it likewise was accompanied by the insistence to whiten both demographically and culturally.

Blanqueamiento/branqueamento, in short, served to sustain, to reproduce, deep lines of social power by diminishing blackness, culturally as much as biologically, as Richard Jackson has observed. This diminution was facilitated by way of the joint mandates to lighten up phenotypically and culturally through the sort of reproductive *mestizaje/mesticagem* characterized earlier and the restriction to the largely invisible social and spatial margins of those not heeding the urge to whiten. These are broad generalizations, to be sure, shifting in ideological commitment and implementation across time, space, and indeed class formation. But *mestizaje/mesticagem* effects a repression of visible blackness in the national self-image, pushing it back into the shadows of both the physical and cultural landscapes, what Toni Morrison has called a "distancing Africanism" in the case of the literary tradition.

Resisting blackness

Whitening or *blanqueamiento/branqueamento*, it should be stressed by extension, is not simply reproductive in the biological or phenotypical sense, the sort of lightening up through successive generations discussed above. It also involves socio-cultural "enlightenment," acquiring the morals and customs, the sensibilities associated with whiteness. And such sensibilities more often than not are to be acquired by shedding the skein of darkness facilitated by socio-geographical movement. Cultural mobility – the movement away from cultural commitments identified as Indian or black – is considered most directly enabled by geographic mobility from areas marked as Indian or black and therefore seen to be lacking urbanity, sophistication, and prospect to areas identified not just demographically but culturally and expressively as white. De la Cadena opens her insight-laden book, *Indigenous Mestizos*, by quoting noted Peruvian writer Maria Vargas Llosa observing that Indian peasants can only acquire the ability "to communicate" by "moving to the cities," "integrating," "becoming mestizos," and thus explicitly shedding their Indianness.

This movement likewise increases the likelihood of whitening through intermarriage. *Blanquiamiento/branqueamento* thus signals for the most part a far more fluid set of racially marking logics and prospects, patterns and contours than one has been used to seeing in rigidly inscribed racial states such as the US or stereotypically conceived South Africa. But it also embeds presumptions, if not prescriptions, regarding blackness, especially, of inferiority and vulgarity, mere physicality and aggressiveness, shallowness and loudness, of thoughtlessness and profanity. Thus France Winndance Twine reports disturbingly that the mixed-race Afro-Brazilians she interviewed generally would avoid reminiscing about the black members of their families, wiping them from publicly circulated memory as well as from enabling public self-identification.

Brazil's experience, while historically molding the pattern outlined here, has come recently to offer threads of an interesting counter-case to this general line, articulating a unique new development in contrast to the more general pattern racial latinamericanization has assumed across the region. Notwithstanding the categorical shiftiness and instability over time, the percentage of the Brazilian population formally categorizing itself as mixed in the official national census counts has substantially increased as the percentage that is black has dropped dramatically. In 1940 the black population was counted at about 15 percent, while in 2000 it was recorded at just 6 percent. The mixed population across this period doubled from about 20 percent to 40 percent, and the white population dropped from well over 60 to a little over 50 percent. At the same time, there has been a slight surge in readiness to claim blackness recently, the percentage of blacks increasing by a little less than 2 percent in the past decade (an increase of almost three million people). This is more remarkable perhaps in light of the fact that Brazilians have traditionally tended to declare themselves lighter or whiter than they might seem on first visual blush, given the associated privileges.

This recent bump in blackness was accompanied by the mildly progressive embrace of affirmative action programs introduced initially, if barely enacted, by President Cardoso and implemented more emphatically by the Lula administration. Lula has also prompted an emergent social discussion around redress, largely undercut by the more recent corruption scandal that has plagued his administration. But the increase among blacks demographically was not the product simply of a relatively high birth rate. It followed also from a modestly diminishing stigma attached to being black and practicing what is perceived as "black culture," or cultural practices embedding African retentions. And this in turn prompted a perhaps even more significant surge in self-assertedness, mobilized by "the *negro* movement," among those increasingly open to identifying themselves as black. Of course, it wasn't always that way, and these are emerging tendencies far yet from fixed patterns. Birth rates have combined with a recent relatively assertive black consciousness and a somewhat more open political climate to turn black Brazilians into a potentially significant if still somewhat embattled political constituency.

The readiness of many Brazilians of all stripes in poll after poll to identify as *moreno* or *pardo* – basically, as mixed in one way or another – reveals more than just an avoidance of blackness and a "somatic preference" for whiteness, as Sansone puts it, although it clearly represents that. It reveals also, and increasingly, an aesthetic appeal for that touch of color noted above, tied to the preference for the elevated structural conditions identified with whiteness. *Moreno* represents the broad "brown" middle, indicative both of racial mixing and cultural *métissage*. Moreno, it could be said, represents a "raceless race," racial reference too easily absent the negativity and burdens increasingly associated with racial characterization, uplift through amalgamated en-whitening. The figure of the *moreno* has come to serve as a sort of modern-day national character, a sense of what Brazil is and aspires to. In short, the *moreno* symbolically stands for the claim, if not always the commitment, to go beyond classically fracturing racial divisions.

The *moreno*, then, is the symbol of racial democracy actualized, racelessness materialized. The proof is in the melt of color and culture. The *moreno*'s popularity obscures discriminations against darker-skinned Brazilians, diluting the possibility of their identification in the alchemical mix. While roughly 40 percent of Brazilians self-identify as *moreno*, as Bailey and Telles point out, youth do so more readily, as do those who are otherwise white, and poorer people. Identification with the *moreno* tends to give way to hardening racial distinctions, by contrast, as people grow older and enter the workplace, and with class mobility, in short, as the experience of racisms materialize and multiply.

Modest mixture as national personality is the legacy of Brazilian racial democracy, at least rhetorically. Under pressures of neoliberal globalization and mobility, mixture as an ideological identity wants to have it both ways, however: looks linked to livelihood, sun-splash on a gold-paved street.

Many analysts of the Brazilian racial lexicon – Sansone and Telles are two recently among a wide range – will comment that Brazilians use varying terms in differing circumstances to make polite reference to people often as lighter or, more occasionally in disparaging terms, as darker than they in fact are. This preference is usually taken to indicate a desire for what whiteness symbolically represents, if not for whiteness itself, not unlike that expressed by the young schoolchildren in *Brown v. Board of Education* (1954) in the US context. But this way of characterizing the matter of course presupposes some objectivity, some fixity, to the racial palette.

Another way of looking at this color flexibility is to tie it less to the "actual" color of a person, whatever that might mean or however it might be fixed, and more to a rhetorics of social characterization racially understood. Thus lighter terms mark the referent in the speaker's eyes (even when it is self-characterizing) as appealing or virtuous, and terms that are characteristically associated with darkness mark their target as the opposite. Sansone reports that his visibly darker survey respondents often referred to parents and partners by way of terms indicating lighter colors than appearance seemed to suggest. And those who are wealthier would more likely be designated by lighter color terms than those who are not.

Here the syntax of racial terms effects a semantic field the significance of which is more in their meaning-making than in any claim to the reductive objectivity of their referentiality. And by casting this as a tendency, I am not suggesting that racial reference in Brazil has come completely unglued from color assumptions about referents, only that these connections are not as fast and fixed as racial characterization traditionally (pre)tends to presume.

To sum up, then: *Mestizaje/mesticagem* clearly is experienced unevenly across Latin America, related as I have been suggesting largely to demographic presence and distribution across racial distinction physically as well as culturally indexed. In those societies where, following abolition, state policy mostly sought to wipe out black and indigenous Indian populations more or less completely (Argentina, Uruguay), *mestizaje* has no real or recognizable role in the national imaginary and social order. In states with significant, even majority Indian presence (especially Andean countries such as Peru, Bolivia, Ecuador, but also emphatically Mexico), the project of placing the stamp of whiteness – most notably through the sort of Europeanizing acculturation I have discussed – becomes the national commitment. Aesthetically, a touch of Indian was considered pleasing, overdetermined however by the presumed superiority of Euro-habitus, polity, culture, and law citizens were more or less encouraged, if not required, to mimic. Mastering Euro-habitus was a ticket to socio-economic status. The project of *mestizaje* could become national policy both because Indians were seen to be closer to whites than blacks in the great chain of being and by the understanding that *mestizaje* ultimately meant euro-mimesis.

In making blacks and blackness, if not invisible, less definitive in the national self-identification and imaginary, *mestizaje/mesticagem* and the dynamics of racial democracy to which it gives content managed to effect two contradictory if complementary political dynamics. For one, it made it far more difficult for those marked as black, as African descended, to organize politically around that self-understanding. Where the nation saw itself as mixed, if lured heavily by euro-mimesis ethnoracially understood, emphasizing blackness as the grounds for political organizing has been seen to fly in the face of national personality, of the being of the nation itself. It is seen as a retreat, as reactionary, as needless recourse to an *ancien régime* of race, and so as verging itself on racism. At the same time, *mestizaje/mesticagem* as metonym for euro-mimesis has tended to render blacks as the unwanted, as the national familia's black sheep, the patria's illegitimate child. Novelist Eliseo Altunaga captures something of this tension in recognizing in Cuba's racial make-up the dissonance between "a white aesthetic and a black ethic."

In the name of progressing beyond race, *mestizaje* thus deeply reinscribes the traditional assumptions not just of racial identification but of racial derogation, denigration, and denial – in short, of racisms. Since the 1980s various social scientists have demonstrated deep racial disparities on almost every significant social index – life expectancy, income, education, employment, residential access, infant mortality, incarceration – most notably but far from only in Brazil. The profound failure to recognize racisms both across the broader publics and by the state evidences also the difficulties facing the necessary and courageous efforts of Afro-Latin political and cultural organizations such as *Frente Negra Brasileira* (Black Brazilian Front) or the *Movimento Negro Unificado* (Unified Black Movement) in Brazil, Ecuador's *Asociacion de Negros del Ecuador* (ASONE: Association of Ecuadoran Blacks), and the Organization of Black Communities in Colombia.

Thus *mestizaje/mesticagem* as *blanqueamiento/branqueamento* and euro-mimesis make organizing and solidarity around blackness and *indigenismo* difficult, almost inconceivable. Denial of blackness and indigeneity, as categories, character(s), or cultures, undermines the possibility of launching a recognizable counter-movement. If a whitening *mestizaje/mesticagem* is actually or effectively the official mandate and domineering (if not altogether dominating) discourse, then Indians mostly and blacks a little less so become inputs in the calculator of mixture. This suggests the inputs themselves are not fixed in place but assume some fluidity, more so historically in the case of Indians than blacks, as I have argued.

This instability, stabilized only in the mixed product, makes almost any organization ordered around the terms of input difficult, though not impossible. For one, the input categories themselves are kept unstable, people dropping in and out of them depending on personal circumstance and prospect, relationships and social relations more broadly. For another, such organizing is largely reactive, and requires considerable conscientizing and consciousness-raising simply to enable the conditions of conceptual possibility for the organization to emerge.

This is not to suggest that ethnoracially based organizing doesn't occur. Often it will emerge in a state depending on local circumstance, though not unusually in relation to energies in states elsewhere, whether regionally or more globally. So the Civil Rights Movement in the US or the anti-apartheid movement might fuel heightened black self-awareness and local political movements, just as broad pan-Indian movements across Latin

America or internationally might energize local groups to identify and galvanize prospects for themselves, as Michael Hanchard has demonstrated. Local alliances whether within or across marginalized groups might be bolstered by seeking out these broader relations, might even become politically insurgent and make a bid for power themselves (as with Bolivia recently). Ethnoracial cross-alliances might form the basis of a class mobilization, as in Venezuela, with visible material effects.

For all of this, however, the legacy to date has been short-lived. Such alliances break down for want of resources or the re-fracturing of interests. The volatility and motility of ethnoracial definition within and across the region undermine the sort of stability necessary for longer-term political effect, exacerbated as they often have been by globally dominant institutions and state powers to geopolitical and lately neoliberal purposes.

Thus, *mestizaje/mesticagem* was married with *blanqueamiento/branqueamento*, the pairing presided over by euro-mimesis and consummated by racial democracy as national commitment. In the longer analysis the marriage stabilized whiteness at the sufferance of any potential competitors. The conjugation of mixture and euro-mimesis extends the political power of whiteness as the prevailing structural condition of racial latinamericanization.

In the past decade in Brazil, to be sure, African-inspired cultures have become increasingly celebrated, and African history is now required in Bahian secondary schools. Fueled by a modestly resurgent black movement and a progressive egalitarianism that brought him to power, the Lula government has made much of insisting on affirmative action in college admissions, and local municipalities have been even more vigorous in promoting black employment. These developments built on earlier efforts, most notably the important clause of the 1988 Constitution outlawing racism as a serious crime, and important if small increases in black political representation at all levels.

Yet blacks – or those of mixed racial background, for that matter – have seldom achieved the status of a coherent political force in Brazil or any other Latin American state, almost never amounting to an effective voting bloc in the way we are now seeing among Indians, for instance, in societies such as Ecuador or Bolivia, or more recently Peru. Organizing around Indian land claims has proved to be somewhat more straightforward, in good part because the land claims are less easily denied, if yet still heavily contested, in their *historical* linkage to indigeneity and their dislocating disentitlement.

The fluidity and motility around racial matters across Latin America thus come with the weight of significant historical and cultural baggage. These historical weights of race are always a drag on possibility and psychology. They are stress-producing and diminish life's prospects by comparison with those not so (directly) weighed down by the burdens of race. The burdens of this weighting mar societies in different ways, marking in their own ways every country across the region. And the burdens may be greater in some cases for women stigmatized by sexualizing innuendo, and at other times for men, dismissed as social wannabes.

In any case, as Peter Wade points out in the case of Colombia in his characteristically nuanced way, the push to lighten up prompts envious resentments across their class divide between those variously marked as black. One could add, by those refusing or failing at euro-mimetic enlightening as by those fueled by it. But also by the latter, who are constantly having to prove themselves, envious and resentful of those at ease with the fact of their blackness, at one with their class and community.

At the same time, *blanquiamiento/branqueamento* undercuts the lure of "passing" so much part of the lore of the United States and to a lesser degree of South Africa. If one can "whiten up," so to speak, by a mix of intercoursing, cultural and even moral *mestizaje* – indeed, where "enlightening" *mestizaje/mesticagem* is projected and promoted as national character, as aspiration – the pull of passing would seem to be largely moot. *Mestizaje/mesticagem*, one might say, is passing made more or less legitimate, manageable, more or less livable, envy and resentment, disdain and denial notwithstanding.

So race in post-abolition Latin America has factored centrally and more or less self-consciously into the project of nation-building. Nations either were articulated by leading national(ist) intellectuals as "a new race" (Freyre, for example, concerning Brazil, or Vasconcelos's "La raza cosmica" in the case of Mexico) or as incorporating all members of the population, regardless of race, into the national body. The nation, in this formulation, was to be raceless (as in Jose Marti's conception in the Cuban case).

This set of commitments represents a long tradition in Latin America. *Mestizaje/mesticagem*, and later racial democracy, were forged as ideas not just uniquely defining the region but as deeply divergent from the reductionism of US racial self-conception, most notably what Jim Crow came to characterize as the one-drop rule. Latin American racial exceptionalism, in contrast to the US (this is how Michael Hanchard characterizes it in the Brazilian case), draws together politicians and intellectuals otherwise as disparate as Simon Bolivar in the early 1800s, Marti in the 1860s, and Vasconcelos, Freyre, and Florestan Fernandes across the long twentieth century.

In these various conceptions and commitments whitening has been a driving force. Blackness – and black people – relationally have been marginalized less by formal legislation than through longstanding structures of social standing reproduced through the articulations of class (gender qualified). Blacks and Indians, I have indicated, occupy different structural positions, are "inserted" differentially into these territorializations of race, into their respective "structures of alterity," as Peter Wade puts it.

Part of this process of differentiated insertion has had to do with the significant demographic differences and the sorts of political and symbolic, eugenic and representational threats those differences have conjured. Axiologically, in terms of the attendant aesthetic and moral values, blacks (in contrast with *mestizos/mesticos*) more often than not are demeaned, cast(e) aside, in the self-characterization of national personality. Indians and *mestizos/mesticos*, *morenos*, or *mulat(t)os* have occupied a more ambivalent terrain, not least in those societies in which their potential political power has been tied to their larger demographic representation as well as their identification with the land both as economic resource and as national imaginary.

The project of a whitening racial democracy, I have argued, has shaped deeply conflicted indigenous and black groups across the region, seeking meaningful standing and mobilizing self-elevation into national narration and characterization, resourceful access and political representation. Marisol de la Cadena suggests that "de-Indianization" – she is talking of Peru but the point can be generalized as "de-indigenization" – is not simply the shedding of indigenous culture and custom in order self-effacingly to integrate or assimilate on the part of the indigenous. It is a self-conscious substitution of reified notions of essentialized culture for more fluid, self-sustaining, mobilizing conceptions and practices of indigeneity, redefining their self-understanding relationally as their circumstances, conditions, and social locations alter.

De-Indianization, thus, does not entail rejecting indigeneity; quite the contrary. It means reconceiving Indianness by stripping it of the fixations of racist culture, updating it in relation to its contemporary circumstances and conditions, casting off its imposed restrictions and delimitations.

At the same time, the indigenous and those inserted into the structural conditions of indigeneity are faced repeatedly by socio-economic and political barriers, racially prompted, produced, and promoted, if somewhat differentially from one state to another. These restrictions have been less formalized across Latin America than those facing people defined by their negation of whiteness in the likes of the US and South Africa. The formal social arrangements excluding those not white in the latter societies were built constitutively and explicitly into the structural definition of the nation-state, as much a feature of the racially exclusionary foundations as of the image of those social formations. In those Latin American societies retaining robust demographic heterogeneity, the fact that blacks and the indigenous came to be seen as belonging in and to the society offered a social footing while too easily discounting the structural barriers they face. Hence the consequent ambivalence experienced by people defined as much structurally as communally in terms of their negation of whiteness.

Racial democracy offered the possibility of belonging and social participation; its definition as *racial*, however, indicated that they could only ever be partial, limited, always begrudging and incomplete. Better perhaps than not or never, but so nebulous as to virtualize the possibilities, making them ever beyond concrete grasp. Motivating and exasperating, seemingly possible but never quite within reach. Like the US now in at least acknowledging racial presence and the mark of race on national histories and contemporary social self-characterization. But like Europe in largely refusing a discussion of debilitating racial effects, evaporating the terms of engagement into seemingly traceless vapors too slippery to hold onto securely.

Latin America, in short, signals the direction of racism(s), the silenced but still gripping debilitations, under the duress of neoliberalism.

Latinamericanizing Racial Neoliberalism

Neoliberal jurisdiction conjures a set of racisms in which mixture constitutes the national imagination, the (self-)image of the nation. Tanned whiteness and euro-mimesis become the national embodiments, the frivolity and conviviality of carnival and soccer its coloring of culture, the whitening of class elevation and the blackening of impoverishment its ends. The racial structuring of life's possibilities and delimitations – ultimately of the conditions of life and death itself – are its unspoken.

It is often taken consequently that across Latin America, as more generally, racism is the product of ignorance. Not knowing better, whether on the part of individuals or institutions, leads to discriminatory expression, to derogatory reference, to failing to address social issues, to the all too easy possibility of ignoring problems because they aren't identified to begin with. But racism also makes possible the not asking, the failure to collect data, the grounds for ignoring the invisible, and by extension the refusal to address deep social inequities which aren't recognized as iniquitous precisely because they aren't recognized at all. Racism, in short, is as much cause as effect. Latin America reveals as well as anywhere these neoliberal failings following from the fog covering over race and its social orderings.

The legacy of a racial democracy that insists on racial incorporation in the name of a new national "race" while privileging euro-mimesis and *blanqueamiento/branqueamento* offered an early experimental prototype for neoliberal raceless racism to emulate and extend. Racial democracy was supposed to produce a new nation amalgamated into a single and singular racial identity through miscegenation, racial intermarriage, and formal equality. It served at the same time to render significant racially marked substantive inequalities – in income, wealth, educational and employment access, criminalization, residential quality, and the like – beyond the reach of reform or redress, if not altogether invisible. Racial democracy throughout Latin America thus has meant democracy in which the historical legacy of racially inequitable structures is inscribed but indiscernible, embedded but intangible, urgent but untouchable. In democratizing substantive inequalities, racial democracy made them seem a matter purely of personal choice or individualized effort.

The US export – ideologically, culturally, economically, and only in an excruciatingly violent sense legally – of "living free, or dying" in the refusal if not in the attempt to free oneself of the imposition, assumes a particular resonance in the Latin American context. There, "living free" has come to mean more or less free of commitments to an insurgent politics with respect to land claims, resource allocation, or indigenous or historical rights. One may be free to be enwhitened, to become white-like, even white, by acquiring education, becoming Christian, working and recreating as those of European descent do, consuming according to their norms of desire and expectation, to their structures of sensibility and sentiment, to the norms of literacy and their attendant forms of "legitimate cultural memory" (to use Canclini's terms), in short, to their preference schemes.

Globalization intensifies the dynamic, by turning Latin America into one of the sites of low-cost production for North America, by rapidly recirculating a lumpen labor force between north and south, and by threatening use and disposability of populations subject to their regulation. Raceless democracy accordingly cements in place as fair and freely established the layered racial inequities of decades, if not centuries, of structural inscription.

Tellingly, while the majority of black Brazilians work, more than half earn less than half of the minimum wage of $200 per month. Eighty percent of children murdered by hired thugs on the streets of Brazil's large cities are black, and police likely shoot black suspects nine out of ten times, twice as often as white suspects. Recent efforts to expand access through explicit affirmative action programs notwithstanding, just 2 percent of black Brazilians make it to college, five times less than whites. Black illiteracy is roughly 50 percent, while about 20 percent for whites, and infant mortality for black babies is double that of the white populace. Telles reports that, in the decade following the 1988 Brazilian Constitution outlawing racism (institutionalized symbolically to commemorate abolition's centenary), researchers identified just three convictions. When it comes to the effects of raceless racism, the reduction of structural conditions of exclusion to individualized instances, Brazil is no exception.

Colombia's Nelson Mandela City exemplifies the effects of this contemporary raceless logic of neoliberalism. Nelson Mandela City is a migrant shantytown of 50,000 people that has grown informally next to the harbor in the celebrated cultural capital of Cartegena. The poor migrants have fled the interior, squeezed out with no prospects between the government-sponsored paramilitaries and the rebels in Colombia's lingering and increasingly deadly civil war. The vulnerable inhabitants of Nelson Mandela City, overlooked and left to eke out livelihoods for themselves from practices such as streetwise micro-vending and micro-mining garbage dumps, are overwhelmingly from the largely denied, all but invisible Afro-Colombian population, a mixed legacy cemented between slavery's denied past and the neoliberal present.

At the same time, those of African descent and the indigenous bring to the mix an acute sense, historically forged and refined, of what it means and takes to survive and revive, faced by the entangled challenges of economic degradation and sometime desperation, by racial antagonism and depreciation, by cultural mis- or non-recognition and nominal oversight. The drive to survive, individually and communally, materially and culturally, politically and legally, in the face of these weights of race offers lessons as well as hope to anyone, any group, similarly challenged.

There is a series of generalizations to be drawn from the notion of racial latinamericanization I have been elaborating here. First, I have been emphasizing throughout that latinamericanization exemplifies most clearly the conceptual and material conditions and implications, effects and challenges of *raceless racisms*, of racist informalisms and individualization, of mannered racisms and racial avoidance. In short, of neoliberalizing racisms. Second, the expansive, almost horizon-less proliferation of racially significant, inflected, or suggestive terms throughout Latin America, many with shifting meanings not only across space and time but also from one user or user-group to another, speaks to the complexity of racial arrangements. Yet it refers also to the varieties and range of racial investment throughout the region.

These two considerations – the historical seepage across the region of raceless racisms and conceptual proliferation – together challenge the possibilities of counting by race. Throughout Latin America just five state censuses, for instance, have enabled African-descended self-classification: Bolivia, Brazil, Colombia, Costa Rica, and Ecuador. Others, such as the Dominican Republic, Mexico, Nicaragua, Panama, or Venezuela, all with at least recognizable African historical presence, do not count in racial terms at all. The case of the Racial Privacy Act in parts of the US, I argued earlier, reveals the debilitating implications of refusing to count by race in the face of extended structural restrictions imposed through race. The problem at least is now recognized: a recent conference organized by the InterAmerican Development Bank and the World Bank in Cartegena began the process of promoting racial counting in national census-taking across Latin America, fueled perhaps by the mix of concerns for social stability and labor shortages.

Racial latinamericanization signals more. Thus, third, it exemplifies the more or less informal identification of race with class formation. It reveals the correlation of whiteness as structural condition with relative wealth, education, social privilege, standing, access, and advancement, and blackness structurally with exclusion or restriction on these indices. As illustrated, individuals elevating along these dimensions are taken to be white(r), to be whitening up. In this regard, racial latinamericanization offers the model for such developments in other regions, most notably but far from only post-apartheid South Africa. Aspects of the Latin American model inflect recent experience both in the US and in Europe.

Racial latinamericanization, I have stressed, models the general structural conditions for racial arrangement and social order neoliberally fueled, structured, elaborated, and circulated in and across other site-specific applications.

Fourth, latinamericanization racially conceived exhibits the trials, tribulations, possibilities, parameters, and rewards of *mestizaje/mesticagem*. It reveals how the otherwise attractive celebration of mixture threatens to draw attention away from the materialities of racial injustices, of the debilitating exclusions produced and effected by racisms. It follows, fifth, that the individualizing of discrimination and exclusion, and the slipperiness as well as ghost-like quality of racial terms, make it an often thankless, even burdensome task to point out racist discrimination. Critics of racisms are taken as akin to whistleblowers, and often treated analogously – as spoilsports, or paranoid, or just plain delusional, seeing wrong by invoking ghostly terms the prevailing social order claims to reject (which is not to deny that in some cases they may be). Racist exclusions accordingly become unreferenced even as they permeate sociality. They are society's unspoken because unspeakable, often unrecognizable because lacking the terms of characterization or engagement, but where recognizable more often than not in deep denial. The ghost in the machine of neoliberal sociality.

Antiracist social movements are those movements to mobilize for greater social recognition, access and equality, and protection from discrimination when focused on and around race as principal organizing feature. They will more likely succeed, where at all, in enabling greater recognition than they are likely to produce any significant material benefits or dramatic social improvements, as Michael Hanchard has demonstrated in the case of Brazil's *Moviemiento Negro*. Vigorous access, equality, and diminished discrimination require ongoing, relentless, scaled social challenge and change around residential improvement and interraciality, significantly better educational opportunities from the earliest age, steady employment, public recognition and general enforcement of the importance of anti-discrimination regimes.

Post-apartheid South Africa in the past decade has been struggling with just these concerns, and with the tensions between antiracist transformation, racelessness, socio-class divisions, ongoing debilitations, and the devastating of everyday life. I turn now to consider post-apartheid South Africa's experiment in the context of its long duration of racial unfolding, as the fifth and final focus in my study of racial regionalizations.

Bibliography

Aidi, Hisham 2002: "History Notes: Blacks in Argentina: Disappearing Acts"; www.cwo.com/~lucumi/argentina.html.

Anderson, Benedict 1991: *Imagined Communities: Reflections on the Origins and Spread of Nationalism.* London: Verso.

Andrade, Oswaldo de 1928/2001: *Anthropophagite Manifesto (Escritos antropó-fagos: selección, cronología y postfacio).* Alejandra Laera and Gonzalo Aguilar. Buenos Aires: Corregidor; www.coleccioncisneros.org/st_writ.asp?IDLanguage= 1&ID=17&Type=2.

Appelbaum, Nancy, Macpherson, Anne, and Rosemblatt, Karin, eds. 2003: *Race and Nation in Modern Latin America.* Chapel Hill: University of North Carolina Press.

Bailey, Stanley, and Telles, Edward 2006: "Multicultural versus Collective Black Categories: Examining Census Classification Debates in Brazil," *Ethnicities*, 6, 1 (March), 74–101.

Balibar, Etienne 1991: "Is There a Neo-Racism?", in Etienne Balibar and Immanuel Wallerstein, *Race, Nation, Class: Ambiguous Identities.* London: Verso, pp. 17–28.

Barraclough, Colin 2002: "Race-Hate Groups Find Virtual Haven in Argentina," *Christian Science Monitor*, August 23, 3; www.csmonitor.com/2002/0823/ p07s02-woam.htm.

Bhabha, Homi K. 1994: "Of Mimicry and Man: The Ambivalence of Colonial Discourse," in *The Location of Culture.* London: Routledge, pp. 85–92.

Briggs, Charles and Mantini-Briggs, Clara 2003: *Stories in the Time of Cholera: Racial Profiling During a Medical Nightmare.* Berkeley: University of California Press.

Brunner, Jose Joaquin 2004: "Notes on Modernity and Postmodernity in Latin American Culture," in A. Del Sarto, A. Rios, and A. Trigo (eds.), *The Latin American Studies Reader.* Durham, NC: Duke University Press, pp. 291–309.

Buckley, Stephen 2000: "Brazil's Racial Awakening," *Washington Post*, Monday, June 12, A12; www.hartford-hwp.com/archives/42/133.html.

Canclini, Nestor Garcia 2000: "From National Capital to Global Capital: Urban Change in Mexico City," *Public Culture* 12, 1, 207–13.

Center of United Marginalized Populations, Brazilian Institute of Geography and Statistics: www.lbge.gov.br.

Chakrabarty, Dipesh 2000: *Provincializing Europe: Postcolonial Thought and Historical Difference.* Princeton: Princeton University Press.

Cheng, Anne Anlin 2001: *The Melancholy of Race: Psychoanalysis, Assimilation, and Hidden Grief.* New York: Oxford University Press.

Chomsky, Noam 1999: *Latin America: From Colonization to Globalization.* New York: Oceans Press.

Comaroff, Jean and Comaroff, John L. 2000: "Millenial Capitalism: First Thoughts on a Second Coming," in Jean Comaroff and John L. Comaroff (eds.), "Millenial Capitalism and the Culture of Neoliberalism" (Special Issue), *Public Culture*, 12, 2 (Spring), 291–343.

Da Silva, Denise Ferreira 2007: *Toward a Global Idea of Race*. Minneapolis: University of Minnesota Press.

Dávila, Jerry 2003: *Diploma of Whiteness: Race and Social Policy in Brazil, 1917–1945*. Durham, NC: Duke University Press.

De la Cadena, Marisol 2000: *Indigenous Mestizos: The Politics of Race and Culture in Cuzco, Peru, 1919–1991*. Durham, NC: Duke University Press.

De la Cadena, Marisol 2005: "Are Mestizos Hybrids? The Conceptual Politics of Andean Identities," *Journal of Latin American Studies*, 37 (May), 259–84.

De la Fuente, Alejandro 2001: *Race Inequality and Politics in Twentieth-Century Cuba*. Chapel Hill: University of North Carolina Press.

Del Sarto, Ana, Rios, Alicia, and Trigo, Avril, eds. 2004: *The Latin American Cultural Studies Reader*. Durham, NC: Duke University Press.

Eng, David and Han Shinhee 2003: "A Dialogue on Racial Melancholia," in David Eng and David Kazanjian (eds.), *Loss*. Berkeley: University of California Press, pp. 343–72.

Enwezor, Okwui et al., eds. 2003: *Creolite and Creolization: Documenta 11_ Platform 3*. Ostfildern-Ruit, Germany: Hatje Cantz.

Essed, Philomena 1991: *Understanding Everyday Racism: An Interdisciplinary Theory*. Newbury Park, CA: Sage.

Essed, Philomena 2005: "Gendered Preferences in Racialized Spaces: Cloning the Physician," in Karim Murji and John Solomos (eds.), *Racialization*. Oxford: Oxford University Press, pp. 229–46.

Essed, Philomena 2006: "Aggressive Tolerance: The Peculiar Career of Racism in the Netherlands," Keynote Address, International Cross-Disciplinary Conference on "Racism, Postcolonialism, Europe," May 15–17. Copy on file.

Fontaine, Pierre-Michel, ed. 1985: *Race, Class and Power in Brazil*. Los Angeles: Center for Afro-American Studies (UCLA).

Foucault, Michel 2003: *"Society Must Be Defended": Lectures at the Collège de France, 1975–76*. Trans. David Macey. New York: Picador.

Freud, Sigmund 1927/1953: "Mourning and Melancholia," in *The Standard Edition of the Complete Psychological Works of Sigmund Freud*, Vol. 14. Trans. and ed. James Strachey. London: Hogarth Press.

Gund, Rosemary 1996: "Not Black and White," www.brazzil.com/p16oct96.htm.

Gund, Rosemary 2005: "Discrimination Out in the Open," May 14; www.brazzil.com/content/view/9228/0/.

Hall, Stuart 2003: "Creolization, Diaspora, and Hybridity in the Context of Globalization," in Okwui Enwezor et al. (eds.), *Creolite and Creolization: Documenta 11_Platform 3*. Ostfildern-Ruit: Hatje Cantz, pp. 185–98.

Hanchard, Michael 1994: *Orpheus and Power: The Movimento Negro of Rio de Janeiro and São Paulo, 1945–1988*. Princeton: Princeton University Press.

Hanchard, Michael 2006: *Party/Politics? Topics in Black Political Thought*. Oxford: Oxford University Press.

Holt, Thomas 2003: "The First New Nations," in Nancy Appelbaum, Anne Macpherson, and Karin Rosemblatt (eds.), *Race and Nation in Modern Latin America*. Chapel Hill: University of North Carolina Press, pp. vii–xiv.

Hume, David 1964: "Of National Characters," in *The Philosophical Works*. Ed. T. H. Green and T. H. Grose III. Aalen, Germany: Scientia Verlag.

Jackson, Richard L. 1992: " 'Mestizaje' vs. Black Identity: The Color Crisis in Latin America," in David Hellwig (ed.), *African-American Reflections on Brazil's Racial Paradise*. Philadelphia: Temple University Press, pp. 216–24.

Katzew, Ilona 2004: *Casta Painting: Images of Race in Eighteenth-Century Mexico*. New Haven: Yale University Press.

Katzew, Ilona and Goldberg, David Theo 2004: "Race and Classification: The Case of Mexican America," A One-Day Symposium, Los Angeles County Museum of Art, May 1; www.uchri.org/page-no-cat.php?page_id=1196.

Levine, Robert and Crocitti, John, eds. 1999: *The Brazil Reader: History, Culture, Politics*. Durham, NC: Duke University Press.

McGuinness, Aims 2003: "Searching for 'Latin America': Race and Sovereignty in the Americas in the 1850s," in Nancy Appelbaum, Anne Macpherson, and Karin Rosemblatt (eds.), *Race and Nation in Modern Latin America*. Chapel Hill: University of North Carolina Press, pp. 87–107.

Morrison, Toni 1992: *Playing in the Dark*. Cambridge, MA: Harvard University Press.

Peters, Troy 2005: "Understanding Pickaninnies and Improving the Race," *Black Commentator*, 147, July 21; www.blackcommentator.com/147/147_guest_peters_pickaninnies_pf.html.

Phillips, Brian 2005: "Brazil's Racial History: Democracy or Discrimination," *International Journal of Diversity in Organizations, Communities and Nations*, 5, 1, 117–24.

Phillips, Caryl 1987: *The European Tribe*. London: Faber and Faber.

Pierson, Donald 1942: *Negroes in Brazil: A Study of Race Conflict in Bahia*. Carbondale: Southern Illinois University Press.

Quesada, Charo 2005: "Invisible Citizens?" *IDBAmerica: Magazine of the InterAmerica Development Bank*, June 11; www.iadb.org/idbamerica/English/JUL01E/jul01e7.html.

Quijano, Anibal 2000: "Coloniality of Power, Eurocentrism, and Latin America," *Nepantla: Views from South*, 1, 3, 533–80.

Randall, Vernellia 2001: "Racial Discrimination in Argentina: Executive Summary," Human Rights Documentation Center, September; academic.udayton.edu/race/06hrights/GeoRegions/SouthAmerica/argentina01.htm.

Reichmann, Rebecca, ed. 1999: *Race in Contemporary Brazil: From Indifference to Inequality*. University Park: Pennsylvania State University.

Ribeiro, Darcy 1971: *The Americas and Civilization*. New York: Dutton.

Sansone, Livio 2003: *Blackness without Ethnicity: Constructing Race in Brazil*. London: Palgrave Macmillan.

Sarduy, Pedro Perez and Stubbs, Jean 2000: *Afro-Cuban Voices: On Race and Identity in Contemporary Cuba*. Gainesville: University of Florida Press.

Sawyer, Mark Q. 2006: *Racial Politics in Postrevolutionary Cuba*. Cambridge: Cambridge University Press.

Schwarz, Roberto 2004: "Brazilian Culture: Nationalism by Elimination," in A. Del Sarto, A. Rios, and A. Trigo (eds.), *The Latin American Studies Reader*. Durham, NC: Duke University Press, pp. 233–49.

Seed, Patricia 1982: "Social Dimensions of Race: Mexico City, 1753," *Hispanic American Historical Review*, 62, 4, 596–606.

Spence, Glenys 2000: "The Wages of Whiteness in a Sinful Paradise: Blacks in Costa Rica," *Black Diaspora* (July/August), 48ff.; www.weyanoke.org/BlacksInCostaRica.htm.

Stephens, Thomas M. 1989: *Dictionary of Latin American Racial and Ethnic Terminology*. Gainesville: University of Florida Press.

Telles, Edward 2004: *Race in Another America: The Significance of Skin Color in Brazil*. Princeton: Princeton University Press.

Torres, Arlene and Whitten, Jr., Norman 1998: "General Introduction: To Forge the Future in the Fires of the Past," in Arlene Torres and Norman Whitten, Jr. (eds.), *Blackness in Latin America and the Caribbean*, Vol. 2. Bloomington: Indiana University Press, pp. 3–33.

Verrisimo, Carlos 1994–5: "Apartheid in Americas," *CrossRoads*, December/January; www.hartford-hwp.com/archives/42/035.html.

Wade, Peter 1993: *Blackness and Race Mixture: The Dynamics of Race Mixture in Colombia*. Baltimore: Johns Hopkins University Press.

Wade, Peter 1997: *Race and Ethnicity in Latin America*. London: Pluto Press.

Wade, Peter 2003: "Race and Nation in Latin America: Afterword," in Nancy Appelbaum, Anne Macpherson, and Karin Rosemblatt (eds.), *Race and Nation in Modern Latin America*. Chapel Hill: University of North Carolina Press, pp. 263–81.

Warfren, Jonathan 2001: *Racial Revolutions: Antiracism and Indian Resurgence in Brazil*. Durham, NC: Duke University Press.

Winddance Twine, France 1998: *Racism in a Racial Democracy*. New Brunswick, NJ: Rutgers University Press.

Wipert, Gregory 2004: "Racism and Racial Divides in Venezuela: Chucho Garcia Interview," Venezuelanalysis.com, January 21; www.venezuelanalysis.com/articles.php?artno=1091.

7

A Political Theology of Race
(On Racial Southafricanization)

When the Europeans came, they brought the Bible, and we had the land;
now we have the Bible, and they have the land.

South African proverb

Modernity, I have been suggesting throughout, cast(e)s long shadows. The shadows deepen to the periphery, fading into a lighter shade of projected off-white the closer to the metropolitan modern is the cast(e).

From the earliest moments of encounter and unequal exchange, the colonial prehistory of South Africa introduced effects with more or less permanent and interacting impacts: modern urban-making and the politics of its contestation, its remaking according to a blueprint of ruled division; the knotted, contested, often tragic politics of more or less robust mixture, ethnoracially, miscegenationally, socio-culturally; and the threatening political economy of racial division, separation, and segregation, with their invariably, even inevitably, tragic effects.

Vasco da Gama's first voyage around Africa in late 1497 may have signaled the sort of violence European colonization was yet to institutionalize in southern Africa. European settlement on the mainland Cape, however, only followed a century and a half later. Between the beginning of the sixteenth century and Dutch settlement of the Cape under the direction of the Dutch East Indies Company (VOC) initiated in 1652, perceived indigenous hostility, treacherous maritime conditions, and European enamorment with the spice and porcelain trade of the East Indies restricted the southern end of Africa to a way station on a long sea-journey. Conditions were considered so challenging that European seafarers avoided the mainland altogether. They preferred using Robben Island, that small piece of then uninhabited land in Table Bay within easy view of the Cape mainland. The island – later a leper colony, mental asylum, and political prison of such infamy – was made a source of fresh vegetables and sometime mail station. This casual if crucial restocking site – salt-splashed, wind-whipped, and weather-worn – produced less than enough. By the mid-seventeenth century it had given way to larger, more dramatic designs by the Dutch intent on expansive geo-economic domination.

So 1652 dramatically altered the siting of southern Africa in euro-modernity's global trajectory, much as 1492 had done in the case of the New World. Seafaring had transformed under the water-soaked hands of the Dutch from simply adventurism, the carrier of cargo, and wealth enhancement to assertion of global military and political power. The sea had become the means not just to wealth but to military might and geostrategic positioning, in short, to the quest for dominant and lasting imperial power. Control of sea passage and traffic was the key to power over land, resources, people. But the pursuit of sea control in turn entailed also harbors, restocking stations, and so produce as well as access to livestock. These things likewise led to local trade.

Traffic and trade, then, were the necessary if not sufficient prompts of the first settler buildings on the mainland. The fear of native hostility meant that the first act of settlement was a gated community, a fortress for housing the fearless settlers. Towning, and later urbanization, subsequently (one could even say consequently) more or less inevitably were to follow. By the late seventeenth century, Cape Town was already in the making.

The Cape was a strategic gem. For one, it offered breathtaking landscape, and abundant agricultural promise. (For the first 50 years or so of settlement, unfamiliar soil and social challenges meant the Dutch settlers had to import more food than they could provide in fact.) More strategically, the southern corner of the Cape offered a sentinel to monitor traffic across the southern Atlantic and Indian Oceans, long preceding the availability either of the Suez or Panama Canals. Indeed, outlook posts along the Cape Peninsula came later – under the British – to bear names such as Signal Hill and The Sentinel. In keeping perhaps with its nomination, *De Kaap van Goede Hoop*/Cape of Good Hope effectively controlled flows – of sea traffic, goods, people, arms – across the southern hemisphere, west to east and back again.

In the Mix

As the crossroads of vigorous traffic, the settling of the Cape quickly came to mean, effectively to produce if not encourage, robust interaction, emergent ethnoracial and cultural mixing. Mixing came early in the struggles around settlement. Van Riebeeck's five boats included 90 Europeans, 82 men, and just 8 women, one Van Riebeeck's wife. It wasn't long before what later would become some prominent Afrikaner family names were being spawned in mixture.

Along with early European dispositions regarding race, the Dutch settlers brought with them the skill of formal record-keeping, whether through public or church records, noting marriages, births and deaths, thus offering a glimpse into pre-segregationist culture. Racial dispositions were already being forged in intra-European intellectual debates, emanating a century earlier most notably from Spain and Portugal. Dutch experience with the slave trade and piracy predated settlement of the Cape by nearly a century and a half. Early racial disposition was forged from the amalgam of biblical equality and a sense of cultural superiority born of projected environmental differences. Seven years into settlement, the Dutch tried to build a border hedge separating themselves from what Van Riebeeck had characterized as the "brutal," "wild," "thievish," and untrustworthy Khoikhoi, more an act of Lockean property enclosure than an early prototype of apartheid, as some have suggested.

In any case, even if early enclosure was an attempt at racially driven segregation rather than simply an assertion of property rights, it failed dismally. The first recorded mixed marriage occurred 12 years into settlement, bringing together Pieter van Meerhof, a Danish member of Van Riebeeck's landing party, and Kratoa, a Khoi woman working as interpreter for the settlers.

Close working relationships notwithstanding – or perhaps enabled by imbalanced power and status relations – no doubt turned into intimacies of another sort. A larger list of offspring followed, leading to the Zaaiman family line that later included significant characters in apartheid's political history such as Paul Kruger (Boer leader and president of the rebel South African or Transvaal Republic from 1880 till its defeat in the Anglo-Boer War in 1900) and Jan Smuts (twice prime minister, most notably as an Allied Force member during World War II). But it included more recently also F. W. de Klerk (the last president of the apartheid republic and the man credited, with Nelson Mandela, for handing power over peacefully to genuine majority rule; it signals deeply significant change that today Mandela rather than De Klerk is far more readily and properly remembered as both symbolic of and critical contributor to apartheid's demise).

The lasting demographic differences, racial *and* gendered, of this increasingly robust heterogeneity were entangled with extended inequalities in power, effectively leading to ongoing sexual relationships between European men and women of color (reverse relationships were *almost* altogether unthinkable). Dutch colonization was effected by the VOC, a private trading company, licensed by the Dutch state to represent its colonial interests initially in Asia and later more broadly even as it sought to maximize profits for its principal shareholders. Under Dutch company rule, lasting until the end of the eighteenth century when the Company went bankrupt, mixed marriages were permissible in the colonies, though restricted from returning to the Netherlands for fear of unsettling the political order of the metropole. Across the period, there were something like 1,300 legally recorded unions between European men and local women of color at the Cape, no doubt considerably more unrecorded if not thoroughly unacknowledged.

Well-known Afrikaner families followed from these liaisons across race, gender, and class, among them the Bassons, Berghs, Brits, Carstens, Claassens, Cloetes, Combrinks, Fischers, and Slabberts. Simon van der Stel, Dutch Governor of the Cape from 1692 and after whom the town and university of Stellenbosch came to be named, was the offspring of a Dutch father, himself commander of the island of Mauritius, and a mother in part Malay. The later legacy of these relationships included prominent Voortrekker and ultimately Nationalist Party leaders, the ancestors, architects, and sons of apartheid Afrikanerdom, bent on repressively excising memory of the darker side of their family heritage. The number of white Afrikaners with mixed race heritage today no doubt runs in the thousands, and has been estimated by Afrikaans demographers at about 6 or 7 percent of the ethnic group.

Early Cape mixing is notable for a number of reasons. Settlement of the Cape came a century after the famous debate at Valladolid between Las Casas and Sepúlveda, a half-century of robust slave trading from Africa to the New World, and at least a century of Dutch activity in the far East Indies. The monogenism associated with the Catholic Church still reigned, equating all before God, and the connected challenges of both polygenism and pre-Adamism were yet to be registered, as too the emergent philosophical influence of John Locke, not least regarding race. Race was not yet quite so threatening, its reach not quite so universal or restrictive as it would become a century later yet. The rise of Protestantism, and most notably the strict Calvinist strain among the Dutch, elevated the notion of divine election, made conversion more difficult, and mixture between those considered chosen and those deemed doomed subject to greater constraints than they had been earlier.

In the first 50 years or so of settlement, intercourse with those considered racially inferior was not yet quite so deeply taken to fly in the face of nature, to be procreating with animals, as it would be by the mid-eighteenth century. Slaves were soon imported by the Dutch, first from Angola and West Africa, later from South Asia. The enslaveable were visibly different, to be sure, not European, not or not fully Christian but not yet regarded as in- or pre-human, perennially or inevitably lower inhabitants of the hierarchy of being.

The slave-house, home at its height to 500 or so Dutch East Indies Company slaves, became a brothel for a brief period each night, frequented by Company agents, employees, and even burghers. Rest time was disrupted for women and men slaves alike, women forced into a second bondage of the body, the men reduced to helplessness in the face of these visits. Notable Afrikaner families that followed from such patronage included the DuPlessis, Myburgh, and Pretorius clans. These at least were the acknowledged, the identifiable progeny of mixture. Touched more heavily and over a much longer time by the sun and the harsh geography of Africa, Africans were different enough to warrant enslaveability but not yet considered so different that they couldn't be profitably (re-)productive, socially, economically, or sexually. State policy and regulation – its governing rationality – were not (yet) principally fashioned by, through, and in terms of race. All that would come, ironically, with the Enlightenment and later with the British takeover of Cape governance.

Marriage was quickly defined as a bond between those baptized into Christianity, restricting marriage thus to the free, though not sexual intercourse, of course. And men and women, once baptized, were free to enter into cross-racial conjugal relations, even where concubinage and out-of-wedlock intercourse were frowned upon, if more or less widely practiced. Men became attracted to, or lustful towards, the women who worked for them, not yet completely inhibited by the threats race later came to carry: perceived primitivity in custom and condition, projected lack of fertility, degeneration, and ultimately inhumanity. Women gave into, were even attracted by, the relative privilege and modicum of power such relationships of intimacy licensed. Intimacies, as Ann Stoler has commented upon extensively in the case of the Dutch in the East Indies, enabled a negotiation of the field of modern morality and sociality, the laboratory of modernity.

Dutch colonial rule, of course, also predated the Victorian British will to global power more than a century on, and the forms of racial subjection and proto-segregation the latter entailed. Colonizing Dutch men, from Batavia to the Dutch West Indies, were unbounded by the formalities of strict segregation with which British settler rule later came to be identified. Intermarriage in other Dutch colonies, while hardly widespread, conjured at least an ambivalent response, and mixed offspring were more widespread than the officializing of any miscegenating intercourse.

Early instances of mixing at the Cape were for obvious reasons relatively small in number. Reliable data are tough to come by, ranging at any one time between roughly 3 and 10 percent of European men for whom formal relationships with local (usually Khoisan) or imported women of color were recorded, strongly suggesting (as I must keep insisting) a larger number of unrecorded relationships. But, as I've indicated also, of lasting if repressed significance. Colonizing Dutch men no doubt experienced similar desires to those of Spanish *conquistadores* in Latin America, but found themselves subject perhaps to greater socio-cultural and by extension self-constraint.

If early modes of cross-racial sexual intercourse could more or less be acknowledged, cultural influence was thought to run in one direction. Those considering themselves superior do not admit to cultural influence or impression from below. By the same token, the impact on Europeans by the indigenous and imported is in many ways obvious: food, clothing, language, visual art, music, perhaps occasionally also survival skills in unfriendly environments. The robustness of cultural mixing is reflected in the fact that at the onset of the eighteenth century the languages that could be heard at the Cape included Dutch and Khoikhoi, to be sure, but in addition French, Portuguese, Hindi, Malay, Malagasy, Mandarin, and Javanese, not to mention a local patois. The lure of cultural promiscuity may have had sexual implications too. Once tasted, it may have been that sexual intercourse with non-European women was considered more satisfying because less inhibited by stultifying European manner, dress, and morals.

From the outset, European culture was taken by the settlers to be elevated, where the indigenous were recognized to have culture at all. As in Latin America, euro-mimesis set the imposed cultural standard, the horizon of rationality, of intellectual prowess and aesthetic metric. No matter, though. *Cultural métissage*, policed as it is, nevertheless usually far outstrips the miscegenational. Not least because it creeps up unsuspectingly, takes hold unexpectedly, and settles in unmentionably.

As it emerged over the next two and a half centuries, South Africa came to exemplify the effects of more or less intense cultural mixing, in denial perhaps but nonetheless undeniable. The settlers may have thought themselves European, and Europeans may have considered the Cape Colony an extension of Europe, civilization beset by premodern discontent, the perceived hostility of the landscape notwithstanding. But it is equally the case that from Europe the settlers generally were thought provincial, more or less marginal in thought and habit, debased perhaps not just by distance but by proximity of and to nativity too.

Mixing, miscegenational and cultural, was never simply just between European settlers, first Dutch and then British, on one side, and the indigenous, initially Khoisan and more than a century later Xhosa and Zulu, on the other. And of course mixture with the already mixed was always more robust, from both sides of the divide. Intercourse was always multiply, complexly interactive. On the European side, as the case of Meertens indicates, the Dutch settlers brought with them some non-Dutch Europeans, seeking adventure, wealth, power, but also simply survival from life's trials and tribulations in economically challenged Central Europe. Before long, and especially with decline of Dutch control in the late eighteenth century, slaves were being imported from socio-cultural horizons further afield, including Madagascar, India, and Malaysia, driven by formal East India Company restrictions on the enslavability of the locals. Thus came Hinduism and Islam to the Cape. The British followed at the close of the eighteenth century, bringing in their wake sources of labor from their other colonies, most notably India, and interacting with both Xhosa and Zulu as settlement seeped up the east coast.

Far from a *terra nullius*, the land that came to be the laboratory of apartheid was from almost the outset of euro-modernizing and largely as a result of practices endemic to colonization a *terra mixta*.

This prompts a more general point. Much less than an anomaly of social being arising late in the record of social history, heterogeneity and mixing are actually marks of human being. The Cape offers a case in point. Khoi, perhaps even more so than San, are now commonly thought from the archaeological evidence to have emerged from many thousands of years of miscegenation with equally mobile East African groups before finding their way to the southern part of Africa. Mixture and its outcome, cultural as much as miscegenational, are products of human movement, as old as homo sapiens. Movement and so mixture may have become more robust with the euro-modern, and so more noticeable. But that's not to say they are absent earlier. Quite the contrary. Biodiversity is as much a human condition as one marking plant and animal life. It would be surprising if it were otherwise; it is shocking that so many have thought to the contrary.

And yet the unstable status of the mixed is revealed in the fact that those of mixed descent could be indentured as apprentices to masters until they turned 25. The category "capturing" this status is revealing: *Ingeboekte Bastaard Hottentoten*, literally, registered persons (or apprentices) of mixed ("mongrel" or "debased") background lacking recognized paternity. Those of mixed parentage, especially in cases where the white father remained anonymous, were more or less automatically considered debased and as such easy targets of indenture. This presumption lingered long: in 1950s and 1960s South Africa, the term "bastard" continued to have the presumptive connotation of a person (usually a man) lacking paternity. Class debasement approaching the implication of racial defilement; and emasculation in a society in which manliness was the presumptive measure of all things human.

There are larger linguistic ironies at work here. The creole language that would later be consolidated into Afrikaans emerged as much in the kitchen to enable enslaved women to communicate with the wives of those owning them as around the campfires of the frontier. A very large percentage of burgher (citizen) households owned at least a small amount of slaves, who pretty much serviced the entire household economy from cleaning and cooking to childrearing and market-shopping. In these originating linguistic sites the language of apartheid was born in the demands of cultural translation. If post-apartheid South Africa has a lingua franca, an indigenously prompted language more or less universally available to its heterogeneous population, it may now be Afrikaans rather than – or at least alongside and interactive with – the more globally prompted commercial and administrative univeralism of English. Or at least a patois at the inter-tongue, so to speak, of various local languages. Masculinity as the social measure of man has fallen flat on its face.

Two obvious oversights mark most historians' accounts of the role of race and racism in the early formation of South Africa. First, virtually no historian of southern Africa (Giliomee and Maylam are two very modest exceptions) looks to the impact on Cape settlers in the seventeenth and eighteenth centuries of changing ideas of race in Europe. Historians who discuss at length whether slavery gives rise to racial rationalization, in the Cape as elsewhere, or whether race may have been formative in the negotiation of social relations from early settlement onwards, restrict their discussions in the very posing of the binary completely to conditions at the Cape. The hold of national history fixes fast. But the counter-conditions cut against this fixation.

Company agents, administrators, *arbeiders* (workers), and adventurers were coming and going quite frequently between Europe and the colony, and these Europeans no doubt carried with them from metropole to province and back again the latest understandings and representations of racial conception. Ideas travel, as and with the people who do. Metropolitan ideas more often than not are looked to by the provincials as fashion, influence, inspiration, even as those in the provinces adapt them to their own purposes, experiment with them, return them revised to sender. It surely was no different with race.

Second, and relatedly, the overwhelming assumption among historians of South Africa is that racial ideas were somehow *un*changing across time, a view completely at odds with the historical record in Europe itself, as I have argued at length elsewhere and hinted at above. As ideas about race in Europe shifted and these ideas circulated globally, so ideas at the Cape changed too. Indeed, we can say something more complex.

European ideas around race were largely fashioned and were in fluctuation over time in response to travel narratives and administrative and existential experiences recounted from the colonies, the Cape included. Not to be too simplistic or reductive about it, one could say that the "evidence" and experience for racial theorizing were drawn by Europeans in good part from what they took to be their colonial experience. But by the same token, racial theories largely crafted in Europe and changing over time were exported to the colonies to be deployed in relation to local circumstance, ordering modes of governance, administrative regulation, spatial arrangement, and social intercourse.

Underlying the absence of these assumptions from the dominant historiographical record is the view, widespread among historians of South Africa, that somehow racism takes firm hold only in the nineteenth century. There may be evidence of strands of racial thinking and racist dispositions towards "the native" before, but it is really only with the rise of scientific racism, on this view, that the impact of European racism can be considered to kick in. This, I have been insisting, is not simply mistaken, it also fails to recognize the changing forms of racial thinking, its differential social implications, and its variant effects over time.

It likewise fails to comprehend how racism and racial thinking by the eighteenth century, at the Cape as in Europe, start to assume the status of a compelling *political theology*. A political theology of race begins amounting to the impact of a compulsion increasingly in the eighteenth century, both as the insistence that people believe and as the forcing – or oftentimes the reinforcing – of compliance, ideologically and behaviorally, culturally and socio-politically.

Race as Political Theology

The force of race begins to take hold among Europeans as the social hold of religion shifts in face of increasing individualization and the emerging power of scientific rationality, epistemological auto-foundationalism, and the grounds of moral self-generation. Race assumes increasing social hegemony as monogenism gives way initially to speculations around polygenesis, differentiated origins, and species proliferation from the later sixteenth century on, then to elaborations of evolution and eugenicism in the latter half of the nineteenth century. The thick resonances of the theological are evident in the underlying referent points of both monogenism (Adam as the source of all humanity, differentiation thus the effects of environmental determination) and polygenism (there are human beings whose origins predate Adam, which accounts for their more animal-like characteristics). Over time, race comes to generate a secularized theology and a civic religion, underpinned initially by appeals to God's dictum but increasingly resorting to claims to scientific validation.

The political theology of race seeks to account for origins, circumscribes rationality, motivates the social fabric and its constitutive forms of exclusion, orders politics and grounds power, liberating cruelty from constraint.

Race, in short, grants embodiment to the will to power.

If religion is a project of inherent self-servitude, of subjection to God's will, then religion's supposedly secularizing repression under modernity by killing off God is a project of self-liberation, an *abolitionist* project. God is done away with in the name of humanity's self-willed power. But it is a humanism that co*term*inously constrains its extension, delimiting its license to those just like me, the familiar and familial. The family of man previously conceived in and by religious order is now animated by the absolutes of racial representation. Where group slaughter was hitherto prompted directly in the name of religious demonism, for the modern project mass slaughter becomes mediated through the motivating threat of racial *term*ination.

Race accordingly is a perfect exemplification of the sort of sacred violence Achille Mbembe finds critiqued by St. Paul in his Letters to the

Galatians. It "purchases order by means of victims and scapegoats," offering laws of purity, acts of purification, and profanity (as Mary Douglas famously has elaborated it), on one hand, while identifying the sacrificeable, on the other. It licenses violence against those who violate, who fail inherently or even contingently to belong to the sacred community, to the Heavenly City, the City of God.

Pariahs are those who are seen to have invaded the Heavenly City of the elected community, to have soiled it by their presence. They are considered threatening by their very presence, by who they are, what they are taken to stand for, by the threat of polluting mixture they represent. They threaten, in short, to reduce the City of God to that of earthly sins, of pollution, of the fall from Eden, to the heterodox carnivality – the profanity – of Jericho. They must therefore be expelled or expired so as to secure the familial in their chosen, their self-elevated status. The history of race, it could be said, is the history of that securitization against the dirt of the non-belonging and -believing. The history of racial theo-politics is the legacy of *disposability*.

The theological law of race is thus constitutively violent, divisive and dividing, modernity's Curse. The history of anti-racism, of its abolitionist commitments, is that of a refusal to be bound by this law, by its political theology and theologically mediated politics. South Africa offers the exemplary landscape of the political theology of race, and of its resistance, its ambivalent rejection.

Settlers brought with them prevailing European conceptions of race at the time. Giliomee reports a letter of 1707 from a group of European burghers residing in Stellenbosch, for example, characterizing "untrustworthy" blacks as "the blood of Ham." This biblically charged view attributing the mark of physically signifying difference was circulating increasingly in European intellectual circles of the day, indicating the fixing of political distinction in terms of religious curse. References to the myth of Ham dot written characterizations by white administrators, clergymen, and travelers at the Cape through much of the eighteenth century.

This is not to suggest that the "curse of Ham" is characteristic of Afrikaner Calvinism, a view André du Toit rejects only half-convincingly. Rather, it indicates the ways in which a variety of racially ordering views imported from Europe is circulated to sustain or rationalize white political, economic, cultural, and moral control in the Cape context. In similar vein, the letter Giliomee cites also offers the first written record at the Cape of the Arabic term *kafir* to refer to Khoi as black heathens. This is a term generalized later in South Africa to characterize all black inhabitants, assuming much of the historical significance that "nigger" does in North America.

By the 1730s in Europe, monogenism was giving way to the likes of pre-Adamism and the view that differentiated kinds of human beings enjoyed multiple origins. Increasingly, the story of Adam was taken to account only for European origins and African origins were considered by a growing number of European intellectuals to be closer to those of animals. As such they could be variously devoured.

Racial views at the Cape began coterminously to reify, no doubt a mix of European intellectual influence and the micro-details of local grudges and resentments. The bulk of new European settlers at the time were German laborers and tradesmen. Fleeing poverty and unemployment as a result of the Thirty Years' War, they were lured to the most powerful European economy of the day. Their salvation was to sign up with the Dutch East Indies Company for a five-year commitment to work at the Cape, much as French Huguenot families had done to escape anti-Calvinist persecution by Catholic-dominated France in 1688.

Status differences between Europeans and non-Europeans at the Cape were becoming more fixed in the first decades of the eighteenth century too. There remained free blacks, mostly innkeepers, fishermen, and artisans, some themselves slave-owners, though few successful farmers, squeezed out by the premium on available land, the lack of access to capital, and a monopoly over the lucrative supply of meat to passing Company ships. There was also an emergent, growing class of mixed descent. Nevertheless, effectively pretty much only Europeans or those of recognizably European descent could become members of the citizen class (*burgher*) or rise to hold office.

The population of the Cape increased steadily throughout the eighteenth century, among both whites and recorded blacks. As farmland in the Western Cape grew scarce in the face of fierce burgher competition, boers began expanding inland. The further they spread from the port and trading capital of Kaapstadt (Cape Town), the more tenuous grew the hold of administrative rule over them and the more independent and self-governing they became. And as the interior opened up, asserting governmental and administrative control over indigenous groups became a challenge, as did too so basic a bureaucratic task as identifying existing groups and where they resided.

The trekboers – stock farmers who had moved to the interior to make lives for themselves – interacted closely with their Khoisan servants and slaves, even as they continued to draw fast distinctions between themselves and "the Bushman-Hottentots," to use the phrase of one Dutch traveler of the time. The deepest defining distinction well into the eighteenth century continued to be religiously prompted, that is, between the God-fearing and the heathen. Heathen was taken polygenically to occupy the categorical space between human and animal, marking out as pre-Adamite the non-Christian, and so the non-European, from the children of Adam, on one side, and the animal kingdom on the other. Race was still religiously delineated and defined.

Culture more broadly conceived was likewise invoked to demarcate those who continued to insist they were European from those who were not, though in reality cultural practices came to intersect, overlap, interact. Thus practices that would later be identified as definitively Afrikaner culture – *biltong* (sun dried and salted meat) and *veldschoene* (literally shoes for the wild fields or cowhide shoes, sandals) are two notable examples, as Giliomee reiterates – were actually adapted from the Khoikhoi locals.

Like biology, culture can claim no lasting or often even initiating purity. These sorts of entanglement counter-hegemonically grew thicker through personal relationships, whether economic, defensive alliances, sexual intercourse, or culturally, the further from the Western Cape and especially from Kaapstadt that the trekboers wandered. Thus, in contrast with the eastern Cape frontier, where a more or less hard line was drawn between boer and native, interactive relationships and alliances grew thick along the more remote northern Cape frontier, where the farmers asserted an autonomy stressful to administrators back in the city. Thus preachers, councilors, and company agents worried aloud and in apocalyptic terms about the cultural and religious degeneracy of the frontiersmen, their "indolence," a "wild nation," polluted by their interactions with the natives and displaying increasing signs of moral and political disobedience, if not ascribed dementia.

The frontier landscape was dotted with small boer farm settlements and Khoi circulation, both seeking self-determination from central Dutch rule. They engaged each other and African groups further afield where self-interest warranted it. Some mixed offspring of course followed, but *métissage* seems in retrospect to have been more largely cultural than leading to sexual generation. The frontier was rough. There were few roads of any note and, where they did exist, linking frontier outposts or farms not so much to each other as to towns more than a few days' ride away. The stretch of sociality is revealed no better than by the fact that a couple of hundred families were strung out across thousands of square miles, and local Khoi, Baster, and African groups were equally sparsely located. Interactions were thin, driven by needs for supplies, self-protection, or service labor and only then by emotional ties.

What could be characterized as a Hobbesian state of nature prevailed, rendered less extreme perhaps only by the force of necessarily cooperative reason on all sides. Cooperation, when not trumped by narrow self-interest or salacious desire, more likely promotes a longer life than does belligerence. The common challenges of survival pulled people together, just as racially exacerbated suspicion kept conflict little more than a stone's throw away.

Khoisan resistance kicked in quite early. Suspicious already from nominal Portuguese encounter at the close of the fifteenth century, Khoi fears were exacerbated dramatically in the first half-century of Dutch settlement, marked by sometimes brutal slave practice and extensively stolen livestock. By the early eighteenth century various Khoi groups, fed up with the heavy hand of settler intrusion, began raiding Dutch farm outposts more or less frequently, sometimes in alliance, making off, often brazenly, with a considerable bounty of cattle and sheep. The Company occasionally mediated these conflicts, formalizing peaceful coexistence momentarily until a further round of debilitating treatment of the Khoikhoi by bartering boer raiders organized in commando units, Company officials more often than not turning a blind eye, and counter-clandestine raids on the part of the Khoi. Tensions grew more heated as boers stretched their thrust more deeply into the hinterland wilderness.

The middle years of the eighteenth century saw a notable shift in proto-racial sensibility. The relative casualness in earlier years about interracial interaction and certainly about intermarriage, at least between European men and women of color, began all but to disappear. In the first half of the eighteenth century, Company rule had insisted on a modicum of civil treatment of Khoikhoi. Boers were occasionally prosecuted for mistreatment on the basis of Khoi evidence, and there are cases of boers convicted of murdering Khoisan and being sentenced to Robben Island incarceration.

By the second half of the century, religiously, culturally, economically, and governmentally, race was taking much firmer hold of social convention, intercourse, and interaction, but also of how those of European descent were conceiving or disposed towards those who were not. This hardening of socio-racial divides was cemented by still strong links among the boers to the metropolitan center and its ideas of sociality, civility, and raciality, as well as by the sharp resultant recession in social status and the consequent inassimilability of any mixed offspring.

This shift to a hardened racial sensibility was prompted no doubt by the spread of an emerging European hegemony about racial hierarchy and its resonance with what boers took to be their local experience. In France Voltaire could claim with confidence at mid-century that "Whites, Negroes, and Albinoes . . . are totally different races," descended as he put it "from different men." His views in this respect were no longer unique, and far from apocryphal.

Trekboers were tied to metropole by the need to record land claims, to register and baptize children, to secure tutorship (which also meant in European civilities, however provincially understood) for their offspring. But also by the perceived need to seem civil by consorting with "their own," increasingly racially conceived. Proximity to the indigenous and the mixed – spatially, occupationally, in terms of certain cultural habits such as clothing, food consumption, living conditions – reinforced the need for distinction, for stressing symbolic distance and social self-elevation. Race increasingly and definitively was invoked to mark the elevated from the excluded, the (relatively) privileged from the demonized, the civil(ized) from the heathen, the blessed community from the cursed. In short, sons of Abraham from those of Ham.

At the same time, mixed race groups established and enlarged themselves as coherent, unique, stand-alone, and self-determining. They too were cast as different, as in-between people, forming separate frontier communities that came to be known by the characterization "Basters" (a shortening of the Dutch *bastaard*). In time, these communities cohered on one hand into the Griquas of the central Cape and on the other formed the basis of free-standing villages and small rural towns, surviving more or less quaintly intact to this day.

Robert Shell has shown that slave demography within the Western Cape, under firm Company control, had grown increasingly heterogeneous by the later 1700s. Cape slaves hailed from a range of different societies, spoke different languages, were culturally distinct. This undermined the emergence of any cultural solidarity among slaves, thus resulting in the fact that any rebellious slave activity was overwhelmingly likely to be individual rather than collective. Locally born slaves were considered more loyal and less likely to rebel, especially those mixed, those whose fathers were European or of European descent and whose mothers were slaves. They lived longer, spoke the local language, and a young woman, little more than a girl, might be given permission to marry a European man who would bear some of the costs of her upkeep and yet whose children would remain the slave property of the slave-master, at least until they turned 25. Creole slaves, not least the pubescent, accordingly fetched a significant premium, costing nearly half as much as foreign slaves.

Khoi and increasingly Xhosa raiding both within and across the blurred frontier boundaries, by contrast, was cutting into the capability of the Company in Kaapstadt to meet its meat quotas and claims to protect burghers. Khoikhoi farm labor was especially ill-treated, involving beatings, withholding of pay, and refusal to release the worker and his family no matter how long or loyally they had served. Basters and Khoikhoi were pressed into commando service to stave off these raids, at the same time as their rights were being curtailed. The result, inevitably, was rising resentment and less than half-hearted effort on the part of Khoi and Baster commando members. Successive rebellious resistances ensued.

The Cape administration faced a series of corrosive crises in the 1770s. Khoi resistance had shifted from individual rebelliousness to unacceptable treatment of person and family under slave or indentured conditions to a more sustained collective effort. Adam Kok, having self-purchased his manumission from Western Cape slavery, moved his family northwestward, attracting a growing following as his family wealth spiked and his leadership asserted autonomy for the group. Over time, the growing group blossomed into full-fledged Baster maroons, self-defining and self-governing as the Griqua nation.

While wars occur at any and all times, they tend to take on millenarian significance as a century ends or takes off. Somehow the promise of a stretch of culturally significant time awaiting definition calls forth millenarian visions of a new beginning, of messianic perfectibility, of the Heavenly City under divine guidance yet to come. As the eighteenth century was drawing to a close at the Cape, conditions seemed especially conducive to millenarian conjecture and creation.

Trekboers sought a degree of independence from the Cape administrators, whom they viewed as representing the interests more or less exclusively of wealthy Western Cape estate holders, white more or less by definition and law, and as unwisely protecting the humanistic claims of Khoikhoi labor and the land claims of Khoi and Baster freemen. The Cape administration at times sought to act as neutral judges in such disputes and from time to time asserted the moral insistence to civil treatment of Khoikhoi and Basters. But even in these instances the claims were more often than not undermined by lack of institutionalization and inaction on the part of the administration or its individual agents and aggressive

counter-assertion, even violence, on the part of the trekboers and frontiersmen. Urban–rural tensions, culturally as much as economically,
dispositionally as much as devotionally, were taking firm root, fanned by
the fervor of racial belief.

In a heated frontier land dispute between a boer who settled Khoi
ancestral land and Khoi community representatives in 1787–8, increasingly
typical at the time, Jan Paerl (Parel) emerged as a local Khoi leader and
self-proclaimed spokesman for the Almighty's will. Born of a Khoikhoi
mother and probably European father, Paerl navigated colonial conditions
with ambivalent fluidity. A speaker of divine command and Dutch
fluency, prophet to his people, Paerl ordered rebellion against colonial oppression. In a prophetic precursor to the disastrous Nongawuse dream some
70 years later, Khoikhoi were urged to begin throwing off the yoke of white
subjugation by slaughtering all their white cattle, building new homes with
two doors (presumably one for chasing out the colonial devil, the other
for welcoming in divine rule), and burning all their European cultural
clothing. They were to gather in the nearby Cedarberg mountains to await
their collective invasion of the local colonial administration, seize their land
back, and destroy all European settlers and their kin (including cutting up
their children into pieces). The date for collective action and the reassertion of self-rule, for what he called "the ending of the world" (he might
have added "as we have come to know it"), was prophetically precise: October
25, 1788. No more than a dream, the vision of a seer, the plot failed.

Paerl was arrested, and spent a couple of years in prison before working
first as a farm laborer and then converting to Christianity – translating his
messianism into missionary good work, to be precise. He spent much of
his mature adult life as a guide to Moravian missionaries, both advising
and assisting them in their missionary project to convert the inhabitants
of the interior. In his earlier millenarian manifestation, Paerl nevertheless
had seized on the chafing sensibilities of the oppressed and given them voice.
He was able to demonstrate to his brethren and to white oppressors how
effective organization and religious zeal could prompt collective resistance
to imposed settler control. He thus was among the very first at the Cape
to channel rage against racially coded subjugation, the alienation of property, and exploitation into the kind of collective social movement that would
come later to mark resistant responses to the South African racial order.

Prior to Paerl, resistance to racial humiliation, infantilization, and
group subjugation was largely a mix of individual rebelliousness (running
away, slow work, damaged equipment, occasionally counter-violence,

personal complaints to colonial administrators or courts) and small group banditry at the frontier (stolen livestock, destroyed property, occasionally physical violence). In initiating collective resistance politics in the southern African theater, Paerl's performance prompted a number of considerations traces of which would later come to haunt all debates about collective resistance in South Africa: how far to refuse engagement with the totalizing and ultimately destructive state institutions regarded as thoroughly racist and so unmitigatedly unjust; whether violence and armed struggle are the appropriate responses to racist institutional violence; whether race-conscious or nonracial politics are the most viable modes of resistance to racist social arrangements, in terms of effectivity or ethicality; whether a politics of self-determining secession and unilateral declaration of independence guarantees self-protection and self-promotion more robustly than the messy politics of heterogeneous racial interactivity; how religiously driven resistance preconceives the wrongs to be resisted, structures the horizon of possible outcomes, shapes the imagined community to come, orders the after-life of liberation, and conditions affective responses; and, finally, it signals both the potentially generative and probably debilitating implications of charismatic leadership, following, and fellowship for the longer-term success of collective resistance movements.

Membership in the Dutch Reformed Church in the closing decade of the century, perhaps not unrelated to this surge in millenarian resistance, increased notably, and became overwhelmingly if not exclusively white. Loss of formal power and easy access prompted a cross-class coherence among Dutch descendants threatened otherwise with dispersal. Afrikaners were born of the double threat of ethnoracial evaporation to boer identity. Conjured as *interactively* British and black, this threat was to become, with the arrival of the surging British as the old century closed and the new one opened, the troubling catalyst of Afrikaner self-conception, but also its distinction, its rupture, from its classically Dutch origins.

The development from Dutch to Afrikaner was motivated and mobilized substantially in reaction to the projected threats of mixture. Where the Dutch came to pride themselves as robustly individualistic, Afrikaners were nothing if not invested in a homogenizing collective; where the Dutch deemed themselves diplomatic, Afrikaners were dogmatic; where the Dutch were entrepreneurial, Afrikaners were dour, even paranoid; where the Dutch are famously marked by their particular brand of repressive tolerance, Afrikaners collectively came to be known for their intolerant repression. Or so the stereotypes suggest.

Racial sanctification elevated Afrikaner society in self-assessment, self-selection, and increasingly separation as God's children, visions of modern-day Israelites wandering in the deserted hinterland. Self-selection is often the cohering response to the paranoid threat of evisceration or extinction. Baptism was almost exclusively restricted to children of white parents, whether burgher (largely) or the expanding class of poor whites. Baptism furnished the mark of belonging to the sanctified class of the self-nominated, and so of maintenance, promise, or possibility of ascendancy. The stamp of salvation came to define power and privilege, elevation and exclusion, linking them ontologically and theocratically to racial conception and comprehension. Theo-political self-ordination and the unstinting drive to domination came to be increasingly firmly forged from this moment.

This was not, or not only or simply, a frontier phenomenon. Kaapstadt was emerging as a regional city, a trading place in its own right and strategic port at the crossroads of global sea-going circulation. And yet it produced its own class distinctions, partly racially defined, between Company people and independent burghers, city men and boers, between the propertied and those serving the landed, between free blacks and slaves, the elevated and the diminished, white, mixed, Malay, Hindu, black, and ultimately also the British, but in addition and relatedly between Christians and pagans. Jews in significant numbers came later, at the close of the nineteenth and into the twentieth centuries. Abundant heterogeneity, under managed care of increasingly racially inscribed and determining definition.

Racial sanctification elevated the Chosen, those of European background, over the Cursed, Japheth over Ham but also over Shem (ascriptively those of Asian descent). Sanctification was directed at "the collectivity," not at "the individual" (to use Stokes's terms though to different purpose), thus reinforcing sustained group membership. Increasingly, then, sanctification entailed purification, fusing apparent biology with assertive ideology, the physical like the landscape always invested with cultural and in this case sustained theological significance. The halo of whiteness had to protect itself from impurities, from pollutants, ultimately from degeneracy. Racial self-sanctification after all is a project of paranoid self-defense, of social prophylaxis, from demons of its own manufacture. Afrikaners made local the global self-importance of European racial configuration, fusing it with locally adapted Euro-theological conception.

In any case, the last quarter of the eighteenth century saw the firming up of racial modes of delineation at the Cape. Record-keeping became more formal, its categories of counting more starkly defined. As in US census-counting, "white" became the default category of delineation, carrying with its expression increasingly the presumption of superiority, as much on moral as on biological criteria of counting. Mixture increasingly came to be squeezed out of the self-portrait, erased from ideological self-representation in ways it couldn't possibly be from the historical record, as I have argued above. Any vocal hint of mixed background came increasingly to be repressed, as much from family histories as from group articulation. And most revealingly, as Robert Shell points out, the bulk of the Cape's 63,000 slaves were imported from venues east of Africa in the wake of rising Khoikhoi resistance, between 1784 and cessation of slave trading under the British in 1807–8.

By the closing decade of the eighteenth century, then, the Dutch at the Cape – even and perhaps especially at the frontier – had become visibly more religious and more pious, drawn no doubt to the apocalyptic millenarian appeal of late-century predictions. Dutch colonial and economic power had slipped seriously, and global power was shifting to the burgeoning British. The French Revolution was followed immediately by a period of unrest, at the Cape as in Europe, leading to increased French shipping activity around the Cape, including expanded slave trading, and to French invasion of the Netherlands in the mid-1790s. Following an economic surge in the 1780s, the economy of the Cape had become deeply depressed by the early 1790s, and the Dutch East Indies Company fell into bankruptcy.

The British took advantage of Dutch weakness, landing at the Cape with little resistance in late 1795. Cape rule thus tilted to the British, formally first in 1796, and then following a brief interlude of renewed Dutch rule and the Battle of Trafalgar more firmly and long-lastingly a decade later.

The coming of the Christ appeared, counter-predictably, in the arrival of: the *Anglicans*.

Missionaries and the Messianic Spirit

With British arrival, the Cape could put up the sign: under new management. And yet while the British introduced some liberalizing initiatives, this should not be overplayed, as some notable historians have misleadingly insisted. The usual account of South African historiography has the boers representing the *ancien régime* of old-style racism, thinking of indigenous Africans as radically inferior, even less or non-humans, totally devoid of intelligence, skill, or the possibility of their acquisition. The boers on this view thus trekked away as much to free themselves of British liberalism vis-à-vis the indigenous as to secure their own freedom from grating British rule and regulation. Apartheid in the making.

The British at the Cape, by contrast, are taken in this narrative, not least by themselves and their legatees, to represent the source and force of racial progress, of standing not for inherent incapacity but for educability and possibility. Of inherent equality in reason's and God's name. The British were the bearers of civilization to those not yet provided it but who had no inherent incapacity preventing them from such acquisition. Supporters of evolution versus the spoilers of racial regression, the advocates of a civilizing Christianity. This, I have argued in *The Racial State*, represents the racial historicism of Millian progressivist liberalism contra the racist naturalism of Carlylean conservatism. It sees itself as level-headed Anglican liberalism set against the arrogant legacy of radical continental Reformation.

The record is not so straightforward. The Enlightenment stressed the Rights of Man, to be sure, and insisted more or less on humane treatment of human beings in the name of universal human rights. Thus, the British indeed declared unacceptable the widespread practice of torture and the physical abuse of slaves, a welcome development. British rule at the Cape, after all, took root as news of the Haitian Revolution circulated, and the abolition-ist movement was gathering strength across the empire, fueled in part by the likes of Equiano's autobiography, on one hand, and the biting moral criticism of courageous figures such as the Abbé Raynal in France or the London Missionary Society's John Philip (who was to play such a large role later in abolishing slavery at the Cape) and James Beattie, on the other. By 1808 the British had banned the trading of slaves throughout their empire, the newly acquired Cape now included. God's children, human beings endowed with the potential of reason all, were not to be bought and sold at market.

However, key Enlightenment figures – Voltaire early on, Hume and Kant most notably as the century progressed, but far from only – were quick to curtail the domain of the human, and in explicitly racial terms. Thinking through race paid no heed to the English Channel.

Liberal abolitionists like Mill and Anglican missionaries more generally may have resisted the base bestialization of "the Negro." But they presumed Africans largely to represent a less civilized stage of humanity. Presumed to be less schooled by far in civility and the virtues of civilization, "natives" were to be uplifted by European schooling and religious conversion. The 1820 British settlers at the Cape, Shell reports, found that characterization of slaves individually by their countries of origin, and in terms of stereotypically presumptuous national character, had been replaced significantly by explicit delineation according to *racial descent*. In this vein, leading European intellectuals of the Enlightenment, British representatives included, more often than not evicted Africans and their offspring from at least full human or historical extension, from moral protection, reducing them to animalized characterization, biblically referenced (e.g., "Negroes" as pack animals, "hewers and carriers of wood").

The British were drawn to the Cape initially to secure geopolitical sea power through control of the passage of global trade at the time. They soon found, like their Dutch predecessors, that the Cape was not simply a cartographic crossroads, a controlling point in the passage of global power. The Cape offered opportunities and challenges of its own, possibilities for local wealth generation, the provision of raw materials to fuel British industrial growth, and a site for expressing imperial power locally asserted. But those opportunities also offered forbidding if not foreboding challenges: contestation over the land as much from indigenous folk as from Dutch settlers gone local, competition to control trade across the Cape landscape and increasingly further afield, and struggles over self-assertion, self-determination, and different comprehensions of governmentality.

Having mobilized more or less robust heterogeneity into the region, Europeans sought to restrain and contain it, ultimately to restrict and repress it in various and vigorous ways. Restraint and restriction of hybridizing heterogeneity were a response to perceived immorality and the threat to presumptuous scientific perversion, to possible constraints on land enclosure and on the unskilled labor supply, and to sustaining order and power shaped by and through race.

Restraint and restriction were led by cultural condescension and control. For Europeans, the indigenous had very little culture worthy of the name (and for the British the boers had only marginally more). Driven especially by the eighteenth-century naturalizing impulse regarding racial non-Europeanness, not only were the indigenous thought to inhabit nature; they were, in their very being, creatures of nature, akin to the animal world. If for Europeans culture was taken to triumph over nature, for non-Europeans and especially for those deemed naturally primitive, culture withered in the face of nature. It never got off the ground. While already articulated before the British took over the administration of the Cape, these views assumed an expression both more varied and heated with their arrival.

Upon settlement, the British quickly turned to transforming De Kaap fully into The Cape. J. M. Coetzee, the noted and now notably alienated South African Nobel novelist, insightfully identified a form of representation among European settlers in the seventeenth and eighteenth centuries found especially in "white writing." Coetzee characterizes this mode of representation as "white pastoral." "White pastoral" is the representation of an idyllic, edenic landscape, the aesthetic articulation of European gardens if not of little England itself being lost to industrialization, quite at odds with the harshness of the actual environment. White pastoral resonates with theological significance too, biblical meaning inscribed on the landscape itself. Thus Cape Town's landmark Table Mountain, shrouded by the southeasterly table cloth, is the imagined site of the Last Supper, biblically bookended on each side by magisterial mountainous peaks aptly named Devil's Peak and the Twelve Apostles respectively.

Hinting at the possibility of a wider expression of a white pastoral in painting, Coetzee nevertheless denied its applicability in early South African cultural expression. It was left to others to take up these wider articulations of white pastoralism in painting and arguably later in photography and even film. Thus Gavin Lucas rightly extends "white pastoral" to broader forms of visual and material culture, including maps and crafted landscapes – what places are emphasized or enlarged in the former case, the layout, imported fauna and flora in the latter. The founding of Kirstenbosch, the botanical gardens at the then edge of Cape Town, by Anne Barnard, the Cape Governor's wife, towards the end of the eighteenth century exemplifies the point. The Cape was imagined as, if not quite completely metamorphed into, the shrinking Kentish countryside, Kaapstadt indeed into Cape Town.

Mapping is central to this imagined landscape. Maps not only enlarge some places over others; they name or don't name places according to the perceived permanence of their settlement by human beings, as I illustrated in relation to the metamorphing of Palestine into Israel. The designated emptiness of places on the map otherwise known to be inhabited by natives thought simply to be passing through in their seasonal or whimsical migrations, these vast swathes of space are designated empty Lockean lands awaiting European enclosure and labored industriousness. The extension of European sensibilities colonially elaborated.

British infiltration of the Cape following its resumption of rulership in 1806 remade both the map and the landscape. They transformed the sensibility of what was to become South Africa over the ensuing century as much as they shaped the European imaginary of what later in the century was widely called "the dark continent" more generally.

This remaking was especially notable after the significant British settlement of 1820. For one, the charm of old Cape Dutch architecture was steadily replaced by much stodgier Victorian buildings. Under the Dutch, houses for the working and free classes close to the town center, white and black alike, consisted of plain whitewashed rectangular and flat-roofed buildings, their only mark of frivolity perhaps a modest gable. For the landed gentry, homes on large estates were stretched out in dazzling whitewash bedecked with ornate gabled façades and in a nod to indigenous industry expertly thatch-thick roofs. It is perhaps revealing that if there is a single cultural mark on the landscape broadly symbolic of English presence, by the mid-nineteenth century it was represented not in architecture but in commercial culture: the bright red fluted mailbox. Settlers were always thinking about their connection to their English elsewheres, dreaming invertedly of home away from home.

Within little more than a decade of British takeover, all positions of government and their agencies had replaced Dutch with English, persons as well as principal administrative language. In 1820, 4,000 British settlers were brought to the Cape, largely to settle at or close to the eastern frontier to reinforce territorial control in the face of continuing and increasingly bold indigenous raids, on one hand, and growing boer disgruntlement, on the other. The British settlers mixed a small cadre of wealthier adventurers looking for long-term investment opportunities and a much larger contingent of economically distressed and socially alienated families.

Lord Somerset, British governor of the Cape across the period, instituted a policy of insistent anglicization, as much to downplay the cultural influence of the Dutch as to stave off the paranoid threats of degeneration as a result of native mixture or "pollution." Subsequent governors through much of the nineteenth century – D'Urban, Maitland, Smith – considered the Xhosa "inherently barbarous" (terms explicitly invoked by D'Urban), untrustworthy, prone to pillage and theft. They were consequently to be pushed further and further back, beyond the expanding boundaries of the British Cape. Here, then, segregation's incipient initiation, its emergent imaginary.

Twenty years into sustained British rule, English had become the sole language of the courts, later of the legislature (even if promulgated laws were announced also in Dutch), and increasingly the medium of pedagogical instruction. Anglican missionaries journeyed to the Cape in swelling numbers, encouraging the locals – indigenous especially but the Dutch too – to convert as much to Anglo-culture as to the Anglican Church. Cultural conversion became a crucial feature of colonial control. Anglo-mimesis came to be the form of European domination, culture and polity effectively mirroring one another. But Anglo-mimesis was also its particular expression of racial rule, of extended racial Europeanization, its peculiar political theology. The Dutch, and boers especially, were aghast, as much at the creeping hints of formal legal equality – in courts, in land tenure, in laboring conditions – that indigenous and especially mixed people within the Cape's borders were beginning as a consequence to experience as at boers' own loss of access and control.

British expansion beyond the formally existing boundaries of the Cape by the second half of the nineteenth century nevertheless had led ironically to the closing down of opportunities for miscegenation: policing the social boundaries, imposing Christianity by missionary mobilization, and refining euro-mimesis into Anglo-imitation. The British took themselves to be buffeted on both sides, though by different forms of boorishness. Faced by the challenges of enforcing colonial control in territory embodying multiple hostilities, the British found themselves resorting to tactics on the ground little different from those of the boers, distinctive ideological dispositions notwithstanding. And while abolition may have endeared black people locally to the British, at least in the abstract, unfolding forms of racially institutionalized or implied constraint, restriction, and curtailment produced a much deeper ambivalence.

Just as racial historicism was taking root in the metropole and its satellite cities as racism's counter-history, fueling especially the abolitionist movement, racial naturalism in Europe and the US was hardening into species distinction, elevating the idealized Anglo-European above all else. So, on one flank, the non-European, whether indigenous or imported, was increasingly taken not only as culturally inferior but as species deficient, naturally incapable of cross-species fertility (that, after all, was the very definition at the time of species differentiation). It wasn't long before customary discouragement of interracial mixing, physical and cultural, calcified into formal policy. Restricting miscegenation was at least indirectly encouraged by the circulation of influential European racial theories of the period, notably polygenism and later eugenicism, referenced to local conditions.

By mid-century, claims to native historical immaturity and Euro-inspired progressivism that constituted the content of racial historicism were infusing Anglo-colonial administrations from Calcutta to Cape Town. The emergence and impact of assertive racial theories of natural difference, by contrast, took their toll more readily outside of Cape Town's provincialized urbanity. In the city, the seat of colonial government, the *contre-histoire* of Anglo-infused racial historicism identified above all with John Stuart Mill's liberalism came to have some traction. Its influence, however, waned the further one traveled from the local metropole, itself a site of more or less robust mixture, as I have been arguing.

Outside the city, not only did the affect of civility and the lack of anonymity increase the cultural stigma of mixing, but the hold of cultural Englishness became more tenuous, not least as one moved inland, challenged on its other flank by a resilient, resistive, repressive boer independence. In Cape Town and perhaps for a brief period after their initial founding in other towns of the Anglo-Cape in the wake of 1820 settlement, such as Port Elizabeth and East London (the names themselves are give-aways), one might lose status as a result of mixed intercourse but remain a social member of at least some standing. Outside of the Anglo-urban shadow, however, racial mixture was becoming much less well received. Urban and frontier dispositions perhaps were brought closer together in antagonism towards racial mixing by the official drive to establish unfettered and unchallenged colonial control over the entire territory, a drive emanating from the seat of city government in Cape Town but implemented insistently all the way to the frontier.

Under early British authority at the Cape, racial rule was formalized initially through the instrumentalities of law, administrative policies, regimes of labor supply, and spatial control. Less formally, racial regulation was enacted through the shaping of cultural interaction. The mission of missionaries was to convert the uninitiated not simply to belief in the Anglican God and the sorts of religious rituals associated with such belief. It was to instill also the godly virtues of self-discipline, hard work, cleanliness, and service, thus cultivating in the name of civility and civilization a new subjectivity.

In the Anglo-provincial coastal cities developing along the eastern frontier things began to alter 30 years into British administration, with dramatic implications for the future of the territory and its expansion. Black people of all backgrounds were to be restricted residentially to "locations" at the urban edge, areas "reserved" for them. The practice actually grew out of initial missionary instigation. In 1834, the year of abolition after all, the London Missionary Society – the chief anglicizing body knotting together religious conversion, civilizing enculturation, and colonial rule as the emergent racial theo-politics of the territory – founded a separate settlement for blacks outside Port Elizabeth.

Commercial mingling came to mean no more than a steady labor supply, expanding control over land, and securing the supply of livestock. Residential mixing was soon to be more or less out of the question. Religious intercourse came to mind only on the road to conversion.

British settlement entailed intensifying ambiguities and ambivalence for the Dutch already living at the Cape: subsequent loss of power and self-determination, gestures of creeping equality, the arousal of insecurities, and ultimately abolition in late 1834, with its consequent effects on raising indigenous expectations and shattering boer reliance on a cheap source of farm labor supply. Combined and interactive, these factors prompted outright boer rebellion as the decade approached a mid-point. Formal abolition brought these factors to a boiling point, prompting strong self-determining secessionist sentiments among boers at the frontier. The result: waves of treks by groups of boer families across the border and into native land.

Into native land deemed unsettled, unclaimed by people considered to be constantly on the move and incapable of settled industry and untrustworthy because unanchored. Trekkers forged alliances with each other against the common enemy (British and natives), and with natives against the British or to secure appealing conditions, land acquisition, or safe passage for themselves. But no sooner made than these agreements were often broken in the drive to guarantee territorial access and control, to fuel a secure labor supply or replenish livestock, and to wreak vengeance or some perverse sense of godly justice. No wonder trust among indigenous people with whom boers came in contact was shattered early on.

Trekking up the east coast into native territory, boers established an early republic, Natalia, in the late 1830s by first subduing justifiably suspicious, resistant, and ultimately aggressive Zulu groups and then carving out land in indigenous territory. From this territorial base, boers moved quickly to secure landholdings for themselves, and to restrict the vote to white men. They forced onto segregated land at the edge of the republic those Africans not directly employed by the boers themselves. A guaranteed labor supply was underpinned by unsettling sedentary African agriculture and shaping a marginalized reserve labor supply.

Boer political domination was effected by electoral restriction defined at the interface of race and gender. And the conceit of a demographic purity morally rationalized was secured by segregative exclusion, fueled in the name of Godly edict. Obviously these commands of boer racial theology occasionally fell into contradiction, the call for labor exploitation drawing into circulation the very people whose enticing presence might undermine the paranoid drive to demographic purity.

Concerned with loss of control and protection of developing ports from boer and Zulu alike, the British responded to boer self-determination by annexing to the Colony in the 1840s the swath of territory known as Natal. The boers sought once more to extend their autonomy and amplify their articulation as a self-contained and -constrained culture. They moved further inland, establishing two more settled and self-governing states in the 1850s, the South African Republic (or Transvaal, 1852) and the Orange Free State (1854). The former was centered in 1855 around the establishment of administrative headquarters in Pretoria. Once more rule and regulation – the electorate, land, and labor – were explicitly racially delineated. The spring of Afrikanerdom.

Afrikanerdom accordingly grew up in rebellion against the British and cut-throat competition with the indigenous, anyway thought inferior, over land, labor, and livestock. There was no doubt pragmatic politics on both sides, boer and indigenous alike, as deals and alliances were occasionally cut between emerging Afrikaner and established African leaders (Dingane first; his half-brother Mpande later; even to a degree Moshoeshoe, founder of the Basuto) to advance political self-interest and group security, on both sides. But for all of that, much blood inevitably flowed in the founding of self-governing Afrikaner republics.

All blood is shades of red, even as the British thought theirs blue, and the boers definitely took theirs not to be black. Blacks wisely gave no credence to race as such before having it thrust upon them by Europeans. Saul Dubow rightly comments, however, that prior to the twentieth century there was little if any locally sustained work formally undertaken in southern Africa on the "science" of race. For one, local universities in South Africa only emerged in the latter part of the nineteenth century, and so there was almost nothing by way of the institutional apparatus of science until the twentieth century.

At the same time, in the nod to the global circulation of racial ideas, Robert Knox began his racial anatomies at the Cape before 1820, and Darwin's cousin and the first to formulate eugenics, Francis Galton, spent two years at mid-century mapping the physical attributes and cultural habits of racial groups in Damaraland and Ovamboland (both now in Namibia). Their southern African scientific beginnings set the stage for later elaboration of their racial theories back in Britain. But they also hint at least at an intellectually driven conversation around racial ideas in the colonized provinces too. Racial ideas certainly circulated, traveling back and forth between metropole and colony, transforming as they traveled.

By the second half of the nineteenth century, though, what was becoming South Africa was more a political and cultural laboratory for elaborating modern racial understandings and orderings, not yet a laboratory to assess or really to "advance" claims of the day's racial science. It would add the latter conceit later, only with the approach of the twentieth century. If travelers returning to Europe in this period brought back with them reinforcing stereotypes of black people, standard ideas of scientific racism tended to flow in the counter-direction, from Europe to southern Africa where they might be tried, placed into practice, and tested at least politically and in popular culture. The laboratory was already the generator and incubator of racial arrangement and state policy.

In 1860, the South African Republic – following the British administration in Natal half a decade earlier – mandated passes for all African men seeking work in the territory. Boer republicans readily placed African women and children in indentured servitude, and rapacious imposition by boer men upon black women was not uncommon. Settler colonials par excellence, boers were not above the very bestiality they themselves projected onto "the natives," though now in every sense of the term.

In contrast to Cape rulers, then, both British in Natal and boer in their republics, if in idiosyncratic ways, shared the mix of racial ideas circulating widely across European societies and their satellites in the second half of the nineteenth century. But they shared also more than this, namely, harsh regimes of territorially segregated control, racially restrictive electorates, and a guaranteed supply of cheap black labor. Thus both invested in themselves the embodiment of racial superiority and saw "the native," more or less invariably characterized under the sign of "the kafir," as "savage" and subject to "witchcraft," as inherently inferior, those whose primitivity was ordained by awesome dual authorities: racial science and God.

The Cape was characterized by a far larger mixed race population and a much smaller African demographic presence than boer and British found as they moved north. Under British rule at least in and around Cape Town, as a consequence, amalgamationism as demographic horizon was joined to assimilationism as political and cultural mandate. Racial uplift of those deemed not white was to be achieved through intercourse, cultural as much as demographic (though in the latter regard still overwhelmingly between white men and women of color). The British Western Cape was not so unlike Latin America.

In British Natal and the boer republics, by contrast, African presence was more palpably felt as threatening, conjuring insecurities regarding not only land and labor but likewise and perhaps more pressingly of physical and cultural degeneration. Indigenous groups vacillated between openness to the boers or the British, depending on who would extend them greater respect, resources, or simply peaceful coexistence, and outright hostility. Indigenous resistance was inevitably folded into the pre-existing set of colonizing dispositions regarding race, re-enforcing the dominant sense of primitivity and naturalized hostility. Once the British left the south-western security of Cape control over political economy for the less settled northeast, their ruling disposition came quickly to emulate that of the boers. South Africa's future lay ultimately in the racial dynamics of the territory's more northern field of vision.

Here, then, the resurrection in the nineteenth century of racial naturalism became foundational, assuming an insistent inherent inferiority, over time inscribing an arm's-length segregationist polity joined to securing a cheap and guaranteed labor economy and proscribed intercourse. Entangled with an intense religiosity, polygenesis and later eugenics took on their own populist expressions at the outer limits of settler colonialism, seeding the early lineaments of a novel *political theology of race*. Within emergent South Africa, an elaborating racial theo-politics began to unify white coherence across these differences into the ruling racial class. If the missionary mode was to convert to belief and culture one soul at a time, the messianic was invested in group salvation all at once.

The missionary modality served well a political economy of the Protestant ethic and the social self-discipline of labor, contribution, and charity. The messianic, by contrast, mirrored the spirit of group rule and racially driven domination. The Anglicans turned out to represent false promise. Intent on self-sustenance and self-direction, the boers would manufacture the messianic in the spirit of segregation. The second coming would later be codified as apartheid. The differences between a liberalizing historicism and a more strident rationalizing scientistic racial naturalism, in the wider scheme of things, assumed the form of a family squabble over the legacy of the racial estate. Who in the end would be sharing the pie, who controlling the distribution? Knowing each other all too well, boer and Britain knew each other barely at all.

Of the locals both were more or less in abject because studied ignorance.

God, Glitter, and Racial Governmentality

British rulers soon understood what the Dutch had taken decades to come to terms with, namely, that economies of scale at the Cape required local forms of revenue generation for its own upkeep so as not to drain the imperial treasury in the metropole. That meant a product appealing to the global market. Colonies in the West Indies had sugar, until that market collapsed in the wake of slavery's demise. The East Indies had silk, porcelain, and spices, perennially in demand. Parts of Latin America glittered with the lure of gold. The Cape, it came to be realized not long after the significant settlement of English immigrants in the 1820s, was an effective source of wool.

Wool demand back in the British Home Counties took off in the industrializing 1830s and flourished between 1840 and 1870. It offered significant opportunities for a settler industry, imperial investment, and international trade. The port of Cape Town flourished both with passing trade, wool export, and reimported woolen products. Natural port towns like Port Elizabeth and East London along the east coast, close to wool production, took off. This carried the colony into the 1860s, when the agricultural economy and its racially inscribed division of labor and forms of rule faced the pressures of global industrialization. The imperial leadership began to worry about the long-term viability of wool to sustain the colony.

Not a moment too early minerals were discovered, and in large deposits: diamonds (1867) in Griqualand, close to the northern Cape border, and then gold in the Transvaal (in small deposits in 1870, but extensive findings by 1886). More or less guaranteed by government both at the Cape and in the boer republics, mine ownership inevitably came under white control. Fueled by connection to British traditions of union organizing and scientific racial inferiorization of non-whites, white mine-workers in South Africa managed to secure skilled positions largely for themselves, and to restrict blacks mostly to unskilled mine work. The territory quickly transformed into a crown jewel of another kind.

The boer republics, by the same token, were soon up for grabs. Their independence was quite quickly undone in the name of extending imperial control over the spiraling treasury the land was promising to spill forth. South Africa was amalgamated into a single administrative and political entity on the spine of mining and industrialization, a repressive regime of guaranteed cheap labor supply to sustain staggering profitability, and a logic of irrepressible modernizing urbanization. The source simultaneously of segregation and its resistance, ultimately of apartheid and in time of its formal demise.

Land settled. Labor supply (to be) secured. Wealth beyond the wildest dreams was to be generated. But staggering racially produced, ordered, and more or less managed poverty too. The south of Africa was soon to be South Africa, a union brought under single governance. The southern end of Africa was being catapulted deeply into global capitalism. But not before struggles of epic, of global proportion. The source of such wealth could not be left to the vicissitudes of unpredictable individuals of untrustworthy, inexperienced, and unregulated (not to mention alien) provenance. It would have to be brought under state domain.

Missionary conversion is arduous. Until the born again revolution of neoliberally inspired mass evangelism in the past two decades, souls were to be saved largely one by one. Missionary work may have had the stamp of the good Lord's approval, but it was slow going. Too slow for the temporality of mining minerals or mass production, to be sure. The demands of a secured labor supply for a capitalist political economy required more than just personal discipline and individual loyalty, though these sensibilities would prove productive as well for the cause. It demanded something more than a Protestant economy of enculturated subjects. The serial individualization of saved souls could never deliver on demand for a mass-producing economy. A steady, sturdy, and cheap labor supply demanded a different regime for its reproduction and regulation, one more immediately responsive.

At the outset, the labor regime for mineral capitalism urged *homo minimalis*: strength over skill, youth over experience, physicality over intellectuality. In any case, an individualized relation to the deity might just as well spawn a sense of self-worth and equal standing, and so a disposition to reject, resist, or rebel against exploitative labor conditions as it did discipline, following orders, and deference. The political theology of race, drawing into common orbit British expansionist and boer settler in mineral-rich South Africa, was far more conducive to delivering labor, securing power, and controlling land – in short, producing the wealth of power through governing heterogeneity – than any simply individualized modality, whether of the missionaries or finance capitalists.

Religious conversion could serve as supplement, to be sure, regulating subjects once in place. But it was ultimately racial rule and repression that produced and sustained the hierarchical regularities of the labor supply. The political theology of race was not simply an ex post facto rationalization of an already and anyway repressive regime of labor supply. It was constitutive of that regime, determining and delivering who the masters and madams and who the mine-workers, manufacturing labor, the farm-workers, gardeners, and domestics.

This was the moment too, it should not be overlooked, that Benjamin Disraeli, between his two British premierships, declared in 1871 that "everything is race"! Provincials often take their cue from the metropole even while expressing disdain, settlers from their colonizing source, even while insisting on their independence. South Africa would naturalize that unnatural racial condition, making it more than an act of faith or expression of the "best that has been thought and said," rendering it the foundational principle of a political economy, of law and society, of culture and its discontents. South Africa was to become both laboratory and lived condition, the trial run and testament of racial theo-politics, ultimately its crucial experiment.

Diamond and gold discovery initially produced headlong rushes by individual wealth seekers, overwhelmingly men, as much from the northern hemisphere as locally. Local black folk largely serviced their needs even if they too were lured to the glitter to seek their fortunes. The mining rush fueled an economy of service provision from supplies to services, unskilled labor to brick producers, domestic labor to sex. It didn't take long for governing forces to assert their authority, to control both the conditions and conduct around spiraling populations in founding and quickly expanding cities, most notably the diamond dig of Kimberly and then especially the gold field that became Johannesburg. But the overriding drive was to bring the source of potentially enormous wealth under official jurisdiction.

Johannesburg 1886, a long day's hike to the south of the established boer republican government in Pretoria. The rush to gold wealth. Scarcely a city worldwide at the time that could claim such rapid rise. In a decade the population had surged to 100,000, tents giving way to corrugated iron, as Van Onselen has pointed out. Two decades later again the population had spiraled by 150 percent. City growth of bricks and mortar was spiked by boom and bust industrializing development. Funded by the ups and downs of mining revenue, expansion was underwritten by capital investment more foreign than local as the price of gold fluctuated on global markets.

By the outbreak of World War I, the Rand mines were producing fully 40 percent of the world's gold output.

Heterogeneity and perhaps with it heterodoxy were the city's mark. The glitter of gold reeled in wealth seekers from across the country and all across Europe. Local and not so local labor poured forth, keen to cash in on working opportunities and secreted gold, helped along by the introduction of cash taxes on rural huts and polls that forced them to seek wage work. Jews arrived in the rush to escape repression in Russia and its neighbors. Skilled workers, fortune seekers, adventurers, and hustlers showed up from Britain and continental Europe.

The city mushroomed along the gold-yielding ridge of the extended Vaal plain, a cauldron of industrialization and the circulation of finance capital. The crossroads of comings and goings, fortunes quickly accumulated and just as quickly evaporated, the pressure cooker of cultural contrasts and political clash. The site of labor strife and repeated racial tension, where men lived hard and women were tolerated to do little more than service men's self-perceived needs. Where "underground" came to mean so much more than mining. The sexual license of Sodom and the greed of Gomorrah, of waste and want. The bondage of Egypt, but always the hope too of the Promised Land.

From the outset Johannesburg embodied the lure of the modern, in all its contradictions. Modernity's second greatest city, as William Kentridge remarks with a touch of loving irony, after Paris.

A tug-of-war marked relations between Paul Kruger's administration of the Transvaal Republic and the Randlords controlling the goldmines, over infrastructure, investment, and not least labor conditions. But perhaps also over cultures of control and dispositions to industrializing development. The boer government consisted of settler farmers, pioneer stock, wedded to land and constrictively religious. The mining magnates were English, German, and Jewish entrepreneurs, vested above all in expansive industrialization and wealth generation, religiosities of another kind. Black labor had virtually no political representation at all. Their one abiding strength would prove to lie in their numbers.

The Jameson Raid in 1895 was cooked up as a conspiracy between goldmine magnates and Cape Government elites under Governor Cecil Rhodes to wrest administrative control of the Transvaal from the boers under Kruger's leadership. It failed hopelessly in its immediate goals. But in the short term it made the Kruger administration more amenable to gold industry demands. The devils' dealings were consummated over the bodies of black mine labor, leading for instance to the instigation of the Pass Regulations, the successors to a series of rules introduced for the diamond and goldmines in the 1870s and 1880s and early precursor of the burdensome Pass Laws later so definitive of the apartheid state. Though on the face of it definitionally neutral, the Pass Regulations, as the name suggests, sought to regulate the supply of *black* labor for the mines.

From the closing years of the 1870s, more or less formalized residential segregation came to define the conditions facing mining labor. Black mineworkers, almost exclusively unskilled, were restricted to living in tightly controlled compounds on the mines. Their daily lives were ordered by mining demands in terms of both immediate living conditions and recreational possibilities, including provision of alcohol. White workers, by contrast, mostly more skilled recent arrivals from Europe, lived either in boarding houses close to the mines or, in some instances, in housing villages constructed by the mines especially for them.

Racial segregation thus was a fact of South African mineral production almost from inception, establishing the segregative foundations of industrialization more broadly. The industrializing underpinnings of formalized segregation in South Africa and the United States in this sense more or less mirrored each other. Prompted by the interaction between demand for labor discipline and the prevailing conceptions circulating in European racial science of the day, these segregative conditions were cemented in place over time by white workers seeking to guarantee their advantages. Everything was indeed quickly being turned into race. Race now overwhelmingly was providing the prism, the shorthand for social reference, the default disposition.

In the more extended term, then, the failed Raid nevertheless unsettled the boer republican government. It loosened boer grip on power along the Rand, leading ultimately to its undoing, the boer Republic's dismantlement, and incorporation into the union that soon was to become South Africa. It was a matter of time before the Cape colonial government, commanded by their metropolitan imperial masters in London, thought it necessary to bring the Transvaal and its lucrative underground economy of gold production firmly under direct control, culmination of a 25-year dream of British administrators at the Cape. The Anglo-Boer War, 1899–1902, was the sharp instrument by which such control would be secured.

The deep mines of the Rand ridge required large capital investment, overwhelmingly from London, and a steady and more or less reliably – or at least reliably renewable – source of unskilled labor. The boer republic government was less than reliable in delivering on either condition. It hardly had the resources or access to capital markets to sustain the investments necessary for mine expansion. It was seen as not sufficiently assertive regarding the labor supply, satisfied as it was with the slave modality of farm labor considered totally unsuited for the needs of the mines. And it was eyed suspiciously by the British and the Randlords as potential competitor, if not so much as a source of capital investment certainly in terms of profiteering from the mining and ancillary sources of the industrializing revenue stream. Time for the political middlemen to go. They at least had to be replaced by a regime more responsive to the invested demands of industrialization.

The Anglo-Boer War was fought over control: of the source of gold; over returns on capital investment; over inserting the region into globalizing modernity; over laboring conditions, skilling and deskilling; and over competing conceptions of the racial. The boers and their political representation stood for the *ancien régime* of racial naturalism, inherent inferiority, and extended enslaveability. British political representatives and Randlords saw themselves by contrast as committed to modernization and industrializing progress, post-emancipation racial historicism, and market forces of demand and supply for educable free labor. The latter was seen as the surest way to depress wages even of skilled labor given the potential abundance of workers.

British capital, local Randlords, and colonial administrators thus sought initially to maximize the labor pool more or less no matter color so as to undercut wage costs of both skilled and unskilled white labor. Boer political representatives, by contrast, sought to ensure job color bars out of a deep entanglement of self-interest and ideological investment. But capital's representatives soon relented, not only to the pressures of white workers intent on securing self-interest but also to the renewed reassertion of the discourse of inherent inferiority.

Social Darwinist dispositions began taking firm hold of intellectual, commercial, and political leaders as well as of the prevailing political imaginary, in Britain and by extension also among its key colonial representatives. The grip of scientific racism and its more casual effects reached deep into the colonial administration of the Cape and its northerly extensions, most notably in the person of the Cape Governor and imperial entrepreneur, Cecil John Rhodes, and then of his racially strident successor, Alfred Milner.

Rhodes's racial imperialism was committed to extending British rule over as much of Africa as he could ensure. In the case of South Africa-in-the-making, this was to be effected where necessary with the help of the boers, more or less European equals. And it was to be effected, Rhodes emphasized, for the good of the natives (though nobody asked them), for the power of Britain, and only then and instrumentally for personal wealth and prestige. Rhodesia (1897) was the outcome; *its* racial politics would come to rival that of South Africa's. Under the influence of his teacher Toynbee at Oxford, Milner sought a federation of South African territories committed first and foremost to combining "the Anglo-Saxon race" scattered across the landscape, and only by extension bringing whites more generally under a single governmental umbrella. Slightly differing political projects, racially mediated; but the same end.

The immediate impact of such commitments was to temper if not to terminate the earlier commitment to historicizing assimilationism. The refashioned sense of black bestiality, inherent incapacity, slothfulness, and threat, reinforced by rapidly rising black urbanization and a long series of vicious and violent wars in Natal, prompted a deep-seated stereotypical skepticism about ability, responsibility, and reliability, if not an unqualified commitment to inherent incapacity.

Thus, by the 1890s the Rhodes administration was formally restricting skilled apprenticeships to white workers only, and legislatively was producing increasingly robust and rigid segregation in the cities. The 1894 Glen Grey Act Rhodes shepherded through the Cape Parliament was designed not only to prompt blacks off the land to earn cash wages, thus securing a steady labor supply for mining and industrialization. It also limited the size and scope of individualized native landholdings beneath a ceiling it set too low to qualify for the electoral roll on property-ownership grounds. In a single legislative flourish, the Cape administration thus reduced black landholdings in the name of securing black property rights, radically circumscribed the size of the black electorate in the name of a free and open franchise, and maximized both the unskilled labor pool and wage tax base in the name of freedom to work. Racial commitment produced as much as rationalized segregation, exploitation, and political restriction.

Short on formal education, capital, and political power – other than the threat of numbers – black people were increasingly finding themselves squeezed into the class of super-exploited labor, containerized reservations and ill-serviced townships, resourceless schools and massively delimited recreational spaces. Considered mostly as animals by the boers, blacks were treated marginally better by the British administration who at least recognized their humanity. In this the Cape and the Randlords were somewhat better than the Natal colonial administration, the latter like the boers in their contempt, antipathy, and debilitating treatment towards black groups under their jurisdiction.

The Natal colonial administration and the boer landowners in the area reinforced their respective drives to marginalize blacks politically and socially while maximizing exploitation of their labor power. Somewhat haltingly, both the Cape and Natal colonial administrations nevertheless insisted on segregative legislation from as early as the 1850s, fully 30 to 40 years before the South African Republic and Orange Free State followed suit, even if British-sponsored segregation proved more ambivalent and less complete. In due course, though, segregation directed at blacks was extended to apply to Indians (in Natal) and Asians more generally, as all registrations of non-Europeanness came to be identified in racial fabrication to some degree as naturally or historically inferior on one index or another.

In this the Anglo-Boer War rehearsed at least the philosophical conflicts of the American Civil War some 35 years earlier, as Maylam remarks in a somewhat different context. It's no wonder that blacks took to the fight, where they felt compelled to fight at all, on the part of the British, notwithstanding British equivocation or even sometime duplicity. Nor that the boers would thrust weapons into the arms of their children, girls and boys alike, as soon as they were sufficiently strong to bear the weight of defending the homestead while men were out on the battlefield. Nor again that anti-imperialists, such as an Irish Republican battalion, took to the battlefield in behalf of the boers. Ironies are sometimes so obvious as not to be noticed.

Differences in racial disposition of whites between the various regions of what was becoming a unified country if not yet under single cohering rule were a matter mostly of degree more than kind. Regional unification into a common country cohered under one government was effected through race. Racial cement collected settler Europeans and their legacy into a wall of common whiteness, notwithstanding ethnic sub-division and different emphases in racial conception. British, Dutch boers, Italians, Greeks, Irish, Germans, East European Jews, and later Portuguese largely lost their emphatic ethnic heritage. Together they became much more firmly and unambiguously, even unambivalently, vested in the religiosities of whiteness and its sources of wealth and privilege than in the US case, notwithstanding the long-simmering and long-lingering contest between British and boer legacies.

Barney Barnato was the poster child of these possibilities. An East London Jewish kid born to immigrant parents, he was a happy hustler, city clown and pavement juggler, sometime pugilist and street smart, a classic and charming mix of East End Yiddish and Cockney. But also at the racial margins of London life. Scraping together a boat ticket to the Cape, Barnato's arrival could not have been better timed. Quickly taking advantage of mineral discovery, his street savvy soon cashed in handsomely on a small capital investment. Before long Barnato was in partnership with Rhodes, both becoming founding shareholders and lifetime directors of De Beers. The well-heeled British politician and Oxford graduate in bed with the scrappy working-class immigrant son from London's equivalent of the Lower East Side, class dismissal and disdain notwithstanding.

Where Rhodes's wealth was put to work in expanding the British empire, Barnato's was always reinvested in individually expansive industrialization and capital formation. Barnato's spiraling wealth bought him firmly into the class of whiteness with which his ethnoracial immigrant beginnings always made him ill at ease. When in 1897 he fell to his death from the top deck of an ocean liner on the way to London, just 45 years old, he ranked among the wealthiest of Britons, white privilege having served him superlatively well on some measure while the culture of its elevated and exclusionary class distinction rankling to the point of suspected suicide. Rhodes's larger legacy was a racially troubled country in his name, Barnato's ultimately the frustrating resentments of finance capital incapable of dressing up his humble beginnings. Modernity's competing religiosities, messianisms without quite identifiable messiahs, to riff on Derrida.

The Anglo-Boer conflict. A civil war. A millennial struggle with global implications, fought out on a local stage. A fight between Europeans, one group still wedded to the farm, the other committed to urbanizing industrialization. One deity the lord of the land, the other the godless deity of gold and glitz.

Ruling Theology

If the British won the century-closing war, militarily and perhaps ideologically, the boers would come to prevail politically, for most of a century yet to come. Long-simmering memories of mistreatment during the war and even older antagonisms from the ashes of colonial clashes. Messianic politics prompt a persistence, an eschatological patience, likely to see its day in the political sun sooner or later. Political tensions of the time fanning the flames of collective narratives of national affliction and historical trauma. David against the great colonial Goliath. If God is thought to ordain a political outcome, you can more or less bet on it being pushily pursued, hardly ever for better and ultimately for far worse.

Competing theo-politics of race thus vied for mastery over South Africa's coming into being and emergence into modernity as the nineteenth century came to a close. Blacks found themselves squeezed between two cultures of political theology seeking to texture the forces of modernizing proletarianization: a culture of missionary conversion and a culture of political messianism. These two forms of political theology both contest and curtail, structure and stream conditions of proletarianization in the region. They shape who counts and who is simply instrumentalized, who can serve in the Kingdom of Heaven and who banished to underworlds of spirits variously conceived and consumed.

The only significant ethno-hyphenation in emerging South Africa reiterated the long-running family feud between British and boer – English and Afrikaans – heritage. Lingering tensions between cultural languages long in the making. Any discernible non-whiteness, by contrast, suffered segregating differentiation, attempting formally to compel the threat of resisting coherence into the disarticulating artifice of competing ethnoracial groupings nationally conceived. Ethnoracial divide and rule long preceded formalized apartheid, disarticulating blackness into fragmented parts as whiteness in contrast covered over the Anglo-boer split.

In the almost decade-long drive to unifying the south of Africa into the Union of South Africa in 1910, British concessions effectively turned the collective boer into the self-conscious national group of Afrikaner with ruling aspirations. The language of Afrikaans was not only codified but granted more or less equal bureaucratic standing with English; an Afrikaans anthem was later composed (1918), newspapers circulated, a growing literature encouraged. The former boer republic, now the Transvaal, was granted local self-rule in 1906, and its sister republic, the Orange Free Colony, a year later. A peoplehood put firmly in place.

The eighteenth century closed and the nineteenth century opened with the arrival of the Anglicans. The nineteenth century passed into the twentieth with British victory over the boers, Anglicanism seemingly imposing itself over Calvinism. As some might have it, this consolidated the power of capital, local and especially foreign, over a system of agrislavery. But with this assertion of mining and manufacturing capital in the wake of the Anglo-Boer War the British in fact cleared the way for elaboration of the logic of a racially driven social order, of an intensified racially predicated political economy.

From this point on an increasingly cohesive and assertive political theology of race came to structure social belief, polity, economy, and law, including the supply of labor, education, residential space, and voting rights. Overall dispositions were still riven by tensions between racial naturalism and historicism, messianism and the secularized mentality of a missionary moralism. But the way was opened up to the emergent march, the culmination of a century-long trek, if not quite straightforwardly or inevitably, to the apartheid state. Far from anomaly, far from oddity, the apartheid state had roots deep in the modernizing history of South Africa, if not in Europe's colonial extension (of) itself.

The Anglo-Boer War gave way to Union, bringing all of the region up to the Limpopo River, all four colonies now, under united domain ruled beneath British jurisdiction. The British rulers locally were consumed by the question of racial arrangement, of how to rule racially, how to extend control through race, how to manage heterogeneity.

British governmentality, as South Africa was being unified, was fueled by a quartet of racially energizing pressures: The eugenic and social Darwinist self-elevation of European – and especially English – genius in contrast with native inferiority; British imperial policy across Africa (and one could say the same of other European powers with imperial design in Africa at the time) was increasingly setting indigenous people apart from Europeans (the "European" and "Native" cities, as Fanon marked it); mining capital demanded a steady, reliable, and cheap source of labor, while skilled white labor refused any constraining conditions on its own wellbeing, most notably, any skilling of the black labor pool which would drive down working conditions and wages for whites; and the segregationist drumbeat more or less incessantly pounded out by Afrikaner politicians and polity alike. Race was the cement, uniting whites in a cause invested overwhelmingly in its own welfare, a commons exclusive of the wellbeing of the country's overriding majority.

The outcome was a stream of segregationist legislation from 1910 onwards. Africans were set aside in rural reserves, formally restricted from entering urban areas for any reason other than licensed labor needs. The

Pass Laws from the 1870s were effectively extended. Notoriously, 90 percent of the landholding of the country was reserved by a 1913 law to whites,
making up just 10 percent of the population, a proportion tempered less
than a decade later to 80 percent. Given that most of the white set-aside
was held by the state in common for whites, it reinforced the understanding
that the new state existed to serve the interests of whites. It was, in short,
a state of whiteness, a white state. Unionization was famously negotiated
on the basis of a franchise compromise: Each province would determine
the racial scope of the franchise for itself. Natal, the Transvaal, and the Orange
Free State restricted voting to qualified white men; the Cape extended its
limited race-neutral franchise, endorsing a voters' roll predicated on property requirements. In time, the limited racial liberalism of the latter too
would be eroded. The Union of South Africa (another USA not so racially
distant at the time from the better-known one) exemplified the principle
at the basis of every racial state: the elevation of whiteness to the overriding state interest could be purchased only with the coin of repression.
From the outset, violence and its resistance, its pushback, were the coin of
the realm.

Milner, now effectively the governor of the merging union prior to
its formalization, clearly inherited a deep racial historicism tied to a sense
of abiding and arrogant English superiority, only slightly less in relation
to Afrikaners than to blacks. His unqualified insistence on anglicization
through education not only alienated Afrikaners, it ultimately served as fuel
for their nationalist fomentation, a rallying cry of sorts. In the end,
having lost the war, Afrikaners inherited a polity increasingly, if not to their
liking, certainly in their interests and open to their shaping. Afrikanerdom
sought political power in the name of a project of its own ethnoracial purity
and self-promotion. But already in the reach for defining what the new
Union would look like, by the middle of the first decade of the twentieth
century, Afrikaner leaders were emphasizing the making of a *South African*
South Africa.

Once firmly in power some four decades later, the Afrikaner ideological project of ethnoracial purity and power logically sought to extend its
scope to include all whites. Apartheid was a racial, not simply a narrowly
ethnic, project. *Whites* were elevated as the ruling class, as the overriding
beneficiaries of apartheid, not simply ethnic Afrikaners. Nor was this
reductively dictated as a matter of the demographic realities, though that
proved a prompting consideration. After 1948, apartheid legislation
declared unqualifiedly and explicitly what had in fact transpired in the

previous half-century. Even as Afrikaner leaders incessantly fretted over survival of their peoplehood, and ethnocultural and political divisions – sometimes deep – lingered between whites ethnically defined, apartheid as such was formulated to advance the perceived interests of whites, almost never only of Afrikaners. It could succeed, of course, because non-Afrikaner whites were largely, if ambivalently, open to white superiority, in cultural and historical if not always in naturalistic terms.

As the new century opened, those increasingly formally marked as black were torn asunder between the warrings among political theologies, the wars of world-views and ways of being. They too were bound by messianic legacies of their own imaginary making, visions of driving devil figures into the sea in the urge to be left alone in a land being taken from under their feet. But banging up against an immediately other-worldly messianism intent on establishing its Heavenly Kingdom on land long the lifeblood of African meanderings. As these meanderings became constrained on all sides, blacks were converted, to some degree, by a political theology and political economy seeing itself as progressive, turning the unbelieving or anti-faith into the disciplined and faithful. This was a political theology striving to exit from bondage by hard labor and the promise of liberty, Zion as the delivery from slavery, a liberation if not for quite some time to come yet. The commitment to uplift through effort, ultimately blocked through emerging and institutionalizing apartheid, became fused quite quickly with the quest for a sort of salvation, of deliverance from bondage, the messages of mission and messianism finding their resolution in the convictions of struggle. The reach of political theology is everywhere, its traces deep in the political psyche, the historical ontology, of South Africa.

This liberating conversion was constrained by the competing theological conception, one seeking to make of blacks an exploitable labor force, unskilled and in large part reserve. It amplified itself through a political projection of inferiorization, of constraint and delimitation. And it sought to train those of whom nothing more was to be expected in minimal skills only of digging down and building up, reproducing solely to generate massive surplus value to the benefit of the chosen among whom they are taken not to number.

If the missionary position retained some resonance at the level of the economic, it was ultimately sublimated (without being fully subsumed) into the political messianism of segregationistically inclined apartheid-yet-to-come. Civilizing culture and the social intercourse of mixing more or less gave way to keeping everyone in their racially ordered place, so long as economic security and a sense of extended wellbeing for whites at large were the social metrics. While segregation was long fueled by a sense of superiority, that sense was just as easily sustained by presumptions of racial historicism as by racial naturalism, even among Afrikaner leaders. Thus the more liberal likes of Jan Smuts, F. S. Malan, and Jan Hofmeyr nevertheless espoused white cultural elevation over blacks. The latter two went so far as to call in their own ways for at least a limited black franchise, if only on pragmatic grounds. Smuts, by contrast, insisted on long-term trusteeship for the supposed sake of black wellbeing, ostensibly for promoting their own interests. As I have suggested in other regional contexts too, this range represents the classic commitments of racial liberalism.

Segregation, then, received its boost from two grades of fuel fusing to common combustion. The larger and more direct kick came from the perception, not least among hardcore Afrikaners fearing they would dissolve in a sea of blackness but far from only, that blacks demographically, intellectually, and so politically constituted a threat to white wellbeing. (In this, Afrikaners took themselves, as they did whites generally, to occupy a position analogous to Jews in Germany.) The core ingredient here is the lingering presumption of degenerationism. The second fuel, extracted from the tradition of racial historicism, energized a commitment to separate racial development of blacks under white direction and domination. This was driven by the underlying presumption of cultural distinction so deep as to mark group-defining differences in temporalities, sensibilities, and possibilities the promotion of which called for separate supporting institutions, much as different religious institutions support different denominations.

While there's a sense in which separation as a political fact on the ground developed incrementally – bit by policy and legislative bit, institutionalization upon conceptualization, institutional reification upon cementation – the fusion of these fuels drove such processes forward after Union. The pace quickened in the 1930s and 1940s even as black, Coloured, Asian, and to some extent worker resistance (ambivalent as its compromised position always made it) was more or less vocally expressed. By the mid-1940s, separate Councils had been established to deal with – nominally to represent – "Natives," "Coloureds," and "Asians." To a degree these Councils became advocates for the interests of each racially designated group, serving at the same time to institutionalize separation.

The Asian case is instructive. Before the end of the 1940s, Asians (overwhelmingly Indian) owned nearly 20 percent of the country's retail business, though just 3 percent of the population. Asian businessmen, a distinct minority within the population group, were purchasing property liberally, especially in Durban. In 1946, then-prime minister Smuts introduced legislation limiting Asian residence and business enterprise to restricted areas and ending all property purchases between Asians and whites. The pieces that would become apartheid were already discretely in formation if not firmly in place by the time its vocal and unifying orchestrators would launch themselves to political power in 1948. South Africa lunged to resurrect and redirect racial domination in a formal political system just as decolonizing movements were beginning to bear fruit.

A sociality of the skin

As south Africa unified institutionally into a single state known as South Africa after 1910, accordingly, it came increasingly to embody, to exemplify, to represent and reproduce in formal terms and institutions "life at the frontier of the skin," to invoke Salman Rushdie's compelling phrase from a very different if comparably manic fabrication. A *sociality of the skin* serves as the signifying referent for a political theology of race, not unlike relation to the body and blood of the Savior in a more traditional theological politics. The skin situates its bearers in racially predicated societies. It sites and restricts, it announces and delimits, it allows and disables, it fixes relation and relates fixations, orders belief and anchors belief in order. The skin thus is more than epidermal. It bears significance and suggestibility, coding information and informing social codes. It is the turnkey to social relation, in short, the principal reference point for a sociality the state of which is reductively racial, which immediately references place and places reference.

But this fixing, fixation, anchoring, and mediation are, if simply skin deep in imagination, depressingly more deeply cemented in the foundations of social architecture. A sociality of the skin paradoxically limits life and its social possibilities – most all that happens in life and at death – to the inflexibilities of the social surface, denying depth and relying on the policing of superficial relation, while grounding the social infrastructure all the way down on nothing but racial cement. A sociality of the skin disposes its subjects to seeing little else, to comprehending pretty much only in terms of its codes even in resistance, to living life largely if not exclusively on its terms. To sustain itself, the sociality of the skin can only fall back on and into a political theology of compulsion. The thicker grows not just the form but the substance of relations, of inter-relationality, the likelier looms the demise of such sociality.

A sociality of the skin, thus, is one of threat. It is predicated on social relation in which the lives – the livelihood, the social conditions of life's reproduction, the social positioning and self-determination – of the subjugated are threatened at every turn. But it is a sociality, in addition, in which the domination of the dominant is fueled by the threat they invest in the very existence and expression of the subjugated. The potential self-determination of the powerless and subjugated, the potentiality of which is always immediately if far from completely signified in a racial state by the invested significance in the skin, is taken as threatening to the continued domination of the powerful. The relations of and through the skin in a racial state inevitably imply potential revolt and possibility of resistance, collective action against the impositions of racial threat. But then always also the racial targeting and pre-emptive profiling of the presumptive threat underlying which is the drive of the dominant to cohere itself as a single, unified racial entity. In a sociality of the skin, threat, threatening, and being threatened are inextricably intertwined in the psycho-social dynamics of power's racial articulation.

By the 1920s, as a broad generalization, English-speaking whites in South Africa came to represent, to stand for, capital, industry, and liberal capitalism. Blacks had little else but their collective labor power, constrained as it was. And Afrikaners held land, where they held anything at all, and were forging both a world and world-view – the segregating sociality of skin – compelling not just to Afrikaners but increasingly to other whites also. This sociality of the skin represented for whites generally the threat of dissolution in a sea of proliferating blackness, of competition over jobs for poor whites of every ethnic background, of disease promising to seep out from every corner of surging urban slum life (this, after all, was the time too of the "sanitation syndrome"), of crime, moral devaluation, and cultural pollution. For Afrikaners, in particular, so caught up with concerns about group extinction, it meant above all survival and self-securitization, as much as a group as individually. The sense of self-superiority whites took to be identified with this sociality of the skin in relation to black groups was a superiority so threatened by contamination and fear that one can only conclude that the sense was more wish and worry than wisdom, more projection than prospect. The heightened form of separation, racially predicated, that came to be known as apartheid was nurtured out of these senses of threat, survival, and security.

Ministers and administration

The Church – in particular the Dutch Reformed Church (*Nederduitse Gereformeerde Kerk*) – played a defining role in apartheid's articulation, elaboration, and rationalization in the century's first half. The skeletal socio-legal structure of the state that would become apartheid, as I have suggested, was already stitched in place by the British and various administrations from 1910 to 1948: restrictive and increasingly eroded Native reserves set apart, Pass Laws, job color bars, segregated schools and delimited educational opportunities for those not white, divided recreational facilities and racially restrictive public accommodations, discrete voters rolls and differentiated political representation. That said, however, apartheid – as a term and as an idea, as a structure and as a set of practices, as an ideal and aspiration, as dream and nightmare, in short, as political theology – was projected as coherent conception from the Church, from God's projected word, down.

"Apartheid" was coined – the vision conceived – almost 20 years before the Nationalist Party took power more or less on its platform in 1948. At a Dutch Reformed Church conference on missionary work in 1929, Giliomee points out in his voluminous work on *The Afrikaners*, the Rev. C. J. du Plessis made the case for missionary work in "the spirit of apartheid that has always characterized [the Church's] conduct." He understood this "spirit of apartheid" as driving the separate development of a nation's unique spirit, its "own" (*eie*) sensibility. That of blacks differed from whites', and apartheid sought not only to recognize this but to center it as the grounds for national development. If there was equality in this, it was the sort of equality articulated in the US Supreme Court's majority decision in *Plessy v. Ferguson* (1896), namely, the equal right of access to unequal resources, possibilities, accommodations. At the heart of apartheid, black people had a right equal to that of white people: to their own language(s), sensibilities, cultural expression, places of habitation, schooling, recreation, even places or pews of worship, no matter the radical inequalities, supposed and produced, of those resources relative to whites'. Because those differences were seen as God-ordained, the divine command of the deity.

For the mainstream Dutch Reformed Church, souls may be equal in principle before God. But equal souls could occupy different rungs on the scale of development, different levels of intellectual prowess and cultural advancement. This entailed an equality not to mix or interact but one of socializing in groups apart, with one's own, one's equals; and development along separate tracks while inhabiting separate tracts. Johann Kinghorn quotes another church leader, F. S. de Klerk, writing in 1939 that

> Equalization leads to the humiliation of both races. Mixed marriages between higher civilized Christianized nations and lower nations militate against the Word of God. . . . This is nothing less than a crime.

Those ahead should not be held back by those behind; those behind should not feel deflated by those running ahead. The strong and leaderly should lead the weak and needy. One's proper place is among one's own, the familial and familiar, those the good Lord had made to be like one. Race was divine provenance, the horizon of spiritual community.

At the threshold of taking power and becoming apartheid's first prime minister, D. F. Malan could be explicit about the theological grounding of the racial order in 1947:

> It was not the state but the church who [*sic*] took the lead with apartheid. The state followed the principle laid down by the church in the field of education for the native, the coloured and the Asian. The result? Friction was eliminated.

H. F. Verwoerd, who played such a key role in articulating apartheid as governmentality and would follow D. F. Malan as prime minister, added at the same moment, "It was in accordance with God's will that different races and *volke* (nations) exist." (I owe both quotes to Giliomee's book, an enormous source of information if an extended and ultimately unsuccessful attempt to render repressive Afrikaner history more palatable.)

Originally referring to the self-governance and self-determination of the separate – or separately conceived – churches that were supposed to minister to these differentiated national communities, the doctrine of apartheid quickly came to be generalized across the entire polity. The separateness of a theological community committed to developing the authenticity of "one's own" came to ground the political theology of separate development. The spirit of self-determining national differentiation fueled the power of political segregation ordered by and in the overriding interests of whites. The pernicious legal order and political practices identified as apartheid were in the first instance anchored in this belief structure, the set of convictions (to use Thomas Blom Hansen's useful term), I am marking by its political theology. Apartheid as separate development had become its messianic message, the mission of differentiated education for the respective good of each group its instrumentalization.

In this expansion across the polity, the religious and secular are inextricably entangled with each other, the presumptive secularity of governing modalities in many ways dripping with religious definition and legacy. The Lord's Prayer was recited daily in public schools:

> Our Father, who art in Heaven
> Hallowed be Thy Name
> Thy Kingdom Come, Thy Will be Done
> On Earth as it is in Heaven.

Taken literally. The terms of the secular assumed and silently extended already existing religious significance, in both senses of the term.

> God Bless the Nation.

Secular modernity, such as it came to be, resonated with the terms of the religious, considered premodern though giving those terms new meaning. The nation reveals itself, announces its deepest commitments, in the anthem it adopts and has its children sing at every occasion.

> Ringing out from our blue heavens . . .

It is not just that religion shaped the national articulations, rationalizations, and aspirations of governing beliefs in and structures of the racial, though that too.

> Teach us, Lord, to trust Thee still:
> Guard our land and guide our people
> In Thy way to do Thy will.

More broadly, a totalizing racial investment itself assumes the form of theological embrace, no more so than in South Africa.

> We will answer to Your calling
> We will offer what You ask
> We will live
> We will die
> We for Thee
> South Africa.

The "we" here that of religious whiteness. Race and nation, for whites only, inextricably intertwined. Starting with a theological transcendentalism underpinning the claims to an ontological status for race (it can sustain itself in no other way than transcendentally), racial belief structures the frames of reference as the theological does: it "commands" belief, exactly.

> Fatherland!
> We will bear your name with honor
> Dedicated and true as Afrikaners
> Children of South Africa.

Afrikaners as inheritors of the land and its treasures. Afrikaners as European Africans, boer and British alike. Afrikaners, modern-day Africanders, as Europeans become African.

But, of course, one can – of one's own will – obey or not (there the very problem of the "free will" in the face of command). For the belief to hold, to be commanded by it, one has to make it one's own, it must become one, so to speak (again in both senses), one has to *have* it move one (this way of putting it indicating the relation between self-motivation and compulsion). That "*I* have to" indicates it is me that is making it so, it is I that compel myself to be so compelled. I am free in my compulsion, I freely choose to compel myself, to be compelled. The theological concerns the consuming order of belief *that would have it so that I have it so.* And the political is my thrust – the way I am having it thrust me – into social relations ordered by such belief. Racial compulsion in South Africa came to be that entangled web of social self-urging.

Apartheid accordingly turned these convictions, this self-urging, into an urgency to complete its edifice, to order all social arrangements in and across racial terms, to orchestrate racial relation and restrain racial intercourse. The racial terms of this set of convictions – broadly set at the foundations if not always settled, shifting in content, subject to negotiation as much personal as political – represented deep-seated commitments. They were immanent in presumption, if instrumentalized in relation to material conditions. They offered the a prioris of a sociality that were both rationalization of their social history, their guiding historical narratives, and the broad terms of engagement of their contemporary conditions. They were, as such, as much political principle as economic rationalization.

At the same time, this constrained social architecture, racially conceived and constructed, inevitably and quickly – from its pronouncement, from the earliest inklings of it expression – became countered by all those who took their lives to be crimped, delimited, impoverished by the vision and its enactment. Antiracism, as I have commented in Chapter 1, in South Africa as much as anywhere, became coalitional, cross-racial, and inter-coursing. If at times racially reifying (for instance, in the sometime elaboration of Pan Africanism), in large part this resistance has proved to be more or less de-racing without becoming deracinating (that, at least, has been the challenge). Along the way, the original urgency of apartheid's articulation necessarily and predictably became defensive, increasingly violent as its terms were quickly seen to be broadly offensive on every register. Urgency devolved into emergency, attempting frantically to keep at bay the perceived barbarians, the ghosts of its own making, at the gate.

Brotherhoods and bondage

The founding of two organizations, the one representing Afrikaner national(ist) aspirations, the other facing down the terms of that articulation and reach for power, reveals these very contrasts. In 1912, the South African Native National Congress (which changed its name, famously, to the African National Congress in 1923) was established, initially to counter the proposed legislative confinement of almost 90 percent of the African population to just 10 percent of the country's land. This stakeholding, amounting effectively to an inverse enclosure act, was the grounding also of the migrant labor system. Landholding and the Bible indeed were being clasped together in the devil's handshake. The ANC was born of resistance to the repressive racial configuration of restrictions on property and prosperity, mobility and miscegenation, education and employment, life's resources and recreation.

In 1918, by contrast, the more educated among Afrikaners – initially teachers, civil servants, and Dutch Reformed Church ministers, then shortly after academics and lawyers – bandied together in the *Afrikaner Broederbond* (Brotherhood) to debate Afrikaner policy and political commitment. The Broederbond grew out of concerns over the dilution of Afrikaner national, cultural, and linguistic interests, the impoverishment of Afrikaners and the expansion of the poor white class, demographic swamping and the fear of degeneration, and out of the emergence of farming cooperatives as a way of coping with insurance, investment, and banking. The Bond, a somewhat secretive salon, under the guiding hand of its academic leadership in the 1930s and 1940s, would come to exercise considerable if largely informal influence on the vision of Afrikaner nationalism, the fixation on which grew into apartheid. It had a large hand in outlining the more strident expressions of Afrikaner political philosophy, the direction of state policy, the shaping of the emergent Afrikaner state, and the architecture of apartheid. But it had considerable influence, not least through its extensive interpersonal networks, equally across public life and civil society, in commerce and ultimately high finance, in journalism, throughout industry and education. The ANC, of course, would soon come to be the principal resistant group, ultimately articulating a profound counter-conception of South African polity and sociality.

The contrast between the two organizations is revealing. Both emerged out of the religious formation of their founders. For the Broederbond leaders this was the anticipatory messianism of a self-directed state by, for, and limited to members of the *volk*, Afrikaners above all and whites more broadly. For the ANC forefathers like John Langalibalele Dube and his cousin Pixley Seme, their missionary education was as formative as their later education in the US and Britain and their influence by Booker T. Washington, most notably under the civilizing guidance of the American Zion mission. Where the Broederbond was always uni-representational, ethno-nationalistic, segregationist, racially restrictive, and inward-looking, the ANC came quickly to be pluralist, multi-racial, coalitional, integrationist, and internationalist. If both started out as "brotherhoods," exclusively male organizations, the ANC developed a compelling section driven by women as early as 1948, whereas the Broederbond pointedly has remained to this day an exclusively male domain. Where the Broederbond saw in mixture civilization's ultimate fall from grace, the threat of its decadence and disgrace, the ANC came to see in nonracial social intercourse, effectively in non-restrictive mixing, the fuel for future national flourishing.

The Broederbond came to be identified with the messianic spirit of Afrikaner national fulfillment, its inevitable destiny, its calling. In the words of one well-placed commentator, General Secretary I. M. Lombard (and quoted by Dan O'Meara), "The Afrikaner Broederbond is born from a deep conviction that the Afrikaner nation has been planted [in South Africa] by God's hand and is destined to remain here as a nation with its own character and its own mission." Afrikaner rule was at once calling and destiny, endowed by nature and yet to be brought about, to be realized. Afrikaners are chosen by God, set to rule though his irresistible grace and guiding wisdom. The Bond was unstintingly local and isolationist by inclination, self-sufficient and segregationist by conviction if not perfectly in practice. Mines needed labor, railway lines needed laying, farms needed a hand and gardens needed tending, homes needed to be cleaned and food had to be cooked. Conviction only produced so much; political pragmatism in the service of a religious nationalism would be the grease of governing. Racial repression ruled the realm.

However instrumentalized its sometime expression, the designer racial order and the repression necessary to sustain it – the physical and intellectual violence, the humiliations, the sense of divine power and complete control, of absolute self-righteousness and moral self-elevation, of being the bearer of God's word and carrying out His command – were at basis taken to be inspired, natural law, God's plan. The need formally to rationalize, legitimate, or even to represent predefined interests or commitments in terms of the articulation of racial superiority was secondary and soft, at best. The ratiocination was principally direct: we are ordained by God, the Chosen, driven to self-determination to preserve ourselves and all that is dear to us, suffering – as Donald Moore aptly puts it in a neighboring and reversed context – for territory. "[The Bond's] sphere of operations," in the words of its Constitution (as quoted by O'Meara), "is the work of the Afrikaner people as *a separate historical, Protestant-Christian language and cultural community*" (Clause 4c, my emphasis). The rest was instantiation, application, materialization.

The ANC was founded on the rejection of this vision. It came to see in the doctrine of "trusteeship," as the mission statement establishing the ANC Youth League by Mandela, Sisulu, Tambo, and others in 1944 had it, the consolidation of power in the hands of whites, the complete conquest of Africans, and their consequent denial of freedom. Where there are theological traces here, they are fleeting and peripheral, as in the opening acknowledgment of "the *divine* destiny of nations." Their resonance fades quickly, though, both within the document and in future resolutions of the major resistance organizations. Thus the Freedom Charter, adopted in 1955 (and a major influence on the post-apartheid Constitution of South Africa ratified at the close of 1996), is shorn of all explicit theological reference, as too the various ANC Constitutions from 1958 onwards.

The Freedom Charter is especially significant. Adopted by the thoroughly multi-racial Congress of the People representing a very broad consensus of South African society and organizations, including the ANC, it rejects all "racialism." The Charter articulates by contrast a vision of fair, equitable sharing of all resources and wealth of the country, and equal rights and treatment in and by the law. Like the Constitutions of the ANC and its key constituent organizations such as the Youth and Women's Leagues, the Freedom Charter represents what could be called the *secularization* of government, if not of South African society, as a key consideration in governmental deracialization. The grip of racial theology on the governing architecture and institutional arrangements of the society is prised loose, de-emphasized, and discarded to the garbage heap of history. But as with secularization generally, theological traces nevertheless linger, as I'll return to reveal, the shadow effects of race continuing to cloud social conditions and relations, if informally.

Living apart together

The social and political interests represented by the Broederbond prevailed from the 1940s until the close of the 1980s, translating Afrikaans experience into the governing philosophy underlying state policy and structure. Under its deific directorship, formulated largely by the guiding hand of a group of academic intellectuals, apartheid gripped state and society, assuming formalized power in 1948. It was translated into a series of concrete and codifying legislation soon after. Mixed marriages were outlawed in 1949, and mixed intercourse – especially sexual – legally immoralized a year later. From 1950 also, every person was required to be racially classified and registered at birth, racially defined groups were to be set aside in formally and forcefully segregated residential areas mapped out by the state, and any resistance to state rule – characteristically charged as "Communist" – was outlawed. A year later again, "Native homelands" were established on the basis of "Native reserves" created under British rule that would come to be known as "Bantustans," job color bars were cemented in place, and "Coloureds" were denied participation in the common (now effectively all-white) voters roll.

If racial classification of "Whites," "Coloureds," and "Africans" in the legislation was definitively incoherent and circular, residential segregation was brutally executed, and resistance was violently suppressed. The more incoherent the legislation, the more repressive the violence it took to enforce. Mixed residential, commercial, and recreational space was brutally purged, the prime locations reserved exclusively to white ownership; homelands were established as repositories of black poverty and desperately cheap migrant labor for mines and manufacturing; and any political resistance to these state regimes was more or less immediately suppressed. Parties and people were banned, one could effectively say "excommunicated," treated as proverbial pariah, the racial equivalent of the witch.

Beyers Naude provides the classic case. A Dutch Reformed Church minister and former Broederbond member (his father had helped to form the Bond), Naude became deeply disillusioned with apartheid especially after the Sharpeville massacre (in 1960, police shot dead 69 black people protesting their lack of free movement). He "converted" as a consequence to a caustic critic of apartheid and an extraordinary advocate of nonracialism, at great personal cost. The government first imprisoned and then banned him, condemning him to house arrest from 1977 to 1984. Following his release in 1985, Naude assumed the chairmanship of the South African Council of Churches, the association of leading anti-apartheid church organizations, succeeding Archbishop Tutu in the position. He played a formative role with Desmond Tutu, Alan Boesak, and others in 1983 in shepherding into the forefront of South African democratic nonracial resistance the leading umbrella anti-apartheid organization in the mid-1980s, the United Democratic Front.

Black political leaders and leaders of the South African Communist Party (many secular Jews), by contrast, were largely driven underground, imprisoned, permanently exiled, or murdered. The ANC leadership, when not in exile, languished for decades in prison, often in solitary confinement, under various pretences of treason, subversion, and Communism. Indres Naidoo's harrowing account of torture and chains on Robben Island is a living testament to just how far the apartheid regime would go to terrorize people for the sake of securing itself. Steve Biko, the person most credited with formulating the intellectual vision for South Africa's articulation of Black Consciousness, was left to suffer a slow, strangulating death in 1977 lying undressed and unattended in the back of a police van on a long cross-country drive after a particularly brutal set of beatings under interrogation in prison. The height of apartheid sought to foreclose any dream of social mixing or black self-determination other than at the command of white benefit. Racial mixing – socially as much as sexually, politically as much as personally – became the counter, the resistant, the underground.

Perhaps nothing more symbolizes the crusading spirit, subjugating domination, and repressive suffering which apartheid sought to impose than the legacy of Sophiatown. Founded at the edge of spreading Johannesburg as the twentieth century opened up, it became a site of freehold property first by whites and then increasingly by blacks and mixed race people as the Johannesburg city council established a sewage plant in the area and upwardly mobile whites sought better living conditions in less polluted environments of the city. By the 1940s Sophiatown had become Harlem-like in hosting a vibrant avant-garde culture of writing, music, art and poetry, the font of a vernacular cultural expressiveness unmatched elsewhere in South Africa. Home to kwela and penny whistle street corner jive, to the dramatic photography and writing of *Drum Magazine* and convivial dance halls, to the great saxophonist Kiepie Moketsi and the street sense of writer Bloke Modisane, to Jewish watchmakers and The Jazz Epistles, to the grittiness of smoky shebeen life and the unstinting humanizing commitments of Anglican archbishop and apartheid arch-critic Terry Huddleston. The site and standard-bearer of intense, vibrant, lived South African *mestizaje*, Sophiatown stood for everything apartheid found repulsive and sought to deny. The living spirit and symbol of another way of being, for the protectors of apartheid Sophiatown was the site of sin, the Earthly City. It had to be destroyed.

So, starting in 1955, destroyed Sophiatown was. With little forewarning, the bulldozers arrived under army and police protection. Houses were flattened with much of their possessions still in them. Furniture and photographs, dolls and pet dogs, clothing and cooking utensils, cups and crockery were crushed into the soil, to be excavated years later by treasure hunters, as Maureen van Niekerk's claustrophobic saga recounts for us in the guttural vernacular of Sophiatown's Afrikaner replacement residents. The township flattened, its lively people forcibly removed, scattered to more squeezed, controlled, discomforting, and less threatening corners of Johannesburg's outlying reaches, Sophiatown vanished but for its fragmented traces pressed into the unforgiving earth. Rebuilt by the apartheid government as a housing tract of lifeless cement block, red tin-roofed houses cut through by wide empty streets, the remodeled township was intended to house poor whites, civil service workers, and policemen's families whose collective vote brought the apartheid government to power in 1948. In a melancholically Riefenstahlian twist, the nominal softness of Sophiatown was replaced by the trumpeted terrorizing of Triomf ("triumph").

This moment of apartheid's triumph, nevertheless, was the initiating mark also of its undoing. As Triomf was declaring the thousand-year Reich of apartheid, the Congress of the People was committing to apartheid's undoing, to calling tyranny to its termination. That undoing would have to endure almost another four decades: of repression and resistance, of subjection and struggle (Sharpeville in 1960, the crippling Durban strikes in 1973, the youth uprising of 1976, the uniting of anti-apartheid efforts in 1983 in opposition to the divide-and-rule strategy of tricameral elections the following year, and so on). But the bell for apartheid was tolled that fierce February day of forced removals in 1955, the ghosts of Sophiatown continuing to haunt the apartheid city at its pinnacle of proclaimed triumph. As the edifice of apartheid was being erected, if not resurrected, so it would be resisted, brick by blood-splattered brick.

In sacralizing race, apartheid extended new definition to nineteenth-century high colonialism (when Disraeli could declare all to be race), assuming at the same time especially aesthetic elements of fascist ideological representation (*volkisch* factors and godly ordination, youth brigades, the social role of the uniform, the appeal of the Volkswagen and the German Shepherd, the construction of huge granite grey monumental blocks of buildings). Apartheid was the social absolutization of race, rendering its conceptual frames foundational in defining the body politic and its terms of relation. Race defined all, was everywhere present. Black and white lives intersected almost ubiquitously – in the home (overwhelmingly but not only of whites), at the workplace, in public space, even recreational sites, and to some degree in educational institutions. But those intersecting relations were not just deeply managed; they were as thoroughly ordered on hierarchical racial planes in their conceptual and organizational structure as they were behaviorally policed. In declaring independence from Britain as a republic in 1961, then-prime minister Verwoerd hinted at this ordination: "We'll work out our own salvation here on the southern tip of Africa, by the light we have, and with the help of the Almighty."

This salvation was predicated on the presumption that whites were always privileged, always in charge – the *baas* (boss), always serviced, ever the beneficiaries. Black people worked for whites; the reverse was legally prohibited. They cleaned homes, washed soiled clothes, scrubbed floors, made the bed, polished shoes, cooked food. They nursed babies and the elderly, provided childcare until teenagers could care for themselves and then still, tended gardens, delivered goods, provided services. They chauffeured, carried, made sure bathrooms – public as much as private – were always spotless. They were trusted with all but the most intimate of details while castigated as trustless. They kept swimming pools and beaches pristine pure where prohibited from using the facilities themselves, even those where white unmarried couples were required moralistically by local ordinance to remain a foot apart from each other. They mined gold and diamonds they had no hope of affording, manufactured clothing they would never adorn save as second-hand charitable donation. They pumped gas for automobiles they could only dream of owning and washed windows of buildings they could never occupy.

For black people of any stripe under apartheid, race was the burden always borne on the back. Inferior health care, where health care at all. Life filled with the likelihood of disease, if not one's own then of those close to one. It was a life likely much more pain-filled than that of any white counterpart, always at the whim of another, a life of demand and command. Of some time in prison if for nothing else than violating the conditions of the Pass Laws when it wasn't for political resistance. A life of dramatically reduced education through no lack of effort or ability of one's own. One where employment more often than not meant leaving one's family for extended periods, where one might spend as much time traveling to work as working, where what one took home barely covered what one needed to get back to the workplace the following day. It was a life, in short, of disposability, of absolute vulnerability, of physical and intellectual exhaustion. Where survival meant knowing those in charge better than they knew themselves, and yet sharing that knowledge only with those sharing the same condition as one. Where life expectancy of blacks was nearly 15 years shorter than that of whites. Where civil society kills, but not so softly. A life of bitterness likely washed away by *spiritual* consolement of one form or another, remarkably producing much less bitterness than critical observers could expect.

Whites would live out their lives denying dependability while absolutely dependent. Sharing familial intimacies with those who knew them better than they knew themselves but whom they knew scarce at all. They could confess their deepest fears and secrets as though confiding in a priest to those whose humanity and certainly dignity they scant acknowledged. They could request a favor of their "boys" or "girls" in the same breath as chiding them knowingly to strangers or intimates alike as lazy or stupid or inept. White men could eye, even sexually abuse, black women or solicit black prostitutes yet joke about black animality with their friends. White men and women could declare solutions to insoluble political situations half a world away while oblivious to conditions in black townships barely a stone's throw from home. They could drive by endless miles of shantytown shacks invisible to their gaze while bemoaning how terrible the favelas in São Paulo or the bustees of Bombay. They could decry the petty crime of black youth seeking to survive in total ignorance of the serious crimes of racially inscribed sociality. And they could claim absolute "knowledge" of "the black man" – the "kafir" – completely ignorant of the most basic conditions under which black people survived right before their eyes. To live as a white person in apartheid South Africa was to live a life of more or less large-scale, if never perfect, denial.

Apartheid's absolute sacralization of race, accordingly, established the grounds of a civic religion reaching into all strands of sociality. It sought to mark all racial relation, defining behavior and thought for most features of a sociality of the skin. It provided the terms of engagement at the color lines, for in South Africa they were multiple, and shifting. The modes of moralizing sociality, the codes for negotiating social space and mores, for inhabiting the cathedral of color. But it provided more than that. For it shaped and secured also sovereignty, vesting in whites the more or less absolute determination not only of who could live and who would die, of letting live and letting die, but equally of the conditions under which life could be lived out, of who had standing in the community and who merely served and serviced it.

Racial sacralization assumed the absolutization of the sovereign, unleashing cruelty towards the demonized without constraint. Condomizing the sacred community of the pure from pollution, moral degeneration, and dissolution licensed limitless violence by the guardians of the sacred against the perceived forces of debilitation. The self-elevated not only exercise absolute power; in assuming such absolutization they aspire to deific status. They thus mimicked God, becoming His rival, assertive in their absolutization shored up by their hegemonic reproduction of consent in and to their power. The more challenged their absolutizing power, the more assertive their resort to violence, ultimately deciding who should live and who suffer physical or social death.

In short, racial sacralization set the terms for defining who could be sacrificed, and to what purpose.

Like religious conviction, apartheid animates belief and conduct in and on its terms, prompting the committed to protect the convicting community above all else, to be guided if not driven by its terms, to give of oneself and to sacrifice others for the wellbeing of the committed, the brotherhood, the *volk*. The committed gave of themselves through service – intellectual, military, police, civil, even sports – renouncing material gain for the sake of communal uplift. Sacrifice – of oneself, of food, of others treated as if food – became a measure of conviction, a mark of committal.

Security forces in the service of the apartheid state notoriously sacrificed black men in just these ways, as Allen Feldman has argued in a series of articles, treating them as meat, softening them up by way of torturous interrogations, seasoning with sweated beatings over *braaivleis* (barbecuing) fires in farflung fields just out of social sight. (Township rebels towards the bitter end of apartheid's duration responded in kind to the provoking call by publicly "necklacing" police informers, sacrificing the complicit of the community to the struggle in the township streets by lighting a car tire around their necks and burning them to death.) The police-tortured bodies were burnt to a crisp, often hacked to pieces, so as to destroy the evidence, devoured almost literally in all but body. The sacrifice was oiled with considerable inebriation, as much to obliterate the memory as to loosen any inhibition, to disqualify any qualms as symbolically to imbibe the blood of the Savior. To cleanse the spirit of the burden of memory, to save the soul by deleting conscience.

This instrumentalizing of apartheid, whether through intellectual work or physical violence and terror, is less a matter of complicity than the servicing cogs of conceptualization and its materialization. Complicity is a matter of joining forces with or supporting those who initiate thought and action. There no doubt were many complicit with apartheid, to use Mark Sanders's term, thus making its extension possible, both across the country and beyond its borders (intellectuals, journalists, corporate leaders, and service providers of all racial backgrounds, indeed, politicians at home and abroad alike). Nevertheless, those complicit with and accordingly complicating apartheid should not be confused with those central to its definition and implementation, those for whom it was first and foremost a commitment of principle, a conviction, a kind of religious embrace if not exactly a conversion, and not just an instrument of profit, commercial or personal.

Nor should they be confused, as Sanders properly points out, with those, not least intellectuals, equally committed to bringing apartheid to an end. Whether interested in producing a nonracial polity under liberal democratic principles of justice as fairness, a socialist state considerably more equitable for all, or a society fashioned on religious principles of fraternity, anti-apartheid forces combined to oppose the Nationalist government in power. Struggling against intense repression, anti-apartheid became the global *cause célèbre*. By the later 1980s, trade union and church leaders, artists and musicians, educators and students, politicians and civil rights leaders scrambled to the cause. Official apartheid was doomed.

Counter-Conversions

State apartheid was doomed as a result of decades of struggle by long-suffering political prisoners and those exiled, excommunicated from apartheid's version of the Heavenly City. By trade unionists slowing the economy to unproductive pace. By township dwellers and rent boycotters resisting apartheid's repressive apparatuses and committed to making the townships unruly, impossible to be governed. By activists, students, and military evaders in and out of South Africa prepared to renounce apartheid's partial privileges alongside its insufferable burdens. By boycotters economic, civic, and intellectual, institutional and individual alike.

By the late 1980s the South African economy was deeply depressed, foreign economic and political support had taken flight. Globalizing forces of political economy were emphasizing the neoliberalizing individualization of social life with which collective emphases of apartheid were considered deeply at odds. Along ironically with soviet collectivism to which it took itself to be so opposed, and for intersecting reasons, apartheid had fallen dramatically out of step with the times.

Curiously enough, religious organizations played a key role, both in helping to force the dissolution of apartheid and in the transforming period of the 1990s. Religious organizations were able to work in the country in ways more radical political groups such as the ANC and the South African Communist Party were not after their bannings in the early 1960s. So deeply religious by conviction, Afrikaners were challenged to treat those equally committed to the language of the Lord with a modicum of respect even where they found their scriptural interpretation, religious conviction, and earthly resolve fundamentally at odds with their own.

The United Democratic Front (UDF) was a coalitional social movement of religious leaders, trade unionists, and community organizations. Together they fashioned a front of sorts on the ground for the banned ANC, giving the latter a leading voice for strategizing among the disaffected and the hopeful from its founding in 1983 until the ANC's unbanning in 1991 when the UDF folded. It was inspired by if not reducible to humanizing religious leadership. Their influence was felt – not least but not only through the inimitable energy, moral courage, insight, and human pathos of Desmond Tutu, so usually categorized by white South Africans comfortable with apartheid as "the black devil" – in two transitional moments of producing the "rainbow nation" that proved the turnkey for shaping the "new South Africa."

Jeremy Seekings rightly concludes his formative history of the Front under Tutu's guidance by commenting that "The whole character of the overall post-apartheid political system reflects, in some respects, the influences of the UDF. The legacy of the UDF can be seen in the character of South African democracy, the contours of political society and the chequered emergence of civil society." Under its lingering influence, the language of God crept back – in a prefatory and suggestive rather than substantive way, to be sure – into the new Constitution of 1996. "May God protect our people," echoing the new national anthem *"Nkosi sikelel' iAfrika"* ("God bless Africa"), closes the Preamble to what by all accounts is the world's most liberal democratic Constitution today, the more notably so given the ANC's studiedly secularized Constitutions of the previous half-century.

> God, bless Africa
> May her spirit rise high up
> Hear thou our prayers
> God bless us Your family.
>
> Chorus
> Descend, O Spirit
> Descend, O Holy Spirit
> God bless us
> Your family.

The anthemic family now inclusively interpellating all members of the rainbow nation.

More pressingly, though, it was a political theology of the truth setting its people free and forgiveness grounding national reconciliation that came to define the extraordinary institutional apparatus that would heal the nation. This theologically resonant politics – more open ended and empathic, universalizing and humanistic than apartheid could ever allow itself to be – would subvert the country's history of intense violence under and transitioning from apartheid, cement the rainbow polity, and draw South Africa back as an exemplary member into the community of nations. The heterogeneity of the rainbow nation, of a humanized Noah's arc, would replace the (in)sanitizing homogeneity of the apartheid *volk*, the gritty lived city on earth the antidote to the antiseptic Heavenly City attempting to flee or repress all the complexities making up its challenges. The Truth and Reconciliation Commission (TRC) offered the ladder by which South Africa would climb out of its hellish history. It was, not to put too fine a point on this, the national purgatory.

The TRC was set in place in 1995 as part of the negotiated transition from apartheid to an inclusively and constitutionally democratic South Africa so as "to heal the nation's wounds." It sought a forum for bearing witness to the human rights abuses suffered by those under apartheid, and an opportunity for perpetrators on both sides fully and publicly to confess their violations, to seek redemption by apologizing, for the victims and their families to forgive them, and thus for the former to be granted amnesty from prosecution. The public national forum was designed to establish reconciliation between perpetrators and sufferers, thus to spare the country from the sort of violence apartheid had imposed upon it and which had gripped it in the early years of transition leading up to the first free elections of 1994. Recognition and confession of these atrocities, as TRC commissioner Pumla Gobodo-Madikizela puts it, would help to heal by restoring to victims their dignity and respect, and allow perpetrators "to reclaim their own humanity."

To qualify for amnesty, perpetrators had to confess fully and with conviction for crimes during apartheid considered to be political. Amnesty would preclude prosecution for crimes so confessed, though not for other crimes, political or criminal. The Commission's official report of 1998 revealed that of the more than 7,000 requests for amnesty, only 849 or a little over 12 percent were granted. The TRC is generally credited with going a long way in helping South Africans to come to terms with one another and the legacy of apartheid. It made political killers sit eye to eye across the table, as Albie Sachs memorably puts it, from those they sought to kill.

The country was riveted by the public hearings which, as John de Gruchy commented, had a distinctly "liturgical character" (including Tutu's well-timed calls to prayer and collective hymnal interventions). The performativity of individual expressions of remorse notwithstanding, the hearings especially disabled white South African deniability about the depth of apartheid's abuses. But they also produced, if not a numbing effect, certainly the public disposition especially among whites to equate perpetrators on both sides, identifying wrongs done by street activists and liberating forces with the intense abuses of human sacrifice touched upon above. It left the bereaving families, often poor and almost invariably black, whose loved ones were horribly killed or maimed, with little or no restitution beyond an individual apology in a public forum, however heartfelt. And perhaps above all, it left the leaders of apartheid's worst atrocities, its architects and arbiters – not least former President P. W. Botha, the quintessential symbol of apartheid abuse, aggression, and arrogance – pretty much completely untouched. (As Antjie Krog correctly points out, it also left Inkatha Freedom Party "warlords" who had licensed atrocities by their followers on ANC supporters in the early 1990s free to thumb their noses at the entire process, to march into the future free of conscience or conviction.)

The blind eye now forced to see somewhat, South Africans largely began to turn the other cheek, to face towards each other racially by moving away from the past. Reconciliation, restoration, and reconstruction, one might say, pretty much without redistribution or recompense.

The rewards for truth-telling in this public confessional, and for repentance at the individual level, then, were (at least public) forgiveness and amnesty; and at the national level they were reconciliation and the foregoing of violence to achieve political ends. If the conventional registers for comprehending the work of the TRC have been science (objectivity, truth, rigor) and law (evidence, judgments, individualized outcomes), the religious pillars have been only a little less remarked. Besides the central confessional dimension to the Commission, and the importance to the Commission's effect of forgiveness, the etymology of reconciliation has to do with "bringing back into" or "reuniting with" the Church, of "resacralizing" a Church that had been desecrated or polluted.

Now if restorative justice hinges on memory, on re-membering or putting the past back together, effective nation-making too often presupposes forgetting, foregoing the memory of past injustice as prelude to living together. National reconciliation in the context of the TRC thus concerned itself with reuniting a country sharply set apart by the divisive violence and human rights violations perpetrated by the pursuits of separate development, resacralizing the body politic by bringing its divided communities into accord and harmony. Some would say at the longer-term cost of justice. The TRC was, in short, a national purification rite, South Africa's redemption song.

Together, the newly crafted Constitution, exemplary in protecting individuals and minorities, and the TRC, despite its various shortcomings exemplary in baring the deeply divided national soul for itself and all the world to see, went a long way to purging the political theology of race from the political order. They were able in their public processes of articulation and arrangement – their combined stagings – to shake loose the grip of racial absolutization. This in turn enabled the movement of social mixture and the interests of unbounded intercourse to spur national sensibility, to assume the expected, the cultural everyday, thus to redefine the nation-state as a vigorously nonracial democracy. The result, still in the process of being socially negotiated in daily, institutional, and political life, is what I will call the *secularization* of race.

Yesterday's Tomorrow: Apartheid's Afterlife

Apartheid, it should be clear by now, conceived and constructed the architecture founded upon the supreme sacralization of race. It exemplifies a civic religion defined and operationalized fully in racial terms. Race under apartheid operated not merely *like* or *as if* a religion. It was also, and more basically, a theology in the classic conception. It offered, as Habermas characterizes religion more generally, "a comprehensive conception of the world." Racial sacralization was both predicated upon and reproduced the idea of a constrained sense of community, of whites as ordained to lead and be served by those set apart as not white, and by Afrikaners as the Chosen among whites to steer their course through the messiness of history while lording over the land of plenty. A plenitude the sustained abundance of which required strict constraints – restrictions – on who amount to its proper beneficiaries. This plenitude of the Heavenly City could be sustained only by limiting its membership, its citizens. Absolutized race imposed the rules, regulations, and rights shaping the practices by which membership and its privileges were to be assigned, reproduced, and maintained.

Racial sacralization and secularization

The sacralizing of race could resort ultimately only to violence to sustain the messianic community. Messianic communities, *qua* messianic, are always in the making, always in process of becoming. That process of becoming includes converting the qualified non-believing to its vision, and keeping the non-belonging, the non-qualifying, at bay. Race both naturalized the boundaries of membership and licensed the rules of maintenance. The secularizing of race on and in terms of which the New South Africa was to be founded, by contrast, had to reconfigure the sense of community, fashioning an expansive and incorporative national unity.

Yolande Jansen points out that the emergence of French secular republicanism, of *laïcité*, forged itself on the twinned conditions of a secular

Constitution and on creating a body politic, a citizenry, conceiving itself in and through republican terms. The public voice of secular republicanism had to become also the preferred expression of its individual citizens. Analogically, a nonracial polity in the South African instance would find itself wedding a Constitution devoid of appeal to race and its divisions with a citizenry, social subjects no longer reaching in the first (or last) instance to racial determinants as the drivers of privilege, access, or power, of significance and standing. The appeal to authoritative reason, the god of race, was to be replaced by the appeal to secular reason, to the racial equivalent of laicization. The arbitrariness of racial appeal was supposed to give way to the refusal to judge or assess people and their worth on the basis of morally inappropriate or irrelevant categories like race.

Secularization, as Habermas remarks, has the potential for releasing new social meanings. These meanings now are mobilized, if not generated, through markets, media (including information technologies), and novel forms of secularizing administrative modalities. Where belonging was the driving force of racial sacralization, equal citizenship is the standard-bearer of the secular state. Bonds of belonging alter from those of racial birthright to those of formal qualification and earned commitment, including cultural knowledge. Categorizing and counting by race, alongside stressing racial distinction and separated development, were to give way to a common national culture qualified by weak cultural differences in private social life.

In absolutizing race, apartheid's agents sought to create the illusion of a timeless, naturalized set of social divisions, even as state representatives shifted the categories and criteria to serve white or Afrikaner self-interest as it suited them from time to time, updating their modes of racial management and rationalization according to the dictates of governmentalizing instrumentalities. The rainbow nation, by contrast, takes social identities and selves to be figured relationally. They are worked out in the world, in the time social subjects actually inhabit, configured in intercourse across every sphere, in the relational interactions that constitute sociality on a daily basis – in language and learning, culture and commerce, play and politics, residentially and recreationally, socially and sexually. (Proponents draw on the traditional notion of *ubuntu* in spelling out this vision.) From the vantage point of a sociality figured on mixing, taking itself to be grounded on freely chosen interactions and relations, the fixations of race would amount to the negation of the rainbow nation, as that from which its robustness could be measured. The nonracial could be heralded only insofar as it took its leave from the racial, but in doing so has kept the ghostly terms of race ironically alive as implicit yardstick.

In little more than a decade, then, post-apartheid South Africa has come a long way from the depths of apartheid. Certainly since the discovery of massive mineral deposits in the nineteenth century, and arguably for much longer than that, the Cape first and then South Africa played a central part in mobilizing and expanding global modernity. Pilloried and pariahed at the repressive depths of apartheid, South Africa has now been fully reinserted into the global geopolitical economy and its contemporaneous reordering of race. (Perhaps no greater sign of its global status is the fact that it is the first African country slated to host football's World Cup, in 2010.) On the face of it, racial mixing is now its mode, its public accommodations – hotels, lodges, bed and breakfasts, restaurants, malls, casinos, beaches, playing fields, airports, and undergraduate university classrooms – far more robustly integrated than are likely to be found almost anywhere in the US. There is, on television sitcoms and in the very visible sites of its consumptive and especially public recreational culture, a conviviality about its intermixture, as though thoroughly enjoying its new-found intercourse (the culture of the mix, the mashup, the piecing together, after all, very much of our time). South Africa, perhaps as much as anywhere, hints invitingly at the genuine irrelevance of race.

But beneath the giddy exuberance of this ethos, of this released spirit and talking in many tongues harkening back to a much earlier time, lurks the legacy of deeper separations, residentially, educationally, commercially, and medically. These divides are reproduced so readily also in informal spheres and settings through implicit and sometimes explicit appeal to racial preference schemes or racially charged political agendas. Race has lost its religious authority, its sacralized status, to be sure, but freeing racism at once of its institutional constraints. The apartheid of race has been replaced by – better yet, subsumed into – a spiraling apartheid of class, to riff on Patrick Bond's terms.

In negotiating the contours of the rainbow nation, the prevailing question has remained, "Who *properly* qualifies and who does not?" Bounded – indeed, to a troubling degree driven – by the coterminous neoliberalizing thrusts of post-apartheid sociality, full membership of the new polity extends to the healthy, to those who can pay-as-they-go, and to those who own property. The vast numbers of people stricken by AIDS (almost 20 percent of those between 19 and 45 are living with HIV, over 10 percent of the population overall, dropping life expectancy distressingly to 54) and those marked as criminals have qualified, even partial, begrudging membership, where membership at all. Migrants are mere guests, aliens hosted begrudgingly by South African generosity, often seen as little more than a drain on the fledgling and so fragile hospitality of the new nation. If the former have citizenship with diminished standing, the latter have little civic standing beyond the abstract formalism of habeas corpus. More perhaps than they did as migrant workers under apartheid, but that's a diminished measure.

But at times even less: The deadly Johannesburg township violence against migrants from other parts of Africa, especially Zimbabweans, the poorest of the poor characterized as criminals and job thieves, evidences the limits of neoliberal sociality. Reminiscent of collaborator necklacings from the 1980s, these migrant murders and beatings signal in the most extreme mode the furious frustrations over neoliberal disposability and invisibility, pitting the socially poorest against the most precarious, both with little if anything left to lose.

Post-apartheid sociality, accordingly, is about channeled choice, under-taking (as Neil Lazarus puts it) to reconstitute both the familiality of South Africa, the national family, and public subjectivities in perhaps expanded but hardly expansive terms. It ascribes to choice the pretense of refashioning membership without resentment, reconciliation without responsibility, redress without sacrifice, without giving up privilege or at least economic power.

The land of apartheid supposedly has become that of deracialized choice. On this account, one can live, school, work, consume, recreate, and even die anywhere and with those more or less of one's choosing – so long as they'll have you, of course. Less the choice of freedom than the freedom of choice, this latter liberty is all about affordability. One can be almost anywhere so long as one can buy one's way in. A society on the make is a society above all on the take. Even a city street parking space requires coining the palm of an otherwise unemployed and all too helpful parking "supervisor" ("consultant" might be a better, if ironic, characterization). Failure to pay will leave one at least with a guilty conscience, if not a gutted car. A small example of the neoliberal economy at work, where the failure of support by a state crimped by global financial institutions such as the IMF insistent on diminished tax revenues is displaced onto a private sphere of informal employment fueled by a pay-as-you-go revenue stream diffused across the economy. In one gesture, consumers are paying for a parking space, for their parked car to be watched, for informal employment of a casual class of otherwise lumpen labor, for diminished urban crime and defused political anger. Quite a fix for a few quarters.

One can only concur with Grant Farred's comment, then, that the "new" society of post-apartheid South Africa is characterized by the pretense of choice. The pretense of choice, its formalistic possibility, concerns the partial parameters facing those for whom the conditions enable choices freely to be made. This pretense of choice perfectly characterizes the neoliberal condition. It is choice within the limits of one's means and networks, one's inheritance and education, one's class and gender, all of which are racially marked if much less deeply and directly determined than under apartheid. While hardly a perfect analogy, it is perhaps revealing to note that one can move through South African society today marked by race to something like the extent citizens were mobile in mid-twentieth-century America marked by religion.

Wealth has spiraled in South Africa in the last decade, supported by a sustained economic expansion, all the challenges notwithstanding. Relatively more people are wealthier, and more have entered the middle class. But as wealth has expanded, the gap between wealthy and poor has exploded. South Africa is now second only to Brazil in negative income distribution. And that gap is racially revealing for a state supposedly paying almost no formal heed to race. While the income gap initially narrowed between black and white, perhaps unsurprisingly given the ending of color bars on employment possibilities and the contested stress on affirmative action, it has grown again in recent years and it has exacerbated dramatically among black people. As a small percentage of black entrepreneurs have acquired enormous wealth, the overwhelming percentage of blacks have been driven more precipitously into deeper poverty. The official unemployment rate runs just short of 25 percent, but it is closer to double that in some township and rural areas inhabited exclusively by black residents and where the HIV infection rate more or less matches the unemployment rate in the area. The state has encouraged privatized home ownership, even among the poor, it has made water and electricity more widely available to more people, and expanded health insurance commitment. But at the same time it has reduced utility subsidies, a prelude perhaps to privatization, dramatically raising the cost to consumers, making them increasingly unaffordable to larger and larger groups of almost exclusively black residents.

When more means less, dashed hope follows raised expectation, the long fuse to a potentially explosive future. The default(ed) meaning of freedom may indeed end up being nothing left to lose.

Vigorous local resistance organizations have resurrected to challenge community disempowerment in townships and squatter camps, drawing on their robust resistant tradition and resilient experience under apartheid. They have been especially active facing down rent and utility increases, the decrease in local services, and successfully insisting on the long overdue provision of inexpensive retroviral cocktails to those living with HIV. But the local emphases of these boycotts and protests have meant that they have less of a national profile, and so less impact at the state level, than the anti-apartheid movement had. These resistances are more like being against the local parish than at odds with the Vatican. Groups come out against the local rent or utility increase, rather than against the state as such, the protest dissipating once the increase is staved off, let alone joining the anti-globalization forces and marching against neoliberalism in any numbers likely to be noticed more broadly. At least not yet.

Post-apartheid South Africa, then, has come to exemplify neoliberal racial articulation. It has transformed racial apartheid into a more generic and so supposedly less pernicious class apartheid. Presumptively less pernicious because more like the class apartheid racial neoliberalism has unleashed in cases like racial americanization and latinamericanization, in the US and Brazil especially. Its racial arrangements are thus seen to fall within the parameters of what has come to be considered the global normal and so acceptable. But acceptable because the terms of recognition now exclude the analytics of racial articulation, because the state no longer takes itself so ordered even if the structural informalities of the society continue to embed their legacy. With the secularization of race, the language of racial order disappears even if its outlines and impressions, its structural imprint, its threats continue to have social force. Much like a shroud in its ghostly appearance, race still exercises a magnetism, modes of referentiality and divisive effects, if now more informalized and sublimated into the body politic, just as it is shrugged off.

Like religious group denominations in the wake of secularization, post-apartheid has had the curious effect of rendering some of the principal ethnoracially defined communities more oblique and opaque to each other. They retreat, as Shaun Irlam observes, into more self-contained, insular, self-consuming projects of examining roots, self-identity, reductionist if not chauvinistic group histories. The romance with Afrikaner identity and its (re)fashioning is the most obvious case in point, but one could make a similar argument regarding "Coloureds" too. Familiality and familiarity get knotted together anew. This is a resurrection, if not redirection, of an older concern: how to negotiate one's now unsettled place in the new South Africa. It conjures an anxiety especially acute for those who thought they had settled the question by a mix of self-asserted superiority and brute force, but for whom the walls of separation had so suddenly come crashing down about them; and for those taking themselves to embody the very condition of mixing but whose status in the new South Africa, while formally equal, nevertheless failed to become any more central.

In the new South Africa, as Irlam concludes, then, neoliberalization has meant not so much the demise of race as the displacement of its meanings, first from biology and then cultural difference now to the market-mediated value of commodifiable condition: can you dance, do you look good, are you healthy (looking), what fashion do you drape about you, what car do you drive, what bills do you bear in your wallet? But also what mega-church have you joined, what born again experience to hold at bay the effects of the born again racisms, what evangelical salvation are you seeking as cloned salve to the cutting competition of radically individualized neoliberal life? Class maps race, hardly unhinged from its older anchors of reference.

Contemporary references to a largely emptied out religious rhetoric of race offer a stark contrast with the political theology of apartheid. But they point quietly also to the resonances of race the language of which has been officially purged from the self-identity of the new rainbow nation. A society caught between expansive wealth and abject poverty, between visible conviviality and daily death, between hope and creeping hopelessness, official non-racialism, still self-confident white economic power, and an opportunistic black nationalism. With so much historical baggage to bear, facing the future unhooked from the heavier questions of the past has seemed like a safer bet.

But is it? Mahmood Mamdani scathingly criticized the Truth and Reconcilation Commission for stressing only individualized transgressions under apartheid, failing to address the institutionalized technologies of the state apparatus that cemented apartheid bureaucratically in place. A sociality so taken up with the temporality of revolutionary transformation, with transforming itself into the new, breaking with the heavy hold of tradition, is likely to forget remembering, to bury its memories in the foundation of the forward looking, to refuse the pain of the past. The TRC, for all its importance, thrust the society towards the future. Only to have its exhumations haunt it in facing the future yet to come.

Here too Afrikaners have been a chief beneficiary of the post-apartheid secularization of race. They are inheritors of post-apartheid largesse, cashing in on the extension of the privileges of apartheid to all whites, *makelaars* (businessmen and businesswomen, hustlers, opportunists) of the post-apartheid moment, return on the risk investment of nowhere else to go but stay and make a thing of it. Putting a stake in the ground, once the rallying cry of the settler, the pioneer trekker, and separate development, now the billboard for property ownership and commercial development. The new pink-stucco-red-tiled-roof-fenced communities dotting the countryside of lakes and golf courses reminiscent of West Bank Israeli settlements cloning California. We are South Africans, above all. We join you in making South Africa ours. The ambiguity of "ours" the perfect expression of the ambiguity of our time(s).

An Afrikaner innkeeper driving us to the Oliver Tambo International Airport in Johannesburg admits to not knowing who Tambo was or why he deserves an international airport in his name ("Why was Jan Smuts not good enough, hey?"). Responding to our explanation that Tambo led the ANC in exile throughout Mandela's imprisonment, our entrepreneurial Afrikaner chauffeur, bereft of memory, suggests that South Africa should "mine" its rich history of anti-apartheid struggle for tourist commercial appeal, much as Israel has done in the case of Masada. That site of suicidal self-sacrifice, of supreme heroism or mass insanity, as Avi Mograbi makes so clear in his painfully insightful documentary, *Avenge But One of My Two Eyes*. I wonder to myself what that would mean for the future of the ANC. The surging Afrikaner middle class – once South Africa's poor white problem of Triomf legacy – provides many of the middlemen for its current tourist trade. Neoliberalism's racial secularization turns out to fuel some of the very same people apartheid's racial sacralization was supposed to uplift. Only better so, neither history nor conscience withstanding.

Post-apartheid secularized race purged the terms of its convictions much as modernity was supposed to have done for religious order and governmentality more broadly. Secularization in the case of race has been carried by a critical oppositional disposition towards any mode of racial absolutization. Dispositional mobilization may assume a wide range of expressions, consonant with the absolutized expression from which it seeks to take leave. Racial secularization has come to mean that there is no Heavenly City, that all South Africans are compelled to negotiate the earthly cities of its landscape with all their complexities, contradictions, and class distinctions.

But modernity did not so much render the religious obsolete as it drove it into the realm of private choice and personal arrangement, of

Augustinian desire, mediating between Hobbesian fear and Machiavellian manipulation of power. Religion became the state of personal being rather than the driving force of formalized rule, the touchstone of authorization, the key to legislation. It became, until the recent turn of events, a matter of personal conviction, of private habitus, its signs nevertheless continuing more or less vocally to inhabit the offices of the state. In God we trust. God bless the country. Guide this nation, dear Lord, its leaders and its people. Racial revivalism remains a distinctly private expression in the post-messianic culture of South Africa after apartheid, its shrouded signs softly resonant in offices of state too.

A people stricken of AIDS told to chew on beetroot and garlic. A thousand deaths a day and nearly two million children orphaned to a disease and abandoned to inadequate state care and private charity (another 4 percent of the population facing almost certain impoverishment). The return of drug-resistant tuberculosis in a country with the best healthcare system on the continent. Non-stop corporate construction, facing away from non-ending shantytowns across town if not across the street, stretching cities well beyond their limits, landless across rural landscapes. Prison incarceration rates second only to the US, institutions run by the same private global enterprises, and still not known for respecting human rights. In each instance, those suffering these social conditions under racial secularization are racially related to those who suffered it under racial absolutization. Racial southafricanization makes evident that relation between the centrality of race to modernity and its invisible indispensability to neoliberalism.

A society living so overwhelmingly with death struggling so valiantly to cope with life. Those inhabiting structural whiteness consumed by barbecues and conspicuous consumption while those struggling to survive a system designed for the benefits of structural whiteness attend funerals of family and friends almost daily. Zakes Mda's professional funeral mourner shuffling between grieving groups, the grief both symbolic of and distraction from the grievances of social conditions under the burdens of neoliberalism. A social sadness masked by the convivial even as it grapples in its public debates with the diabolical legacy.

Neoliberalism and nonracialism

In a society so stricken with the legacy of racial absolutization, what finally, then, does nonracialism amount to? Where race has marked every thread of social life and its ends, what does racial irrelevance mean, add up to, what will it take to effect? Those tensions – between absolutization and turning away, turning away and rehabilitation, rehabilitation and reconstruction, lurching from the one to the other – is what racial southafricanization still has to teach us.

In the context of South African politics, as Michael MacDonald's useful critical survey reveals, nonracialism has meant three things, singularly or in combination. First, it is commitment to the claim that race has no reality, races do not exist, they are social fictions explaining nothing. Second, there should be a commitment to a singular nationality as unifying attachment, no matter the number and kind of subsumed subgroups. And third, nonracialism signals the commitment to negating racism and its effects, purging race from the explicit commerce of the state, and committing in principle and practice to universal citizenship.

Nonracialism, then, like the emperor's clothes, is what the state wears to represent itself to the world, how it looks. Joseph's technicolor dreamcoat, not the high priest's uniform of any one subgroup or sect. The cloak of national citizenship should be for all to see, for any citizen to take on. At home, in private, one can assume any sectarian uniform, in concert or competition with others, so long as the multi-colored public cover of national unity is respected, indeed embraced, particular identities no matter. Liberal democracy's nonracialism accordingly is the inversion, the turning inside out, of apartheid's absolutizing of identity politics. A reversible coat leaves the original on the inside.

Biko's Black Consciousness nevertheless characterized nonracialism as a "white politics," an empty universalism that placed racial strategizing and organizing off limits to antiracist resistance, thus limiting its effective reach and range. Nonracialism in this sense offers the perfect conceptual partner for a neoliberal politics bent on delimiting state power and empowering the interests of privately preferred partnerships and projects, where the already familiar are the trusted and tried, if passing only the loyalty test. Race continues to exert social effect, even where the category is placed under official erasure. The assertively critical attacks on affirmative action are a case in point. "The Native Club," an exclusive and racially exclusionary intellectual forum established recently to resurrect and advance what its leaders characterize as "African identity," is born of the same logic, if the other side of the coin. It is something of a reaction to neoliberal formalism, a local version of Afrocentric response to US-style colorblindness.

Racial irrelevance, by contrast, is the recognition that there really can be no (racial) uni-form, that race fails to map the body politic either directly in its own terms or more obliquely through cartographies like those of class; and that the categories of race will neither structure nor shape state institutions, animate state agencies and practices, or inflect the making, thinking, seeing, or acting of social subjects. The social sphere and its inhabitants are (to be) free of racial reference or resonance at the very least in ways that affect how social subjects relate to and interact with each other. And where commercial and state spheres are (to be) unstructured, uninhibited, and unfueled by racial category or energy. Race becomes not so much an empty category – its long history in any case is that of this emptiness being filled by divisive, demeaning, and destructive social commitments and convictions. Rather, it is irrelevant because literally meaningless, without significance, perhaps even unrecognizable, socially incomprehensible, certainly lacking any force. It simply ceases to count, to effect, to make any mark in any and all social spheres and contexts.

The intermediate challenge, of course, is how to code for recognizing racially inspired or inflected discrimination in the spirit of promoting racial irrelevance. How to effect irrelevance without either giving in to empty universalism and licensing unreachable privatized expressions or reifying the very terms social policy is seeking to render irrelevant?

Carl Schmitt famously declared the sovereign to be he who decides the exception. Less noticed is his qualification that allows him to draw so *compelling* a conception of the sovereign. A sovereign will be clearly identified, he says, where his act "is not hampered in some way by [constitutional] checks and balances," this placing him "outside the normally valid legal system." There are two senses of sovereignty embedded here, only one of which is recognized as "real." Schmittian sovereignty is outside the law, the Hobbesian sovereign not bound by the law he himself makes and so can change, the commanding sovereign of Austinian legal positivism. By contrast, Schmitt renders liberal democratic sovereignty the exception to commanding the exception, an inversion that reduces to a sovereignty somehow lacking power, constrained, incomplete.

But to deem it powerless is to measure it against an omnipotence, an embedded theological conception, no earthly sovereign could possibly exhibit, as Hobbes pointed out. A sovereign assumes absolute power only in virtue of surrounding himself with sufficient and sufficiently loyal protection to prevent the approach of threat. But in so surrounding himself he immediately renders himself vulnerable, at least to the paranoia that no protection is foolproof.

Racial absolutization exemplifies and embodies Schmittian sovereignty: racial purification and anti-pollution controls, separation, ghettoization, the declaration of emergency law to stave off increasingly successful resistance, a death order for anyone considered a threat to social order and power. Racial secularization, by contrast, seeks to bring sovereignty back under constitutional constraint, "hampering" it in principle by "checks and balances" designed also to ameliorate the paranoia or at least to undercut its likelihood. But this hampering, far from being simply to chain the omnipotent sovereign, constitutes a different conception of sovereignty, one less omnipotent than bounded in conception by guiding principles and generalized delimitations. The latter is the sovereignty of the autonomous, self-determining individual, supposedly guaranteed to reach a common conclusion or outcome by drawing on the universalizing dictates of reasons in the comparable circumstances.

Sovereignty in South Africa today is caught between these two conceptions, vacillating between the possibility of an absolute, and absolving, power, on one hand, and a delimited and diffuse system of moderating authorities, on the other. Between the absolutization of self-ascribed heavenly power and the earthly power of secularized relation and ramification. The extensive power of sovereign authority shifts between a more or less abstract possibility and its concretization in daily practices, over the quality of people's living and dying, and perhaps a little less directly over whether they live or die, the decision concerning which it has largely absolved itself by removing the constraints of race to the past. Secularization replaces the symbolic commitments of race through which authorized citizenship recognized itself as empowered citizens under apartheid, as Talal Asad might say, for less partial, more universal symbols of state commitment and loyalty: the multi-colored flag, the hymn-like anthem *Nkosi sikelel iAfrika*, Madiba himself (Nelson Mandela) who above all else stands for apartheid's demise.

Driven by racial absolutization, apartheid fueled a commanding and unqualified sovereign power. It exercised the limitless juridical power it ceded itself so as to depersonalize through racial ascription, absolutizing state power and undercutting or delimiting the "right to have rights," as Arendt puts it. Racial secularization, by contrast, could be said to depress the sovereignty of the sovereign, deflating power by dismantling a technology key to modernity's assertiveness while leaving its traces – its structures, effects, relations, social differentiations – imprinted into the social landscape of power and privilege. Racial absolutization played a central role in expressing and extending modern sovereignty, defining whose life was worthless and whose was to be encouraged, a register for privilege, power, indeed, life's limit, expendability, and extension itself. The shift from sacralization to secularization for which racial southafricanization today stands reveals that the neoliberalizing of race displaces that sovereignty from the state to the realm of the economic, diffusing it from state authority to less identifiable, at once more open and less resistible structural forces. The constitutional constraints on state sovereignty are circumvented to some degree by the privatization of social power.

South Africa is unique, then, in demonstrating in a historical blink the self-conscious shift from – or between, as the shift is hardly complete – racial absolutization and racial secularization, between "all is race" and racelessness, explicit racial emphasis as state architecture and neoliberal privatization as individualized relation. It offers, in a nutshell, a crucial experiment of – a social laboratory for observing – what the shift might look like.

It is to a more extended reflection of the global convergences around racial neoliberalism to which I now turn in conclusion.

Bibliography

Adhikari, Mohamed 2005: *Not White Enough, Not Black Enough: Racial Identity in the South African Coloured Community*. Athens: Ohio University Press.

ANC Youth League Manifesto 1944: www.anc.org.za/ancdocs/history/ancylman. html.

Arendt, Hannah 1973: *The Origins of Totalitarianism*. New York: Harcourt Brace Jovanovich.

Asad, Talal 2006: "Trying to Understand French Secularism," in Hent de Vries and Lawrence E. Sullivan (eds.), *Political Theologies: Public Religions in a Post-Secular World*. New York: Fordham University Press, pp. 494–526.

Austin, John 1861/1995: *The Province of Jurisprudence Determined*. Cambridge: Cambridge University Press.

Beckford-Smith, Vivian 1995: *Ethnic Pride and Racial Prejudice in Victorian Cape Town: Group Identity and Social Practice, 1875–1902*. Cambridge: Cambridge University Press.

Bond, Patrick 2004: *Talk Left Walk Right: South Africa's Frustrated Global Reforms*. Durban: University of KwaZulu-Natal Press.

Bond, Patrick and McInnes, Peter 2007: "Decommodifying Electricity in Posta-partheid Johannesburg," in Helga Leitner, Jamie Peck, and Eric Sheppard (eds.), *Contesting Neoliberalism: Urban Frontiers*. New York: Guilford Press, pp. 157–78.

Boraine, Alex 2001: *A Country Unmasked: Inside South Africa's Truth and Reconciliation Commission*. New York: Oxford University Press.

Buntman, Fran Lisa 2003: *Robben Island and Prisoner Resistance to Apartheid*. Cambridge: Cambridge University Press.

Butler, Judith 2006: "Critique, Coercion, and Sacred Life in Benjamin's 'Critique of Violence'," in Hent de Vries and Lawrence E. Sullivan (eds.), *Political Theologies: Public Religions in a Post-Secular World*. New York: Fordham University Press, pp. 201–19.

Davenport, Rodney and Saunders, Christopher 2000: *South Africa: A Modern History*. Houndsmills: Macmillan.

Davis, David Brion 2006: "Blacks: Damned by the Bible," *New York Review of Books*, 53, 18 (November 16), 37–40.

Desai, Ashwin 2003: "Neoliberalism and Resistance in South Africa," *Monthly Review*, 54, 16–28.

Douglas, Mary 1966: *Purity and Danger: An Analysis of the Concepts of Pollution and Taboo*. London: Routledge and Kegan Paul.

Dubow, Saul 1995: *Scientific Racism in Modern South Africa*. Cambridge: Cambridge University Press.

Du Toit, André 1983: "No Chosen People: The Myth of the Calvinist Origins of Afrikaner Nationalism and Racial Ideology," *American Historical Review*, 88, 4 (October), 920–52.

Eldredge, Elizabeth and Morton, Fred, eds. 1994: *Slavery in South Africa: Captive Labor on the Dutch Frontier*. Boulder, CO, and Pietermaritzburg: Westview Press and University of Natal Press.

Essed, Philomena and Goldberg, David Theo 2002: "Cloning Cultures: The Social Injustices of Sameness," *Ethnic and Racial Studies*, 25, 6 (November), 1066–82.

Farred, Grant 2004: "The Not-Yet Counter-Partisan: A New Politics of Opposi-tionality," in "After the Thrill is Gone: A Decade of Post-Apartheid South Africa" (Special Issue), *South Atlantic Quarterly*, 103, 4 (Fall), 589–606.

Feinstein, Charles 2005: *An Economic History of South Africa: Conquest, Discrimination and Development*. Cambridge: Cambridge University Press.

Feldman, Allen 2003a: "Political Terror and the Technologies of Memory: Excuse, Sacrifice, Commodification and Actuarial Moralities," *Radical History Review*, 85, 58–73.

Feldman, Allen 2003b: "Strange Fruit: The South African Truth Commission and the Demonic Economies of Violence," *Social Analysis*, 46, 3.

Gibson, James L. 2003: *Overcoming Apartheid*. New York: Russell Sage Foundation.

Giliomee, Hermann 2003: *The Afrikaners: Biography of a People.* London: Hurst.

Gobodo-Madikizela, Pumla 2003: "Alternatives to Revenge: Building a Vocabulary of Reconciliation Through Political Pardon," in Charles Villa-Vicencio and Eric Doxtader (eds.), *The Provocations of Amnesty: Memory, Justice and Impunity.* Trenton: New World Press, pp. 51–60.

Goldberg, David Theo 2002: *The Racial State.* Oxford: Blackwell.

Goldenberg, David M. 2006: *The Curse of Ham: Race and Slavery in Early Judaism, Christianity, and Islam.* Princeton: Princeton University Press.

Goldin, Ian 1987: *Making Race: The Politics and Economics of Coloured Identity in South Africa.* Harlow: Longman.

Graubard, Stephen, ed. 2001: "Why South Africa Matters," *Daedalus: Journal of the American Academy of Arts and Sciences,* 130, 1 (Winter), 1–296.

Graybill, Lyn S. 2002: *Truth and Reconciliation in South Africa: Miracle or Model?* Boulder, CO: Lynne Rienner.

Habermas, Jürgen 2006: "On the Relations Between the Secular Liberal State and Religion," in Hent de Vries and Lawrence E. Sullivan (eds.), *Political Theologies: Public Religions in a Post-Secular World.* New York: Fordham University Press, pp. 251–60, 93.

Hansen, Thomas Blom 2007: "Cool Passion: The Political Theology of Conviction," Inaugural Professorial Address, University of Amsterdam, May 25. MS on file with author.

Hofmeyr, Jan H. 1945: *Christian Principles and Race Problems.* Hoernle Lecture. Johannesburg: South African Institute of Race Relations.

Irlam, Shaun 2004: "Unravelling the Rainbow: The Remission of Nation in Post-Apartheid Literature," in "After the Thrill is Gone: A Decade of Post-Apartheid South Africa" (Special Issue), *South Atlantic Quarterly,* 103, 4 (Fall), 695–718.

Jaffrey, Zia 1998: "Interview with Desmond Tutu, Chair of South Africa's Truth and Reconciliation Commission," findarticles.com/p/articles/mi_m1295/is_n2_v62/ai_21280695.

James, Wilmot and Van de Vijfer, Linda, eds. 2000: *After the TRC: Reflections on Truth and Reconciliation in South Africa.* Athens: Ohio University Press.

Jansen, Yolande 2006: "Laïcité, or the Politics of Republican Secularism," in Hent de Vries and Lawrence E. Sullivan (eds.), *Political Theologies: Public Religions in a Post-Secular World.* New York: Fordham University Press, pp. 475–93.

Keegan, Timothy 1996: *Colonial South Africa and the Origins of the Racial Order.* London: Leicester University Press.

Kinghorn, Johann 1990: "The Theology of Separate Equality: A Critical Outline of the DRC's Position on Apartheid," in Martin Prozesky (ed.), *Christianity Amidst Apartheid.* London: Macmillan, pp. 57–80.

Krog, Antjie 2003: "The Choice for Amnesty: Did Political Necessity Trump Moral Duty," in Charles Villa-Vicencio and Eric Doxtader (eds.), *The*

Provocations of Amnesty: Memory, Justice and Impunity. Trenton: New World Press, pp. 115–20.

Kuperus, Tracy 1999: *State, Civil Society, and Apartheid in South Africa*. Houndsmills: Macmillan.

Lazarus, Neil 2004: "The South African Ideology: The Myth of Exceptionalism, the Idea of Renaissance," in "After the Thrill is Gone: A Decade of Post-Apartheid South Africa" (Special Issue), *South Atlantic Quarterly*, 103, 4 (Fall), 607–28.

Leasor, James 1997: *Rhodes and Barnato*. London: Leo Cooper.

Lester, Alan 2001: *Imperial Networks: Creating Identities in Nineteenth-Century South Africa and Britain*. London: Routledge.

Lucas, Gavin 2004: *An Archaeology of Colonial Identity: Power and Material Culture in the Dwars Valley, South Africa*. New York: Kluwer.

Mabula, Nthabiseng 2000: "The Truth and Reconciliation Commission: An Interview with Pumla Gobodo-Madikizela," www.sapartners.org/sa/pumlagobodo.php3.

MacDonald, Michael 2006: *Why Race Matters in South Africa*. Cambridge, MA: Harvard University Press.

Malherbe, Vetrees 2006: "Illegitimacy and Family Formation in Colonial Cape Town, c.1850," *Journal of Social History*, 39, 4 (Summer); www.historycooperative.org/journals/jsh/39.4/malherbe.html.

Mamdani, Mahmood 2000: "A Diminished Truth," in Wilmot James and Linda Van de Vijfer (eds.), *After the TRC: Reflections on Truth and Reconciliation in South Africa*. Athens: Ohio University Press, pp. 58–61.

Marks, Shula and Atmore, Anthony, eds. 1980: *Economy and Society in Pre-Industrial South Africa*. New York: Longman.

Marshall, Sharon 2006: "What's in a (South African) Name?" *South Africa: The Official Gateway*, International Marketing Council of South Africa; www.southafrica.info/ess_info/sa_glance/history/mixedmarriages-genealogy.htm.

Mathews, Anthony 1972: *Law, Order and Liberty in South Africa*. Berkeley: University of California Press.

Maylam, Paul 2001: *South Africa's Racial Past: The History and Historiography of Racism, Segregation, and Apartheid*. Aldershot: Ashgate.

Mda, Zakes 1995: *Ways of Dying*. Cape Town: Oxford University Press.

Moodie, T. Dunbar 1975: *The Rise of Afrikanerdom: Power, Apartheid, and the Afrikaner Civil Religion*. Berkeley: University of California Press.

Moore, Donald 2005: *Suffering for Territory: Race, Place, and Power in Zimbabwe*. Durham, NC: Duke University Press.

Mostert, Noel 1992: *Frontiers: The Epic of South Africa's Creation and the Tragedy of the Xhosa People*. New York: Alfred A. Knopf.

Naidoo, Indres 2005: *Island in Chains*. Harmondsworth: Penguin Global.

Oldfield, Sophie and Stokke, Kristian 2007: "Political Polemics and Local Practices of Community Organizing and Neoliberal Politics in South Africa," in Helga Leitner, Jamie Peck, and Eric Sheppard (eds.), *Contesting Neoliberalism: Urban Frontiers*. New York: Guilford Press, pp. 139–57.

O'Meara, Dan 1977: "The Afrikaner Broederbond 1927–1948: Class Vanguard of Afrikaner Nationalism," *Journal of Southern African Studies*, 3, 2 (April), 156–86.

Penn, Nigel 2005: *The Forgotten Frontier: Colonist and Khoisan on the Cape's Northern Frontier in the 18th Century*. Athens: Ohio University Press.

Posel, Deborah and Simpson, Graeme, eds. 2002: *Commissioning the Past: Understanding South Africa's Truth and Reconciliation Commission*. Johannesburg: Witwatersrand University Press.

Prozesky, Martin, ed. 1990: *Christianity Amidst Apartheid*. London: Macmillan.

Roberts, Brian 1987: *Cecil Rhodes: Flawed Colossus*. London: Hamish Hamilton.

Rotberg, Robert 1988: *The Founder: Cecil Rhodes and the Pursuit of Power*. New York: Oxford University Press.

Rushdie, Salman 2000: *The Ground Beneath Her Feet*. New York: Vintage Books.

Sachs, Albie 2002: "South Africa's Truth and Reconciliation Commission," *Connecticut Law Review*, 34 (Spring); www.connecticutlawreview.org/archive/vol34/spring/Sachs.pdf.

St. Augustine 1967: *The City of God*. New York: Everyman's Library (Dutton).

Sanders, Mark 2002: *Complicities: The Intellectual and Apartheid*. Durham, NC: Duke University Press.

Schmitt, Carl 1922/2005: *Political Theology: Four Chapters on the Concept of Sovereignty*. Trans. George Schwab. Chicago: University of Chicago Press.

Shain, Milton 1994: *The Roots of Antisemitism in South Africa*. Charlottesville: University of Virginia Press.

Seekings, Jeremy 2000: *The UDF: The History of the United Democratic Front: 1983–1991*. Cape Town: David Philip.

Shell, Robert C.-H. 1994a: "The Tower of Babel: The Slave Trade and Creolization at the Cape, 1652–1834," in Elizabeth A. Eldredge and Fred Morton (eds.), *Slavery in South Africa*. Boulder, CO: Westview Press, pp. 11–40.

Shell, Robert C.-H. 1994b: *Children of Bondage: A Social History of the Slave Society of the Cape of Good Hope, 1652–1838*. Hanover, NH: Wesleyan University Press.

Shriver, Jr., Donald W. 2003: "Truth Commissions and Judicial Trials: Complementary or Antagonistic Servants of Public Justice," in Charles Villa-Vicencio and Eric Doxtader (eds.), *The Provocations of Amnesty: Memory, Justice and Impunity*. Trenton: New World Press, pp. 61–91.

Stokes, Eric 1963: *The English Utilitarians and India*. Oxford: Clarendon Press.

Stoler, Ann Laura 2002: *Carnal Knowledge and Imperial Power: Race and the Intimate in Colonial Rule*. Berkeley: University of California Press.

Stoler, Ann Laura, ed. 2006: *Haunted by Empire: Geographies of Intimacy in North American History*. Durham, NC: Duke University Press.

Stoles, Randall 1975: "Afrikaner Calvinism and Economic Action: *The Weberians: A Harold Wolpe Memorial Lecture Collection*, ed. Amanda Thesis in South Africa," *American Journal of Sociology*, 81, 1 (July), 62–81.

Thompson, Leonard 2001: *A History of South Africa*. New Haven: Yale Nota Bene.

Tleane, Console 2006: "Is There Any Future in the Past? A Critique of the Freedom Charter in the Era of Neoliberalism," in Amanda Alexander (ed.), *Articulations: A Harold Wolpe Memorial Lecture Collection*. Trenton: AfricaWorld Press, pp. 157–80.

Truth and Reconciliation Commission 2000: *Amnesty Hearings and Decisions*, www.doj.gov.za/trc/amntrans/index.htm.

Van Niekerk, Maureen 1999: *Triomf*. New York: Little, Brown.

Van Onselen, Charles 1982a: *New Babylon: Studies in the Social and Economic History of the Witwatersrand, 1886–1914*, Vol. 1. Harlow: Longman.

Van Onselen, Charles 1982b: *New Nineveh: Studies in the Social and Economic History of the Witwatersrand, 1886–1914*, Vol. 2. Harlow: Longman.

Viljoen, Louise n.d.: "*Triomf*, by Marlene van Niekerk"; www.scholars.nus.edu.sg/post/sa/viljoen/8.html.

Viljoen, Russel 2006: *Jan Paerl, a Khoikhoi in Colonial Society, 1761–1851*. Leiden: Brill.

Villa-Vilencio, Charles and De Gruchy, John, eds. 1985: *Resistance and Hope: Essays in Honour of Beyers Naude*. Grand Rapids: Wm Eerdmans.

Vora, Jay and Vora, Erika 2004: "The Effectiveness of South Africa's Truth and Reconciliation Commission: Perceptions of Xhosa, Afrikaner, and English South Africans," *Journal of Black Studies*, 34, 3, 301–22.

Welsh, Frank 1998: *A History of South Africa*. London: HarperCollins.

Wilde, Marc de 2006: "Violence in the State of Exception: Reflections on Theologico-Political Motifs in Benjamin and Schmitt," in Hent de Vries and Lawrence E. Sullivan (eds.), *Political Theologies: Public Religions in a Post-Secular World*. New York: Fordham University Press, pp. 188–200.

Wilson, Richard A. 2001: *The Politics of Truth and Reconciliation in South Africa: Legitimizing the Post-Apartheid State*. Cambridge: Cambridge University Press.

Wines, Michael 2005: "Shantytown Dwellers in South Africa Protest Sluggish Pace of Change," *New York Times*, December 25; www.nytimes.com/2005/12/25/international/africa/25durban.html.

Worden, Nigel 1985: *Slavery in Dutch South Africa*. Cambridge: Cambridge University Press.

8

Enduring Occupations
(On Racial Neoliberalism)

Mankind is not a whole; it is an inextricable multiplicity of ascending descending life-processes... the strata are twisted and entwined together... Decadence belongs to all epochs of mankind: refuse and decaying matter are found everywhere.
Nietzsche, *The Will to Power*, 1888

The surplus populations would have to die...
Marx, *Economic and Philosophical Manuscripts*, 1844

In looking back across the terrain of arguments threaded throughout this book, I have set about bringing interactively together two sorts of mapping. In the first instance, I have laid out a broad, spatio-temporally sensitive *conceptual* mapping of race-making and racist structures. I have undertaken here to signal analytic markers, signposts or pointers for reflecting critically upon the complex experiences of racially prompted, produced, and experienced oppression across time and space.

In the second instance, I have been concerned in the central body of this book with an inductive cartography of racial fabrication and racist exclusion across five broad regional terrains, historically indexed. These regions largely have dominated and determined the historical and contemporary legacies of racial definition, shaping the principal routes of exclusionary racist experience and the main modalities of racist conception and counter-practice. This second mapping exemplifies the shifting terrains of race, racially fueled threats and violence, debilitation, terror, and prompted profiteering, personally and socially, politico-economically and culturally. It traces the key threads, in some cases even the main routes, in a global geography of racisms and their resistances in the face of claims about the demise and death of the category of race. And in doing so it informs, as it is informed by, the conceptual cartography in complex and sometimes contradictory ways.

In general, then, I have been plotting how modern state and regional arrangements have come to form, fashion, make, and mold – in short, how they manage – their heterogeneous populations. These modes of management shift over time, varying from place to place. But they converge at moments too, overlapping and informing each other in the conceptual and commercial traffic between and across the racially inflected and interacting globe of modernity.

Foucault speaks in *Security, Territory, Population* of the knowledge of the state, the knowledge it comes to acquire, diffuse, and circulate as "necessary" for governing. This is not just a knowledge of the law, but a knowledge – as he puts it – of the state's reality, of its population, deemed necessary to govern. Such knowledge includes "forces and resources" comprising the state – its demography, its conditions of being and distribution, but also its social and natural ecology. Foucault calls this summation of knowledge "statistics." At the very least, statistics synthesize the information comprising the state, making it up, offering a snapshot of state composition. But statistics also inform state-making, providing the data inputs fashioning it, making possible the modalities by which it governs, its modes of doing or carrying things out. Statistics, in short, order the state's constitution of and relation to *population*.

The principal charge facing the modern state, then, has been how to conceive of and manage its population. What is the population, who makes it up, how to recognize it, put it to work, secure it from threats both without and among its body politic? And how, at the margin, to do so under transforming modes of political economy, cultural representation, new legal regimes, and regimes of truth? Modernity is marked by novel modes of globalizing reach and so transforming modes of population definition and regulation. As these emergent modes became entrenched, establishing normative structures of sociality, population, and regulation, they licensed resistances. This, in turn, prompted revised technologies of power, coordination, and control in the face of broader, more global challenges.

Globalizing Racial Horizons

If the eighteenth century was considered the age of enlightenment or reason, and the nineteenth century that of imperialism, the twentieth century (especially the second half) has been identified as the age of globalization. But there have been various versions of globalization historically, multiple globalizations. Early modes of globalization were those stretching across known worlds in their day, across the states and city states of the east that, among others, Gunder Frank analyzed in *ReOrient*. These globalizations included trade routes that stretched into what today we call the Near East. They overlapped with those among the states and cities of the medieval Mediterranean Near East. There are no doubt others, linked to various empires. These might be called regional globalizations.

The first globalization with fully planetary stretch and pervasive world-making – or world-transforming – implication was the expansive reach of Europeans circulating in their voracious explorations. They came ultimately to magnify European power through acquiring new access to existing mineral sources elsewhere, and to revive and remake European social life through renewed supplies of raw materials, new markets and pools of exploitable labor. They challenged old modes of being, prompting novel objects of desire. This proved so far-reaching and transforming for the world that it came later to identify itself as the period of "modernization." Not that earlier periods in other sites hadn't experienced moments of rebirth, updating themselves, flourishing, and wilting – of deeming themselves modern, precisely, as Habermas among others has long pointed out.

The enormous reach, range, and redirection of the European impact across the middle of the last millennium, nevertheless, signal a quality and quantity to the globalizing project that was genuinely novel. Consider the impacts on learning, commerce, war-making, technological innovation, production, consumption, and political organization. On consumptive capacity, avariciousness, resource destruction. On being and belonging, identity and interactivity, modes of thinking and existence, sensibility and sociability. The notion of modernization at work here signals less a measure of evolutionary success than a mark of re-making, of breaking away and initiating, with all its attendant challenges and pitfalls, assertions and assertiveness as well as its devastations and destructiveness.

Race has been commonly assumed in the popular imagination to be an antique notion, long predating this planetary globalization. In this, it is considered a vestige of premodern or at least not adequately *modernized* social assertions and arrangements. I have written extensively against this understanding in earlier work, arguing that race is an irreducibly modern notion defining and refining modern state formation as this new form of planetary globalization takes shape. Race is a foundational pillar of modernizing globalization, both shaping and coloring the structures of modern being and belonging, development and dislocation, state dynamism and social stasis.

Because race is so conceptually pliable and elastic, since its earliest explicit expression in the sixteenth century it shifted in meaning over time and space. It came to assume significance in terms of – determined by – prevailing social conditions in the region in which it is invoked. It has been taken up to account for and comprehend, to shape and order – in short, to manage – the demographic, political, cultural, and economic heterogeneities particular to a region at a given time. These meanings overlap and "converse" (sometimes converging) with other regional landscapes. It is possible as a consequence more often than not to draw generalizations, to identify broad transnational meanings for racial meaning-making and social ordering within a historical time-slice.

World War II is commonly taken to have revealed for all to see the extreme dangers of racial conception and thinking, what such commitments entail if not inevitably bring about. By the late 1940s race was being challenged as a scientifically vacuous, morally repugnant, and politically dangerous notion. European societies especially sought to expunge race from social reference, at least locally, at home. But this rejection presupposed racial conception and its political order to be predicated pretty much exhaustively on its naturalistic and biologistic interpretation. Following first the anti-colonial and then the civil rights struggles, increasingly the counter-commitment regarding race in social arrangements came to be expressed as colorblindness, or more generally as racelessness.

In Western Europe this purging of race followed almost immediately its painful wartime experiences and the drive to reconstruct, reconfiguring as much Europe's imagination of itself as the material conditions of its wellbeing. In the US, the stress on colorblindness took a couple of decades longer to solidify, given the firm hold race exerted over social life. Colorblindness accordingly materialized fully first as a characteristic expression of the civil rights regime and then as a reaction to its commitment to affirmative action. One was not supposed to judge intellectual or moral competence, or for that matter physical prowess, by the color of a person's skin. Colorblindness – or racelessness more generally – claimed to judge people according to individualized merit and ability. Where members of a racially identified group were generally and repeatedly judged to fail, or to be less qualified, it would be attributed to cultural deficiencies of the group, historically developed, rather than as naturalistically, biologistically determined.

In South Africa, nonracialism became the rallying figure of the Freedom Charter in the mid-1950s. It expressed much the same commitments as colorblindness in the US, fueling anti- and post-apartheid organizing. Racelessness, far from inconsistent with racial historicism, was its contemporary extension, as I argued at length in *The Racial State*. In one sense the perfect representative and outcome of expansionist globalizing space-time-compression, racelessness came to conjure the cultural corollary for emergent neoliberal political economies.

Neoliberalizing Race

The increasing stress on individualized merit and ability in the name of racelessness was coterminous with structural shifts in state formation away from welfarism and the caretaker state following the mid-1970s. As globalization took on dramatically new form, its regimes of management and rule developed novel strategies. Eventually, these cohered under the rubric of neoliberalism. Neoliberalism accordingly took hold of political imaginaries as capitalism vigorously sought to expand its market reach, as the institutional structures underpinning capital and their fueling came under pressure, as technologies of travel, communication, and information flows became speedier and more sophisticated, further shrinking distances and compressing time.

Neoliberal commitments became increasingly institutionalized in the late 1970s and 1980s as the respective rules of Thatcher, Reagan, and Kohl sought to restructure the state. This restructuring became the rallying cry as much of the institutions of globalization as of the overdeveloped states of the global north. From the 1930s through the 1970s, the liberal democratic state had offered a more or less robust set of institutional apparatuses concerned in principle at least to advance the welfare of its citizens. This was the period of advancing social security, welfare safety nets, various forms of national health system, the expansion of and investment in public education, including higher education, in some states to the exclusion of private and religiously sponsored educational institutions. It saw the emergence of state bureaucracies as major employers especially in later years of historically excluded groups. And all this, in turn, offered optimism among a growing proportion of the populace for access to middle-class amenities, including those previously racially excluded within the state and new immigrants from the global south.

Since then, and as reaction, the state has been molded into a counter-structure. This counter-movement has sought to delimit the impacts of globalizing deracination, both to maintain a competitive edge within and between states and to secure itself from perceived threats, almost invariably if more or less silently racially perceived and shaped, from without. Accordingly the state became increasingly troubled with securing privatized interests from the projected contamination and threat of those deemed for various reasons not to belong. Of those considered to have little or no standing, the welfare of whom is calculated to cost too much, economically or politically.

Neoliberalism, accordingly, seeks to elevate privatization of property, revenue generation, utilities, services, and social support systems, including health care, aid, and disaster response and relief. The privatizing of services is particularly revealing, shifting the traditional caretaking functions of the modern state – emergency relief most notably but far from only – increasingly to charitable institutions. This inevitably produces bifurcated experiences of social goods and access such as health care, education, even public highways. In turn, privatized property – equated with nationalist identification and supplementing state enforcement – has functioned to re-homogenize the body politic. Where the welfare state, with all its contradictions and failings, produced a modicum of social egalitarianism, the neoliberal state exacerbates inequality, further privileging the already privileged.

Neoliberalism is the undertaking, then, to maximize corporate profits and efficiencies by reducing costs – most notably as a consequence of taxes, tariffs, and regulations. It has touted itself as the defender of freedom. But it is a peculiar sort of freedom to which neoliberalism is committed. It seeks above all to protect and expand the freedom of *flows* of capital, goods, and services, and more recently of information. It is expressly for letting the market regulate itself so far as the artificial constraints of politics will allow. It thus places faith in the market's capacity to optimize resource allocation and expand employment capacity as a result of sustained profitability, subsequent economic growth, and "trickle-down" charitability. It follows that neoliberalism is committed to denationalizing industry and deunionizing labor power in the name of limiting state regulation, reducing public costs, and freeing capital and its interests from constraint. The perceived result is dramatically if not completely to roll back the need for public funding, institutions, and resources.

So neoliberal states are restricted to securing conditions for privatized interests to flourish, and of shaping – policing may not be too strong a term, as will become clear momentarily – the flows of information, capital, and consumer goods to these ends. Grover Norquist, the person most identified in the US as articulating the convictions of neoliberal commitment, famously boasted that his "goal is to cut government in half in twenty-five years, to get it down to the size where we can drown it in the bathtub." The rhetorical flourish and disarming bluntness of Norquist's expression notwithstanding, the claim is somewhat misleading, if not downright disingenuous.

Neoliberal emphasis is less to get rid of the state – what, in any case, exactly would that mean? – than radically to shift its priorities, to redirect it to represent different interests, to do different work. While committing to the flows of commodifiable entities, contemporary modes of control have been decidedly circumspect about freedom of movement for multitudes of *people*. If developing economies have traditionally seen the dramatic movement of people from rural to urban locations in search of work, neoliberal movements have been threefold. First, they have been largely of jobs to sources of cheap labor, reversing the usual direction. The *legal* movement of people *to* highly capitalized societies has been increasingly curtailed. As a result, second, large-scale movements to highly capitalized societies have been prompted by economic and social dislocations in less capitalized regions. And third, movements to less from more capitalized countries tend increasingly to be tourist prompted and so temporary, fleeting, mostly uncommitted.

These shifting modalities of movement have prompted novel arrangements of demographic management in neoliberalizing states. Consequently, support for state institutions of violence and repressive control – their enactment, enlargement, and (re)enforcement – has spiraled at the cost of a diminishing treasury burdened by dramatic tax reductions for the wealthiest and consequently crimped state revenues and squeezed social welfare commitments. Social welfare commitments (including subsidized education, health care, and pensions) are increasingly under- or defunded, the resources sustaining them shifted to shoring up repressive state functionalities. The latter include the police, military, prisons, homeland security, border control, and the like.

Far from dismantling the state, or drowning it, then, neoliberalism would remake it. The state would become more robust in its controlling than enabling or caretaking conditions, more intrusive, more repressive. Neoliberalism, as Jean Comaroff has succinctly stated it, is not so much a break with capitalist state formation as "an intensification of some of its core features."

The social ends of state emaciation accordingly are not that social spending should terminate. Rather, in being redirected into private hands when not underwriting repressive state apparatuses, social spending and charitable giving are fashioned by and for the social and political interests of those with capital to spare. Those recalcitrant states or population factions not willing to support or which resist the neoliberal political economy of structural adjustment, debt creation, and regulation are subjected to more direct forces of militarized or policed imposition.

In the extreme, "uncooperative," "rogue," or unruly populations (states, communities, groups, individuals) are to be subjected to necropolitical discipline through the threat of imprisonment or death, physical or social. These forces of unruliness – those taken to be unbounded by the force of law – are likewise defined through racial extension and rearticulation. Exceptions to normativizing practice, they become the targeted subjects of states of exception. A state of exception licenses the state reserving to itself extraordinary power in the name of securitization to treat such subjects in any way deemed necessary to restrict, restrain, or disappear them.

In short, 9/11 hastened and heightened the shift already well under way from the caretaker or pastoral state of mid-twentieth-century welfare liberalism to the traffic cop state of the millennial turn. Race, I have been suggesting, now also operates at a different and less obvious if still crucial register than it once did. As a technology of determination and population management, race is now mobilized in different ways when applied inside and outside the contemporary state.

In its extra-territorial dispositions – as a technology of geostrategic positioning external to state boundaries – racial implication and significance are actively if often implicitly mobilized as a mode of securitization, control, expansion, and competitiveness. Within the state, by contrast, race has been socially desacralized, rendered part of the profane (and not now just in South Africa). But here, too, it has hardly disappeared. Rather, it has been placed behind a wall of private preference expression, of privatized choice. The more robustly neoliberal the state, accordingly, the more likely race would be rendered largely immune from state intervention so long as having no government force behind it.

Neoliberalism, then, does not reduce the state sphere of government regulation and intervention altogether. It dramatically shifts the relation of state to private sphere. It serves to protect the private sphere from state incursion. In doing so it thus also ensures a space for extending socio-racial interventions – demographic exclusions, belittlements, forms of control, ongoing humiliations, and the like – difficult or impossible any longer for the state to carry out baldly in its own name. Given the legal regime of equality before the law or of government-protected rights, the state can no longer be seen to engage in or license racially discriminatory acts with respect to its own citizens or legitimate residents. To do so would call into question the grounds of its legitimacy as the defender of both freedom *and* equality. Instead, state reach is more or less curtailed, making privatized preference expression and action, most notably in this instance racial expression, mostly beyond state delimitation.

The differences in social welfare and neoliberal state commitment are revealing. Where the welfare state was committed to ameliorating what were deemed structurally produced or magnified deficits for individuals, the neoliberal condition is committed to calculating optimalities in reductively economic terms, to speculative financialization, and to what Peck and Tickell characterize as "selective 'deregulation.'" Where the prevailing social commitments for the liberal democratic state had to do with social wellbeing revealed in the registers of education, work, health care and housing, the neoliberal state is concerned above all with issues of crime and corruption, controlling immigration and tax-cut-stimulated consumption, social control and securitization.

So the contemporary slogan of neoliberalism might as well be: The state looks after your interests by encouraging you to choose to lock yourself in(to gated communities) while it locks up the undesirable (in prisons) or locks out the externally threatening (by way of immigration restrictions). Where the liberal democratic state was concerned in the final analysis with the welfare of its citizens, all the contradictions of its arrangement and application notwithstanding, the neoliberal state is concerned above all with their security. The "social security" state has morphed in meaning from prevailingly economic significance to its more assertively disciplinary interventions. If the social welfare state could be seen as modestly paternalistic, the neoliberal state has proved invasively repressive. The latter's robust and deregulating libertarianism has turned out to apply only in the realm of the economic, playing up the fears of insecurity by playing down welfarist convictions regarding social security.

These transformations in the structure of the social are rationalized to secure individuals, their families, and those for whom they choose to care. At the macro level, neoliberalism expresses itself in terms of the nation over – even at the expense of – the state. The state is to stand for protecting me, and those like me, my national family, the rest be damned. The traditional language and objects of racial humiliation, expunged from social characterization because at odds with this rabid individualized communitarianism, are not so much erased as similarly structurally transformed. They now silently reference those who threaten the fiscal wellbeing (notably the perpetually unhealthy) or the social security of the nation (as I have indicated, for example, in the European instance of those deemed *death approaching*, especially young Muslim men and those, even entire ethnonational or religious groupings, identified as or with them).

In the US, the Minutemen, a vigilante border patrol group fueled by Latin American anti-immigrant sentiment with tacit approval from the Bush administration, have been protesting recently under the slogan, "This is America, get off my property." In this emphatic privatization, the Minutemen perfectly represent neoliberal state commitment, even as they explicitly resist neoliberalism's more expansive global reach. The traditional state function of border enforcement is at least partially abrogated to a private, self-promoted vigilante group. The claim to America is staked as a national one, the belonging to which is implicitly characterological: one is taken to belong because one embodies the characteristics – the character – of presumptive Americans, their rugged individualism, racially coded as white. And public land, the property of the nation, is privatized, becomes symbolically enclosed, closed off, from which the group can expel those taken not to belong. There is a privatizing, too, of extreme political expression, encouraging private sphere expression of views that the formal representatives of the state, with its nominal commitment to neutrality and formal equality, cannot be seen to express, to stand for.

If the Minutemen trade on racial presumption implicit in the representational codes they readily express and circulate, racial meanings have animated neoliberal attacks on the welfare state. The most obvious example is the strident attacks, notably but not only in the 1980s, on the "Welfare Queen." She is projected as the stereotypic single black mother of multiple children, usually portrayed as having different fathers, minimally educated, irresponsible, refusing work, and collecting welfare while partying all night long. Sex, drugs, and rock 'n' roll, at state expense.

Where the figure of the Welfare Queen suggested that the welfare state did nothing but support idle, undeserving, and overly fertile black women, the image of state support for the undeserving poor of color was branded into the social imaginary by the determined attack on affirmative action from the later 1970s onwards. Affirmative action was considered unacceptable to the neoliberalizing stress on individual merit because it was taken to reward undeserving people on the basis of group attributes or achievements, not on individual effort and excellence. Indeed, for neoliberals committed to privatizing individualization, the standard racism – rewarding people for no reason other than their membership in a racial group – came to be affirmative action (or "positive discrimination" in Europe). Liberalism's very instrument for undoing the effects of racism became neoliberalism's poster child for the condition of racism itself.

These attacks on affirmative action reveal a deeper critical concern for neoliberals troubled over race. In the US, neoconservative critics of the state implicitly identify it as representing blackness and the interests thought most directly to advance black life (the book's cover image most directly and dramatically represents this sense of inverted threat). As a result both of at least moderately serious application of anti-discrimination legislation and of affirmative action policies, the state became the single largest employer of African Americans. The perception among critics of these programs accordingly devolved into the view that black people are either employed because the beneficiaries of affirmative action or they are supported by welfare. In short, from the 1970s on, the state increasingly came to be conceived as a set of institutions supporting the undeserving (recall the identification of Bill Clinton as "the first black President," first by Toni Morrison but taken up quickly by neoconservatives out to do him in). Fear of a black state is linked to worries about a black planet, of alien invasion and alie*nation*, of a loss of the sort of local and global control and privilege long associated with whiteness.

Neoliberalism accordingly can be read as a response to this concern about the impending impotence of whiteness. Neoliberalism is committed to privatizing property, utilities, and social programs, to reducing state expenditures and bureaucracy, increasing efficiencies, and to individual freedom from state regulation. As the state was seen increasingly to support black employment, to increase expenditures on black education, and to increase regulation to force compliance, white neoconservatives found neoliberal commitments increasingly relevant to their interests.

It was but a short step from privatizing property to privatizing race, removing conception and categorization in racial terms from the public to the private realm. It does not follow that the state purges racism from its domain. Rather, the state is restructured to support the privatizing of race and the protection of racially driven exclusions in the private sphere where they are set off-limits to state intervention. California's defused experiment with the Racial Privacy Initiative best represents the sort of structure proponents of neoliberal commitment seek accordingly to put in place.

The Racial Privacy Initiative was a ballot proposition placed before the California electorate in the November election of 2003. It was intended to restrict state government from collecting any racially identified data save principally for criminal justice investigations (police profiling) or certain sorts of medical research. It was designed to make it impossible to track ongoing racial discrimination across a wide range of social indices, including residential, educational, and employment. While the proposition failed significantly to garner electoral support, its terms of conception should be noted. The Racial Privacy Initiative was not a proposal to outlaw racial discrimination, to address past or to redress structural racism. It was, to put it bluntly, the "protection of private racial discrimination initiative," the undertaking not just to privatize racism but to protect ongoing discrimination in private, to restrict it from scrutiny and from intervention.

An example from a different social context will suffice to illustrate the implications of a policy such as this. In Paris, having run out of beef one day, a privately run soup kitchen discovered by accident that if it made soup with pork, neither Muslims nor Jews would eat it. This "identity soup," as it came to be called, served as the rallying cry for those explicitly considering Europe to be white and Christian, for those calling jingoistically for "Ours before the Others." The outcry for or against this expression of continental nativism notwithstanding, this sort of private expression would be beyond the reach of state restriction in the US and elsewhere (though a number of municipalities in France subsequently banned it). The neoliberalizing of race accordingly entails the delimitation of public interventions to curtail racisms and the discriminations on which they invariably rest.

The social traumas of post-Katrina New Orleans, as elaborated in Chapter 3, and of privatized utilities in South Africa, as referenced in Chapter 7, offer ample illustration of these shifts from the pastoral care of welfarism to the curtailed neoliberal state. The US, in particular, has led the way both in definition and in implementation of what can properly now be marked as the Age of Neoliberalism.

I am suggesting accordingly that race is a key structuring technology not just of modern state formation but also more contemporarily of neoliberalism as the driving condition of late modern capitalist state formation. Neoliberalism, as I have been elaborating it here, represents the shift from the caretaker or pastoral state of welfare capitalism to the "traffic cop" or "minimal" state, ordering flows of capital, people, goods, public services, and information.

In diluting, if not erasing, race in all public affairs of the state, neo-liberal proponents nevertheless seek to privatize racisms alongside most everything else. They seek, that is, to protect preference determination and expression behind a wall of privacy, untouchable by state intervention, the outcome of which is to privatize race-based exclusions. Categories of race disappear as much from keeping account of discrimination as from producing the discrimination itself, thus leaving the condition it is supposed to articulate, to mark and express as well as identify and assess, as untouchable as it tends now to be untouched. Devoid of race in the public sphere, racism – as modes of racially driven subjection and exclusion, debilitation and humiliation – is freed up to circulate as robustly as individuals or non-government (or non-government-funded) institutions should choose in private.

Managing Heterogeneity

Throughout modernity, race has fashioned "the population." It has shaped membership and standing in the nation-state from the patchwork of those present. It has ordered inclusion and exclusion, the shaping of taboos and prohibitions that sustain the Chosen and those set apart, the sacred and moral community against the pariahs and outcasts. It has molded demographic diversity, sculpting population heterogeneity to the reproduced benefit of those structurally in power, invariably identified in the racial scheme as white. Race, thus, has defined and refined the population, who makes it up and how to recognize its contours, its boundaries, how it is put to work, how its maps of living, learning, policing, and playing are drawn, how legal regimes and regimes of truth molding the population are constituted. It licenses who is recognized, whose interests and indeed individuality are rendered invisible.

World War II was the most global of wars, pulling almost every nook and cranny, every corner of the world not yet visibly incorporated into the orbit of geostrategic arrangement and play. It was the war, as I have commented elsewhere, pitting racial good against racial evil, the future of race – colorblindness, racelessness, formalized equality as the placebo of significant and sometimes increasing substantive inequality, desegregation over robust integration, affirmative action reductively equating with reverse discrimination – against its *ancien régime*. But the ending of the most global of wars brought with it a new order of globalization. While neoliberalism became explicit only some 35 years later, the closing of that global war opened up the movements making neoliberal strategies of political economy, its regimes of truth and governmentality, ultimately conceivable.

The postwar moment was one of intense anti-colonialism. The Pan-African Congress of 1945, as I mentioned in Chapter 1, significantly brought together almost every future leader of major postcolonial liberations. India and Pakistan attained independence and statehood. Israel came into being. China quickly followed with its long march to its own revolution. Independence movements swept across Africa: Ghana, Kenya, Algeria, and so on. British, French, Portuguese colonies in more or less that order were swept away. Cuba threw off its yoke of gringo economic colonialism. Direct rule of the nineteenth century gave way to indirect rule in the first half of the twentieth. The latter was swept aside for independence by mid-century.

Empire, however conceived, had struck back not just in the assertion of nominal independence but in increasingly large numbers of now excolonials showing up at the metropolitan door. Extension and renewal of economic, political, and cultural dominance conjured a different set of engagements. Race could no longer be seen simply as the "out there." By the late 1960s, visible heterogeneity was becoming remarked in Europe and finally undeniable in settler societies such as the US, Canada, and Australia, just as civil equality was being insisted upon.

The reach of transformative forces remains impressive: civil and economic equality, racial diversity and robust anti-segregationism, broad access and expanding political claims if not power itself. Heterogeneity at the time was still dramatically transgressive: "guess who's coming to dinner, in my class at school and college, moving in next door, sleeping with Barbie (and it ain't just the old Ken), even running and ruining the place?" Enoch Powell's "rivers of blood" speech in Britain, and the earliest hints of anti-affirmative action in the US, signal the sorts of racially indexed resentments that would spiral by the 1980s.

It would take another decade after these early expressions before a coherent counter-attack would be sustained. All this called forth, for those traditionally exercising modernity's long reach of power, new modes of managing heterogeneity. That "we are here because you were there" coupled with "we are still here though you are no longer there" conjured new modes of postcolonial (re-)arrangement and racial management. That counterattack came to cohere under the sign of still *racial* neoliberalism.

With neoliberalism, I have been suggesting, race is purged from the explicit lexicon of public administrative arrangements and their assessment while remaining robust and unaddressed in the private realm. Neoliberalism, as I elaborated most explicitly in the case of post-apartheid South Africa, sought expression as racial secularization. Race faded into the very structures, embedded in the architecture, of neoliberal sociality, in its logics and social relations. Race lost its social sacrality while retaining its personal cache and privatized resonance, even in the public sphere. Michael Richards's rant about "niggers" onstage at a comedy club in Los Angeles is just one prominent instance of a much wider cast(e), even as the state remains vigilant about equal protection law.

One can ask, accordingly, how heterogeneity and its challenges are managed anew under neoliberal conditions of racial privatization.

At the center of neoliberal commitment is the principle that people should be free to express and exercise their preferences as they see fit. Given that preference expression throughout modernity was to greater or lesser degree fashioned and formulated in racial terms, preference expression and its products continue to carry racial weight. Cultural preferences, for instance, remain to a considerable extent racially predictable, even if internally various and overdetermined. The preference of the overwhelming percentage of whites in the US to live exclusively among themselves, as I indicated in Chapter 3 (and the same could be said about contemporary South Africa, the Netherlands, France, even Britain, not to mention Australia and Canada), exemplifies just this point. At the interfaces, cultural preference expression can be the cause of tension, if not friction. It thus requires some massaging, if not persistent management, at the very least in the interests of extending power. And power, wherever it manifests racially, remains structurally white, as I have been arguing throughout.

Racial management for neoliberal sociality today tends principally to be twofold: mixture; and duress or invasive violence. Elaboration of each reveals something unique in turn about neoliberalism's commitments.

Racial mixing

Racism for Europeans, as Bernard Chazelle insightfully points out about France, concerns restrictions and repressions of those racially identified who *refuse* to "be us." American racism, I suggest by contrast, concerns limits and blocks on those who *would* "be us." The notion of the "we" here, whether the people of Europe or America, is both normative and constraining, metric and malleable, aspirational and refusing, clone-commanding and traffic cop. In each instance, the refusal of normativizing mixture is the issue, the first explicitly, the latter by implication, the boot on the other foot.

Without facing up to it in these terms, late modern modes of social management have taken increasingly robust heterogeneities to pose pressing challenges. Managed mixture has become a principal response: who and how, where and when, under what constraints and conditions?

Free choice, on the neoliberal account, is best informed and exercised through interactive engagements with others. Through the free flow of commerce checked and bounded only by the security of agents, their social arrangements, and property. Commerce thrives when people can interact and mix. And preferences, after all, can only be successfully expressed and exercised in secure environments.

Mixture on this picture is considered to express and expand market possibilities. Not unbounded mixture, to be sure, which can spiral out of control. Mixture subject rather to well-established controls long set in place, bounded by racial presumptions now more or less implicit – sublimated, rendered explicitly raceless – about merit, excellence, and beauty taken as unquestioned givens. Racial mixing may be deemed desirable, but its product, while embedding determining inputs from each of the ingredients, is exhorted ultimately to mimic the cultural and performative standards of those embodying historical power. In short, to mimic or emulate the standards and habits of whiteness, of Euro- or Anglo-mimesis racially preconceived. Performing parrots presupposed.

The Brazilian notion of *racismo cordial* provides a revealing conceptual summary of heterogeneity's management of mixture, neoliberally licensed. The concept of "cordial racism" explicates exclusion or devaluation though in terms carefully and self-consciously race-neutral. It is, as raceless, a mannered racism, even exaggeratedly mannerist, civil to a fault, behavior by the book, racism knowingly in denial.

The denial can assume two forms. The first claims that I cannot be racist (saying or doing something racist) because it is not in me, I am not intending it, how should or could I have known it to be racist, what I have said or done is not directed at any individual, and in any case I have treated you as I would anyone in such circumstances. The other form is to deny one means anything mean: It's just a joke, I say these things about all kinds of people (races, genders, people from other parts of the country, indeed, about members of my own group). A recently popular song in Brazil characterized a black woman as "stinking like a skunk." In the uproar that followed the song was banned and the singer charged with racism, now a felonious crime in Brazil, leading one comedian to quip dismissively that "It is natural that people stink, independently of their race."

Here, curiously, the claim to equalize meanness serves to negate, in two related ways. It is a negation, first and obviously, of the specific wrong – racism – directed at this target. And it is a failure to recognize, to comprehend, the ways in which traditional targets of racism – almost invariably shades of black-brown, or black-associated people – are targeted over and over. It fails to consider how this particular targeting at this time reinforces the accumulated targeting (both historically and contemporarily), exacerbates the vulnerability, reiterates the charge of inferiorization, of exclusion and excludability, concretizes and cements in place again and again the targeted group's or individual's marginalization. That's in fact how everyday racism works, as Philomena Essed has demonstrated so effectively.

Racismo cordial is racism's everyday equivalent of humiliation with a human face. A survey in 2000 indicated that more than 90 percent of Brazilians think that racism exists in Brazil though only 10 percent confessed to expressing their own prejudices. Yet the overwhelming majority surveyed agreed with various more or less vicious expressions of stereotyping prejudice listed in the study. So "cordial racism" as a concept softens the edge of structural degradation racially ordered. It is to contemporary racial latinamericanization what "born again racism" is to racial americanization. Each alchemizes racial reference and the conditions for racist exclusion from the asserted authority of state sponsorship to the distributed and dispersed diffusion across the population individualized. It is civil society's racism without responsibility, civility fronting for terms of extended dismissal. Structural dislocation, exclusion, debilitation, racially indexed, are buried, but buried alive. Racial reference vaporizes, racisms evaporating into the very air we breathe.

In the last decade, to be sure, Brazil has backed into acknowledging the weight of racisms and responded especially under Lula to prising open access to education and employment for those racially excluded. Others – across the region but more broadly too – have inched forward even less vigorously (most notably Venezuela and even more ambivalently Cuba) with respect to African-descended populations. Recently, indigenous Indians in

Bolivia and Ecuador, and to a lesser extent Mexico, have asserted themselves politically, heightening expectations. At the same time, the informalities of *racismo cordial* have seeped across the region, much as they have across other increasingly racially mixed regions, the shadow condition of whiteness. It has blinded the privileged to debilitation of life's conditions, possibilities, and prospects racially predicated. To the foreshortening of life itself, racially indexed. To drudgery racially doubled in the name of individual decency, privatized effort, personal cordiality, charitable donation.

The state, as might be expected, offers little counterweight here, on two interactive accounts. For one, as political economist Fernando Cardim Carvalho has commented in the case of Brazil (though the insight applies perhaps also not only to some other Latin American societies but increasingly to those enamored with neoliberalizing militarization), the state is widely identified across civil society with the debilitating years of military dictatorship and more and more with corruption. And second, the pressures of neoliberal global institutions – the World Bank, IMF, multinational corporate investment and bank loans, etc. – to denationalize, to privatize key institutions, intensify as states intervene to redress past inequities or to render economic distribution more equitable. So the state remains the nemesis of civil society and its social movements, while continuing to provide little if any prospect for even identifying – let alone curtailing – racisms rather than prompting new modalities of their expression.

Cordial racism trades on race without naming it as such. For where no race, no racial harm. So no racism. Evaporation alchemizes the structural into the individual, the pernicious into the cordial, the public behind the veil of ignorant privacy, racisms into the virtues of *mestizaje/mesticagem*. Into mixture. Mergence is emergence from the chilling fog of race – into denial, the left behind, the new untouchable, the shadow of the shadow. We no longer need to do anything about this, for there is nothing to do. And there is nothing to do because the index to the condition is no longer. No longer thinkable, so no longer to be bothered about. A new day. Race is so . . . yesterday, racism so . . . not us.

Racisms denuded of their conceptual referents in the final analysis are racisms deregulated. In their mutedness unspoken, unapologetic. But cordial to the bitter end.

Racial evaporation prompts racial skepticism. It prompts skepticism in the context of robust mixture of the very wrongs being claimed to offend in the first instance. Where's the offense? How bad can it be? The offense, if admitted, is less about the exclusions, inequities, or iniquities prompted by the racial characterization so much as it is an offense against society as such for invoking the offending term to begin with. The harm identified is less that to the individual or group who have consequently suffered loss than to the society for having to deal with the nonsense of race itself. Can we just get over it, ignore it, will it into oblivion as though it never existed and left no legacy? It once marked individuals, to be sure, but now it has (and should have) no reference point, no measure, no determination.

So mixing mediated by mimesis offers one of the principal ways of re-regulating heterogeneity in different social circumstances, globally configured. Understood thus, mimetic mixing establishes the horizon of possibility, the limits for heterogeneity, while making it seem as though there are no limits. In the absence of racial configuration and its pernicious histories of social arrangement and order, an unmarked and certainly unremarked racial mixing would no doubt be the norm. Mixing not even recognized as a mixing. There might of course be other constraints on who would (likely) engage, but what falls under the spell of race would offer no delimitation. To think otherwise amounts at least implicitly to taking up the cause of racial distinction and naturalized homogeneity, protestations to the contrary notwithstanding. Racial histories in Brazil have been at least ambivalent about mixing, delimiting and diluting mixture through the filter of euro-mimesis (as I elaborated in Chapter 6). Relatedly (as I argued in Chapter 7), post-apartheid South Africa has grappled more recently and openly with leaving its racial legacy to the past by turning to mixing, but doing so through the coin of cashing in race for class distinction, a kind of class mimesis or socio-cultural cloning though often with a local ironic tweak and twist.

Now the terms of racial neoliberalism seek to satisfy both socio-conceptual masters: that of personal preference and power, and that of racial histories shaping preferences. Fused, the historical outcome is a racial regime of mixing mediated by mimesis. But people, whole populations, refuse to be bound by these constraints, refuse to subject themselves to the discipline of financializing debt regulation and structural adjustment, of denationalization and state restriction, of presumptive homogeneity and cultural cloning, deracination and constricting racelessness. They refuse, in short, to give up their compelling identifications for the sake of greasing neoliberalism's tracks. Where mimesis and the mixing it filters and frames are refused, a different if complementary toolset for racial management is refined. In the face of such resistance, more invasive technologies of control are invoked by the traffic cop state. The *force* of flows becomes more assertive.

Racial duress

Since at least the 1980s what has materialized is not a withering of the state, as some had predicted in the 1990s, nor of its importance. Rather, there has been an increasingly profound if checkered shift in state function and form – what it does, who it is for, what modes of power it draws on, what regimes of regulation it stands for and promotes. So where the state previously had served as a more or less porous container looking out, if somewhat intrusively and imposingly, for the wellbeing of those contained, of its citizens, it is now a regulatory node. It is – and since 2001 more and more assertively – an intrusive and invasive regulator, what earlier I called a traffic cop state, invested in directing and ordering flows of goods, people, information, capital. So it is less concerned than it once was, and increasingly less, about the wellbeing of citizens than it is with the regulatory forces and flows internally and across states.

On this state schema, states intervene at crucial switching points, obviously tied to and overlapping with older state regimes and forms. As traffic cop, the state works to ensure smooth flow (sometimes getting in the way, as traffic cops can) to impose and collect regulatory fees not least in moments of violation, and to generate the power to initiate, direct, and channel interchange. These circuits and flows of traffic may be placed in jeopardy when states or other non-state groups and movements threaten or choose more or less partially to opt out of neoliberal regimes of accumulation and their relations of order, interaction, and circulation. Dominant states and inter- and trans-state regulatory mechanisms and institutions accordingly may be severely challenged or restricted, the circuits in danger of disruption. The state's contemporary caretaking commitments may now be reinterpreted less as looking after citizens' wellbeing for its own sake than as the instrumental concern about delimiting systemic disruption.

Once identified as a general condition or state of being and not simply as a passing moment of exasperation or disconnection, disruptiveness assumes the characterization of "outlaw" or "renegade" state, as "deviant" or "perverse." It becomes, in short, as Jacques Derrida late in his life elaborated it, a "rogue." Derrida points out that, in English, "rogue" came to characterize not simply humans but plants and (importantly for the point at issue here) animals also. The rogue is the member "violating the customs and conventions, the customary practices, of *their own* community" (the emphasis is Derrida's). The rogue, in short, is one who "[i]n the animal kingdom . . . is defined as a creature that is born different. It is incapable of mingling with the herd, it keeps to itself, and it can attack at any times without warning." Born different, a creature apart, of savage character, untrustworthy because prone to irrational, intemperate, and unpredictable violence. Monstrous, even deformed, in Armand Marie Leroi's provocative characterization *mutant*. Bacon's aberrants of nature, nature's mistakes. The anomaly, beyond reason because beyond human speech, uncomprehending and incomprehensible. Beast, pariah, terrorist.

Rogue states are those that have "proved" for a variety of reasons that they cannot be controlled or managed by the "soft power" of debt regulation, structural adjustment, persuasive investment, and ideological rationalization in the new global scheme of neoliberalism. These are the sorts of states identified by George Bush as representing the "axis of evil": Iran, Iraq, Syria, Palestine, North Korea, Venezuela, Cuba. If the euro-mimesis at the heart of racial mixture holds out to those engaged in the mixing a possibility of entering even a diminished whiteness, then rogue states are states (where properly states at all) of various sorts of non-whiteness, structurally understood. Mutant states, they are states, that is, of anti-whiteness, which is to say, anti-Americanism. In short, of debilitated racial definition. Inferior, savage, untrustworthy.

Rogue or mutant states supposedly represent a more radical difference or otherness than those states properly plugged into the neoliberal global network of robust and unrestricted trade, free markets, and exploitable labor forces and natural resources. Their management is seen logically to require a greater degree of invasiveness, of surgical strike, of the imposition of duress or violence to control, to transmogrify or metamorphose, than those states where intercourse is considered more appealing and effective. Falling outside the reach of control through commerce, debt regulation, structural adjustment, and cultural or ideological suasion, they are subjected to increasingly invasive measures of regulation. Their supposed racial distinction renders them vulnerable to external imposition, restraint, and ultimately violence.

This, then, suggests a new modality of (potentially) invasive, even occupying state formation made possible conceptually by the projection of permanent racial infantilization, humiliation, what in Chapter 4 I called philistinianization. This cast(e)ing as infantile, "philistine," mutant or rogue – in short, as aberrant – makes such states, where states at all, vulnerable to what in the case of Palestine has been characterized as the first "permanently temporary" state. Somalia may be another, and Iraq and perhaps Afghanistan arguably are being turned into more recent iterations.

Permanent temporariness entails that such geostrategic sites are states without (self-)sovereignty, always in formation and deformation. They are permanently unsettled so that they can be violently disciplined at any and all moments, their resources destroyed or redirected, their inhabitants always on edge, their cartographic boundaries porous and shifting, their jurisdiction open incessantly to renegotiation. Their temporariness will remain permanent – lasting, continuous – unless and until accepting of the terms of neoliberal indebtedness economically and politically predicated. Permanent temporariness instantiates what in Chapter 1 I elaborated as born again racism at the level of the geostrategic state *system*.

The regime of container states froze space and relativized time. Those considered racially less developed within or as states could become more so by progressively taking on the qualities and qualifications of those deemed more advanced, of the racially more mature. By contrast, the regime of traffic cop states out to order flows freezes time and controls through special regulation, through normalized exception. It makes static the racially dismissed (the *permanently* temporary state) and undertakes to control through spatial regulation and geostrategic coordination. It seeks to route flows of goods, capital, waste, weapons, but also pipelines for strategic resources such as oil and water; to shape movements of people and service providers; to site placements of information systems, financial markets, and military bases; and to position satellites, weapons systems.

Those thus seen as threatening to disrupt these authorized economic, informational, and cultural flows, movements, placements and positionings – the media of value and significance, of capital, after all – become more or less explicitly racially marked, racial rogues, mutant states. They are racially marked in belonging to one or other group, racially conceived, considered threatening. The racial marking of the targets serves to rationalize – both to economize and legitimize – the invocation of *violence*. The racially targeted are represented as beastly, roguish, unruly because ultimately unrule-able. Out of the ordinary, errors of nature, they remain beyond the reach of the regular rule of law, narrowly or metaphorically conceived. They are (to be) subjected to racial duress.

Dominant regulatory regimes almost invariably resort to harsh or severe force, with invasive violence to move or remove, to contain, restrain, or detain. But, to generalize Derrida's point about the sovereign, in resorting to assertive and uncontrolled violence, in their own unruliness and shedding of self-restraint most directly and limitlessly in "making war on rogue states," sovereign states themselves become rogues. The tendency towards hegemony, towards the abuse of power in its exercise of law, reveals the sovereign (state) qua sovereign as rogue.

Violence invariably involves force, but it is more than just force. Violence is force the effect of which is to leave a debilitating mark on its "object." Violence leaves the objects on which it is acted enervatingly transformed, at least in the immediate wake, rent from the state it was in previously and made different by the marking of the force on it. (Daniel Ross has called this a *"rupture,"* a rupturing.) This "acting on" need not be only from points external but could be an entity, a being or organism, acting on itself, unraveling its auto-immunity from inside itself, literally an unraveling. The thing, the body, the being on which violence has effect is forcibly changed, thrown into a new state, whether physically or experientially, psychically or epistemologically (depending on the nature of the being). The more violent the effect, the more likely will it be a combination of those interactive outcomes, transformations, ruptures.

Violence thus doesn't simply open up to allow the external in. It tears apart – skin, the psyche, space, society. In short, ways of being, ways of knowing, and ways of acting. And in this tearing apart it doesn't simply rupture; it *disrupts*. It brings those affected up short. It redirects – not always an appealing condition. Though as emergency also often opens up possibility, is a possible site of emergence, so the forced disrupting that is the more or less immediate effect of violence can spin those affected into new directions, themselves sometimes debilitating but also possibly renewing. Violence can thus open up, or close down. And often it does both, even simultaneously. (So there are both immediate effects, which I am characterizing as debilitating or enervating for its objects, and more extended effects that can spin in either debilitating or renewing directions. By contrast, those who act violently, disruptively, may thus be or become more or less immediately excited. They may be exiled as a consequence, in any number of explicit or extended metaphorical ways.)

Prevailing conceptions of violence tend to be predicated primarily on its physicality, on producing physical injury through force. Even principal dictionary definitions privilege this sense, reducing to "weakened" and so dependent status meanings that are not or not so directly physical in their force. But as the preceding remarks suggest, this is too constrictive. For there is, at the very least, violence that is psychic, emotional, indeed conceptual. The notion of "violating" sensibilities, of profaning or defiling, bears witness to this latter sense. This could be teased open a touch to consider what might be called "representational violence" through acts – speech acts, of course, but more broadly various sorts of expression, or articulations – that belittle, that make small simply for the sake of diminishing, of reducing in power, stature, status, standing. The notions of be-rating (B-rating), of de-grading (D-grading) indicate the violence, the disruption, and oftentimes the associated humiliation as well as the bringing up short I took above to be central to the sense of violence.

Representational violence in the more hardened sense serves to humiliate, so to reduce as to make disappear, to be erased in crucial regard, to be rendered invisible. It is the violence that closes out and locks down. The violence of closing down is that of reinforcement, of constraint and containment, of stricture and restriction. There is a counter-violence too, one that undertakes to prise open. The violence that opens up looks to prise apart the restrictive, transgressing the strictures that contain and constrain, violating the reified and the "given." It offers some sort of possibility where none or little had prevailed or been thought to exist previously (at least not productively).

Thus while violence presupposes power it is not identical with it. It takes power both to constrain and to disrupt, though no doubt of different kinds. The institutional power of an office need not disrupt (though of course it may); its institutionality is likely designed precisely to effect ends with as little disruption as possible. Institutional establishment may have disrupted – rent those it effects – at its founding moment, but once settled in may prove enabling and not constraining. Though its enabling power might also be predicated on its power to constrain.

Race, I have insisted, is a structuring conception of the modern state. Modern states become modern in and through the various technological apparatuses of race. Race takes on and embeds in its onto-logical conception some of the key contributing elements of theological conception – of belonging and othering, friend and enemy; of the familial and familiar, the exogenous and strange; of origins and differentiation, the distinct and demonized; and so too of sacralization and sacrifice. It looks to schemes both to differentiate and divide the wanted from the unwanted, the qualified from the disabled, the productive from the dependent, the healthy from the diseased and polluting. The National Unity Party, radical nationalist members of the Israeli Knesset (Parliament), promotes the "National Uprightness Movement" to provide a public platform for zealots to call for the resettlement of all Arab inhabitants of Israel *and* Palestine in Arab countries. They insist too that all non-Jews, because of their polluting influence, should have the right neither to pass through nor to reside in Israel.

There is a broader, more provocative sense too in which race historically doesn't just take over these terms. Even as it embeds and embodies various theological meanings, race is counter-historical in disrupting and displacing the historicity of the theological, usurping in key ways its modes of rationality, its orders of sociality, its conditions of possibility for making and counting as human. And so too its modes of exclusivity and exclusion, its abstracted forms and conditions of privilege, its logics of disruption, of violence.

Race, in short, becomes par excellence the political theology of and for modernity, as I argued in the exemplifying case of apartheid South Africa in the previous chapter. And in so doing, it licenses institutional violence that seeps into and across the key apparatuses of the state while directing both the shape and content of social subjectivity. Race, in brief, lights the fuel sparking what Achille Mbembe provocatively calls the "spirit of violence." It accordingly sustains systematic social conditions of exclusion, and the varieties of more or less visceral violence underscoring and extending them. It turns a blind eye to, when not encouraging, state-tolerated individual violence, silently licensing individuals to do the work with which the state should not be associated. Since Silvio Berlusconi's re-election, residents of Naples, materializing the polled preferences of more than two out of three Italians to expel Roma from the country, have taken to burning down Roma residential camps in the city, with little if any official resistance. Gyanendra Pandey characterizes this as the "total social fact" of "routine violence," cracking and crumbling under the weight of its own modes of maintenance.

Routine violence is not just violence routinized but the shaping, directing, and filling of institutional dispositions, sensibilities, and cultures of the society by those of state-repressive apparatuses such as the military and police. Where the military is socially sacralized (the US, Israel), social subjectivities become formed by, through, and with(in) these modes of violence, routinizing them into daily life, making them default dispositions of seeing, feeling, and doing. Social subjects become immured to socially expressed violence in their collective name, walled off against even the recognition while bemoaning the condition of those whose lives have been disrupted directly or indirectly by such violence. Profiles of the wanted, the qualified, the productive, the healthy and able and their antonyms articulate racial classes of social incorporation and dislocation, rules of engagement and taboos determining distantiation. Violence, as Talal Asad remarks, is constitutive of how liberty itself is conceived, elaborated, lived.

Disruption likewise resides in the insistence on a set of conditions to keep people socially, economically, recreationally, sexually apart – to restrict intercourse in every sense of the term – in a set of social affairs that persistently throws them together subject to constraining rules of what can or cannot be done together. That orders taboos and rules of regulation, prohibitions and permissions, that insists through the sociality of the skin on keeping people in awkward ways and degrees disengaged from each other, both within and across states.

States that take themselves as reasonable, peaceful and peace-loving consider those states seen as racial rogues to be anomalies. It follows that the violence required to bring them into line or to keep them at bay must be anomalous too. It is this doubled sense of anomaly that undertakes to legitimate the violence necessary to rogue control. That racial rogues are supposedly exceptional requires exceptional grounds – extended states of exception – to reign them in or wall them off so as to protect the sacredness of the civilized, of civilization itself, as Pandey insightfully puts it. And that the violence necessary to reign them in is exercised only in the limit cases, because supposedly all other reasonable alternatives have been exhausted or are destined to failure, renders violence in this instance necessary, regrettable, caused by the roguish behavior to begin with.

The supposed anomaly of the counter-violence suggests also that it is more likely hidden, less visible to public scrutiny even when in plain view, and so less obviously troublesome. But insofar as less visible, less conscious across civil society, it is also likely to become more routinized, sewn into the institutional structures of state security and its logics of response, and so making possible even more violent interventions. Violence against the rogue in the name of exceptionality at once reveals the sovereign licensing the violence to be as rogue-riddled, as beastly, as the target.

That states reserve to themselves, in the name of protecting their liberty, the use of violence to do so has implied a readiness also to invoke violence pre-emptively against other states or their citizens. The sanctity of national community, its sacredness, becomes the grounds for insisting on the universalization of its values. Asad provocatively generalizes this point: some may be treated violently so that "humanity can be redeemed." If in the case of the religious suicide bomber redemption turns on disregard for the victims' humanity, then in the more general case of state violence for the sake of its citizens' national redemption the humanity of the non-belonging, the non-citizen, is discounted. Compassion, as Asad remarks in a related context, is indeed coupled in the case of redemptive politics always with cruelty.

Sacred violence is that expressed for no reason other than to extend and protect the sacralized community. Such violence becomes itself as much the sacral condition as the community itself (in this context, the racially ordained nation-state). Often, the condition of sacralization overshadows the interests of community members, supposed spiritual wellbeing trumping other valued considerations. But conceived so nebulously and more or less indiscriminately, sooner or later such violence is likely to redound, kicking off reciprocal cycles of vengeant violence. What René Girard tellingly calls "purifying violence" – violence "sacrificing" outsiders to sustain the bounded sanctity of the community – breaks down, becoming "impure." The desacralizing of violence as a result of this reciprocating (in)toxi(fi)cation undermines all distinction, throwing into crisis the very infrastructure of the culture the distinctions sought to sustain. Securing violence against the different and non-belonging ultimately fuels in this breakdown of distinction a crisis of unpredictability, of contamination and fear of pollution, of discernibility. It becomes in short, as Girard implies, the crisis of judgment itself.

The securing of distinction is sought, then, by holding at bay or disrupting those forces seen to threaten the grounds – the culture – of judgment's possibility. Distinction and the forms of judgment it enables are thus extended by delimiting or destroying the sources of its insecurity, its challenges, its vulnerabilities. And yet all forms of violence for the sake – the sacralization – of security ultimately exacerbate insecurity. The production and exaggeration of non-belonging over neighborliness, of strangers over interlocutors, of enemies over conceivable collaborators inevitably materialize (into) the objects most feared. Born of insecurity, purification invariably prompts its intensification. Racial americanization and racial palestinianization have provided abundant evidence.

Racial neoliberalism signals two further considerations barely discernible but buried in the preceding line of analysis. The history of racial configuration, I have been arguing throughout this book, is deeply linked in its emergence, elaboration, and expression to death and violence, variously articulated. Fred Moten has noted that black social life is one angled towards death, both physical and social. Blackness, historically conceived, is "being-towards-death."

One could perhaps generalize this eschatology of racial ontology, without diminishing the particular and particularly pressing exemplification of the principle embodied in the modern histories of blackness. So any group the intense modern experience of which has been conjured principally as the object of racial configuration will find its sense of self mediated, if not massaged and managed – in short, *threatened* – through its relation to death, as earlier chapters have elaborated. What traces do voluminous legacies of racially prompted death and violence leave in the making and making over – the remaking – of racially marked communities imagining themselves anew?

Different minoritized groups react to this mediation in different ways. For Jews, the "never again" articulated by Emil Fackenheim as the 614th biblical commandment internalizes a vigilant aggressivity expressed as survival at almost any cost. Radical Muslim political theology rationalizes the violence of its response to what Philomena Essed revealingly identifies as humiliation in terms of the lure of liberatory reward in the afterlife. Native Americans suffer the liquidation of their interests first in the melancholy of disaffected sociality and in some regional states more recently in the turn to conventional electoral politics. Blacks respond to their persistent minoritization and repeated (often spotlighted) invisibilization variously by a turn to an insistent visibility of cultural performance, sometimes celebrating a counter-violence in the wake of a persistent challenge to self-confidence, by racially driven political organizing, by assimilating or integrating as best as conditions allow, or (as in the case of Latin America) by an effort at amalgamating through mixing, all with decidedly mixed results.

In each instance, the valence of death lingers, if only as a negative dialectic, modulating the inevitable melancholy or aggressivity vying for the sense and sensibility the group comes to have of itself.

Racial latinamericanization reveals something significantly contemporary in its response to this relational, racially inscribed "being-towards-death." In its insistence on euro-mimetic *mestizaje/mesticagem*, it once more minoritizes the contributions and concerns of the historically diminutized and devalued. It thus reinstates the racially excluded as secondary social citizens, as burdens of state largesse, suppressing their contributions in their own right to state formation or social reconstruction, silencing the terms of reference even for registering such contribution. In short, racial latin-americanization offers both the precursor and perfect exemplification of neoliberal commitment to consumption sans the source of production, to pleasure denuded of guilt, excess unrestricted by constraint, fabrication disanchored from fact.

The conceptual and material conditions and implications, effects and challenges of *raceless racisms*, of racist informalisms and individualization, of
mannered racisms and racial avoidance amount, in short, to the complex
of neoliberalizing racisms. The expansive, almost horizon-less proliferation
of racially significant, inflected, or suggestive terms globally distributed, many
with shifting meanings not only across space and time but also from one
user or user-group to another, speaks to the complexity of racial arrangements. Yet it refers also to the varieties and range of racial investment.

As an abstract conception of social categorization, then, race perhaps
need not be exercised to exclusionary, debilitating, and humiliating ends
against those taken not to belong to the designated privileged group. But
historically it has been invoked throughout its half-millennial histories to
these ends. It carries the prospect if not the promise of violence with it. It
follows historically that when invoked to mark the human, race almost invariably operates as *threat*, as pernicious, as disruptive. Racism, of course, always
incorporates race within it as basis of conceptual differentiation. In that
sense, racisms can be said to order race, to require and to fabricate it. But
the related point I am pushing here, the one to which the reach of arguments throughout the book draws, is the complementary one, at once
simpler and more obscure. Race, in short, is never far from racism.

Racial distinction, categorization, projection – in short, the threat of race
– makes if not inevitable certainly easier the assertion, application, and
targeting of terror. Race lubricates much modern institutional violence. This
is not to say it does so as a stand-alone concept of production, regulation,
and legitimation. It interacts with, magnifies and multiplies other categorical
conceptions, formations, and rationalizations of structural privilege and
denial, social elevation and exclusion. The weighting race has brought to
modern social arrangements. But as a routine social fact shaping modern
state violence, race is not an antiquated institutional apparatus, an antique
hangover, an unfortunate holdover. Absent race, modern – and now late
modern – social life would look dramatically different than it has.

Enduring Occupations

Race, I am suggesting, has been an enduring occupation of modernity.
Its structural legacy, institutional articulation, and social implications
have lingered despite racial conception becoming less pressed or formally

elaborated, less a default of social pronunciation, arrangement or order, more invisible, coded, and proxied. The elasticity of race – its mutability, adaptability, and motility – enables the continued insinuation of racial meanings, arrangements, and orderings into metamorphosed social circumstances. This racial marking has continued as race, under neoliberalizing pressures, has become less explicit, less visible, less obviously a mark of formal state formation. "Invisible man" has deepened into invisible racial arrangements of social conditions. In short, race is now circulated more readily and openly in private spheres than in formal public ones.

Occupation has multiple meanings and racially coded references in play here. First, it signals *places of living*, the places and spaces people occupy, fill, inhabit. These are occupational spaces – sites or places – that "give" residents their habits, shape their relations to others, their habitus, their dispositions to their world(s), immediate or more extensively. Such spaces of habituation in turn have been partly fabricated throughout modernity by racial architecture, its form-giving force articulated with other social moldings, within and across the lived conditions, the forms of life, of modern or modernizing societies. The regional focus of the analysis throughout this book points to the interplay of spatial definition and historical transformations, to the continuities and distinctions marked by race. This focus spotlights the generalizations and sharpens the divergences it is possible to draw regarding registers – economic, political, technological, and cultural – of racially coded spatial exclusions.

Occupation speaks relatedly to one's *work*, to what one does "for a living," how one provides for oneself and those one regards as one's extended self, how one gets by. Here occupation concerns what more literally consumes one's life-sustaining time, with which one "occupies" oneself. As with spaces of habitation, occupation in this sense too is deeply racially indexed. Throughout modernity, racial meaning and presumption have deeply marked not just where one can work but what one can do, from slavery and ownership to unskilled labor and professional license, artistic expression and intellection. While no longer so explicit, racial determination still structures occupational possibility, through codes of class, inherited wealth and poverty, cultural presumptions about ability, and socio-physical conditions of inheritance. Like a noxious but odorless gas, race silently and invisibly strains and signifies the limits of "employability." Less explicit perhaps, racial figuring of occupational possibility nevertheless now is not only less remarked and visible but to that degree also less easy, even less possible, to challenge.

Stated thus, "occupation" also concerns *ideas* with which one is currently consumed: "I am occupied by/with these ideas." These are one's pre-occupations, the things by which one – or what one takes as one's group, culture or society – is driven before taking action on them, as a prelude to taking action, sometimes even a foreclosure on the possibility of doing something, or of doing it otherwise. As a set of transforming ideas over time and in place, race has set distinct horizons on what is – if not possible or impossible – licensed to think about social groups and their members, where they can be or the modes of work in which they can engage. Race, accordingly, not only licenses or encourages but equally forecloses and discourages thought and action.

Increasingly, the racial horizon of these enablements and delimitations has become silently circulated, less noticed perhaps even to oneself, defaults often denied, not least because in denial, when made visible or conscious. The revealing limit case here is evidenced by what it is in response to that people in power express themselves too occupied to respond, too busy to acknowledge. At work here is a silent hierarchy of (in this context often racially indexed) value at the basis of dismissal or (in)attention. Examples abound: the impatient dismissal or casual inattention of the colonial bureau-crat, public housing official, or bank loan officer, the skepticism of a police officer in the face of black youth enjoying themselves or the quickness to deploy a Taser, the itchy finger of Blackwater security guards in Baghdad.

Finally, and perhaps most pressingly given the latter example and the contexts with which I have been pre-occupied throughout the book, "occupation" suggests *invasion* and *control* of a place not one's own, as assert-ing and governing a place presumed to "belong" to others. And this latter sense – or attempt to force sense – as a prelude perhaps to making that place one's own through settlement. A settlement, in turn, which could never be complete, the grounds of tension between organic being with its longstanding, its deep local historicity, and the ahistoricity of invasive or settler presence. Here occupation is always frozen, a noun or substantive imposition: "*the* occupation."

Occupation as settling in(to) another('s) place as a movement of modernity invariably has a racial resonance to its prompt and enable-ment, elaboration and extension or prolongation. This racial fuel is now increasingly silent and almost always today denied, spilling out awkwardly in unguarded and invariably embarrassing expression. "They are in no position to govern themselves" or "They constitute a threat to the rest of us" or "They need us to guide them to democracy" immediately and unselfconsciously articulate an "us" and a "they," the better or ill prepared, the challenged or the violent placing everyone else at risk.

Occupied states, as I suggested earlier, are states today that have unraveled, states damned or dismissed as mutant. But their mutant condition is ambiguous. Not just aberrant, they are muted states. They are, in short, states that have – are made to have – no voice of their own. They are states (to be) filled with the occupier's loudspeaker, literally or metaphorically. Denuded of their own voice, they are reduced to a counter-whisper, either explicitly or mimicking clones of the occupier's pre-occupations – in law and law-making, in commerce and intercourse, in expression and culture more generally. In enduring occupations, occupations (to be) endured, even the voice of the occupied becomes forced.

Occupation accordingly generally concerns place: being in a place, taking a place, exercising oneself in or over a place, inhabiting a place whether concretely or abstractly, conceptually. Race defines, molds, predisposes what can occupy one and what can be occupied, where and over what being occupied can take place and under what conditions. Racial occupations bear significance as varied as the senses of occupation itself. They have morphed from the extractive and denuding force of a colonizing occupation claiming to discover empty lands for the taking, Lockean enclosure acts claiming ownership over *terra nullius*, via the civilizing mission of occupying native territory "for their own good" to neoliberal occupation to ensure democracy and stave off terrorism.

The interactive energies between these varying senses of occupation are evidenced in the ways the Bush administration has repeatedly rationalized its "war on terror." "We are fighting them there," George Bush has reiterated, "so we don't have to fight them here." If we can just seed democracy "there" we will not have to struggle with *their* disaffection "here at home." But far from a democracy denuded of race, this articulation is quietly predicated on it. The price of blindness is blowback. The slippages between "war *in* Iraq" and "war *against*" and "*on* Iraq" offer the terrain of "race war" in denial, war through racial proxy rendered invisible. Occupation and the making of permanently temporary states are conceivable only in the case of local indigenes whose fullness of being, claim to sanctity of place and dignity of person can be racially discounted.

One abiding occupation – an enduring commitment – of those who have lived through especially the larger traumas of racial colonization, racial derogation, and subjection has recently been bearing witness, giving testimony. Testimony and bearing witness are possible only for those with first-hand, direct experience of and immediate proximity to death and deathly violence. In the past decade or so, formal fora have emerged to facilitate bringing witness, as evidenced by the popularity of various national truth commissions. And yet renewed racial terror and trauma become that much more possible, and the formal fora serve as rationalizations at worst or partial exercises in national reconciliation at best, unless a broader circle of commentators – historians, concerned citizens, political activists – are prepared coalitionally to draw attention to the horrors and cumulative burdens (spectacular or everyday) to the weights of race, elsewhere in but enduring across time or place.

Bearing witness from a distance of time and place is a different mode of testimony than first-hand witness. It is produced out of and encourages a different sensibility or passion, another sort of disposition, even distinct sentimentalities. It is, in short, another kind of pre-occupation than that of immediate victims or witnesses. It concerns more mediated knowledge, a commitment to be informed rather than a drive to share if not shed a burden. It often turns on a passion to pass along historically a sense of outrage over injustice rather than an effort, often melancholic but sometimes manic, to externalize. It involves a civic commitment to take social equality seriously across time rather than to elevate disinterested and dispirited self-interest as the driving principle of sociality above all else.

Race, then, is itself an enduring occupation, one which in raceless contexts a critic takes up at risk, on pain of marginalization, being maligned, being considered almost mad. Its deepening invisibility is evidenced in its prevailing proxy articulations – its fixations, its pre-occupations – today in the powerful polities of the global north: migration and immigration, terrorism, contagious disease and viral spread.

The threat of invasion implicit in each set of these concerns is racially indexed. Those from the global south are threatening to take those jobs "here" they haven't already grabbed through outsourcing; mutants from rogue states are threatening "our" wellbeing by plotting terror attacks or seeking nuclear arms; and those from unsanitary societies threaten "our" health by prompting the emergence of new viral diseases circulated as a consequence of global migrations and mobilities. The bearer of threat as condition of presumptively distinct ways of being in the world equates implicitly – implicatively – to racial otherness under a different description, under descriptive distinction.

A critical focus on race may be said accordingly to be an occupational hazard – or given the ambiguity many hazards. One is bound to speak out when others would rather have one silent. Race here signals different kinds of bother, situationally determined. One may invoke a category increasingly considered off-limits or socially off-color, on pain of dismissal, unpopularity, recrimination, not being heard. Patricia Williams once remarked that speaking out against racism may entail ruining a good party – or war, interrogating torture, or the comfort of homogeneous sociality. Organizing in the name of a category so widely socially maligned is often taken as "identity politics" or for the sake of "recognition" – as though it is a bad thing to be recognized – and not in the more traditional terms of interest group or lobby politics. In short, in taking on and up race, one risks being castigated and isolated as a troublemaker.

Racisms without Racism

As *race* conceptually is made to disappear, is made invisible in and to the landscapes of life, loves, and labor, what has happened to what we know as *racism*? There has been a twofold, interactive dynamic: On one hand, there has been an increasing reluctance to acknowledge its traces, the legacy of its structural conditions, its continuing significance. William Julius Wilson's *The Declining Significance of Race* signaled an emerging emphasis, more insidious by far than Wilson was intending, of what since has become a widespread – and I am suggesting globalizing – social trend. As race is rendered irrelevant socially, racism *conceptually* becomes stigmatized so that only the obviously bigoted – extreme individuals – get to qualify. On the other hand, racism is redirected to malign those who invoke race, implicitly or explicitly, but now to undo the historical legacies of racisms, even modestly to redress its effects.

Here racism is reduced in its supposed singularity to *invoking* race, not to its debilitating structural effects or the legacy of its ongoing unfair impacts. Not to the refusal to racial mixture, or the violence of such avoidance. As race evaporates from the socio-conceptual landscape, racisms (in their plurality) are pushed further and further out of sight, out of "existence," unmentionable because the terms by which to recognize and reference them recede, fade from view and memory.

As the terms of articulation, analytic and critical, are dimmed and deleted, distorted and redirected, the kinds of conditions once referenced by the term have not disappeared so much as they have assumed new form, taken on new significance in more or less novel social conditions. The new modes of debilitation and degradation, humiliation and dehumanization, often directed at renewed clusterings and groupings of what once were identified in explicitly ethnoracial terms, requires a new analytic vocabulary, new referential articulations. They are not just raceless racisms, as I have argued in earlier work and other analysts have made much of. Not just racisms without race. Nor simply racism without racists, the refusal to acknowledge racist expression, as Eduardo Bonilla-Silva has declared. They are *racisms without racism*.

This is not to say that what can be identified as traditional racisms have disappeared; quite the contrary. There is here the condition without the category and mode without the (same) meaning. The modes, forms, sociologics, even their rationales more often than not mimic classic racisms. But they lack the sharpness of their identifying account or defining contours, torn as they are from the classic conditions of their articulation. These anthraxic racisms without the ostensive reference of racism exacerbate humiliation and degradation, debilitation and desecration, desacralization and distortion. They underpin torture in denial ("We don't torture" even as "we" waterboard) and collateral damage under apology ("Sorry, we didn't mean it, they got caught in the firing zone"). So as racisms have become more difficult to track and trace, more blurred, new targets and their rationalization have appeared.

The post-human, post-anthropic ontology of our time has rendered more vague any barrier to processes and expressions that can be characterized as racist. Dehumanizing is no longer so readily recognizable when "the human" is either only recognized as those like us or the limit conception is so porous, so nebulous, as to make no one sure of who counts and who does not, of who is first person and who avatar. In the case of past racisms, sub-classes – for example, young black men, Jewish bankers – might be more or less easily identifiable "suspects," their stereotypicality supposedly generalizable to the group at large. Today, as the referential language of race is placed under erasure, made to evaporate, all Muslims are more or less suspect in America or Europe, all North Africans in France, all Palestinians in Israel or Iraqis (to Americans) in Iraq.

That torture is even conceivable to some at the supposed limit so as to elicit information where there is "pending attack" – the case of "the ticking time bomb" – must necessarily take its cue from such silenced racisms. That *they* are planning such an inconceivably horrifying act – suicide bombing, beheadings, and so on – licenses extreme counter-action to limit possible devastation. These after all, as Alan Dershowitz emphatically insists, are rare instances. But how to know whether the person under inter-rogation has such information in the first place? So contemplation of tor-ture can only be pursued on suspicion. And that suspicion is predicated if not altogether fabricated on presumption of a stereotypical preconception, invariably indexed to or insinuated about a group gone ghostly, of what a terrorist must look or act like.

"We know him to be a confidante of Bin Laden."

But that's not the same as knowing him to know. The rare instance of one in the know can be conjured only because he is (presumed) like all those who are taken to be like him. He is under suspicion of special knowledge of the pending attack because those like him are, always, under suspicion. After all, such intense interrogations are conducted never to pre-vent attacks against Iraqis or Palestinians in their marketplaces but solely to uncover plots against America or Europe or Israel. *Their* lives don't warrant the torture necessary to save them as *our* lives do. The post-colonial hymn that "We are here because you were there" has given way to the neo-globalizing holler that "We are fighting *them* there so we don't have to fight them *here*, at home." Our cityscapes, social infrastructure, and civil society are sacred; theirs can be wiped out on whimsical suspicion.

Racisms without racism, then, is the peculiar expression of neoliberaliz-ing globalization. It is the way of governing distinction, in the global scheme of enduring freedom, considered too different and difficult to deal with. It is the (re-)institutionalizing of racism gone private, the priv-atizing of institutionalized racisms. Racisms cut off from their historical fertilizer. Racisms born again, renewed. But shorn of the referential language. The wolf in sheep's clothing, speaking of sheep while deeply ambivalent about defanging the wolf. They are political expressions unre-cognized as free because driven by forces outside of themselves, illegible to those external to its circles of persuasion. At worst, beastly violence against the inevitable advance of freedom and democracy.

The consequent counter-violence of containments cannot possibly be racist not just because no races exist but also because the threatening expressions it seeks to contain are unrecognized as properly human. It – the projected action as metonym for the person, for the (national) character – is beastly, monstrous, mutant, after all. It places itself outside the bundle of legiti-mate human preference expression or instrumentalization. As such, *we* can't be racist just as *we* don't torture. Even as a bad apple, even two perhaps do. The individualization of wrongdoing, its localization as personal and so private preference expression, erases institutional racisms precisely as conceptual possibility. The bad faith of deniability is dismissed as the demands of ensuring the necessary flows of worldly commerce, the possibility of global liberties, the stabilizing of securities. Apartheid was state racism's last word, the closing act of racism's institutionalization. Nothing left to it but the individual variety of a few rogues in the private sphere.

The curtaining off of the racial from the public domain, from the formal sphere of politics, and restricting it to the privacy of occasional individual choice and (self-)determination make race and by extension the effects it produces as racist discrimination and exclusion matters of personal morality rather than public law. Race is rendered accordingly before, beneath, or beyond the law. The racial dimensions of crime, social practice, and ultimately state action (from profiling to genocides) are cordoned off-limits to the law. They may be moral or ethical matters, as Agamben puts it, tied ineluctably to the private choices of individual preference. They accordingly are not issues of legal responsibility. As strictly and reductively moral matters, racist acts and institutional patterns or effects are less likely to be prosecuted by the law; they are regarded as personally offensive, morals offenses, more like pornography than injurious. Even "hate crimes" are crimes exacerbated by hate, recognized as crimes first and accentuated by a condition that makes the matter worse, the potential sentence longer. The personalization of hate is an add-on, a legislative after-thought, institutionalizing a matter that on the premise ought not to be but just won't quite go away. These are the awkwardnesses, the inconsistencies, produced ultimately by restricting racist expression to the private sphere.

Neo-neoliberalism

If neoliberalism concerns the intensification of privatized preference and experience, *neo-neoliberalism* is the hyper-extenuation of the neoliberal, its decoupling from any conscious modesty or humility, from any finitude. It reaches for absolute and unrestricted mobility and produces irreversible displacement, at once limitless and infinitely restrictive. It concerns unrestricted flow, implacability and irreplaceability at one end, hyper-visibility, invisibility, and unplaceability at the other. Neo-neoliberalism is the reach for the perfect replica and the perfectionism of the momentary, of making the everywhere and anywhere, any and every moment open to financialized investment, immediate and instantly mediated experience.

It commits, where it commits to anything at all, to remaking and replication as the locally Same, as the particular instantiation of the unchanging Universal and therefore recognizable. Its trick is to be anywhere by going nowhere. A culture of pure replicability via a culture of cloning. Stasis and boredom of the changing same racially indexed are undercut only by seeking extreme experiences, risking life and limb where professional and recreational interests meet.

But in this imperious and imperializing reach, in its world-making universalism, its overarching and overreaching aspiration, neo-neoliberalism must necessarily trade on disinvestment and avoidance, displacement and restriction, distance and desolation, damnation and desolation, on destruction and what Naomi Klein generalizes as disaster. On invisibility and violability, secrecy and clandestine operation, occupation and abandonment, shock and awe. It opens up in order to close down, and it puts out of business in order to put into business. It is the manufacture of scarcity and the perfecting of disposability.

Scarcity is manufactured to sustain value through the artifice of desirability. The more available something or someone, the less desirable, and so the less likely to be valued. If a consumer is kept waiting or wanting, even for no apparent reason, it must be made to seem like it's due to competing demand or the failure of nature, human or otherwise. The point is to play the marginal utilities, to determine the moment just prior to diminishing returns. The supplement of production on demand is just in time delivery, recognizing the bounded moments between perceived need and desperate desire. Disposability is supposed to mediate between delivery and desperation, between invisibility and conflagration, ensuring the former before the tinderbox of smoldering dreams ignites into incendiary nightmares. New Orleans buffeted by Katrina. Parisian *banlieue* set alight. Gaza's permanent nightmare, relief from which can only ever be temporary.

Disposability, by the same token, is rendered acutely ambiguous. Throwaway things: commodities, the no longer useful, clutter, all up for sale to become someone else's at one's profit. Disposable people or groups, those who can be discarded because no longer (if ever) considered useful. Perhaps outliving their usefulness or having never lived up to a demand for it. But also collateral damage in wars, or the discardables, *los olvidados*, the throwaways of the urban landscape. The new or new old races of our time. Disposability, in short, signals the disposition to write off people as depreciated consumption goods, reverse-engineering people through their massification into the base metal of presumptive groups, marked by a debased character all their own.

Race, then, oddly enough, becomes a *futurology*, a sign of things to come. Race signals people's prospects. It generalizes the projection of a delimited and delimiting future to a constrained past so as to evade and efface the structural constraints of the present, to detour them. Past condition or genetic make-up group generalized becomes not just a prediction of future prospect but its likely guarantee. The monitoring of characteristic currency and scanning of environmental determinations enable the shaping of emergent trends to mimic established state personality or national character, to clone culture even as it morphs and reproduces power just as it threatens to disperse. Group belonging becomes the index of individual health, of anti-social violence, education and educability.

In ordering and sustaining conviction, in seeking to determine and delineate nature, race even in its erasure, its muting, thus is a political theology. It underpins sacrifice both in the sense of what social beings can be sacrificed and who take themselves to be making sacrifice. It offers (up) a porous social prophylaxis, condomizing society as much against itself as against its constitutive outsides. So race conjures a group theology, a theology of groups. It sets out in religious registers at the outset but increasingly takes on secularized and lately individualizing articulation though in still apocalyptic terms.

Neoliberal jurisdiction and its neo-neoliberal hyper-extension thus conjure a set of racial articulations, arrangements, and their expression in which constrained mixture constitutes the national imagination, the (self-)image of the nation. Tanned whiteness and euro-mimesis become the national embodiments, the frivolity and conviviality of carnival in contrast to skiing, golf, and surfing its coloring of culture, the whitening of class elevation and the blackening of impoverishment its ends. Risking serious injury and death by surviving the vicissitudes of individualized extreme sports are today's adventures in the skin trade, much as colonial exploration might have been in the nineteenth century, indices of the racial prowess of whiteness both. The health and wellbeing of the racially prosperous are uniformly protected by cordoning them off against the various viral pollutants of the racially precarious and degraded. The racial structuring, ordering, and governing – ultimately the violent re-arrangement, the *disruption*, of the conditions of life and death itself – of those taken not to fit, of the unhealthy, physically and economically, socially and culturally, are increasingly its unspoken occupations.

Closures and Openings

Modern states homogenize in large part through territorialization. Boundaries as the codification and institutionalization of power (what Balibar calls "power structures") order not just the spaces they bound but the entire productive and cultural formations they incorporate. These include forces and relations of production, modes of signification and representation, distribution and consumption, patterns of individual and collective desire, linguistic base and facility, cultural expression, and so on. Together they fashion and regulate the state's population. State populations are thus homogenized through territorialized constriction and conscription. The technologies of race discussed throughout this book have played not just contingent but constitutive roles in the making of modern state populations, and also in their global circulation and circumscription.

Race reinforces stated and political boundaries, as it conjures and characterizes their possibilities, reifying and regulating the claim of the common and familiar through the artifice of kinship and the fantasy of the familial. As Balibar comments in an essay on "Europe as Borderland," "territorializing" entails the fashioning of "identities" through structures of power by the joint processes of categorizing them into collective identifications and individuating self-inscriptions, interpellating individuals as collective commitments, as citizens. Homogenization is possible only by exclusion of the resistant or the different, the stranger and the alien, turning the distinct into outsider, excisable from the body politic. Race accordingly has been one of modernity's principal modes, interactive with the likes of class, ethnicity, and gender, of categorization and abjection, incorporation and ablution, citizenship and alienation. In short, of belonging and distantiation, of claim(ing) and reject(ion).

Neoliberalism entails closely guarded mixtures and streamed flows, violently asserted, arranged, and aggressively enforced where vigorously challenged or resisted. Responses to neoliberal order may range from enthusiastic embrace to violent rejection, from instrumental mobilization for the sake of narrowly defined self-interest to equally forceful resistance to the imposition of its regimes of rationality and relationality, its restrictive order of being, its codes of governmentality. Where the sort of strained and constrained mixture is rebuffed in favor of indigenous or local sociality – coded as different, as irrational or antique, religious or premodern – there the force of neoliberal imposition and insertion may be brought to bear.

Indignant refusal more often than not assumes the form of violence too. Invasive disruptions are met mostly with the disrupting of the invasiveness, spiraling into massively exacerbated disruptiveness on all sides. Short of this, resistant responses may vary. They may amount to a mix of the satirical and the more or less quietly derisive, of the counter-derogatory or the ironically nostalgic, of feigned ignorance, even stupidity, or calculated, smirkingly smiling engagement.

Occupations nevertheless are never totally exhaustive, completely ordering lives, fully hegemonic. They often offer opportunities, more for some than for others: of heterodoxies, of less stereotyped mixtures, of breaking out even of preordained mixings, of an inordinate and ultimately uncontainable and unconstrainable range of intercourse. They suggest even in the difficult conditions faced always an inkling, possibilities, or hopes of an unraveling and a restitching of socio-cultural fabrics. And they may prompt the prospect of a destating turn and of resituating in the face of devastating conditions and of pre-determination.

Heterogeneous dispositions

Cultural homogeneity emphatically encourages, if it doesn't presuppose, denial of the multiple and diverse influences on cultural expression. Homogeneity presumes the conviction that everything of cultural significance and value is group determined, fashioned famously from within the confines of the group narrowly defined. It strongly suggests, if it doesn't entail, a presumptive commonality to group members' character, the basis after all of stereotypes. The more self-contained and insulated a culture, the more likely it is isolated and small both in the sense of being restricted to a numerically delimited number and in having very constrained scope and reach.

It follows that every culture develops heterogeneously, whether through social intercourse and interaction, commercial transaction, inadvertent or purposeful borrowing, youthful transgressions, or outright theft. It is of the very nature of culture, accordingly, that despite itself, in spite of its disposition qua cultural identity to repeat and reproduce itself, it could develop into something else. The threat to (a) culture is that it could become something different, lose its (current) identity, cease to be by seeing what it takes as its core convictions, values, or commitments eroded. This range of responses and concerns about cultural homogeneity, retention, legacy, and reproduction points to the power of the heterogeneous just beneath the surface of any seemingly homogeneous sociality. In closing, then, the challenge of heterogeneities calls out for some elaboration.

Heterogeneities lie beneath all claims to purity, order, refinement, and restriction, not just as their negation but even as their prompt. (I obviously have ethnoracial heterogeneities principally in mind here, but the argument reaches more broadly across cultural articulation.) To engage heterogeneities is to shift attention from populations – their statistics, their state management, their constrained formation and social control. The emphasis on heterogeneities, by contrast, stresses and seeks to sustain more or less unconstrained relationalities, activities, inter-actions. It undertakes to conjure, craft, and coordinate collaborations.

Heterogeneities, in short, amount to a disposition against closure. Structured and informed by grids of intelligibility themselves constituted by what Foucault marks in *The History of Sexuality* as a "heterogeneous ensemble" of "discourses, institutions, architectural forms, regulatory decisions, laws, administrative measures, scientific statements, philosophical, moral and philanthropic propositions," dispositions are complexly articulated relations. Heterogeneities thus are grids of intelligibility and variably informed interests, prompts, and practices breaking with those imposed merely as delimitations or constraints, restrictions and delimitations. As complex dispositions, heterogeneities entail a facing towards others in their respective multiplicities.

Heterogeneous dispositions thus express both a variety of dispositions and a disposition to variety. They are dispositions of or towards openness, with no guarantees of outcome, stability, even predictability. Heterogeneities make obvious that no guarantee is foolproof, no security inevitable or for that matter lasting. If predictability is guaranteed only by controlling the variables, the challenge of the heterogeneous is to serve always as a reminder that variables themselves are, well, variable. Heterogeneities offer an antidote to the conceit of holding things constant, to the arrogance of control.

As dispositions of openness, heterogeneities suggest engagements with those not or not like one, vulnerable to the loss of control thus made possible, which might just follow. Disposition to the heterogeneous refuses to give in to others' determinations or delimitations of fundamental rules and regulations, of constraining restrictions. In short, it opens one to the possibility of becoming, to transformation, to undoing and remaking, in the face of stasis and the repetition of sameness. But always without guarantee of the outcome.

Heterogeneity's scope, range, and reach are challenged at both ends: by the curtailments of the homogeneous, what I have called its closures, its closing down, and by the sort of unrecognizability its robust open-endedness may rub up against – the monstrous or teratological, the deformed, the mutant. The shiftiness of the latter across time suggests they are place-holders for the limit, the boundary, the constitutive outside or beyond that normativizes and normalizes, thus rendering acceptable the inside, those taken to belong, the comforting and comfortable stasis of being and belonging. Beasts of yesterday have become – today's avatars!

Why, I am often asked, is heterogeneity to be celebrated, homogeneity berated? What, after all, is wrong with wanting to live among one's own, to be comfortable with kinship, pleased with one's cultural (indeed, "natural") kin, threatened by the unrecognized and alien? Turning away from others, from those not like one, retreating into the comfort of consorting with one's "own," the narrowing inevitably associated with homogeneity is one among other modes of working things out, of resolving tensions.

Besides the fact that such presumed homogeneity necessarily takes for granted the coherence, purity, boundedness, and racial identity of cultural likeness, such homogeneity can only be purchased with the coin of severe repression, of purging difference and denying its influence if not its miscegenating seed. The sustaining of homogeneity necessarily requires restriction, keeping out those one takes to be unlike one, in some ways keeping in those one identifies with or who are at one with one. Hardly a natural condition, the very possibilities of the distinctions require work both to define and to sustain them. Their premise is built upon repression, aggression, blindness to other identifications, cross-seminations. Seemingly safe, the insistent closures and totalizations of homogeneity prompt and promote, mobilize and multiply their counter, resistances, the commitment to undress, transgress, redress. In short, homogeneity is a recipe for constitutive conflict and repetitively destructive, debilitating politics.

Heterogeneities, while no doubt stretching across the spaces of tension and discomfort, nevertheless are open to them, facing up to the difficulties of living together across divides, willing to deal with distinction, open to learning from engagement with the foreign, even the mutant. Heterogeneities do not amount to the flattening or ending of difference but an openness to the latter's forms of sociality, the spaces of its possibilities, the grounds of risibility and revisability in the face of its challenges. Heterogeneities live dispositionally in, across, and between the landscapes of contingency, challenging the limits of engagement, of sociality itself, ready to risk transgression.

The commitment to heterogeneous dispositions accordingly constitutes a threat *to* race in the face of the threat *of* race. And perhaps by extension it amounts ultimately, if not immediately, also to the facing down of racial threat.

Critical regionalisms, critical habit(u)ations

Racial regionalizations of the kind I have mapped here are dispositions to homogenization, in space and across time. What Gayatri Spivak compellingly has called *critical regionalisms* and the habits they engender in the places and moments inhabited, by contrast, embody dispositions to heterogeneity, to heterogenizing, across all places and at all times. They concern those regions that are both crucial to comprehending globalizing impacts of racial states and critical of any attempts to narrow the possibilities of people to define their sensibilities and values, their ways of being, their habits and habitations for themselves sensitive to the full and equal consideration of each.

"Critical regionalisms" accordingly conjures an analytic prism through which to approach and assess the roles of race in the transformations of modern state order, the impact of state form on the perpetuation of racial conditions at different times and places. It is a conceptual shorthand and methodological frame for considering the commonalities and divergences across regions regarding the historical force of race, and the resistances to racially driven exclusions, debilitations, and humiliations. The regional stretch undermines the narrow hold of national determination on racial definition and power, encouraging their critical analysis in the play of relations between the here and its interactive elsewheres.

The central case studies of racial regionalizations – of regional racisms – I have undertaken in this book evidence the repressive embedding of racisms' persistent institutionalizations as their *explicit* terms of enunciation have been socially shed. *Racial americanization* revealed the historical play between segregation and its privatizing born again expression at home and in its neo-imperializing reach. *Racial palestinianization* has concerned the forcing of occupational partition and the dialectics of terror and targeted assassinations, of suicide bombing and collateral killing in the name of securing cycles of partial population safety and frustrated revenge. *Racial europeanization* revealed the shift to categorical erasure and coded reference in the wake of unspeakable destructiveness, attended by the elevation of fixing boundaries cultural as much as territorial as immigration was made the dominant expression of racial threat. And *racial latinamericanization* has conjured the social rules for promoting and containing racial mixture. Finally, where *racial southafricanization* historically revealed the repressive debilitations and restrictions implicated in the convictions of a political theology of race, it has now come to exemplify the post-racial ambivalence between a commitment to nonracialism and a more robust racial irrelevance.

Racial regionalization suggests also the more or less local dynamics by which racial arrangements are given specificity and particularity, again to larger or lesser degree generalized. It likewise conjures the processes by which regions, more or less expansive, are marked by race. Racial regionalization, then, figures the relation between space and time, geographies and their histories of and in the making.

Regions vary, in their scope and nature, their histories of making and their boundaries of being: here, from the subnational (Palestine, Israel) to the nation-state (America, South Africa), from sub-continental geographies (Latin America) to continental reach (Europe). I have allowed the histories of racial shaping and making, and the prevailing rhetorics of racial-regional articulation in each instance to dictate the scope, contexts, generalizability, and delimitation of analytic reach and range.

Other regions could be identified and analyzed variously in their racial formulation, most notably, asianization and balkanization. While elaboration of each is endemic to the place and time of their respective articulations – to their regions, precisely – each represents a modality of racial expression and racist conviction, of racisms and the possibility of an afterlife, of alternative ways of being in the world. In short, of alternative, even counter-dispositions to past, present, and futures.

Two dominant senses of *racial asianization* are evident, as much discretely as interactively. There are, first, those operations of orientalisms analyzed most forcefully by Edward Said, notably under the expressive conditions of colonizing Europeans and their lasting legacy. These include imposed conceptions, definitions, practices, and institutions from the imperializing Outside, or from the Outsider inside in the case of settler colonialisms sometimes internalized throughout the region. But second, relatedly and variously, there are those racial articulations that are distinctly if relatedly Asian, that arise from within national configurations of the region – even if perhaps influenced by the circulation of racially fueled derogations from without. Here I think of Japanese articulations in relation to Koreans or Chinese; of Chinese in relation to most everyone else; of the formulations of Aryans and Dravidians in case of India, or the articulation of race with religion by Hindutva nationalists in relation to Dalits, on one hand, and Muslims, on the other; of the "multicultural" tensions, explicitly racially articulated, in contemporary Singapore between demographically differentiated Chinese, Malay, and Indian citizens on the island or across the peninsula. One could pursue a comparable analysis, historically indexed, for racial *balkanization*.

These generalized mappings of racisms' geostrategic models perhaps are best differentiated by contrasting how they embed a range of considerations central to the racial ordering of states: formal racial classification schemes; inequitable distributions of socio-material resources and access to educational institutions and political power; criminalization and social elevation, group driven and determined; access within and to the territory, nationally or regionally configured through cultural articulation.

The analytic produced and prism pursued here suggest why it remains productive to continue critically to engage the category of race at all. Far from losing all analyticity, race has continued, silently as much as explicitly, to empower modes of embrace and enclosure, in renewed and indeed sometimes novel ways, as much shaping the contours and geographies of neoliberal political economy globally as modulated by them. As em*brace*, race constitutes a bringing in, an engulfing, elevating, consuming, and suffocating hold on populations. It is a holding up and a holding out, a tying and restricting. As enclosure acts, it continues to encircle, closing in and out, to fence off. Perhaps the symbolic sign(post) of race in our (neo-)neoliberal present reads "DO NOT TRESPASS."

***

The legacies of abolitionist, civil rights, and anti-apartheid social movements have made abundantly evident that there is no ultimate narrative of absolute redemptive transformation resulting from racial revolutions. There are just the piecemeal changes and shifts – some small, ameliorative, accumulative; others largely and to lesser or greater degree ground-shifting. But ultimately even the larger changes produce, if not necessarily more often than not, backlashes, changes in racial expression and modes of exclusion themselves. They may become less overt, more subtle, more carefully formulated. They may shift in their underlying presuppositions (for example, from biological to cultural racism, or from racial naturalism to racial historicism). They may even jettison the language of and any reference to race itself, whether covert or altogether. In short, the successes of such social movements often given rise and voice to new expressions, new forms, new structures of racist restriction. The threat of race pays no respect, either to silence or to the celebration of its demise.

Hannah Arendt famously characterized Eichmann less as monstrous or demonic than as involving a "total absence of thinking." It is this she finds most disturbing, because so generalizable. The anti-intellectualism, the war on thinking, on independence of mind, the refusal to read, to think critically or deeply, the rejection of all but one or one kind of book, this is the danger to humankind through which Arendt lived and on which she reflected so compellingly.

It is this danger of threatening thoughtlessness we live so deeply also today. As enduring occupations. As (pre-)occupations endure.

Bibliography

Afzal-Khan, Fawzia and Seshadri-Crooks, Kalpani (eds.) 2000: *The Pre-Occupation of Postcolonial Studies.* Durham, NC: Duke University Press.

Agamben, Giorgio 1999: *Remnants of Auschwitz: The Witness and the Archive.* New York: Zone Books.

Alvarez, Sonia 2003: "Challenging Racism without 'Race': Reflections and Refractions on Brazilian and US Racial Formations and Transnational Antiracist Politics," lals.ucsc.edu/hemispheric_dialogues/papers/7_S_Alvarez.doc.

Arendt, Hannah 1971: "Thinking and Moral Considerations," *Social Research*, 38, 3 (Autumn), 417–46.

Asad, Talal 2007: *On Suicide Bombing.* New York: Columbia University Press.

Associated Press 2005: "Bush Denies Racism in Katrina Response," *chron.com*, December 13, www.chron.com/disp/story.mpl/nation/3520492.html.

Balibar, Etienne 2009: "Europe as Borderland," in Kim Benito Furumoto (ed.), *Race's Ghostly Words.* Durham, NC: Duke University Press. MS on file.

Bonilla-Silva, Eduardo 2003: *Racism without Racists: Colorblind Racism and the Persistence of Racial Inequality in the United States.* Lanham, MD: Rowman and Littlefield.

Bowling, Benjamin 1998: *Violent Racism: Victimization, Policing and Social Context.* Oxford: Oxford University Press.

Braun, Bruce 2003: " 'On the Raggedy Edge of Risk': Articulations of Race and Nature after Biology," in Donald Moore, Jake Kosek, and Anand Pandian (eds.), *Race,*

Nature, and the Politics of Difference. Durham, NC: Duke University Press, pp. 175–203.

Chazelle, Bernard 2006: "France's Colonial Blowback"; www.cs.princeton.edu/~chazelle/politics/france.html.

Comaroff, Jean 2007: "The Politics of Conviction: Faith on the Neoliberal Frontier," paper presented to Conference on "Cool Passions: The Political Theology of Conviction", Amsterdam, May 25–7.

Crenson, Matt 2005: "Katrina Rebuild Hinges on Who Will Pay," Associated Press, December 4; www.redorbit.com/news/general/320400/katrina_rebuild_hinges_on_who_will_pay/.

Da Silva, Denise Ferreira 2007: *Toward a Global Idea of Race*. Minneapolis: University of Minnesota Press.

Derrida, Jacques 2005: *Rogues: Two Essays on Reason*. Stanford: Stanford University Press.

Dershowitz, Alan 2002: *Shouting Fire: Civil Liberties in a Turbulent Age*. New York: Little, Brown.

Dreyfuss, Robert 2001: "Grover Norquist: 'Field Marshall of the Bush Plan'," *The Nation*, May 14; www.thenation.com/doc/20010514/dreyfuss.

Dumenil, G. and Levy, D. 2004: *Capital Resurgent: Roots of the Neoliberal Revolution*. Cambridge, MA: Harvard University Press.

Essed, Philomena 1991: *Understanding Everyday Racism: An Interdisciplinary Theory*. Newbury Park, CA: Sage.

Essed, Philomena and Goldberg, David Theo 2002: "Cloning Cultures: The Social Injustices of Sameness," *Ethnic and Racial Studies*, 25, 6 (November), 1066–82.

Foucault, Michel 1978: *The History of Sexuality: An Introduction*. New York: Vintage.

Foucault, Michel 2007: *Security, Territory, Population: Lectures at the Collège de France, 1977–8*. London: Palgrave Macmillan.

Frank, André Gunder 1998: *ReOrient: Global Economy in the Asian Age*. Berkeley: University of California Press.

Friedman, Jonathan, ed. 2003: *Globalization, the State, and Violence*. Walnut Creek: AltaMira Press.

Girard, René 1977: *Violence and the Sacred*. Baltimore: Johns Hopkins University Press.

Goldberg, David Theo 2002: *The Racial State*. Oxford: Blackwell.

Goldberg, David Theo 2006: "Deva-Stating Disasters: Race and Poverty Post-Katrina," in "Katrina: Unmasking Race, Poverty, and Politics in the 21st Century" (Special Issue), *Du Bois Review*, 3, 1 (August).

Guardian Unlimited 2005: "Drowned City Cuts Its Poor," *Sunday Observer*, December 11; observer.guardian.co.uk/international/story/06903,1664630,00.

Hanchard, Michael 1994: *Orpheus and Power: The Movimento Negro of Rio de Janeiro and São Paulo, 1945–1988*. Princeton: Princeton University Press.

Harvey, David 2005: *A Brief History of Neoliberalism*. Oxford: Oxford University Press.

Kestin, Sally, O'Matz, Megan, and Maines, John 2005: "FEMA Reimbursements Mainly Benefit Higher-Income Groups," Sun-Sentinel.com, December 11; www.sun-sentinel.com/news/local/southflorida/sfl-fema11xdec(2005).

Kim, Claire Jean 2004: "Unyielding Positions: A Critique of the Race Debate," *Ethnicities*, 4, 3 (September), 317–56.

Klein, Naomi 2007: *The Shock Doctrine: The Rise of Disaster Capitalism*. New York: Metropolitan Books.

Leitner, Helga, Peck, Jamie, and Sheppard, Eric. S., eds. 2007: *Contesting Neoliberalism: Urban Frontiers*. New York: Guilford Press.

Leroi, Armand Marie 2003: *Mutant: On Genetic Variety and the Human Body*. New York: Viking.

Lipsitz, George 2006: "Learning from New Orleans: The Social Warrant of Hostile Privatism and Competitive Consumer Citizenship," *Cultural Anthropology*, 21, 3, 451–68.

McAlister, Melani 2001: *Epic Encounters: Culture, Media, and US Interests in the Middle East, 1945–2000*. Berkeley: University of California Press.

McLennan, Gregor and McLaren, Peter 2001: "Debate: Critical Multiculturalism," *Ethnicities*, 1, 3 (September), 389–422.

Marx, Karl 1844/1975: *Economic and Philosophical Manuscripts, Collected Works*. New York and London: International Publishers.

Mbembe, Achille 2001: *On the Postcolony*. Berkeley: University of California Press.

Morrison, Toni 1998: "Clinton as the First Black President," *The New Yorker*, October; ontology.buffalo.edu/smith/clinton/morrison.html.

Moten, Fred 2004: "Knowledge of Freedom," *Centennial Review*, 2, 4 (Fall), 269–310.

Nietzsche, Friedrich 1888, 1901/1968: *The Will to Power*. New York: Vintage.

Ong, Aiwha 2006: *Neoliberalism as Exception: Mutations in Citizenship and Sovereignty*. Durham, NC: Duke University Press.

Pandey, Gyanendra 2006: *Routine Violence: Nations, Fragments, Histories*. Stanford: Stanford University Press.

Peck, Jamie and Tickell, Adam 2007: "Conceptualizing Neoliberalism, Thinking Thatcherism," in Helga Leitner, Jamie Peck, and Eric Sheppard (eds.), *Contesting Neoliberalism: Urban Frontiers*. New York: Guilford Press, pp. 26–50.

Racial Privacy Initiative 2003: www.adversity.net/RPI/rpi_mainframe.htm.

Ross, Daniel 2004: *Violent Democracy*. Cambridge: Cambridge University Press.

Saad-Filho, Alfredo and Johnston, Deborah, eds. 2005: *Neoliberalism: A Critical Reader*. London: Pluto Press.

Sansone, Livio 2003: *Blackness without Ethnicity: Constructing Race in Brazil*. London: Palgrave Macmillan.

Smith, Craig S. 2006: "In Paris Streets, Soup with a Twang of Intolerance," *International Herald Tribune*, February 28; www.iht.com/articles/2006/02/28/news/paris.php.

Smith, Neil 2005: *The Endgame of Globalization*. New York: Routledge.

Spivak, Gayatri Chakravorty and Butler, Judith 2006: "A Dialogue on Global States, 6 May 2006," *Postmodern Culture*, 17, 1 (September); muse.jhu.edu/login?uri=/journals/pmc/v017/17.1butler_spivak.html.

Stanko, Elizabeth, ed. 1994: *Perspectives on Violence*. London: Quartet Books.

Weber, Samuel 2006: "Rogue Democracy and the Hidden God," in Hent de Vries and Lawrence Sullivan (eds.), *Political Theologies: Public Religions in a Post-Secular World*. New York: Fordham University Press, pp. 382–400.

Weizman, Eyal 2003: *A Civilian Occupation: The Politics of Israeli Architecture*. London: Verso.

Williams, Patricia 1991: *The Alchemy of Race and Rights: Diary of a Law Professor*. Cambridge, MA: Harvard University Press.

Wilson, William Julius 1978: *The Declining Significance of Race: Blacks and Changing American Institutions*. Chicago: University of Chicago Press.

Winant, Howard 2006: "Race and Racism: Towards a Global Future," *Ethnic and Racial Studies*, 29, 5 (September), 986–1003.

Winter, Elke 2007: "How Does the Nation Become Pluralist?" *Ethnicities* 7, 4 (December), 483–515.

Index of Authors

Index of Keywords